Migration by Boat

STUDIES IN FORCED MIGRATION
General Editor: Dawn Chatty

Volume 1
A Tamil Asylum Diaspora: Sri Lankan Migration, Settlement and Politics in Switzerland
Christopher McDowell

Volume 2
Understanding Impoverishment: The Consequences of Development-induced Displacement
Edited by Christopher McDowell

Volume 3
Losing Place: Refugee Populations and Rural Transformations in East Africa
Johnathan B. Bascom

Volume 4
The End of the Refugee Cycle? Refugee Repatriation and Reconstruction
Edited by Richard Black and Khalid Koser

Volume 5
Engendering Forced Migration: Theory and Practice
Edited by Doreen Indra

Volume 6
Refugee Policy in Sudan, 1967–1984
Ahmed Karadawi

Volume 7
Psychosocial Wellness of Refugees: Issues in Qualitative and Quantitative Research
Edited by Frederick L. Ahearn, Jr.

Volume 8
Fear in Bongoland: Burundi Refugees in Urban Tanzania
Marc Sommers

Volume 9
Whatever Happened to Asylum in Britain? A Tale of Two Walls
Louise Pirouet

Volume 10
Conservation and Mobile Indigenous Peoples: Displacement, Forced Settlement and Sustainable Development
Edited by Dawn Chatty and Marcus Colchester

Volume 11
Tibetans in Nepal: The Dynamics of International Assistance among a Community in Exile
Anne Frechette

Volume 12
Crossing the Aegean: An Appraisal of the 1923 Compulsory Population Exchange between Greece and Turkey
Edited by Renée Hirschon

Volume 13
Refugees and the Transformation of Societies: Agency, Policies, Ethics and Politics
Edited by Philomena Essed, Georg Frerks and Joke Schrijvers

Volume 14
Children and Youth on the Front Line: Ethnography, Armed Conflict and Displacement
Edited by Jo Boyden and Joanna de Berry

Volume 15
Religion and Nation: Iranian Local and Transnational Networks in Britain
Kathryn Spellman

Volume 16
Children of Palestine: Experiencing Forced Migration in the Middle East
Dawn Chatty and Gillian Lewando Hundt

Volume 17
Rights in Exile: Janus-faced Humanitarianism
Guglielmo Verdirame and Barbara Harrell-Bond

Volume 18
Development-induced Displacement: Problems, Policies and People
Edited by Chris de Wet

Volume 19
Transnational Nomads: How Somalis Cope with Refugee Life in the Dadaab Camps of Kenya
Cindy Horst

Volume 20
New Regionalism and Asylum Seekers: Challenges Ahead
Edited by Susan Kneebone and Felicity Rawlings-Sanei

Volume 21
(Re)constructing Armenia in Lebanon and Syria: Ethno-Cultural Diversity and the State in the Aftermath of a Refugee Crisis
Nicola Migliorino

Volume 22
'Brothers' or Others? Propriety and Gender for Muslim Arab Sudanese in Egypt
Anita Fábos

Volume 23
Iron in the Soul: Displacement, Livelihood and Health in Cyprus
Peter Loizos

Volume 24
Not Born a Refugee Woman: Contesting Identities, Rethinking Practices
Edited by Maroussia Hajdukowski-Ahmed, Nazilla Khanlou and Helene Moussa

Volume 25
Years of Conflict: Adolescence, Political Violence and Displacement
Edited by Jason Hart

Volume 26
Remaking Home: Reconstructing Life, Place and Identity in Rome and Amsterdam
Maja Korac

Volume 27
Materialising Exile: Material Culture and Embodied Experience among the Karenni Refugees in Thailand
Sandra H. Dudley

Volume 28
The Early Morning Phone Call: Somali Refugees' Remittances
Anna Lindley

Volume 29
Deterritorialised Youth: Sahrawi and Afghan Refugees at the Margins of the Middle East
Edited by Dawn Chatty

Volume 30
Politics of Innocence: Hutu Identity, Conflict and Camp Life
Simon Turner

Volume 31
Zimbabwe's New Diaspora: Displacement and the Cultural Politics of Survival
Edited by JoAnn McGregor and Ranka Primorac

Volume 32
The Migration-Displacement Nexus: Patterns, Processes and Policies
Edited by Khalid Koser and Susan Martin

Volume 33
The Agendas of the Tibetan Refugees: Survival Strategies of a Government-in-Exile in a World of Transnational Organizations
Thomas Kauffmann

Volume 34
Making Ubumwe: Power, State and Camps in Rwanda's Unity-Building Project
Andrea Purdeková

Volume 35
Migration by Boat: Discourses of Trauma, Exclusion, and Survival
Lynda Mannik

Migration by Boat

Discourses of Trauma, Exclusion, and Survival

Edited by
Lynda Mannik

berghahn
NEW YORK · OXFORD
www.berghahnbooks.com

First published in 2016 by
Berghahn Books
www.berghahnbooks.com

©2016, 2018 Lynda Mannik
First paperback edition published in 2018

All rights reserved.
Except for the quotation of short passages
for the purposes of criticism and review, no part of this book
may be reproduced in any form or by any means, electronic or
mechanical, including photocopying, recording, or any information
storage and retrieval system now known or to be invented,
without written permission of the publisher.

Library of Congress Cataloging-in-Publication Data

Names: Mannik, Lynda, 1957– editor.
Title: Migration by boat : discourses of trauma, exclusion, and survival / edited by Lynda Mannik.
Description: New York : Berghahn Books, 2016. | Series: Studies in forced migration ; volume 35 | Includes bibliographical references and index.
Identifiers: LCCN 2015042122 (print) | LCCN 2015045252 (ebook) |
  ISBN 9781785331015 (hardback : alk. paper) | ISBN 9781785331022 (ebook)
Subjects: LCSH: Boat people. | Refugees. | Emigration and immigration–Social aspects.
Classification: LCC JV6346 .M49 2016 (print) | LCC JV6346 (ebook) |
  DDC 305.9/06914–dc23
LC record available at http://lccn.loc.gov/2015042122

British Library Cataloguing in Publication Data

A catalogue record for this book is available from the British Library

ISBN 978-1-78533-101-5 hardback
ISBN 978-1-78533-834-2 paperback
ISBN 978-1-78533-102-2 ebook

Contents

List of Illustrations   vii

Acknowledgments   ix

Introduction   1
    Lynda Mannik

Section I. Embedded Memories for Public Consumption

1. Children's Literature and Memory Activism: British Child Labor Migrants' Passage to Canada   27
    Sharon R. Roseman

2. Representing Migration by Boat at the Australian National Maritime Museum   49
    Kim Tao

3. Nước/Water: Oceanic Spatiality and the Vietnamese Diaspora   65
    Vinh Nguyen

Section II. The Artist and the Illegal Migrant

4. Imagining Europe's Borders: Commemorative Art on Migrant Tragedies   83
    Karina Horsti

5. "Washed Clean": The Forgotten Journeys of "Irregular Maritime Arrivals" in J. M. Coetzee's *Estralia*   101
    Jennifer Rutherford

Chapter 6. Unstable Vessels: Small Boats as Emblems of Deaths
    Foretold and as Harbingers of Better Futures in Figurations
    of Irregular Migration across the Strait of Gibraltar   116
    David Álvarez

Section III. Media, Politics, and Representation

7. Memorializing Boat Tragedies in the Mediterranean: The Case
   of the *Katër i Radës*   135
   Daniele Salerno

8. "Where Are Our Sons?": Tunisian Families and the
   Repoliticization of Deadly Migration across the
   Mediterranean Sea   154
   Federico Oliveri

9. Mysterious Refugees: Social Drama Ensues   178
   Lynda Mannik

10. Islands and Images of Flight around Europe's Southern Rim:
    Trouble in Heterotopia   197
    Helen M. Hintjens

Section IV. Stories of Smuggling, Trauma, and Rescue

11. "If We Die, We Die Together": Risking Death at Sea in Search
    of Safety   219
    Sue Hoffman

12. En Route to Hell: Dreams of Adventure and Traumatic
    Experiences among West African Boat People to Europe   235
    Papa Sow, Elina Marmer, and Jürgen Scheffran

13. Re-living *Janga*: Survivor Narratives   253
    Linda Briskman and Michelle Dimasi

Afterword   269
    Lynda Mannik

List of Illustrations

S.1 Vietnamese refugees await rescue from their thirty-five-foot fishing boat. 25

1.1 British immigrant children from Dr. Barnardo's Homes at landing stage, Saint John, New Brunswick. 28

2.1 The Lu family on board the restored *Tu Do* at the museum, 2005. 53

2.2 "Waves of Migration": Digital projection on the roof of the museum, 2013. 57

2.3 Gina Sinozich with her painting, *Our Story,* 2005. 59

3.1 Vietnamese refugee boat people arriving in Hong Kong in 1979. 69

S.2 *The Refugee Ship* (M/S Anton foldt lastet med flygtninge), 2010. 81

4.1 *At Crossroads* by Kalliopi Lemos, Brandenburg Gate, Berlin, 2009. 90

4.2 *Porta di Lampedusa–Porta d'Europa–Gateway to Europe* by Mimmo Paladino, Lampedusa. 93

6.1 The Moroccan coast and the Strait of Gibraltar from the south end of the Rock of Gibraltar. 118

S.3 Melbourne refugee and asylum seeker rights rally, Saturday July 27, 2013. 133

7.1 *L'approdo. Opera all'umanità migrante* (side view). 142

7.2 *L'approdo. Opera all'umanità migrante* (front view). 143

7.3 *L'approdo. Opera all'umanità migrante* (from a distance). 143

7.4 Victim's relative touching the picture of his beloved on the *Infin che 'l mar fu sovra noi richiuso.* 147

8.1 Cemetery of migrant boats in Lampedusa. 159

8.2 Mother of a missing migrant wearing the Tunisian flag during a sit-in at the Italian embassy in Tunis. 163

8.3 Mothers of missing migrants during a sit-in at the Italian embassy in Tunis. 167

9.1 "173 men and one woman are being held at the Canadian Forces Base Stadacona", *The Globe and Mail*. 184

9.2 "Refugees remembered", *The Toronto Star*. 189

11.1 Southern part of Southeast Asia in relation to Australia. 221

11.2 West Java, three hours south of the Indonesian capital of Jakarta, 2007. 225

12.1 Visa Information System, 2014. 238

12.2 Illegal sea border crossing between the Border Crossing Point (BCPS), 2014. 239

12.3 Top ten nationalities of persons entering the European Union or Schengen using fraudulent documents, 2014. 240

13.1 Christmas Island location. 255

13.2 *Janga* Memorial, Christmas Island, 2011. 262

Acknowledgments

My interest in migration by boat began as a child. It was not unusual for family dinner conversation to include stories about World War II and about how two generations on my father's side of the family almost drowned in a small fishing boat destroyed by a fighter plane while attempting to find refuge. Details about their dramatic and dangerous exodus will forever be etched in my memory. Three people died that day and all but a few were severely wounded. Nevertheless, alongside tales of trauma were stories about heroic acts of survival, serendipity, and determination. I would like to publicly thank my father and my grandmother for being the storytellers for our family, for telling and retelling stories that were often painful to recall, and for providing me with richly articulated renditions that fueled a lifelong curiosity, and a rich imagination.

In 2013 I posted an online call to the international academic community to see if anyone was interested in joining me in publishing a book specifically about boat migration and the various public ways it has been remembered. The response was overwhelming and positive. I would like to thank all those who showed interest and encouraged me in this undertaking. In particular, I thank the contributors to this volume who committed to this project and patiently worked alongside me as the book developed. I would also like to thank several colleagues, family, and friends who have provide encouragement in the past and listened to my ideas. In particular, Sharon Roseman, Julia Harrison, Karen McGarry, Joan Sangster, Colin Coates, Teresa Holmes, Cathy Jeffery, Linda Hogarth, Len and Linda Mannik, Steve and Sil Mannik, Jen, Lisa and Andrew, and of course my beautiful daughter, Dylan, and my father, Meinhard. Writing a sole-edited volume seemed like a daunting task at first, so I would like to say a special thanks to David Murray for providing the inspiration to proceed with this project.

Last but not least, a heartfelt thanks to everyone at Berghahn Books who worked with me on this. This list includes Molly Mosher, Dhara Patel, Melissa Gannon, and Jessica Murphy. Your encouragement and cordial e-mail correspondence is much appreciated.

Introduction

Lynda Mannik

In 1948, four years after the end of World War II, 347 Estonian women, men and children boarded the SS *Walnut,* a retired British minesweeper, to find safety, freedom, and refuge in a place that was as far away from the Soviet Union as possible. They left Göteborg, Sweden, illegally on November 16 and landed in Canada on December 11. Their voyage was long and arduous, as well as physically, emotionally, and psychologically debilitating. It was very similar to most migrations by boat undertaken by individuals who have been forced to leave their homelands. Crossing the Atlantic in the winter months was cold and stormy. Many of the *Walnut*'s passengers were extremely seasick for the entire journey and many became seriously ill. There were only two toilet facilities for 347 passengers, very little food and water, a lack of fuel for the engine, and very little space for the passengers to move around in. Each passenger slept for the month-long journey in what they described as "cubbyholes:" a series of wooden boxes, two foot by two foot by six foot, stacked against the walls of the hull of a ship that was originally designed to sleep only seventeen crew members. It was an emotionally traumatic journey, and left an indelible mark on their memories and identity.[1] Thousands of people made similar journeys in the years following World War II. Those specifically carrying Baltic refugees from Sweden are only one example.

For centuries people have migrated by boat. The legalities of such migrations have become increasingly contentious since World War II, which is hailed as a defining moment in the creation of definitions concerning refugees (Malkki 1995; Nyers 2006; Zucker and Zucker 1996). Events surrounding the atrocities of this war left millions of displaced people homeless and stateless. Their necessary relocation precipitated the creation in 1948 of the Universal Declaration of Human Rights. In Article 14.1, it states, "Everyone has the right to seek and to enjoy in other countries asylum from persecution." This is when refugee law became an "inseparable part of the code of Human Rights" (Noble as seen in Malkki 1995: 500). During this period, portrayals of refugees were most often positive. There was a consistent sympathy for so-called displaced persons who were generally represented as hard-working, mostly white, anticommunists in need of, and deserving of, protection, and who had the potential to become excellent and productive citizens with the correct ideological and economic values. Representations paralleled legal ideas about refugees that lasted until the end of the Cold War (roughly between the late 1940s to the late 1980s).

Beginning in the mid to late 1980s, publicized textual representations, visual representations, immigration policies, and laws shifted toward the "myth of difference," as coined by B. S. Chimni, an internationally renowned legal scholar. In 1998 he explained how refugees from the global South captured the attention of Northern policymakers as having a nature and character that was far different from the refugees who had left Europe after World War II. According to Chimni, refugees and migrants from the South were represented in the geopolitics of knowledge productions and legal policy, in terms of overwhelming (and possibly uncontrollable) mass movements of people who were looking for economic opportunities only, and therefore who were serious threats to national and economic security (Chimni 1998: 351). In media reports metaphoric descriptions align people who are forced to migrate with terms such as *tides, waves,* and, *floods,* exemplifying mainstream discrimination.

Refugees and others who migrate by boat have since been considered the most threatening within this schema. The "official" reason behind this designation is that their movements are uncontrolled and often uncontrollable and that their choice to migrate illegally is a criminal act of sorts, whether or not they are involved with smuggling rings. Although these voyages are currently described as "illegal," the passengers on these boats still fall under UN definitions allotted to refugees, and most are granted refugee status following their arrival at their destination. Modern nationalism is founded on a homogeneous system where all global space is marked, named, and accounted for. This nationalism is accompanied by an unspoken ideology that being "rooted" in a place creates necessary morality and balance, and conversely, that being "uprooted" propels individuals to become amoral and, potentially, criminally minded (Malkki 1995). Within this Western obsession with national order, refugees and asylum seekers are viewed as an undifferentiated mass, an aberration. They are in between homeland and nation. They do not yet belong anywhere (Allatson and McCormack 2005). Arriving via the wrong channels or out of the bounds of state control can have devastating effects, even for individuals who fall legally under UN definitions. Traveling via water disallows sympathy for the migrants' plight and in fact often works to support state protectionist policies that are innately discriminatory. Metaphorically speaking, travel via water is viewed as such a threat to the solidarity of national spaces that it has the power to wash away humanitarian sentiments. Michael Pugh (2004: 55) reminds us that asylum seekers who arrive by boat are often associated with natural disasters in international media descriptions where terms such as *engulfed, swamped, flooded,* and *washed away* are used to describe the effect they have on the nations they arrive in. Ironically, all who migrate by boat incur far greater risks, and their survival rates are increasingly shrinking.

Migration by boat is the most dangerous form of movement between nations for a variety of reasons; the scale of human tragedies associated with such migration are often overlooked or kept hidden from view. As explained above in the example of the *Walnut*'s voyage, most of the vessels are ill equipped for ocean crossings or for the large number of passengers they are carrying. Passengers are crammed into small, uncomfortable spaces, such as dark, airless hulls of decrepit ships, for long periods—weeks and even months. The boats often have unreliable engines, and a lack of fuel and appropriate navigational equipment, or equipment that breaks down during the voyage. Basic living conditions are minimal at best. Running out of food and water is common, and there are few if any sanitary (toilet) facilities. Therefore, even if they are successful in arriving at their intended destinations, which many are not, most passengers suffer illness and physical debilitation on the voyage, and all suffer psychological and emotional trauma to varying degrees. As Pugh explains, "Securitization of the issue in destination countries inverts the risks. For it is actually the boat people who are at the mercy of tides, waves, shipwrecks and drowning" (Pugh 2004: 55). There are also countless stories of refugees who have paid exorbitant amounts for these voyages; if they do arrive at their destination, they are left in dire financial straits.

Historic statistics concerning the number of people who have drowned trying to migrate by boat are vague at best. This is due to the clandestine nature of these voyages, the complex channels of migration, and the varying sizes and conditions of the boats. For an example, as Álvarez notes (chapter 6), it is impossible to track all the small duck-hunting boats (called *pateras*) that cross the Strait of Gibraltar, nor those who have lost their lives attempting to cross, which was estimated to be in the thousands by the end of the twentieth century.[2] As well, in the European Union (EU), for example, primary data concerning drownings is collected by organizations such as the United Nations High Commissioner for Refugees (UNHCR) and United Against Racism. Nation–states have not collected comprehensive data until recently (Robins et al. 2014). An unofficial estimate posted on the blog site "Fortress Europe" states that approximately 14,309 people died trying to cross the Mediterranean Sea between 1990 and 2013 (http://fortresseurope.blogspot.ca/2006/02/immigrants-dead-at-frontiers-of-europe_16.html). Other approximations are as high as 17,000 for a similar period (Horsti, chapter 4). It is estimated that approximately two thousand people drowned off the coasts of Australia between 2000 and 2013. Many of the larger boats that sank are discussed in this volume, including the SIEV X (2001), which was carrying 353 passengers (146 children, 142 women, and 65 men, all Iraqi or Afghan); they all drowned (Hoffman, chapter 11; Briskman and Dimasi, chapter 13). The numbers of attempted, successful, and unsuccessful migrations by boat have increased exponentially in the past few years. European statistics are the highest they have ever been, with an estimated 580,000 people attempting to cross the Mediterranean between January and October 2015. For example, in April 2015, within one week (April 10–17), it was estimated that 13,500 people tried to cross the Mediterranean from Libya, most were originally from Syria, Eritrea, and Somalia. On April 19 an estimated seven hundred to nine hundred people (estimated because there were only twenty-nine survivors) all crammed onto one boat, drowned in freezing waters only seventeen miles from the Libyan coast.[3] The International Organization for Migration (IOM) and Missing Migrants Project (www.missingmigrants.iom.int) estimated that over three thousand, seven hundred people have drowned trying to cross the Mediterranean in 2015. Increased numbers and increasing tragedies garnered concern from the international community, but adequate measures focused on organized rescue missions as opposed to border control did not surface. The larger issues concerning the business of international human trafficking rings, and the reasons why people risk their lives to migrate by boat have yet to be tackled.

Over the years several scholars have discussed the myriad ways images and stereotypes about migration by boat marginalizes the people involved. These representations cross a wide berth and can have a profound influence on policymaking and public opinion, setting up a vicious cycle of discrimination. Labels are crucial to the attainment of rights and future citizenship protections. When human identities are naturalized through metaphors, it becomes easier to further subjugate individuals legally. What is left out of public representations is that asylum seekers who migrate by boat often have no other choice, and that this type of migration is their last chance for survival. The authors in this collection remind us of the power of stories, films, performance, and art to address these issues in creative ways for public consumption, but that also allow for shifts and changes to public perspectives, to give a voice to marginalized individuals, and to challenge dehumanizing policies. Even though the global realities concerning migration currently seem insurmountable, the need for fairness with a focus on humanitarian ideals is equally urgent. The physical movement of refugee and asylum seekers through water turns them into scapegoats for the imagined dilution of state power, when in reality these individuals are often forcibly managed, and sometimes kept in motion by state practices that are attempting to ensure an orderly flow.

A Thematic Synopsis

The essays that have been collected for this volume are all published here for the first time. They explore various contemporary case studies, artistic renditions, and literary interpretations of migrations by boat as events where cultures intersect and identities are reshaped, in both painful and creative ways. Each chapter features a particular kind of marginalization that exaggerates aspects of belonging, and the fluid borders that differentiate "us" from "them." Contributors represent a variety of scholarly disciplines and national interests; although the book is centered on refugee and migration studies it clearly contributes to debates in media and communication studies, cultural studies, anthropology, geography (in particular border studies), and history. Sprinkled throughout are conversations about policy directives and histories, and all contributors hope their work will have an effect on future decision-making processes.

The ambiguous nature of memories (both social and individual), media representations, and popular culture productions are highlighted in order to address negative stereotypes and, conversely, to humanize the individuals involved. To this end, it is important to reflect on the nature of terms and labels. Authors in this volume use the terms *refugee, asylum seeker, migrant, illegal migrant, and illegal immigrant,* and each author clarifies his or her individual choices. Generally speaking, all labels or terms are problematic because they suggest a naturalized category and never adequately distinguish specific aspects of identities for social groups such as nationality, political status, legal status, economic status, or intentions. The term *boat people* is currently perhaps the most derogatory term; it was coined in the 1970s to identify the hundreds of thousands of people who fled Indochina. The word *illegal* and the overall emphasis on "illegality" is a central problem because it exemplifies a disregard for international human rights in favor of securitization. In a response to the allocation of labels, Kieran O'Doherty and Amanda LeCouteur suggest the use of the term *unexpected arrivals* to "steer the focus away from claims about the legality of the method of arrival" (O'Doherty and LeCouteur 2007: 2).

To begin, I would like to highlight four themes that connect all chapters in this volume. These are different from the section breakdown that this book is organized around, but are critical to understanding the power and relevance of interdisciplinarity in analyzes of dominant discourses that circulate in regards to nation–state policymaking, and public opinion. Vacillations between well-understood binaries such as citizen/stranger, land/water, and victim/threat can be easily used to justify vacillations in policy according to the current political will of those in power. Simply put, "Elected leaders and bureaucrats increasingly have turned to *symbolic* policy instruments to create an *appearance* of control" (Massey et al. 1998: 288; emphasis in the original), yet, those leaders also manipulate that appearance through rhetoric in the media. Increasingly, scholars are attempting to understand how "transnational flows of people, media and commodities" (Escobar 2001) can be viewed outside of standard dualistic terms and away from the clear-cut juxtapositions of citizen/stranger, land/water, and victim/threat. All the authors in this volume focus on alternative modes of representation to facilitate humanitarian perspectives that are often left out of policy decisions, public conversations, and media reports.

Water as Ambiguous Space

The only spaces considered "free" within the system of modern nations are the high seas.[4] Ulf Hannerz (1997) attempts to piece together a brief history of theoretical ideas associated with the term *flows* by quoting a variety of scholars that have used water-related terms in reference to culture. He suggests that a systematic analysis of the use of such terms needs to take place (Hannerz 1997: 4). Hannerz begins with Alfred Kroeber, who stated that civilizations should be viewed as "limited processes of flows in time" (1952, as seen in Hannerz 1997: 4). He quotes Johannes Fabian and his playful suggestion that scholars have been "liquidating the culture concept" (1978, as seen in Hannerz 1997: 5), and Roland Barthes, who in 1984 suggested that cultural movement could be viewed as "an imagery of streams and currents within a river" that has the power to "transport objects" and "create whirlpools" (Hannerz 1997: 5). Overall, Hannerz suggests that the fundamental importance of cultural "flows" is in their ability to have direction, reorganize, and move without destroying their source, and that words such as *crisscross, multicentric,* and *counter* can act as appendages for further analyzes that attest to notions of freedom associated with bodies of water. He concludes by stating that as a root metaphor for culture, myriad forms of water such as "tiny rivulets," "mighty rivers," and "whirlpools" may work well as primary organizing principles (Hannerz 1997: 6–7). In fact, the word *flows* is used frequently in many forms of textual expression, ranging from academic writing to media reports, as a seemingly well-understood term that exemplifies refugee movement in general.

Oceanic voyages have metaphorically represented liminal periods where human beings are "betwixt and between" (Turner 1964) real lives and identities. It has been argued that the ambiguous nature of liminality, associated with the sea and ocean travel, also facilitates many negative associations for refugees. As mentioned earlier, these ideas are fed by Western obsessions with binarisms and a "categorical order of nation–states," where refugees come to represent an objectified, undifferentiated mass that is in between homeland and outside of other nations; in essence, they do not belong anywhere (Allatson and McCormack 2005: 13–16). On many levels, refugees signify and have come to represent "an emptiness, an incompleteness vis-à-vis the meaningful positive presence to political subjectivity that state citizenship provides" (Nyers 2006: 16).⁵ This is echoed in Jennifer Rutherford's links to ideas about "holing"–"casting refugees out into a state of un-being"– to metaphorically describe the extent of the marginality experienced by asylum seekers (Rutherford chapter 5). Susan Coutin says that during the actual movement of refugees, when they are imagined to be are at their most liminal, they are viewed as non-human, which often leads to extremely dehumanizing treatment (Coutin 2005: 199). Elizabeth Colson and Thayer Scudder list negative emotional responses that are a direct result of relocation including grief, depression, loss, and anxiety. Here, the stress incurred is viewed as a temporary vacuum, which can be extremely difficult to recover from (Colson and Scudder 1982: 269–70). Emotional voids experienced by the Tunisian families of individuals who have disappeared while migrating by boat are brought forward in Oliveri (chapter 8) where even their grief is left unrecognized by state authorities. Therefore, an emphasis on liminality could be considered one of the prevailing problems for refugee identity because of its ambiguous implications. While metaphorically, the movement that is suggested by this concept may aid in understanding shifting cultures and the creation of new identities, the actual experience of physical movement often positions refugees ideologically, psychologically, legally, and physically in a void where marginality, loss, and fear prevail.

Conversely, water possesses the ability to traverse across land in a variety of ways; its movements have always been relegated to powerful ideas about freedom and borderlessness. When fluidity is epitomized in this way, it washes away any remaining trace of grounded existence and as Escobar reminds us, it is imagined that "transnational flows" lead to deterritorialization and that "fluidities of time and space" lead to the erasure of "place" as something we can rely on (Escobar 2001: 146). However, oceans and seas are also social (human) spaces both in terms of social constructions and in terms of geographical borders. Moreover, real life experiences and connections are made while people move through it (Steinberg 2013). As Vinh Nguyen explains, water and mass migration via water have the ability to solidify collective identity, to create "ties, attachments, and relations not circumscribed by terrestrial nationalism" (Nguyen chapter 3). The complex circulations of identities and relationships linked to ocean travel and the positive dynamics of movement through water are also central to understanding the ambiguous nature of metaphors and migrants' experiences. Here, liminal experiences can be viewed in a positive way because they allow for creativity and the production of new meanings. Chapter 12, "En Route to Hell: Dreams of Adventure and Traumatic Experiences among West African Boat People to Europe" (Sow, Marmer, and Scheffran), highlights the fluid and creative connections and human relationships that are forged because of the desperate need to migrate by boat.

Trauma vs. Agency

In 1951 a detailed definition pertaining specifically to refugee status was created. Article 1 A(2) of the United Nations Convention and Protocol Relating to the Status of Refugees determines that a "refugee" is someone, who, "Owing to a well-founded fear of being persecuted for reason of race, religion, nationality, membership of a particular social group or political opinion, is outside the country of his nationality and is unable or, owing to such fear, is unwilling to avail himself of the protection of that country; or who, not having a nationality but being outside of the country of his former habitual residence as a result of such events, is unable or, owing to such fear, is unwilling to return to it" (UNHCR 2014). This definition is based on two core indicators—fear and protection—that resonate in stereotypes applied to illegal migration where individuals are positioned as threatening or victimized. If individuals do not express a "well-founded" fear that propels them into homelessness and helplessness, they cannot expect to acquire protection. This would suggest that any form of agency on their part could be viewed as detrimental to the attainment of refugee status, and possibly put them in the position of an unwanted intruder. However, in reality, fear and agency are most often conjoined in the refugee experience. As Mansouri and Leach state, individuals would not risk "their lives in [an] unseaworthy boats [if] they [we]re not in danger"(Mansouri and Leach 2004: 121). Fear also becomes prioritized where the term *economic refugee* establishes unsuitability and where the declaration of ideological fear is elevated, as in the case of Eastern Europeans and communism following World War II (Nyers 2006: 46).[6] On the other hand, if refugees are viewed as too problematic or too threatening, state control is increased and much, if not all, humanitarian aid is refused. In Australian media and policy discussions, refugees arriving by boat are often described as "queue jumpers," (Gale 2004: 330), viewed as undeserving, and considered "illegal migrants" (Briskman and Dimasi chapter 13). For state policymakers, *fear* and *protection* become key terms that are manipulated to exclude, to manufacture categories of difference, and to strengthen social and political order. The fate of migrants of all sorts are colored by this juxtaposition. All individuals or groups who migrate in a so-called "illegal" way, by boat, are viewed as the most threatening types of migrants, and therefore as having the most agency.

Even though migration by boat is undertaken for a variety of reasons, it is always a clandestine experience. Often family, neighbors, and friends are not told about plans, either to protect them or those leaving. "Push factors" as discussed by Mansouri and Leach (2004: 15), are historically linked with political conflicts that originate internally, regionally, or internationally, as well as with natural disasters. Personal accounts provide gruesome details of torture, imprisonment, death threats, and other forms of persecution that are common to the experience of forced migration. Lan, a Vietnamese woman in her forties, stated, "You want to know why we left Vietnam? We saw no future for the next generation.... We lived in a house with Dan's parents, and we stayed in the house and waited for the communists to come. We thought that if they did not kill us, they would put us in jail" (Gilad 1990: 35). And in Iraq Aisha claimed, "Saddam's people used to come and threaten me, ask about my husband and children. I wasn't staying in the same place, I was always moving. My daughter was fourteen and she couldn't go to school because we kept moving houses. I kept moving because Saddam's people used to threaten me that they'll arrest me and kill my daughter if I didn't tell them about my husband and other children" (Mansouri and Leach 2004: 20). Implicated in these comments is a deep sense of loss accompanied by betrayal, pain, humiliation, and fear. It is very difficult to imagine that there would be any sort of debate about "well-founded fears" in reference to refugee aid for these individuals. It is even more difficult to imagine that "push factors," such as those mentioned above are not specifically reflected in UN designations. A solid argument can be made for the incompetence of critiques in the media and/or arenas of policymaking that fail to explicitly reflect the realities these voices portray. This argument, along with personal expressions of trauma, is clearly articulated in chapters 11, 12, and 13.

Piotr Sztompka (2000: 457) says, "Trauma occurs when there is a break, displacement, or disorganization in the orderly, taken-for-granted universe," and that the trauma of forced migration "touches the core of collective order–the domain of main values, constitute rules, [and] central expectations," and therefore is deeply felt. The depths of this form of trauma is well documented by Briskman and Dimasi in respect to survivors of the sinking of the *Janga* in 2010, when more than fifty passengers drowned (chapter 13). Similarly, stories about incidents of hunger and very uncomfortable living situations accompanied by traumatic, near-death experiences are narrated by Norres and Messar in personal interviews with Sue Hoffman (chapter 11). Colson claims that a perspective that favors the idea that "forced migration releases human energy which can lead to new and better lives for those uprooted" is a dangerous conclusion because it does not take seriously the trauma that continues to plague refugees and the lives of future generations (Colson 2003: 15). Most often refugees and illegal migrants are victims of human rights abuses, and not of ideological concerns. A poignant historic example is the more than one hundred thousand child labor migrants–many orphaned in Britain–who were sent to Canada in the nineteenth and twentieth centuries (Roseman chapter 1).

Refugees and asylum seekers do not confer feelings of empowered upon leaving or while in transit. They are under a great deal of stress and physical suffering, and they are often positioned as pawns of complex political and economic injustices, and of contradictions. Their decision to migrate by boat is often spontaneous, or is a last resort. For most, logical thoughts of political agency, or of having any agency during this period in their lives is not likely because these are acts of desperation. Commentray about agency may be heard years later, once they have left detention centers or other places of transition, and are actually able to work and live in a place they can call "home." This transition usually takes a very long time. The studies presented here illustrate that the traumas experienced during flight remain one of the most enduring aspects of personal memories. One example of the long-term shift from an exclusive focus on trauma toward feelings of newness and agency can be found in Tao's description of Gina Sinozich's artwork that Tao says represents a "compelling intersection" that enables a convergence of memory, history, and a "powerful new evocation of home" (Tao chapter 2). Undertaking, enduring, and surviving this type of migration is a feat of determination and strength. "Strength through adversity" was one of the prevailing themes within a complex web of ideas concerning being a refugee that surfaced in my conversations with the *Walnut*'s passengers in 2006 (Mannik 2012). This is not an uncommon theme for those who have experienced forced migration (Holt 1997: 251). Many of the *Walnut*'s passengers explained to me on several occasions, there was a "certain type of strength" gained from having been a refugee that very few people can understand unless they have experienced it themselves. Some felt they were better people for having gone through it. A few made the same joke: "What doesn't kill you makes you stronger." These conversations took place 60 years after their traumatic voyage. Similarly, Nguyen emphasizes migration by boat as a powerful indicator of community and solidarity for a now diverse Vietnamese diaspora (Nguyen chapter 3). Overall, individuals who migrate by boat incur far greater risks, leave in more-desperate situations and generally arrive in a more dilapidated condition, yet are publicly discriminated against in a more dehumanizing manner. It takes a very strong individual to survive all of that.

Original to this volume are examples of human agency, both in humanitarian acts and in selfish acts that can be seen in the actions and comments of host communities. Karina Horsti explains how the funds for the construction of the Porta d'Europa (Gateway to Europe) memorial on the island of Lampedusa were donated by people and organizations in Italy who wanted to draw attention to the thousands of drownings that had occurred in the past two decades (Horsti chapter 4). Mannik explains how the residents of Charlesville, Nova Scotia, welcomed the 174 Sikh refugees that arrived unannounced in their tiny village in the middle of the night with water, tea, and sandwiches, and, conversely, how many capitalized on this event by promoting tourism in the area (Mannik chapter 9). Briskman and Dimasi explain how many islanders ran to assist *Janga*'s passengers when they heard screams from the shoreline and how their valiant efforts did not coincide with a state-directed rescue plan (Briskman and Dimasi chapter 13). All of the chapters mentioned above provide examples of humanitarian activities that are happening outside of, and often in contrast to, political discourses and state-funded practices.

Control and Protectionism

As noted by Peter Nyers, "To invent the citizen is to invent its opposite, the refugee" (Nyers 2006: 9). This idea is discussed by all authors in this volume either in overt or in indirect ways. One of the primary problems inherent in definitions and representations surrounding refugees in general is that even though UN designations dictate that certain people are entitled to refugee status, there are no state obligations attached to these designations. This sets up a paradox whereby international law confirms that nations are obliged to protect refugees, but that their obligations are only voluntary. Consequently, state leaders have total control over the management of refugee rights to asylum and their own responsibilities toward aid (Adelman as seen in Agar 1999: 93–94). Coutin refers to this as a "legal limbo" (Coutin 2005: 201). In reality, state responsibility is most often predicated on a tension between immigration policies and asylum policies (Mansouri and Leach 2004: 115), which do little to support the specific needs of refugees. In Canada, for an example, refugees can be rejected if they suffer from health problems or cannot financially support themselves (Gilad 1990: 126).[7] Historically, state-supported racial prejudice affects the outcome of "who" gets in. Legal realities place refugees in an "ambiguous 'inter' zone, whereby they are paradoxically included within the realm of humanity by virtue of their exclusion from it" (Nyers 2006: 46). This exclusion is legally malleable and is fashioned and refashioned in myriad ways at the state level.

In particular, political arguments favoring protectionism and state-centered securitization prevail when it comes to refugees who arrive by boat because water borders are often more difficult to police and survey. As well, media representations sensationalize them as a dire threat or crisis to the security of citizens on a variety of levels including economic, health, and basic safety that is translated in direct quotes from politicians The framing of their identities in the media, often suggesting criminality, has an impact on public opinion and government policies concerning immigration, and vice versa. Generally speaking, refugees are positioned as voiceless, helpless victims, or, conversely, "masses" or "waves" that threaten to destroy intact homeland security. As has been already stated, individuals who migrate by boat are usually equated with the threatening side of this dichotomy. Tamara Vukov (2003) explains that "affective processes" that focus on illegal refugees as intruders and as a threat to national security circulate through the media, other forms of public culture, and government logic. There is a "governmentalization of affect itself," where media culture becomes "a key site through which the affective dimensions of government policies and practices can be traced" (Vukov 2003: 339). Arrival by boat has a profound effect precipitated by heightened media coverage, which further translates into justification for policies that attempt to shore up national borders.

Securitization and impromptu controls at the level of state policy have roots in sensationalized media representations, but the power of the media also lies in interpretation of the facts. As Daniele Salerno explains (chapter 7) media narratives can hide just as much as they seem to reveal. Here Salerno is referring to the lack of inclusion of the fact that in 1997 the Italian government chose not to rescue the *Kater I Rades,* and consequently eighty-one Albanian refugees drowned. Mannik provides another example that explains how media representations inspire public opinions that are then manifested in discriminatory public performances. She explains how for weeks large groups protested the arrival of the 174 refugees with slanderous placards, saying, "Deport AND Prosecute" outside a detention center in Halifax where the *Amelie*'s passengers were being held and investigated (Mannik chapter 9). Mannik thus highlights Ahmed's comments about the ways events that are promoted in the media as crises of security invite citizens to police national boundaries—to monitor suspicious others (Ahmed 2004: 76).

In this volume, Rutherford (chapter 5), Hoffman (chapter 11), and Briskman and Dimasi (chapter 13) provide detailed accounts of the history of policy formation in the Australian context concerning arrivals by boat. These authors explain how, over time, offshore camps or holding places have become increasingly decrepit and volatile situations—as Rutherford puts it, "grim realities." They explain how refugees' rights are stripped from them for long periods of time while they wait to be released. In particular, harsh and punitive policies are responsible for locking up more than a thousand children indefinitely in Australian-run immigration detention centers (Hoffman chapter 11), and the callous government attitude toward humanitarian aid for ships in distress. All of these measures are justified by rhetoric that lays claim to the need for tighter state securitization. Álvarez (chapter 6), Oliveri (chapter 8), and Sow, Marmer, and Scheffran (chapter 12) focus on the reinforcement of Europe's external frontiers historically, and in particular since the early 1990s, in efforts to detract so-called illegal migrants from arriving at various points by boat. Arrivals most commonly come from countries in North Africa, providing the perfect example of the contemporary "war on refugees," the term coined by Hintjens (chapter 10) that supports "the myth of invasion" (de Haas 2008). Also, as Sow, Marmer, and Scheffran (chapter 12) explain, dominate discourses that define migration to Europe by boat as a security problem work to obscure underlying structures that demand cheap migrant labor from places like Africa.

Memory: Personal and Public

Language often falls short of enabling a memory of a traumatic experience due to severe confusion over the actual events that cannot be understood in a logically way; emotions take over. Ernest Van Alphen (1999: 32) uses the metaphor of "killing the self" to emphasize the dynamic way that trauma can kill memory and meaning. Nevertheless, it is only through memory and remembering the past that trauma can be understood and negotiated; it is only when traumatic experiences are given a voice through narratives that painful memories and losses can be integrated into the present. The relation between trauma and memory is complex. For example, symptoms of posttraumatic stress dissipate over time, yet acute memories and extreme emotions can lie dormant for a lifetime. In general, we compose memories and retell memories that help us feel at ease with our lives, our pasts, and our identities; memories aid in the creation of appropriate contemporary meanings. However, traumatic experiences are so powerful and unusual that meaning cannot always be allotted to them because there is no appropriate context. Theorists have suggested that trauma can be experienced only in a belated form, "when it returns in the form of dreams or flashbacks" (Edkins 2003: 40), for example.

The details of personal memories, such as those expressed by young Senegalese men in dangerous crossings in small dinghies (Sow, Maramer, and Scheffran, chapter 12), aptly express the impact trauma can have. Similarly, for those leaving Vietnam by boat in the late 1970s and early 1980s, the 1 percent survival rate was obviously deemed less risky than staying. Gilad relates the story of Ly Fang, who was taken by bus in the middle of the night to a small town and who then spent thirty-two hours in a canoe to get to the sea. Once on board the canoe he encountered a litany of life-threatening experiences, including having no food for four days and being beaten by pirates. Fang was forced to watch the rape of a young girl and finally found refuge on an old oil rig with 112 other people for twenty-six days. Fang describes his experience on the oil rig: "It was very hot, not enough water. The Thais do not treat people well so that you will not write relatives to come and join you. The Thais also encourage the pirates to discourage people from coming. We eventually ran out of water even though we had rice. We would die if we cooked with salt water. It looks ridiculous to die on an oil rig. We were very hungry" (Gilad 1990: 64). These detailed accounts, although often difficult to read, give voice to actual experience and enlighten readers to the realities of forced migration, which in turn, hopefully, engenders empathy. These stories remind us that "there are stories lying 'behind' the stories that are told, and the emotions they arouse may never be fully known" (Donnan and Simpson 2007: 24). It could also be argued that migration stories provide the fuel for future creative expression as explained by Nguyen (chapter 3).

Maurice Halbwachs was the first theorist to analyze the importance of social memory. In 1951 he wrote *The Collective Memory*, in which he initiated a discussion concerning the pubic and sharable nature of memory as it differed from dreams (Halbwachs [1951] 1980: 9–13).[8] He is most well cited for his commentaries on the importance of social frameworks as guiding factors in the production of individual memories, made obvious in his renowned quote, "The memory of a society extends as far as the memory of the groups composing it" (Halbwachs [1951] 1980: 82). Roseman's chapter attests to the important social role memory activism can play concerning traumatic migrations that took place as long as a century ago, their relationship to nationalisms, and how individually authored literary genres, such as children's historical fiction, can perpetuate the social memory of mass migrations by boat (chapter 1). This role also extends to the creation of counter-narratives and the ability to initiate social and political agency (Bell 2003; Confino 1997). Federico Oliveri discusses the powerful role those outside of the nation, in this case Tunisian mothers and sisters, can play in depoliticizing national memories in Italy with the intention of shifting public opinion through protest (chapter 8).

The productions of social memory that occur in museums, memorial sites, and in various forms of media are all clear examples of the multiple ways nationalisms are produced. Often these productions provide an alternative voice for public and political debates surrounding migration by boat. In this volume, Mannik provides a detailed analysis of what was described as a media frenzy that took place when the *Amelie* arrived on Canadian shores in 1987, and how it was responsible for much controversial political debate about the nature of Canadian national ideologies and innate tensions between hatred, fear, and tolerance. This event has had a lasting effect on the ways the Canadian public views and reacts to subsequent arrivals by boat (chapter 9). Tao explains how the Australian National Maritime Museum consistently provides an arena for public debates and the memorialization of Australia's long and continuing history of arrivals of refugees and asylum seekers by boat (chapter 2). Horsti compares two outdoor public art installations to demonstrate the pivotal role art plays in critical questions about humanitarianism versus national security for Italian sea borders and islands such as Lampedusa. Greek artist Costas Varotsos's work titled, "L'approdo. Opera all'umanità migrante" [The landing. Art work for the migrant humanity] is built on the wreckage of a ship carrying eighty-one Albanians that needlessly sank off Italy's coast (chapter 4). Salerno explains that this art work/memorial site engendered some debate about issues related to humanitarian aid for refugees migrating by boat, but failed to address a primary issue—the all-too-common lack of government will to finance rescue missions—so therefore, in essence, it created an incorrect public memory (chapter 7).

Fiction and film are also valuable outlets for exploring the depths of remembering. Helen Hintjens (chapter 10) compares media reporting and film to look at the ways islands near Europe's Southern Mediterranean shores are symbolically depicted as both places of refuge and places of horror. Mediated images circulate and infuse public memories with ideas about islands as heterotopic places and islanders as conflicted and divided. Books and novels are also places where this type of migration is imagined and reimagined. As has been mentioned, Roseman provides an original examination of Canadian children's literature, as a neglected medium that aptly inscribes shared social memories about migration by boat (chapter 1). David Álvarez compares a Moroccan novel, *Cannibales,* with a performance piece by an artist from Belgium to highlight the symbolic function of small boats that travel frequently across the Strait of Gibraltar (chapter 6). In chapter 3, "Nuớc/Water: Oceanic Spatiality and the Vietnamese Diaspora," Vinh Nguyen compares two contemporary short stories to explore how literary narratives reflect on, and regenerate, the paradoxical role that ideas about water have played in terms of loss and belonging. When these experiences are given a voice through narratives, it is often with the intention of making sense of painful memories (chapter 3). Overall, the authors in this volume demonstrate how pain and trauma can be intimately linked to creativity and agency.

Conclusions

All of the chapters in this collection are original, and all explore ocean travel undertaken by refugees, asylum seekers, labor migrants, and so-called illegal migrants to show how migration by boat is symbolically aligned with notions of deterritorialization that often support fears of invasion, yet in reality these voyages represent the most physically and emotionally devastating form of forced migration. The contradictions in representation and lived experience are brought forward through stories, memorials, literature, media, and art. Contributions are interdisciplinary, and sometimes multidisciplinary in scope, to empathize the myriad ways migration by boat is imagined and reimagined, lived and experienced, and how the individuals involved are represented in ambiguous ways, which both challenge and reinforce cultural and legal structures. It draws attention to the fact that, symbolically, boats and water are viewed as spaces and places where hopes and fears along with "poetics and politics are mobilized" (Perera 2013: 78). The "boat" as an object, becomes a vehicle for finding refuge, and an experience that can quickly turn into a nightmare, and sometimes end in death. Bodies of water, the only viable spaces between nations, become battle fields; places that primarily foster ideas about human agency in terms of invasion, and only sometimes, foster humanitarian ideals; places where national security is contested and where innocent victims are often hidden and forgotten.

Organization of Chapters

The chapters within each of the four sections are structured to show a comparison between topics and places with the intention of moving conversations about migration by boat from histories and memories to literature and media representations, from artistic renditions to personal accounts, and from politics to popular culture. There is an intentional balance between theory and empirical research. Every chapter is a case study of either migration by boat over time between certain geographical areas, or a certain event(s) within a specific time period and set of locales. All are based on challenging stereotypical representations of individuals who migrate by boat and some, particularly in Section IV titled, "Stories of Smuggling, Trauma, and Rescue," include qualitative interviews. Migration routes are varied and cover the globe: from Britain to Canada, Tunisia to Italy, Iraq to Australia, and Morocco to Spain. In this context, boats carrying asylum seekers, refugees, and so-called illegal migrants not only move people and cultural capital between places, but also fuel cultural fantasies, dreams of adventure and hope, along with fears of invasion and terrorism.

Section I, "Embedded Memories for Public Consumption," consists of three chapters that focus on histories of migration by boat ranging from the nineteenth to the twentieth century. Sharon Roseman analyzes Canadian children's fiction to explore contemporary memory activism concerning the over one hundred thousand British "home children" who were forced to migrate to Canada between the 1860s and the 1930s. Philanthropists imagined at the time that they were involved in rescuing these children, whereas Canadian authorities agreed to this migration program only because of a dire need for farm laborers. The children were either orphans or had parents who were unable to take care of them. The youngest were only three to four years old and labor contracts often lasted until they were eighteen years old. Roseman highlights three literary motifs that inspire this category of historical fiction, to emphasize the power of children's books to affect social memory over time.

In "Representing Migration by Boat at the Australian National Maritime Museum," Kim Tao (chapter 2) explores the centrality of migration by boat in Australia's history and at the Australian National Maritime Museum (ANMM). This chapter examines three different ANMM exhibitions to demonstrate how arrivals of refugees by boat are remembered in the Australian context over time. Various creative interpretative processes are discussed in terms of meaning and practice, all of them aimed at detailing the pain and traumas of forced migration and its central role in Australian history. The individualized case studies cover arrivals from Vietnam in the late 1970s, the broad history of arrivals from British convicts, free settlers, and Indochinese boat people, to seaborne asylum seekers from Iraq and Afghanistan in an exhibition titled "Waves of Migration," and finally, the individualized experiences of one Croatian family in 1957. Collectively, these case studies are intended to challenge mainstream discourses about identity that are linked to forced migration.

In "Nước/Water: Oceanic Spatiality and the Vietnamese Diaspora," Vinh Nguyen emphasizes the symbolic association of water with community and belonging for hundreds of thousands of Vietnamese survivors who fled a new communist government in the late 1970s. "This mass migration captured the world's attention and gave rise to a new cultural lexicon: the 'boat people'" (chapter 3). After years of reflection, memories have surfaced in cultural and literary representations. Nguyen examines two short stories that describe the unique experiences of this group and how, over time, the cultural significance of water as a metaphor and as a particular kind of space has become central to the construction of diaspora memories to produce a contemporary sense of collective identity that was forged through loss and trauma, yet that emphasizes agency, connection, and mobility.

Section II, "The Artist and the Illegal Migrant," examines links between various forms of artistic productions that explore migration by boat in attempts to enlighten the public about the politics and problems for refugees who chose this type of movement. It looks at migration by boat, both historically and symbolically, through fiction and public visual arts. It also juxtaposes European and Australian experience and perspective. In chapter 4, "Imagining Europe's Borders: Commemorative Art on Migrant Tragedies," Karina Horsti draws on theories about borders and the practice of bordering in the context of southern European sea borders through a comparison of two public art works. One is an installation of damaged migrant boats that were collected on the shores of a Greek island named Chois and then displayed in Berlin in 2009, at the Brandenburg Gate. The second is a monument that was erected on the island of Lampedusa in the form of a gate. Both exemplify the gate as a metaphor for borders, liminality, humanitarianism, and state securitization. Her analysis is critical to understanding how art works can effectively commemorate the trauma and suffering associated with migration by boat, yet that nevertheless, become ineffective in eliciting policy shifts and empathy in terms of public opinion.

In chapter 5, "Washed Clean": The Forgotten Journeys of "Irregular Maritime Arrivals" in J. M. Coetzee's *Estralia*," Jennifer Rutherford examines J. M. Coetzee's novel, *The Childhood of Jesus* (2013). In this fictional work Coetzee creates a shadow-land called Novilla, "a cosmos of being *in absentia*" where "there is a room but no key, a place to sleep but no shelter, food but no flavor," a place filled with holes (chapter 5). She links Coetzee's complex use of metaphor to the experiences of irregular maritime arrivals to Australian shores. Accordingly, she demonstrates how holing (the act of propelling an object into a hole) becomes one way to think about stringent legal policies that have become more severe over time, policies that create disparaged subjects and express the will to hole. Although *The Childhood of Jesus* is neither just about refugee policy nor about Australia, Coetzee's mythical Novilla is a place where asylum seekers dwell in limbo, "stripped of all but the barest necessities of life" (Rutherford, chapter 5 this volume), and therefore is a space that allows us to imagine the logic of inhumane practices, ideologies, and policies.

The Strait of Gibraltar is the narrowest waterway between Europe and Africa. David Álvarez looks at migration by boat that takes place in this strait where illegal migrants cross either in duck-hunting boats called *pateras*, or in various kinds of inflatable crafts called by their brand name, Zodiac. These small boats frequently capsize and many people have drowned in their attempts to find refuge in Europe. Álvarez explains the historic significance of the Strait of Gibraltar as a geopolitical site that links the global North and South through a comparison of Mahi Binebine's novel, *Cannibales,* and a performance piece by artist Francis Alÿs, called "Don't Cross the Bridge before You Get to the River." After providing a history of one of the busiest maritime channels in the world, he explains how these two works function to critique increasingly stringent immigration policies that strip migrants of their rights and endanger their lives. Álvarez also brings to light counter discourses about clandestine migration and the important role that boats, as objects, play in fragile circumstances and experiences.

In section III "Media, Politics, and Representation," there is shift toward comparing art and performance with media representations. While making a variety of connections between imagined and real events, section III provides avenues for understating how public opinion is formed by myriad media representations and popular culture venues. As well, resistance to discriminatory state policy is explored alongside explicit racism and indignation toward refugees. Daniele Salerno begins this section by looking at news media, monuments, and art installations that revolve around the *Kater I Rades* tragedy when eighty-one people died in the Strait of Otranto. These individuals were attempting to escape a civil and economic crisis in their homeland of Albania. The meanings associated with this event were "shaped, readapted and rewritten in order to meet the shifting narratives on which Otranto and its community base their collective identity" (Salerno, chapter 7, this volume). Even though the opening of Costas Varotsos's work, "L'approdo. Opera all'umanità migrante" [The landing. Art work for the migrant humanity], was framed by narratives of hospitality and humanitarianism, interpretations in the media surrounding it function to erase the specificities of the event, in particular the fact that eighty-one people died because of the Italian government's refusal to rescue their sinking vessel. In this way Salerno reminds us that representational practices and media reports can often hide more, or just as much, as they claim to memorialize.

In chapter 8, "'Where Are Our Sons?'": Tunisian Mothers and the Repoliticization of Deadly Migration across the Mediterranean Sea," Federico Oliveri looks at the southern European sea borders where it is estimated that 13,000 people have lost their lives since 2000, although the political responsibility and will for searching and mourning for them is rarely apparent. He focuses on the case of missing Tunisians who left after the Revolution of 2010 and reconstructs protests that took place in a variety of ways over time, from the perceptive of the lost Tunisians' mothers and sisters. In this chapter Oliveri combines the analysis of multiple sources, including public petitions, newspapers, press releases, videos, and Web sites to demonstrate how these family members are repoliticizing issues of injustice based on race, class, and gender through demands of respect, which are grounded in parental feelings of love and protection. He argues that even though shifts and changes to Euro-Mediterranean immigration policies will be extremely difficult to achieve, it will be impossible without the active involvement of the migrants and their families.

Some events seem to monopolize the international "mediascape" (Appadurai 1990) for periods of time. Arrivals of refugees by boat are one such event. Often, for weeks following, social dramas are created in representations that rely on systems of shared values and meanings, which are politically charged and highly emotional. In "Mysterious Refugees: Social Drama Ensues" (chapter 9, this volume), Lynda Mannik adopts Victor Turner's theories about social dramas to explore how mass media affects and alters everyday discourses, solidifies public opinion about migration by boat, and inspires public, political performances. In 1987 the arrival of the *Amelie*, a freighter carrying 174 refugees (mostly young, Sikh men) that landed in a small, isolated fishing village (population seventy-seven) on the shores of Nova Scotia, created a media frenzy, and a subsequent social drama. Within the first week, national Canadian newspapers alone had published over 150 articles. This chapter explains how the event brought to light tensions in national ideologies between hospitality and humanitarianism that subsequently highlighted racism and public fears concerning those who arrive illegally in Canada by boat. It also highlights the fluidity between media and performativity in descriptions of individual and collective responses.

Helen Hintjens shifts this conversation specifically to islands and focuses on understanding how media and film work to represent islands, such as Lampedusa and Linosa (both off the coast of Italy), as contradictory places of refuge and horror in "Islands and Images of Flight around Europe's Southern Rim: Trouble in Heterotopia" (chapter 10). Several tiny islands on southern Mediterranean shores have become clearinghouses for the detainment of asylum seekers. Hintjens focuses on the heterotopic nature of these places that are surrounded by water, alongside the conflicting relationships between tourists, island inhabitants, and refugees. In general, islands are imagined as paradises and safe havens, places where it becomes easier to imagine utopian lives. In recent years, hundreds have died trying to get to Lampedusa and Linosa, trying to survive and to escape political oppression from locations such as Libya, Syria, and Tunisia. Subsequently, these islands have become places of increased military securitization where refugees are confined, rejected, and buried.

Finally, the last section, "Stories of Smuggling, Trauma, and Rescue," gives an intimate view of the complex sets of human relationships that are inculcated in traumatic experiences of people who are forced to migrate by boat. The stories of survivors, smugglers, and members of host nations are told in the hopes that discriminatory, stereotypical attitudes will be altered in favor of balanced and empathetic viewpoints. In chapter 11, "'If We Die, We Die Together': Risking Death at Sea in Search of Safety," Sue Hoffman focuses on the Australian context and relationships between so-called people-smugglers and the so-called illegal migrants, who are typically from Afghanistan, Sri Lanka, Iran, and Iraq. Through personal interviews she focuses on themes that are central to the experience of migration by boat, including fear, insecurity, and risk. People smugglers are most often depicted as callous opportunists and their passengers are most often viewed as victims who are preyed upon. Real relationships, however, are varied; and sometimes smugglers concern themselves with the safety of their customers, particularly if they are working with citizens from their own country. Refugees' accounts demonstrate that a small number believe that the smugglers they were involved with did help them find a safe place to live and did treat them with humanity. Hoffman reminds us of the dire need for international aid and protection for refugees, so that ultimately they do not have to resort to trying to find safety in unsafe boats.

Migration from West Africa to Europe has escalated in recent years. In chapter 12, "En Route to Hell: Dreams of Adventure and Traumatic Experiences among West African Boat People to Europe," Papa Sow, Elena Marmer, and Jürgen Scheffran explore the plight of young Senegalese men who undertake clandestine journeys with the aid of complex organizations, including travel agents, ship captains, *touts,* and *borom gaals.* After providing a thorough analysis of sophisticated and pricey passport controls, they analyze qualitative interviews to highlight the individuated complexities of relationships that are forged through the risky experience of migration by boat. They uncover symbolic and emotional elements that explain the associated trauma. Dominate discourses that position migrants who travel by boat as a threat accompanied by restrictive immigration policies fail to deter men who are in search of an income to support families who are living in dire poverty due to the increasing destruction of marine ecosystems. Dominate discourses focused on securitization obscure the fact that these migrations are fuelled by "the structural job demand for cheap migrant labour in informal sectors in Europe" (chapter 12).

In 2010 the *Janga* crashed on the rocks at Christmas Island, killing fifty people. It is one of many such events linked to what has recently been described as a global crisis. In the final chapter, chapter 13 "Re-living *Janga*: Survivor Narratives," Linda Briskman and Michelle Dimasi narrate this event through survivors' stories and the voices of the citizens of Christmas Island. Islanders talked about their courageous efforts to save lives and the trauma of witnessing. Survivors recalled the horrors of almost drowning at sea while watching friends and family members die. Dimasi was conducting research on the island at the time of the crash and the conversations she engaged in contrasted dramatically with successive political discourses that promoted increasingly stringent deterrence and interception policies as life-saving requirements. Both authors argue that the failure of the Australian government to focus on human security, empathy, and compassion was a factor in the deaths of the *Janga*'s passengers, and that lessons can be learned about compassion and humanity from the stories that islanders and survivors told.

Notes

1. I have discussed this voyage in more depth in *Photography, Memory and Refugee Identity: The Voyage of the* Walnut, *1948* (Vancouver: UBC Press, 2012).
2. L'Association des amis et des families des victims de l'immigration clandestine (AFVIC) claimed that 3,286 bodies were recovered from the Strait of Gibraltar beaches from 1997 to 2001.
3. The mass drowning of hundreds on one boat made international headlines and drew attention to what was described as an international crisis in need of UN intervention. The tragedy that occurred on April 19 happened when most of the passengers tried to get to one side of the ship in order to be rescued by a merchant ship. For more details BBC 2015.
4. In 1982 the UN adopted an international agreement called the Law of the Sea. It defines a national boundary of twelve miles from any shoreline as territory, and two hundred miles where state authority has power over resources. Areas outside this range are considered high seas, where there is no national ownership. The high seas are considered mutually owned by all peoples. Having said that, even on the high seas pirates and drug runners (for example) can be detained.
5. Here, Nyers (2006: 46) also reminds us that, as a liminal category, refugees "unhinge" humanitarian ideas associated with citizenship.
6. By this I am referring to the marked hatred of communism following World War II as discussed by Jacobson 1998; Troper 2000; Whitaker 2014.
7. In response to Canada's policy restrictions, Gilad quotes a Polish immigrant: "Now, Sweden is really humanitarian because it takes deaf people and people with diseases" (Gilad 1990: 129).

Bibliography

Agar, Alistair. 1999. *Refugees: Perspectives on the Experience of Forced Migration*. London/New York: Pinter, 1999.
Ahmed, Sara. 2004. *The Cultural Politics of Emotion*. London/New York: Routledge.
Allatson, Paul, and Jo McCormack. 2005. "Introduction: Exile and Social Transformation." *Portal Journal of Multidisciplinary International Studies* 2, no. 1 (Jan.): 1–18.
Appadurai, Arjun. 1990. "Disjunture and Difference in the Global Cultural Economy," *Theory, Culture, Society* 7: 295–310.
BBC. 2015. "Mediterranean Migrants: Hundreds Feared Dead after Boat Capsizes." BBC News, April 19. http://www.bbc.com/news/world-europe-32371348.
Bell, Duncan S. 2003. "Mythscapes: Memory, Mythology, and National Identity." *British Journal of Sociology* 54, no. 1: 63–81.
Chimni, B. S. 1998. "The Geopolitics of Refugee Studies: A View from the South." *Journal of Refugee Studies* 11, no. 4: 350–74.
Colson, Elizabeth. 2003. "Forced Migration and the Anthropological Response." *Journal of Refugee Studies* 16, no. 1: 1–18.
Colson, Elizabeth, and Thayer Scudder. 1982. "From Welfare to Development: A Conceptual Framework for the Analysis of Dislocated People." In *Involuntary Migration and Resettlement: The Problems and Responses of Dislocated People*, edited by Art Hansen and Anthony Oliver-Smith, 267–88. Boulder, CO: Westview Press.
Confino, Alon. 1997. "Collective Memory and Cultural History: Problems of Method." *American Historical Review* 102, no. 5 (Dec.): 1386–1403.
Coutin, Susan Bibler. 2005. "Being en Route." *American Anthropologist* 107, no. 2: 195–206.
de Haas, Hein. 2008. "The Myth of Invasion: The Inconvenient Realities of African Migration to Europe." *Third World Quarterly* 29, no. 7: 1305–22.
Donnan, Hastings, and Kirk Simpson. 2007. "Silence and Violence among Northern Ireland Border Protestants." *Ethnos* 72, no. 1 (March): 5–28.
Edkins, J. 2003. *Trauma and the Memory of Politics*. Cambridge: Cambridge University Press.
Escobar, Arturo. 2001. "Culture Sits in Places: Reflections on Globalism and Subaltern Strategies of Localization." *Political Geography* 20: 139–74.
Gale, P. 2004. "The Refugee Crisis and Fear: Populist Politics and Media Discourse," *Journal of Sociology* 40: 321–40.
Gilad, Lisa. 1990. *The Northern Route: An Ethnography of Refugee Experiences*. St. John's: Memorial University of Newfoundland.
Halbwachs, Maurice. 1980 [1951]. *The Collective Memory*. New York and London: Harper and Row.
Hannerz, Ulf. 1997. "Flows, Boundaries and Hybrids: Keywords in Transnational Anthropology." Originally published in Portuguese as "Fluxos, fronteiras, híbridos: palavras-chave da antropologia transnacional." *Mana* (Rio de Janeiro) 3, no. 1: 7–39.
Holt, M. 1997. "The Wives and Mothers of Heroes: Evolving Identities of Palestinian Refugee Women in Lebanon." *Journal of Development Studies* 43, no. 2: 245–64.

Jacobson, Matthew Frye. 1998. *Whiteness of a Different Colour: European Immigrants and the Alchemy of Race.* Cambridge: Cambridge University Press.
Malkki, Liisa. 1995. "Refugees and Exile: From "Refugee Studies" to the National Order of Things." *Annual Review of Anthropology* 24: 495–523.
———. 1997. "Speechless Emissaries: Refugees, Humanitarianism and Dehistoricization." In *Siting Culture: The Shifting Anthropological Object*, edited by Karen Fog Olwig and Kirsten Hastrup, 223–54. London/New York: Routledge.
Mannik, Lynda. 2012. *Photography, Memory and Refugee Identity: The Voyage of the Walnut, 1948.* Vancouver: UBC Press.
Massey, Douglas S., Joaquin Arango, Graeme Hugo, Ali Koudouci, Adela Pellegrino, and J. Edward Taylor. 1998. *Worlds in Motion: Understanding International Migration at the End of the Millennium.* Oxford: Clarendon Press.
Mansouri, Fethi, and Michael Leach. 2004. *Lives in Limbo: Voices of Refugees under Temporary Protection.* Sydney: University of New South Wales.
Nyers, Peter. 2006. *Rethinking Refugees: Beyond States of Emergency.* London/New York: Routledge.
O'Doherty, Kieran, and Amanda LeCouteur. 2007. "Asylum Seekers," "Boat People" and "Illegal Immigrants": Social Categorisation in the Media." *Australian Journal of Psychology* 59, no. 1: 1–12.
Perera, Suvendrini. 2013. "Oceanic Corpo-graphies, Refugee Bodies and the Making and Unmaking of Waters." *Feminist Review* 103: 58–79.
Pugh, Michael. 2004. "Drowning Not Waving: Boat People and Humanitarianism at Sea." *Journal of Refugee Studies* 17, no. 1: 50–69.
Robins, Simon, Iosif Kovras, and Anna Vallianatou. 2014. "Addressing Migrant Bodies on Europe's Southern Frontier: An Agenda for Research and Practice." Belfast: Queen's University and the University of York.
Steinberg, Philip E. 2013. "Of Other Seas: Metaphors and Materialities in Maritime Regions." *Atlantic Studies* 10, no. 2: 156–69.
Sztompka, Piotr. 2000. "Cultural Trauma: The Other Face of Social Change." *European Journal of Social Theory* 3, no. 4: 449–66.
Troper, Harold. 2000. "History of Immigration to Toronto Since the Second World War: From Toronto "the Good" to Toronto "The World in a City." CERIS Working Paper no. 12, University of Toronto.
Turner, Victor W. 1964 "Betwixt and Between: The Liminal Period in *Rites de Passage*." *The Proceedings of the American Ethnological Society,* Symposium on New Approaches to the Study of Religion, pp. 4–20.
1969. *The Ritual Process: Structure and Anti-structure.* Chicago: Aldine.
United Nations High Commissioner for Refugees (UNHCR). 1951. "Convention and Protocol relating to the Status of Refugees." http://www.unhcr.org/3b66c2aa10.html
———. 2014. "Asylum Trends, First Half 2014." http://www.unhcr.org/
Van Alpen, Ernest. 1999. "Symptoms of Discursivity: Experience, Memory, and Trauma." In *Acts of Memory: Cultural Recall in the Present,* edited by Mieke Bal, Jonathan Crewe, and Leo Spitzer. Hanover/London: University Press of New England.
Vukov, Tamara. 2003. "Imagining Communities through Immigration Policies: Governmental Regulation, Media Spectacles and the Affective Politics of National Borders." *International Journal of Cultural Studies* 6 no. 3: 335–53.

Whitaker, Reginald. 1097. *Double Standard: The Secret History of Canadian Immigration.* Toronto: Lester and Orpen Dennys.

Zucker, Norman L., and Naomi Flink Zucker. 1996. *Desperate Crossings: Seeking Refuge in America.* Armonk, NY: M. E. Sharpe.

Section I

Embedded Memories for Public Consumption

Figure S.1. Vietnamese refugees await rescue from their thirty-five-foot fishing boat. They were rescued by the amphibious command ship USS BLUE RIDGE (LCC-19) 350 miles northeast of Cam Ranh Bay, Vietnam, after spending eight days at sea. May 1984. Courtesy of DefenseImagery.mil.

1

Children's Literature and Memory Activism

British Child Labor Migrants' Passage to Canada

Sharon R. Roseman

In 1869 the SS *Hibernian* carried the first group of children from the Maria Rye homes to Canada (Kohli 2003: 44). It was run by the Allan Line, which had been transporting people and mail across the North Atlantic since 1852. This inaugural voyage of mainly female migrants from this particular philanthropic agency included seventy-eight minors and two adults; it departed Liverpool on October 28. The youngest from this group on board were Mary E. B. Court and Margaret McFee, both at four years of age, and Florence R. Alverez at five (Library and Archives Canada n.d.). The party disembarked in Quebec City on August 11. Their destination: Niagara-on-the-Lake, Ontario, where the institutional distribution home was located (Parr 1994: 47). From there, they would be sent to individual families. The names of many steamships like the *Hibernian* appear in Canadian immigration passenger lists that record the composition of the arriving groups of individuals who came to be known as "British home children."

In this chapter, I consider how the history of this migration of well over 100,000[1] children and adolescents between the mid-nineteenth and mid-twentieth centuries has come to be memorialized very powerfully in a body of children's fiction published in the past few decades in the wake of a memory activism movement. The following two sections summarize the history of child labor migration on which the novels are based and the role of children's literature in the memory movement. The remainder of the chapter comprises an analysis of potent literary motifs found in six children's novels about individual child migrants.

Child Labor Migrants and Canadian History

The home children were brought to Canada from England, Scotland, Wales, the Isle of Man, and Ireland by dozens of charitable agencies led by charismatic individuals such as Annie Macpherson, Maria Susan Rye, John T. Middlemore, and Dr. Thomas John Barnardo. They saw themselves as "rescuing" vulnerable young people and providing them with a better future in another country (see Figure 1.1).

Some of these children were orphaned but others were leaving behind parents who were in some cases themselves confined to institutions, including workhouses (Bagnell 2001; Kershaw and Sacks 2008; Oschefski 2011; Parker 2008; Parr 1994). Once in Canada, while some remained in institutional settings such as farm schools, most of the children and adolescents brought to Canada were placed in private homes purportedly to receive basic care but also to serve as domestic workers and farm workers. These

Figure 1.1. British immigrant children from Dr. Barnardo's Homes at landing stage, Saint John, N.B. Credit: Isaac Erb, Department of Interior photographic records (New Brunswick), Library and Archives Canada, accession number 1936-271 NPC, item N.B.17-1-1, reproduction copy number PA-041785.

placements were covered by contracts between the immigration agencies and locally appointed guardians, and the individual "masters" and/or "mistresses" to whose homes the children were sent. These contracts often spelled out up to three stages to cover different age ranges, sometimes lasting until the immigrant apprentices reached eighteen years of age (Parr 1994: 84–86; also see Kershaw and Sacks 2008; Kohli 2003: 359–361; Parker 2008).[2]

Although Kohli notes that the first child settler workers were brought to the Canadian colonies in the 1830s, the home children period is generally regarded to have begun in the 1860s (Kohli 2003: 12; also see Parker 2008; Parr 1994: 28–29). With time, this migration pathway was facilitated by Canadian policies such as the 1897 Act to Regulate the Immigration into Ontario of Certain Classes of Children. A series of relevant British legislation included the amendment to the Poor Law Act in 1850 and the Custody of Children Act (1891) allowing so-called fit individuals to make decisions about children without their parents' consent, including about emigration (Oschefski 2011; Parr 1994: 28–34). Due to grave concerns about the system, in 1924 the Dominion Immigration Branch banned the entry into Canada of "children under 14 years of age who were not accompanied by parents" (Parr 1994: 153; also see Parker 2008: 192–206). Not only were there some subsequent exceptions to this law, but numerous adolescents who were called home boys and home girls continued to enter Canada via the same institutions through the 1920s and 1930s (Parr 1994: 153). Most authors indicate that this migration scheme had ended by 1939, even though some young people continued to be brought over by the same agencies after that period.[3]

Part of the context for the program was that British and Canadian children from working-class homes helped their parents. They also generally left school at age fourteen, when they were expected to apprentice or begin earning wages full time (Parr 1994: 20–21). The philanthropists who ran receiving homes in Britain and Ireland, and who along with the British Boards of Guardians raised funds to pay the children's passage on boats to Canada, may have genuinely believed that they were engaged in child rescue, However, many Canadian authorities agreed to this migration program only because of a perceived labor shortage on farms in Canada and a racist immigration policy that preferred white British "stock." Home Children Canada calculates that 11.5 percent of the current Canadian population is comprised of descendants of such migrants (Kershaw and Sacks 2008: 230). Roger Kershaw and Janet Sacks (2008) refer to these young people who crossed the Atlantic on boats without their parents or guardians as *child migrants,* while Kenneth Bagnell (2001) and Marjorie Kohli (2003) use the terms *young immigrants* and *child emigrants.* Joy Parr, in contrast, more explicitly uses the categories of *young immigrant workers* or *immigrant apprentices* (Parr 1994: 82). To describe the group portrayed in the six novels I discuss in this chapter, I use the term *child labor migrants* (International Labour Organization 1996–2014).[4]

This phrase highlights that these novels focus on the experiences of children fourteen and under rather than on the older apprentice workers, but that these younger migrants were being brought to Canada as workers as much as they were as minors in need of care, and that it was not clear at the outset that these children would end up as immigrants rather than as temporary residents of Canada. Like many migrant laborers in the past and present, these children were being moved around the globe by boat primarily for the purpose of filling others' requirement for labor (Castles 1989; Cohen and Sirkeci 2011).

Traveling in third-class steerage, many of the children experienced seasickness and confronted immediate physical danger, with some groups becoming lost through shipwrecks.[5] The presence of numerous child labor migrants on ships in this period is evident in this letter written to *The Times* from an eyewitness to an explosion in the coal storage compartment on the SS *Sardinian* in 1878 when it was coming into port near Derry, Ireland: "Miss Macpherson and her little band of Canadian emigrants showed no small amount of true fortitude and heroism. Most of the children behaved nobly under the trying circumstances, and exhibited much of the fruit of their careful training. They kept repeating to one another many of the sayings they had heard from Miss Macpherson about being patient, and brave, and good" (cited in Kohli 2003: 49-50).

Once in Canada these children experienced extensive discrimination, with a widespread idea that they came from problematic ancestry and might be criminals or physically weak, a form of classism and eugenic thinking that intensified rather than diminished in the early decades of the twentieth century. The organizations that brought them to Canada attempted to counter these ideas by emphasizing that they only selected the "best" children to come to Canada, and that they instilled in their charges a moral Christian grounding and work discipline. However, this troubled legacy was suppressed in dominant accounts of Canadian history. As well, many former child migrants did not talk about how they had come to Canada, even in some cases to their own family members (e.g., Skidmore 2012; Snow 2000).

Memory Activism

To counter the silencing of child labor migration as a significant component in Canadian European settler history, a vigorous memory movement emerged in various countries, including Canada and Australia. Organizations such as Home Children Canada, the International Association of Former Child Migrants and Their Families, and the Child Migrants Trust have sought access to formerly closed records and apologies from the governments involved. Their efforts are buttressed by the hard work of individuals such as Lori

Oschefski, who runs a memory activist Web site compiling lists and examples of archival records, and published materials documenting this period and its ongoing impact.[6]

Children's literature has become an identifiable medium through which this migration has become inscribed as part of a shared social memory. As Fentress and Wickham (1992: 26) note, "Social memory is a source of knowledge" that provides a "group with material for conscious reflection." More recently, the term *memory activism* has been used in relation to the reclamation of specific histories in cases where events as a whole, or specific details about them, have been suppressed or distorted. In such cases, as part of re-evaluating and publicizing specific historical events and relationships, there is a reinscription of *lieux de mémoire* (places of memory) or related spatialized histories (e.g., Kreissler 2007: 7; also see Billingsley 2014). In the case of the British child labor migrants brought to Canada, the memory activism movement has focused on recuperating various places of memory, including the locations from which the children were removed, the journeys they took by land and by sea, and the locations where they ended up working in the new country. This has resulted in the publication of transcriptions of oral history narratives (e.g., Harrison 2003[1979]; Staples 2003) and full-length biographies (e.g., Skidmore 2012; Snow 2000), including some produced for children and other young readers (e.g., Pettit 2000; Young 2009). This form of recuperation is psychologically and politically meaningful for survivors and their descendants, who can thus employ autobiography and family history as forms of reappropriating histories of stigmatization and exploitation, while also providing materials for a broad public reflection on this migration (Fentress and Wickham 1992; Mannik 2013).[7] The novels about British child migrants similarly provide a lens through the eyes of individuals. They are examples of both realistic fiction and historical fiction (Egoff and Saltman 1990: 20, 103; Hudson 2003: 28–31). They remind us of the role of children's literature in the politics of memory "to cultivate children's imaginations, their critical thinking abilities, and their sense of history" (Mickenberg 2006: 13).

Thematically, the novels about British child labor migrants share much with other accounts of immigration, including the common nineteenth- and twentieth-century tropes of adventure, hardiness, hardship, and survival of the European settler populations. These are evident, for example, in what is regarded as the first Canadian children's novel: Catharine Parr Traill's 1852 *Canadian Crusoes* (Egoff and Saltman 1990: 6; also see Hudson 2003: 28–29). Narratives promoting the "Romantic structure of loss and return" are found in the autobiographical accounts of Thomas Barnardo about his work of "rescuing" children (Reimer 2013: 4). Works such as his and the more recent critical novels about British child migrants discussed here resonate with the famous book *Anne of Green Gables,* by Lucy Maud Montgomery (originally published in 1908). Montgomery's work documents the transfer of an orphaned home girl not from Britain, but from Nova Scotia, to what turns out to be a loving home in Prince Edward Island. Although written in a different period and with a focus on the good that could come from such arrangements, Montgomery inserts details about the neglect and hardship experienced by Anne in the previous homes where she was placed (Reimer 2013: 10–11). As Hudson notes, in the Canadian corpus many works of historical and realistic children's fiction in the past several decades are "often harsh in tone and atmosphere, showing the physical hardships, relentless labour, prejudices towards cultural groups, and restrictions facing girls and women in past eras" (Hudson 2003: 31). By providing a critical focus on labor exploitation and child neglect and abuse, the contemporary body of novels about the British child migrants' arrival in Canada can also be viewed as sharing with leftist children's literature "a sense of social justice ... ; exploring the histories of peoples and groups previously ignored" (Mickenberg 2006: 7). Finally, the novels examined here also form part of a larger body of works for children that document other, later migrations by boat; these include those by and about former child refugees such as the illustrated book for young children entitled *The Little Refugee,* based on Ahn Do's journey from Vietnam to Australia in the 1970s (Do and Do 2011).

The Novels

To illustrate the role of children's literature in shaping social memory about this migration, I have chosen six novels. In order of publication date, the first is Barbara Haworth-Attard's 1996 book *Home Child* published by the Montreal-based Roussan Publishers. It follows the story of Arthur, an underweight boy from London with no experience of agricultural work, whose Canadian employer Mr. Wilson exclaims when he picks him up at the train station, "'Hmph! Pretty small for thirteen. Look to be ten–eleven at most'" (Haworth-Attard 1996: 21). As in most of these novels, despite neglect and abuse from the farmer couple he works under, Arthur has allies in some of their children and in Grandma Wilson who had herself been an immigrant and openly contests the stigmatization of British child migrants.

Elaine Breault Hammond published *Beyond the Waterfall* in 1997 with Charlottetown's Ragweed Press. It opens with the lead character, orphaned Maggie, traveling back in time and through space, from her familiar surroundings in New Brunswick in the 1990s to the 1890s and a home on a Manitoban farm where she lives for a time as a girl called Ellie. As Ellie she meets Nicholas, a new boy attending their one-room Prairie schoolhouse, who was recently brought from England by a woman he has named "Miss Charity" of the Lost Lambs Orphanage and placed with the brutal neighbor Newt Ebenezer: "'Yep, some English boy's goin' to have a hard life, seein' as he's goin' to the

Ebenezers'. It don't seem fair.' And Pa shook his head at the wicked ways of the world" (Breault Hammond 1997: 38).

Troon Harrison's 2000 book *A Bushel of Light* was published by the Stoddart Kids imprint. It begins with the lead character Maggie just turning fourteen and facing years more in her Barnardo Society contract, after having lived on the Howards' farm for six years. Maggie had been forced to leave her twin sister Thomasina behind in Britain and never stops worrying about her sister's fate until Thomasina is also sent to Canada by the Barnardo Society and they are rejoined at the end of the book.

Another very experienced author of children's literature, Jean Little, wrote the book *Orphan at My Door: The Home Child Diary of Victoria Cope* in 2001 as part of the "Dear Canada" series put out by Scholastic Canada, a specialized line dedicated to teaching specific skills through accounts of Canada's past (Scholastic Canada 2006). This book takes us back to 1897 and uses the device of eleven-year old Victoria Cope keeping a diary when her family brings in the twelve-year old home girl Marianna Wilson to help with housework. Even Victoria's gentle physician father reacts unkindly when he is discomfitted with the situation he confronts when he and Victoria go to pick up Marianna at the train station: "'That girl is nothing but a child. A sickly youngster wouldn't be worth her keep'" (Little 2001: 29). Victoria describes in vivid detail the contrast between the relatively good conditions for servants in their home and the terrifying abuse suffered by Marianna's brother Jasper who escapes from sure death on a Canadian farm.

Louise Ravenhill's novel *Move Smart, Boy!: A Novel about Home Children in Rural Prince Edward Island 1911–1913* was published in 2002 by Luíka in Charlottetown. Like Marianna and Maggie, the lead character Adam Hollyfield is separated from his siblings at the Charlottetown train station where they are picked up by the kind Moore couple. Adam is assigned to the unhappy Lewis Rufford who frequently falls into uncontrolled rages during which he belittles and beats Adam: "Mister's reaction was swift and without warning. His massive hand smashed against my face, toppling me and the chair backward onto the floor" (Ravenhill 2002: 160). This brutal existence is made bearable in snatches by Adam's contact with the farm animals; the youngest Rufford girl, Lucy; the teacher, Miss Tucker; and the kind Granny and the home boy Potter who lives with her. However, Adam also ends up running away, becoming unsure he "could survive another beating" (Ravenhill 2002: 189).

Irene Watts's book, *Flower: A Novel,* was published by Toronto's Tundra Books in 2005. As with the Breault Hammond book, connections across different periods are a device used in the novel. It begins in Toronto in 2005 with thirteen-year old Katie, who had lost her mother when she was seven, setting out to visit her grandparents who have just bought an old house in Halifax, Nova Scotia, that they are fixing up to run as a bed-and-breakfast.

It is in this Victorian house that Katie meets the ghost of Lillie, who had become a Barnardo girl in 1902 when she lost her own mother, and was subsequently sent to Canada. Readers learn about the history of child labor migration from the chapters containing Lillie's narration and from the character of Katie's grandfather, whose own father and mother were brought to Canada as children by immigration agencies.

Aside from the cover art and a few line drawings and reproduced historical photographs (in the case of Little's book), the characters, plots, and imagery in these gripping novels are represented through the authors' texts. They are based on extensive historical research, made explicit in Barbara Haworth-Attard's reproduction of a memory from a survivor of the British child migration process: John Atterbury (Haworth-Attard 1996: 126–27) at the end of book, and Jean Little's (2001) inclusion of photographs, a "Historical Note," and other information such as recipes for food mentioned in the novel. Louise Ravenhill (2002) similarly includes a glossary, an introduction providing a brief historical background to the story, and a bibliography and other resources. There are clear tie-ins with the memory movement evident in some of the acknowledgments and Haworth-Attard's book is endorsed in a foreword by J. A. David Lorente, the chair of the Heritage Renfrew Home Children Canada Committee who comments that the author "has somehow managed to get inside the minds and hearts of Arthur, the Home Boy, and Sadie, his empathetic peer in the family to which he was sent" (Lorente 1996: n.p.).

My coding of the content of these novels revealed a number of common literary motifs. I am following William Freedman's definition of a literary motif as "a recurrent theme, character, or verbal pattern, [that] may also be a family or associational cluster of literal or figurative references to a given class of concepts or objects" (Freedman 1971: 127). As he notes, "The motif, then, may become a part of the total perspective, pervading the book's atmosphere and becoming an important thread in the fabric of the work" (Freedman 1971: 125). The analysis below draws on three of the most dominant and significant literary motifs in the novels discussed: displacement as illustrated through descriptions of the journey by boat, material traces, and silencing. These three motifs comprise a powerful aspect of the plots driving the novels' narratives and of the emotional texture of the children's experiences. They are used skillfully to parallel the details found in the historical data about this period and the ideology underlying the memory movement's call for recognition of the suffering and vulnerability of Canada's "home children."

Displacement: Journey by Boat

As Ahmed et al. (2003: 6) note, "home and migration" can never be understood without attending to "spatialized relations of power." Just as "homes" are often "sites of alienation and violence," displacement attends migration, both in cases when people become mobile as a result of "homelessness, exile and forced migration," and when migration into some regions is associated with the displacement of others being pushed out (Ahmed et al. 2003: 6). In the novels, the children's experiences of physical and existential displacement (Jackson 2005) are transmitted very clearly through references to their journeys overseas.

The accounts of the children's trip across the Atlantic begin with descriptions of leave-taking that include accounts of ritualized performances used to promote the migration program at the highest levels of British society. Just before she boards the boat to Canada, Watts's character, Lillie, participates in a concert at the Royal Albert Hall to raise money to send the "Waifs and Strays" overseas: "The boys went onstage first, showing all the work they'd do when they got to Canada. They cut logs, shoveled snow, fed the animals, loaded hay, and baked bread. Then it was the girls' turn. We mimed washing, hanging up clothes, and ironing" (Watts 2005: 65, 64). Other references to leave-taking reference the visceral experience of sometimes large groups of children boarding the ships, when "feet thundered on the gangway" (Harrison 2000: 44).

Once under way, the rough seas led to children becoming seasick in "crowded and stuffy steerage quarters" (Ravenhill 2002: 3). Lillie talks to her dead mother while on the ship: "I hope good times start soon because there's rats running over our feet where we sleep, down below in steerage, and the smell is awful there" (Watts 2005: 65). And "Nicholas lay on his berth, his eyes closed, feeling the pitch of the ship, his teeth clenched against the urge to throw up when there was nothing left in his stomach" (Breault Hammond 1997: 41; also Haworth-Attard 1996: 52). In contrast, Nicholas recalls that "Miss Charity was not sick for a moment on the rolling ship.... He remembered her lining up all fifty of her charges on the deck for morning prayers and lecturing them on their weakness.... They had a duty to the British Empire and to the Lost Lambs Orphanage to be strong workers for the good families" (Breault Hammond 1997: 41). The character Arthur tells the sympathetic daughter of his employers that he reads to take away the metaphoric feeling that he is still on the boat that brought him from England: "'the deck moving all the time, never still, and the fear of knowing there was nothing beneath me but deep, black water. Well, that's how it feels to me here'" (Haworth-Attard 1996: 69).

Aside from illness, cold, hunger, and fear, other physical dangers of the journey are also highlighted, as when "a great big wave slops over the deck, drenching us both" (Watts 2005: 66) or when a Salvation Army chaperone blows his whistle after a boy climbs onto a ship's deck rail (Ravenhill 2002: 1). The regimented nature of the traveling groups of children also comes out: "We immigrant boys and girls, ages seven to thirteen, resembled chunks of charcoal from the same bin.... The Maddock Children's Home in Birmingham had issued dark gray suits, black woollen stockings and ankle-high, laced girl's shoes and boy's boots, all oversized to allow for growth" (Ravenhill 2002: 5). However, Haworth-Attard's character Sadie notes that, by the end of the journey, "it wasn't only their clothes that made them look similar, it was also their faces; paste white, with deep, purple circles drawn under dulled eyes" (Haworth-Attard 1996: 20).

The seascapes so prevalent in photographs taken by migrants in other historical moments (e.g., Mannik 2013: 39–44) are vividly recounted in the novels, making them easy to picture for readers. Lillie tells a boy traveling with her group that she stands "'looking at the ocean … because I can't abide those waves'" (Watts 2005: 66). Thomasina describes the boat trip as "'miserable, windy and cold. And in the fog we saw icebergs bigger than huge houses, all white and blue!'" (Harrison 2000: 200). For her sister Maggie, the ocean crossing consisted of a stage for her fury: "I strode up and down the decks of the ship, glaring at the wrinkled sea," and "the ribbon of pale wake unfurling to the horizon" was also the thread that kept her tied to Thomasina (Harrison 2000: 45).

The descriptions of arrival are dominated by the linked submotifs of dispersal and the transition from being in a collective body of travelers dressed in similar outfits to being alone and vulnerable. In *Beyond the Waterfall,* the character Nicholas remembers that no one came to get him at first. He had traveled by himself on the train to Winnipeg and then to Valhalla, for all the children heading west were sent on alone: "The other passengers on the train from Winnipeg had stared at him in his tight wool jacket and short wool pants. There was a label pinned to his lapel, as if he were a parcel" (Breault Hammond 1997: 39). The sense of the children now being isolated in the households to which they are assigned is in some cases reinforced by descriptions of the length of rides by train and by horse-drawn wagons to farms: "We went on and on into this alien landscape" (Harrison 2000: 46) "On the long journey, neither spoke. Nicholas stared in amazement at the same landscape he had seen from the windows of the train: mile after mile of prairie grasses. … He had lived all his life in London, with buildings crowding against one another" (Breault Hammond 1997: 42). These descriptions of stages of the journeys that follow the trip by boat reinforce the motif of geographical displacement and underscore the importance placed in mobilities research on examining people's experiences of movement (Cresswell and Merriman 2011; Vannini 2012). The other key moment in the arrival narratives is the moment when the children see where they will live, with whom, and where they will be sleeping: "In the dimness, Nicholas could make out a sagging cot against the wall, with a dirty mattress and one rough blanket" (Breault Hammond 1997: 43). As I discuss in the next section, another key aspect of the novels is the theme of the material culture that demonstrates so clearly the subordinated relationship between the children and their employers.

Material Traces

One of the main literary motifs used in these works are references to specific personal objects associated with the history of the children's migration. Some of these are the standard items issued to the children by the philanthropic agencies such as trunks, Bibles, books such as *Pilgrim's Progress*,[8] and basic clothing.[9] Found as well in museum exhibits about this period[10] and on the Web sites maintained by memory activists, such objects are an important common narrative thread in all of the novels. These books then serve as a way of communicating the past through a "'memory of things'" (Leach 1976: 51, cited in Fentress and Wickham 1992: 18).

The emphasis on the meager material belongings that accompanied these children across the Atlantic serves to represent the traces of their migration journey and of their time in the institutional "homes." A common image is of children standing beside their trunks or suitcases on train platforms or in receiving homes, waiting to be picked up: "All four wore labels with their names written on them, and each of them had a trunk" (Little 2001: 28). Moments are tense when adults grab these trunks that contain all that the children have in the world: "the man swung Nicholas' little metal trunk onto the back of the wagon" (Breault Hammond 1997: 42). "The boy moved with a nervous, jerky walk, like a puppet being pulled on invisible strings ... The man lifted the trunk into the buggy, the boy lunged in beside it" (Harrison 2000: 207). The trunk is also the object that the children regret leaving behind in cases when they run away: "I was sad that I couldn't take the trunk. It was the only really good thing that I had ever owned." (Harrison 2000: 76). The trunk can form a link between the present and the period of child labor migration. In *Flower,* even before she hears stories about her great-grandparents, the early twenty-first-century character Katie discovers in her room at her grandparents' house "a shabby old-fashioned trunk" with "a couple of faded letters on the lid—an *I* and an *L*" (Watts 2005: 36).

When these belongings are lost, stolen, or worn out, the children are saddened. This is illustrated well when Adam's brother Terry loses his woolen cap overboard while they stand on the deck of the SS *Northumberland* ferry that takes them to Prince Edward Island from Nova Scotia: "These visored caps matched our new charcoal suits, and we prized them" (Ravenhill 2002: 1). The trunks and their contents are one focus for cruelty and neglect. In the case of Jasper, the little boy brutally beaten and starved by a Mr. Stone, his new guardian (Victoria's father Dr. Cope) insists on locating the trunk that Jasper reports having been taken from him as soon as he arrived at Mr. Stone's run-down farm: "'No. You have little enough, my lad. That box is your property.'" (Little 2001: 194).

Another category of material traces are personal objects specific to each child's life, objects that more often than not contain memories of their parents, siblings, and original homes. Arthur has a precious photograph of his mother that he keeps beside his bed (Haworth-Attard 1996). Similarly, "Night after night, Nicholas crept silently upstairs to his attic, tired, aching and heartsick. But he was never too tired to reach into his trunk, under his few pieces of cheap clothing, to pull out the cracked, curling photo of his mother, taken before his father died" (Breault Hammond 1997: 47). Harrison's character Lizzie remarks on the "treasured possessions" in her trunk that include not her allotted clothes but her "Bible with its thick black cover embossed with gold lettering, a copy of *Pilgrim's Progress,* a prayer book with pages as thin as petals. Three seashells from a beach in another country" (Harrison 2000: 27). We learn a little later on in the book that the shells are some of the few possessions she and her sister took after her parents died and she was removed from her uncle and aunt's home: "Thomasina had six seashells; she put three in her bag and three in mine" (Harrison 2000: 38). In the novel *Flower,* when the twenty-first-century character Katie looks in the old trunk in her room at her grandparents' house, she finds the precious postcard and dried flower that the early-twentieth-century Lillie brought over from England, which were her only material ties to her dead mother (Watts 2005: 158).

The topic of material culture is also significant in terms of the children being ill equipped to do farm work in all kinds of weather, and in their stigmatization for their appearance at school and other public locations as being evidently less fortunate than their peers. On Nicholas's first morning at the farm in a new country, Mrs. Ebenezer wakes him: "'It's five in the morning, boy. Time for work. You got work clothes in there?' She pointed at his trunk. He nodded. When she left, he quickly dressed in the heavy cotton shirt and long work pants provided by the orphanage. He wore the thin socks and ill-fitting boots he had arrived in" (Breault Hammond 1997: 44).

Watts's character Lillie explains that she has "'grown out of both my work dresses. They're too tight, and too short. I've moved the buttons and let down the hems'" (Watts 2005: 112). In the Harrison novel, when Maggie runs away she is wearing an old, thin dress, and "rocks poked through the thin soles of [her] tight, worn boots" (Harrison 2000: 87). When she takes some paper to write a letter, she defends herself to her friend: "'I've worked for the Howards for years and they've never given me anything they didn't have to. Kathleen always buys the cheapest fabric for my dresses ... even though the Barnardo people have been sending them money for my clothes!'" (Harrison 2000: 121–22). With cruel irony, when the unsympathetic Barnardo Homes inspector comes to visit, Maggie feels as though she is being judged for her appearance:

> I knew that he was glaring at me with cold eyes; that he'd noticed my falling down hair, my torn dress, my fingernails rimmed with dirt.... Mr. Walker noticed everything.
> "I hope you are being a Godly and hard-working girl, Maggie," he said frostily. (Harrison 2000: 135)

This encounter between the neglected, silenced Maggie and a home inspector points to the third motif of silencing discussed in this chapter, which I turn to in the next section. In this part of the essay, I have demonstrated how important the motif of the children's personal material culture is in the novels. Material objects are the key focus in the many staged memorializations of the past that shape social memory, even in cases of ambivalent and contested claims (e.g., Breglia 2006; Herzfeld 1991). In this role, they can be seen in public locations such as monuments, heritage buildings, and museum displays as well as in public spaces in people's homes during and following the periods in which they are created. The personal material objects stored in private physical spaces are of equal importance, including to subordinated individuals such the child labor migrants represented in these novels. A focus on possessions can be an effective motif for literary representations of the operation of memory in the lives of characters of all ages. In the case of these novels, the significance of thinking about sensoriality, materiality, and memory in children's lives in particular is brought out clearly just as it is in the oral histories and written memoirs about this migration (e.g., Staples 2003: 9, 19, 22, 35, 171, 173; also see Brookshaw 2009; Howes 2005).[11] Following Pearce (1995) and others, Moshenska suggests that collecting material culture "can be a coping mechanism for children in traumatic environments" (Moshenska 2008: 112). In the case of child migrants, however, the novels emphasize that it was not a question of accumulative collecting as much as it was of retaining and guarding the few material traces they were allowed. Material objects from the past are also a common way to link the pursuit of family histories with the moulding of social memory. The importance of unearthing the stories attached to ancestors' possessions, especially in cases of buried or silenced histories such as those of the British child migrants, comes across strongly in the novels.

Silencing

A silenced history and the individual silencing of children form an important motif in all of the novels. In a historical note at the end of Little's book, she addresses her readers, letting them know "Some never told their children that they had immigrated as Home Children." She further encourages readers to make inquiries: "Ask the older members of your family," since it is possible that "one of them was a grandparent of yours, or a great-aunt or great-uncle" (Little 2001: 207, 208). In *Flower,* when Katie auditions for a play based on *The Secret Garden* back home in Toronto in 2005, she tells her teacher that one aspect of her motivation for the part is that her great-grandparents were British home children (Watts 2005: 173–74).

Various authors have demonstrated how power relations between groups and regions drive the inscription of dominant histories wherein specific ideologies, events, and individuals are highlighted and others are hidden and distorted (Sider and Smith 1997; Wolf 1982). There is much documentation of the silencing of women, children, and groups oppressed through slavery, colonization, and labor exploitation (Gal 1991: 175; Trouillot 1995). The six novels discussed here portray the microlevel encounters wherein children are afraid to speak because they are socially isolated within relationships of physical and psychological domination.

There are frequent references to the children being intimidated into remaining verbally silent. These include situations when they are striving to avoid additional physical punishment. In such moments, the children are frightened, deeply sad, and angry. Harrison's lead protagonist Maggie "stared at him, speechless" (Harrison 2000: 50) when her employer, Mr. Howard, tells her that he will be sending all of her meager wages to the Barnardo Homes to hold until she is twenty-one. The character Nicholas in *Beyond the Waterfall* "learned to run when he was called, and never to let up at a task, even if he felt his back would break. In this way he avoided beatings, but whenever he said or did something that Newt Ebenezer disapproved of, he got a sharp cuff on the ear" (Breault Hammond 1997: 46). After beatings, he did his best to stifle his sorrow: "he curled up on his hard cot and pulled the blanket over his head so no one would hear him crying" and begged other children to also be quiet: "'Promise you won't tell?'" (Breault Hammond 1997: 47, 86). His lesson was shared by Adam in *Move Smart, Boy!* who was brutally beaten when he tried to explain some of his actions: "'Sass me, will you?' He tore a long slat off a broken lobster trap. Like a man possessed he gripped my arm and began to flog my back and legs" (Ravenhill 2002: 56). In Little's novel, when Victoria finds out that Jasper, the home girl Marianna's brother, has escaped his cruel employers and is hiding out in her house, she initially helps to keep the secret for fear that he will be sent back even though she worries that he needs medical attention due to a fever and a broken arm (Little 2001: 129–35). When a boy tries to defend a home girl in his school from a teacher's insults, he also confronts adult domination: "Tom spoke up though. 'Mary Anna is not a waif or a stray,' he said in a most polite voice.... 'Silence, young man. One more such remark and I'll need to get out my strap,'" (Little 2001: 61). These examples all point to the explicit manner in which child migrants were forced or pressured into remaining completely subservient in verbal and other ways as a result of the abusive behavior of their employers and of other adults they encountered in the rural settings they were sent to once they reached Canada.

Moreover, the hoped-for relief from neglect and abuse as a result of annual visits from inspectors is not generally forthcoming, as with the experiences of Nicholas: "I opened my mouth to protest; ... Then I shut it again. ... I knew that Mr. Walker wouldn't listen" (Harrison 2000: 136). And, of Adam: "I followed, determined to get my chance to speak." (Ravenhill 2002: 163).

However, Adam further explains that he had to be careful in what he said because "my master's wrath would fall on me after the inspector left.... If only he would leave me alone with the inspector" (Ravenhill 2002: 163).

At other times the children consciously choose silence as the only power of the vulnerable (Gal 1991: 175; Mannik 2013: 129). This comes through when Adam hears that he might gain his desire to attend school, something required but often disallowed by employers: "My head reeled. School! I felt my chest would burst, but I tried to restrain myself and continued to pile wood quietly, afraid my charged nerves would show and trigger Mister to change his mind" (Ravenhill 2002: 75). Or when he is given some coins by his siblings' guardian and tries to keep the mean "Mister" from knowing: "I gripped my pocket of precious silver coins to keep them from jingling.... He had stolen my peppermints, but these coins were mine, and I would hide them and tell no one" (Ravenhill 2002: 154).

And, finally, the child migrants and their allies choose to break their silences in strategic ways: "The best time to make any requests was before the day's demands rattled her patience beyond reason" (Ravenhill 2002: 183). Upon her departure from one of her placements, the character Lillie says, "'I have something I wish to say before I leave. You would be doing the new girl a great kindness, ma'am, if you and Miss Alice were to call her by her own name'" (Watts 2005: 138). After discovering what Little's character Victoria was writing about her in a diary, the home girl Marianna (with the nickname of Sparrow) writes her a note in which she proclaims, "'I did NOT feel like Oliver Twist. I felt like Sparrow Wilson with her belly twisting with the pain of hunger'" (Little 2001: 97). At the end of *Home Child,* Sadie shocks her parents when she asserts that the home boy Arthur should eat with the family, breaking a family silence about her own mother: "'You were an orphan, Mama. You must understand a bit how Arthur feels'" (Haworth-Attard 1996: 123).

Fields such as psychiatry, psychology, and counseling have produced a large literature about the impacts of trauma on the silencing or distortion of memory (Sotgiu and Rusconi 2014). These include explorations of the repression of memory or amnesia, dissociation, ways in which memories are incomplete, links between various forms of mental illness such as depression and posttraumatic stress disorder and memory, cultural variation, and the therapeutic value of recovered memories (Brewin and Andrews 1998; Herlihy and Turner 2007; Jobson and O'Kearney 2006; Rosenthal 2003). As Herlihy and Turner (2007) summarize, there is an important body of literature about mental health and difficult migration experiences such as those of refugees seeking asylum. Anthropologists and historians have also examined how traumatic events influence forgetting and the revisiting of the past (e.g., Antze and Lambek 1996; Mannik 2013). Mannik provides an excellent, detailed example of the complex ways in which individuals both recount "Past traumas and the losses associated with forced migration," and acknowledge cases of forgetting as well as maintaining silences about remembered details (Mannik 2013: 106, also see 130–31). As Lambek and Antze have noted, we have to examine "the roles of trope, idiom, narrative, ritual, discipline, power, and social context" in the "production and reproduction" of such memories (Lambek and Antze 1996: xiii). "The inscription of trauma narratives" (Lambek and Antze 1996: xxiv) can be an important step toward achieving political recognition in cases such as that of the memory movement to reverse the historical silencing of the British child migrants' experiences. However, in such contexts it is also important to recognize the specific nuances and complexities of specific accounts within the context of individuals' lives (Lambek and Antze 1996: xxiv; Mannik 2013). Children's novels that use the trope of silencing to provide readers with access to the inner worlds, relationships, and actions of individual characters are one way to relay such nuances and complexities while furthering the need to reinscribe understandings of Canadian migration history. Moreover, there is clear potential for dialectical relationships between memory and literature. As Douglas notes, "Popular cultural forms ... have been instrumental in breaking silences and creating cultural templates for stories to be told" (Douglas 2010: 107).

Conclusion

The memory activism movement calling for recognition of the injustices experienced by the British child migrants has led to a variety of outcomes in Canada and around the world.

In the past decade, we have seen the British prime minister Gordon Brown delivered a public apology for these injustices in 2010 (CBC News 2010). A Canadian stamp representing home children was issued in 2010, with an explanation acknowledging that "while some benefited from the promise of a brighter future that the movement's founders had envisioned, others were abused, neglected and overworked" (Canada Post 2010; Reimer 2013: 8). The home children experience has been documented in a number of on-site and digital museum exhibits and archival information sheets by museums in Canada, Australia, and England (see endnote 10). Numerous Web sites, including social networking Facebook and other pages, have created access to a dense body of important information about this example of long-lasting child labor migration.[12] The migration is also represented in physical public memorializations such as on the gravestones dedicated to the memory of former St. George's Home Children that were erected in 2006 in Notre-Dame Cemetery in Ottawa, Ontario (Oschefski 2012). It is the mistreatment and bad luck of some of the children, counterposed with examples of those children who were fortunate enough to survive and to end up in homes where they were treated with dignity and some respect that is the main message relayed by the six novels discussed in this chapter.

These books demonstrate that children's historical fiction can be one key genre through which histories of migration by boat can become integrated into the social memory of specific countries. The use of a set of compelling motifs across the different novels is what makes these examples of children's literature such an effective vehicle to promote this collective reevaluation of the past. The motif of displacement as emphasized in descriptions of the organizational, sensorial, and emotional aspects of the physical journey by boat that the children took to reach their new homes and work placements in Canada is an effective way to introduce the prevalence in the period portrayed of a large-scale, long-distance movement of child laborers across oceans by external agencies. A second literary motif found in these novels is the significance of the children's few personal possessions, from the standard items such as trunks, Bibles, and identical outfits issued to them by the agencies that brought them to Canada to those belongings that they brought as keepsakes reminding them of their families and their original homes. This emphasis on material traces highlights that these children's displacement is an ever-present aspect of their lives, that material culture is both a way to retain connections between places and a site for the children's struggle for a minimal level of autonomy in the face of economic, physical, and emotional domination. The last motif is the authors' effective employment of descriptions of the threats and fear that led to the prevalent silencing of individual child migrants as a way to transmit the point that theirs was an aspect of Canadian history that was silenced in earlier official records about settler migration. Like films, oral histories, and museum exhibits, children's literature can comprise an important form of memory activism. Novels such as those discussed here can effectively reach thousands of child and adult readers, who will pass on the books, discuss them, and, as a result think differently about Canadian settler immigration history.

Sharon Roseman is professor of anthropology at Memorial University of Newfoundland. Her specializations include historical anthropology; labor history; human mobility, including labor migration, pilgrimage and tourism; memory and heritage politics; and rural studies. She is the author of the monograph *O Santiaguiño de Carreira: o rexurdimento dunha base rural no Concello de Zas* (Baía Edicións, 2008). She is coeditor of *The Tourism Imaginary and Pilgrimages to the Edges of the World* (with Nieves Herrero, Channel View 2015); *Antropoloxía das mulleres galegas* (with Enrique Alonso, Sotelo Blanco, 2012); *Recasting Culture and Space in Iberian Contexts* (with Shawn S. Parkhurst, SUNY Press, 2008); and *Intersecting Journeys: The Anthropology of Pilgrimage and Tourism* (with Ellen Badone, University of Illinois Press, 2004). She is series editor of European Anthropology in Translation (Berghahn Books).

Notes

1. The total numbers vary among sources, due to the use of different start and end dates and access to distinct archives. Parr (1994: 39) notes that 80,000 children arrived in the period from 1868 to 1925. More recently, through the constantly evolving scrutiny of records, Oschefski (2011) and others have placed the number at over 100,000 for the longer period from the 1860s to 1948 (Oschefski 2011).
2. The terms of the contracts that families signed varied across the different organizations and according to the children's ages. However, in general the families that took in children aged between six and ten received a monthly stipend for the children's board. Children this young were not supposed to work so much that they were prevented from going to school. Some children under six were not supposed to work, although it is not clear that this was usually honored. Children between eleven and fourteen were to work enough to earn their keep, some clothing, and supposedly some pocket money. They were also supposed to be allowed to go to school in the winter when there were fewer agricultural tasks (Parr 1994: 85). At fourteen, the children began to earn a small wage that was sometimes cumulative and only provided to the young people after they had finished their indenture as late as age eighteen (Kohli 2003: 359–61; Parr 1994: 86). Although the children frequently changed work locations due to families complaining about their work or other conflicts, they were not allowed to leave their place of employment without the approval or knowledge of the agencies that had brought them to Canada (Kohli 2003: 359).
3. These children include those brought to the Fairbridge Farm located in British Columbia between 1934 and 1951 (Parr 1994: xviiii; also see Child Migrants Trust 2014). Other British children were evacuated to Canada temporarily during World War II (Kershaw and Sacks 2008: 170–91). However, in this period Canada and Newfoundland both rejected pleas to accept some boatloads of child and adult refugee survivors of Nazi concentration camps or those fleeing Nazism before and during World War II (e.g., Abella and Troper 1983; Bassler 1992).
4. The literature uses terms such as *migrant, immigrant,* and *emigrant* in diverse ways. Brettell and Hollifield (2008: 21–22) use the term *international migration* despite noting that others reserve the term *migration* for internal movement and the term *immigration* for international mobility. Jeffrey Cohen and Ibrahim Sirkeci note the value of using the more general and dynamic term *mobility* as opposed to *migration* for cross-border human movements, in part to avoid engaging with "the conventional and static definition of migration offered by groups like the U.N. ('movement from point A to point B for at least 12 months')" (Cohen and Sirkeci 2011: 7).
5. The *Laurentian* was wrecked close to Cape Race off the island of Newfoundland in 1909 (Kohli 1997–2007). Seven years earlier, "The *Huronian* disappeared without a trace in March of 1902, while on her way to Halifax from Liverpool" (Kohli 1997–2007).
6. Lori Oschefski's impressively comprehensive site is found at http://canadianbritishhomechildren.weebly.com/
7. In the present-day Canadian context, the key example of memory activism related to childhood and colonial oppression are the wrenching accounts of Aboriginal children's experiences in residential schools recounted in many formats,

including in testimonials presented to the Truth and Reconciliation Commission of Canada (National Centre for Truth and Reconciliation n.d.; Truth and Reconciliation Commission of Canada n.d.).
8. The children would have been given one of the various condensed versions of the original 1678 work by John Bunyan, *The Pilgrim's Progress from This World to That Which Is to Come; Delivered under the Similitude of a Dream.* These often used the shortened version of the title, *Pilgrim's Progress*, as is mentioned in the book by Harrison (2000: 27, 76).
9. Jean Little (2001: 210) publishes as a form of appendix, "Barnardo Girl's Canadian Outfit in 1898," in which she lists the items issued to these migrants.
10. For example, in the permanent exhibit and Online Story Collection at the Canadian Museum of Immigration at Pier 21 (http://www.pier21.ca/stories/search), the Merseyside Maritime Museum and Archive in Liverpool (http://www.liverpoolmuseums.org.uk/maritime/archive/sheet/10), the 2010 special exhibit "The Fabric of British Home Children" at the Galt Museum (http://www.galtmuseum.com/exhibits-homechildrenquilts.htm), the National Museum of Australia's traveling exhibit (2011–14) "Inside: Life in Children's Homes and Institutions" (http://www.nma.gov.au/exhibitions/inside_life_in_childrens_homes_and_institutions/home).
11. In her analysis of oral history accounts of British children's collections of shrapnel during World War II, Moshenska has also noted that this same theme appears in fiction about the period (2008: 109).
12. In addition to Lori Oschefski's site listed above (http://canadianbritishhomechildren.weebly.com/) and those for the official associations, see examples such as https://www.facebook.com/bhc.chatham.kent.on.ca and http://www.bytown.net/homekids.htm.

Bibliography

Abella, Irving, and Harold Troper. 1983. *None Is Too Many: Canada and the Jews of Europe 1933–1948.* Toronto: Lester & Orpen Dennys, Publishers.
Ahmed, Sara, Claudia Castañeda, Anne-Marie Fortier, and Mimi Sheller. 2003. "Introduction: Uprootings/Regroundings: Questions of Home and Migration." In *Uprootings/Regroundings: Questions of Home and Migration,* edited by Sara Ahmed, Claudia Castañeda, Anne-Marie Fortier, and Mimi Sheller, 1–22. Oxford and New York: Berg.
Bagnell, Kenneth. 2001. *The Little Immigrants: The Orphans Who Came to Canada.* Toronto: The Dundurn Group.
Bassler, Gerhard P. 1992. *Sanctuary Denied: Refugees from the Third Reich and Newfoundland Immigration Policy 1906–1949.* St. John's, NL: ISER Books.
Billingsley, Doc McAlister. 2014. *So That All Shall Know: Memory Activism & Epistemic Authority in Guatemala.* Doctoral dissertation, Washington University, St. Louis.
Breault Hammond, Elaine. 1997. *Beyond the Waterfall.* Charlottetown, PEI: Ragweed Press.
Breglia, Lisa. 2006. *Monumental Ambivalence: The Politics of Heritage.* Austin: University of Texas Press.

Brettell, Caroline B., and James F. Hollifield. 2008. "Introduction. Migration Theory: Talking across Disciplines." In *Migration Theory: Talking across Disciplines,* edited by Caroline B. Brettell and James F. Hollifield, 1–30. New York and London: Routledge.

Brewin, Chris R., and Bernice Andrews. 1998. "Recovered Memories of Trauma: Phenomenology and Cognitive Mechanisms." *Clinical Psychology Review* 18, no. 8: 949–70.

Brookshaw, Sharon. 2009. "The Material Culture of Children and Childhood: Understanding Childhood Objects in the Museum Context." *Journal of Material Culture* 14, no. 3: 365–83.

Bunyan, John. 1678. *The Pilgrim's Progress from This World to That Which Is to Come; Delivered under the Similitude of a Dream.* London: N. Ponder.

Canada Post. 2010. "Home Children." *Details* 19, no. 3, July to September. https://www.canadapost.ca/cpo/mc/personal/collecting/stamps/2010/2010_home_children.jsf

Castles, Stephen. 1989. *Migrant Workers and the Transformation of Western Societies.* Ithaca, NY: Center for International Studies, Cornell University.

CBC News. 2010. "British PM Apologizes to 'Home Children'." http://www.cbc.ca/news/world/british-pm-apologizes-to-home-children-1.916446

Child Migrants Trust. 2014. "Child Migration History." http://www.childmigrantstrust.com/our-work/child-migration-history

Cohen, Jeffrey H., and Ibrahim Sirkeci. 2011. *Cultures of Migration: The Global Nature of Contemporary Mobility.* Austin: University of Texas Press.

Cresswell, Tim, and Peter Merriman, eds. 2011. *Geographies of Mobilities: Practices, Spaces, Subjects.* Farnham, UK: Ashgate.

Do, Anh, and Suzanne Do. 2011. *The Little Refugee.* Sydney: Allen & Unwin.

Douglas, Kate. 2010. *Contesting Childhood: Autobiography, Trauma, and Memory.* New Brunswick, NJ: Rutgers University Press.

Egoff, Sheila, and Judith Saltman. 1990. *The New Republic of Childhood: A Critical Guide to Canadian Children's Literature in English.* Toronto: Oxford University Press.

Fentress, James, and Chris Wickham. 1992. *Social Memory.* Oxford: Blackwell.

Freedman, William. 1971. "The Literary Motif: A Definition and Evaluation." *NOVEL: A Forum on Fiction* 4, no. 2: 123–31.

Gal, Susan. 1991. "Between Speech and Silence: The Problematics of Research on Language and Gender." In *Gender at the Crossroads of Knowledge: Feminist Anthropology in the Postmodern Era,* ed. Micaela di Leonardo, 175–203. Berkeley: University of California Press.

Harrison, Phyllis, ed. 2003 [1979]. *The Home Children: Their Personal Stories.* Winnipeg, MB: J. Gordon Shillingford.

Harrison, Troon. 2000. *A Bushel of Light.* Toronto & New York: Stoddart Kids.

Haworth-Attard, Barbara. 1996. *Home Child.* Montreal: Roussan.

Herlihy, Jane, and Stuart W. Turner. 2007. "Asylum Claims and Memory of Trauma: Sharing Our Knowledge." *British Journal of Psychiatry* 191 (1): 3–4.

Herzfeld, Michael. 1991. *A Place in History: Social and Monumental Time in a Cretan Town.* Princeton: Princeton University Press.

Howes, David. 2005. "Skinscapes: Embodiment, Culture, and Environment." In *The Book of Touch,* edited by Constance Classen, 27–39. Oxford and New York: Berg.

Hudson, Aïda. 2003. "Introduction." In *Windows and Words: A Look at Canadian Children's Literature in English,* edited by Aïda Hudson and Susan-Ann Cooper, 1–10. Ottawa: University of Ottawa Press.
International Labour Organization. 1996–2014. "Migration and Child Labour." http://ilo.org/ipec/areas/Migration_and_CL/lang--en/index.htm.
Jackson, Michael. 2005. *Existential Anthropology: Events, Exigencies, and Effects.* Oxford and New York: Berghahn Books.
Jobson, Laura, and Richard O'Kearney. 2006. "Cultural Differences in Autobiographical Memory of Trauma." *Clinical Psychologist* 10, no. 3: 89–98.
Kershaw, Roger, and Janet Sacks. 2008. *New Lives for Old.* Kew, UK: The National Archives.
Kohli, Marjorie P. 2003. *The Golden Bridge: Young Immigrants to Canada, 1833–1939.* Toronto: Natural Heritage Books.
———. 1997–2007. "Immigrants to Canada." http://jubilation.uwaterloo.ca/~marj/genealogy/allan.html
Kreissler, Françoise. 2007. *"Le Mémorial de Nankin, lectures et relectures de l'histoire." Matériaux pour l'histoire de notre temps* 4, no. 88: 8–12. www.cairn.info/revue-materiaux-pour-l-histoire-de-notre-temps-2007-4-page-8.htm.
Lambek, Michael, and Paul Antze. 1996. "Introduction: Forecasting Memory." In *Tense Past: Cultural Essays in Trauma and Memory,* edited by Paul Antze and Michael Lambek, xi–xxxviii. New York/London: Routledge.
Leach, Edmund R. 1976. *Culture and Communication: The Logic by Which Symbols Are Connected.* Cambridge: Cambridge University Press.
Library and Archives Canada. n.d. "Home Children (1869–1930)–Immigration Records." http://www.bac-lac.gc.ca/eng/discover/immigration/immigration-records/home-children-1869-1930/immigration-records/Pages/list.aspx?ArrivalYear=1869&=&p_ID=75
Little, Jean. 2001. *Orphan at My Door: The Home Child Diary of Victoria Cope.* Markham, ON: Scholastic Canada.
Lorente, J. A. David. 1996. "Foreword." In *Home Child,* edited by Barbara Haworth-Attard. Montreal: Roussan.
Mannik, Lynda. 2013. *Photography, Memory, and Refugee Identity: The Voyage of the SS Walnut, 1948.* Vancouver: UBC Press.
Mickenberg, Julia L. 2006. *Learning from the Left: Children's Literature, the Cold War, and Radical Politics in the United States.* Oxford: Oxford University Press.
Montgomery, Lucy Maud. 1908. *Anne of Green Gables.* Boston: L. C. Page.
Moshenska, Gabriel. 2008. "A Hard Rain: Children's Shrapnel Collections in the Second World War." *Journal of Material Culture* 13, no. 1: 107–25.
National Centre for Truth and Reconciliation. n.d. "Truth and Reconciliation Commission of Canada." http://www.trc.ca/websites/trcinstitution/index.php?p=905.
Oschefski, Lori. 2011. "British Home Children & Child Migrants in Canada." http://canadianbritishhomechildren.weebly.com/.
———. 2012. "The Saint George's Home Memorials, Notre Dame Cemetery, Ottawa, Ontario," British Home Children & Child Migrants in Canada. http://canadianbritishhomechildren.weebly.com/the-st-georges-memorial.html
Parker, Roy. 2008. *Uprooted: The Shipment of Poor Children to Canada, 1867–1917.* Vancouver: UBC Press.

Parr, Joy. 1994. *Labouring Children: British Immigrant Apprentices to Canada, 1869–1924.* Toronto: University of Toronto Press.
Pearce, Susan M. 1995. *On Collecting: An Investigation into Collecting in the European Tradition.* London/New York: Routlege.
Pettit, Mary. 2000. *Mary Janeway: The Legacy of a Home Child.* Toronto: Natural Heritage Books.
Ravenhill, Louise. 2002. *Move Smart, Boy!: A Novel about Home Children in Rural Prince Edward Island 1911–1913.* Charlottetown, PEI: Luîka.
Reimer, Mavis. 2013. "The Child of Nature and the Home Child." *Jeunesse: Young People, Texts, Cultures* 5, no. 2: 1–16.
Rosenthal, Gabriele. 2003. "The Healing Effects of Storytelling: On the Conditions of Curative Storytelling in the Context of Research and Counseling." *Qualitative Inquiry* 9, no. 6: 915–933.
Scholastic Canada. 2006. "Teaching with Dear Canada." http://education.scholastic.ca/product/9780439947244
Sider, Gerald M., and Gavin A. Smith, eds. 1997. *Between History and Histories: The Making of Silences and Commemorations.* Toronto: University of Toronto Press.
Skidmore, Patricia. 2012. *Marjorie Too Afraid to Cry: A Home Child Experience.* Toronto: Dundurn.
Snow, Gordon. 2000. *Neither Waif Nor Stray: The Search for a Stolen Identity.* Universal Publishers.
Sotgiu, Igor, and Maria Luisa Rusconi. 2014. "Why Autobiographical Memories for Traumatic and Emotional Events Might Differ: Theoretical Arguments and Empirical Evidence." *Journal of Psychology: Interdisciplinary and Applied* 148, no. 5: 523–47.
Staples, Michael Anthony. 2003. *Middlemore Memories: Tales of the British Home Children.* Fredericton, NB: Unipress.
Trouillot, Michel-Rolph. 1995. *Silencing the Past: Power and the Production of History.* Boston: Beacon Press.
Truth and Reconciliation Commission of Canada. N.d. http://www.trc.ca/websites/reconciliation/index.php?p=312
Vannini, Phillip. 2012. *Ferry Tales: Mobility, Place, and Time on Canada's West Coast.* New York/London: Routledge.
Watts, Irene N. 2005. *Flower: A Novel.* Toronto: Tundra Books.
Wolf, Eric R. 1982. *Europe and the People without History.* Berkeley: University of California Press.
Young, Beryl. 2009. *Charlie: A Home Child's Life in Canada.* Vancouver: Ronsdale Press.

2

Representing Migration by Boat at the Australian National Maritime Museum

Kim Tao

Migration by boat is a central theme in Australia's history and over the past decade has reemerged as a dominant issue in Australian political and public discourse. This chapter will examine how migration by boat has been remembered and represented in three recent programs at the Australian National Maritime Museum (ANMM) that attempt to move beyond the parameters of the traditional museum exhibition to explore the interpretive possibilities of historic vessels, digital technology, and contemporary art.

The first case study reviews one of the icons of the ANMM's collection—the restored Vietnamese fishing boat *Tu Do* that carried thirty-one refugees to Australia in 1977. It reveals how the boat has become a compelling vehicle for the ANMM to humanize and contextualize the experiences of seaborne refugees and asylum seekers. This notion of contextualizing history was also fundamental to the ANMM's dynamic 2013 digital projection, "Waves of Migration," which is the subject of the second case study. The show was projected on the expansive roof of the ANMM to make a highly visible statement about the continuity of migration by sea in the history of an island nation. The third case study investigates how the sea passage has been narrated and visualized through art, focusing on a series of works that the ANMM commissioned from Croatian refugee artist Gina Sinozich in 2003. Together the three case studies reflect the ANMM's methodology for representing migration by boat in the museum context, with reference to broader discourses of nationhood, identity, forced migration, memory, and travel by sea.

The ANMM's Methodology

Setting the ANMM apart from many other maritime museums around the world is its emphasis on social history. The ANMM considers Australia's links with the sea through the lens of the experiences of people. This approach creates a powerful emotional engagement with its audiences, and is of particular significance to the core thematic area of immigration and the ANMM's methodology of exploring wider historical narratives through personal stories.

Telling migration stories has been a major part of the ANMM's mandate since it opened in Sydney in 1991; until the 1970s nearly all of Australia's migrants had arrived by sea. But it was also influenced by the evolving museological and historiographical methodologies of social history, immigration history, and history from below at the time of the ANMM's establishment, which as historian Ian McShane (2001: 123) argues, coincided with "the political and institutional development of multiculturalism as a dominant national ethic."[1] Today the ANMM has a permanent gallery dedicated to immigration called "Passengers," and holds more than ten thousand objects relating to its collection. The strongest area of the collection is material from the enormous wave of displaced persons and assisted immigrants who traveled from Europe on the great ocean liners after World War II. Over the years the ANMM has presented many of these migrants' stories in its programs.

But the history of seaborne migration did not end with the last passenger liners. It is a history still in the making as people escaping recent conflict in the Middle East and Sri Lanka make the dangerous boat journey to Australia, provoking intense debate about how governments should deal with asylum seekers who arrive on unauthorized voyages. These debates often neglect to acknowledge the number of asylum seekers that arrive by air or the number of asylum claims made in Australia compared to those in an increasingly globalized, migratory world.[2] Nevertheless the fear of the boat still looms large, a phenomenon sociologist Andrew Jakubowicz (2004: 3) has termed "penetration phobia ... [and] the loathing of unauthorized arrivals, who breach the protective skin around the body politic." In recognition of these ongoing debates, one of the priority areas identified in the ANMM's Collection Development Policy is to document the experiences of seaborne refugees and asylum seekers in a changing policy framework (ANMM 2011: 23).

Case Study 1: A Fishing Boat Called "Freedom"

One of the main challenges to representing migration history in museums is that there are often few *personal* objects to tell these stories, particularly in the case of those fleeing conflict or persecution. This was an important factor in the ANMM's decision to acquire the refugee boat *Tu Do* as tangible evidence of the arrival of the first Vietnamese boat people in Australia after the fall of Saigon to communist forces in 1975. The Vietnamese initially received a warm welcome from authorities; their arrival coincided with major shifts in immigration legislation, such as the final dismantling of the restrictive White Australia Policy that had been in place since 1901, and the introduction of the new concept of multiculturalism (adapted from a Canadian model) in 1973.[3] *Tu Do* provides a fascinating contrast to more recent unauthorized boat arrivals in Australia, including the infamous *Tampa* affair of 2001, arrivals that have contributed to a growing culture of fear in both the political and public imaginations. The 2001 affair was the incident in which the crew of the Norwegian cargo ship MV *Tampa* rescued 433 asylum seekers from their stricken fishing boat in the Indian Ocean, but were denied permission to enter Australian waters (Marr and Wilkinson 2003). This first case study outlines the background to the acquisition of *Tu Do* and discusses the ANMM's landmark twenty-year program to research, restore, and interpret the vessel.

When the ANMM purchased *Tu Do* in 1990 little was known about the boat's history. Its name, meaning *freedom* in Vietnamese, hinted at the motives of its passengers. But it was not until 1995 that an ANMM curator was able to locate the boat's builder, Tan Thanh Lu, who was then operating a Chinese restaurant in the town of Lismore in regional New South Wales. The ANMM arranged for Lu and his teenage son Mo to visit Sydney, where they inspected the vessel and provided invaluable information about its construction and original appearance. Since then curators have worked closely with the Lu family to piece together *Tu Do*'s remarkable story.

Escape from Vietnam

Lu had fought with the South Vietnamese during the Vietnam War and knew that his family faced an uncertain future under the new communist regime. In 1975 the thirty-year-old store owner pooled resources with three friends on the southern island of Phu Quoc and built *Tu Do* specifically to escape Vietnam. It was constructed to the design of a dragnet fishing boat typical of the island region, sixty feet long, with a mast forward, and a cabin and wheelhouse aft. Lu initially used it for fishing, to divert the suspicion of the authorities and to help pay for crucial supplies such as food, diesel fuel, and a spare engine.

Prior to departure on September 16, 1977 Lu staged an engine breakdown so that surveillance of *Tu Do* would be relaxed. He installed the more powerful replacement engine, then he and his thirty-eight passengers, including his pregnant wife Tuyet (twenty-seven), daughters Dzung (six) and Dao (four), son Mo (two), and relatives, friends, and neighbors, set off in the dark. The children had been given cough medicine to keep them quiet, but as they reached deeper water, a head count revealed that Dzung had been left sleeping on the shore. They returned to find her and the voyage began.

With gold and cash hidden about the vessel *Tu Do* outpaced the notorious Gulf of Thailand pirates who preyed on boat people. After being turned away from the Malaysian port of Pekan, the group managed to land in Mersing, where eight exhausted passengers were permitted to disembark as refugees. Lu had relatives in the United States, but after weeks of frustrating negotiations with U.S. immigration officials in Mersing, he decided to set sail for Australia with his remaining thirty passengers. Off Flores in Indonesia they rescued another refugee boat, PK3402, which had run aground, and towed it across the Timor Sea. The boats landed near Darwin, Northern Territory, on November 21, 1977. Lu and his crew had navigated more than 3,700 miles using a simple compass and a map taken from the lift up lid of a school desk. The Lu family was transferred to Wacol Migrant Hostel in Brisbane, Queensland, where Tuyet gave birth to a son, Quoc. The family was granted asylum after six months.

In 1978, while still at Wacol, Lu arranged to sell *Tu Do* to a Darwin local, who then sold it to a man in Cairns, Queensland, in 1985. Both owners made minor modifications to the vessel, such as removing its awning and winch, fitting rails and seating, and painting over its simple sky blue color scheme, which Lu had originally chosen to blend into the ocean. However, *Tu Do*'s hull, deck, and cabin structure were still largely intact by the time the vessel arrived at the ANMM in 1990.

Restoring Tu Do

In 2003 ANMM staff developed a Vessel Management Plan for *Tu Do* and commenced a program to restore the boat to its appearance in 1977–the most significant period in its history. It was at this time that the ANMM received the tragic news that Tan Lu had died during a business trip to Vietnam. The restoration program took on even greater meaning–it became a way of preserving Lu's legacy as well as the experiences of all those who have taken immense risks to escape oppression.

The program was underpinned by extensive research into Vietnamese fishing boat construction and wooden boat restoration, and supported by the ANMM's *Tu Do* interpretive collection, which includes oral histories with the Lu family, interviews with subsequent owners, and a series of evocative black and white photographs of the vessel arriving in Darwin taken by photojournalist Michael Jensen.

The first stage (2003–8) involved restoring the engine, and repairing and stabilizing the hull and wheelhouse, while trying to retain as much original fabric as possible. Once the internal structure was sound, the deck planking, engine, and wheelhouse were reinstalled, making *Tu Do* the only fully operational refugee boat displayed on water in Australia (see figure 2.1). The second stage (2009-12) involved reconstructing elements identifiable in Jensen's photographs, including an awning over the deck, makeshift timber barricades on the port side of the vessel, a trawl winch on top of the cabin, and a basic plank toilet at the stern. The final step was to repaint the vessel in its arrival color scheme, which again relied heavily on the visual evidence in Jensen's photographs. Finally, in 2012 replica fuel drums were installed on deck, fishing nets were suspended from the winch mechanism, and a tarpaulin was fitted over the reconstructed awning to restore *Tu Do* to its configuration when it docked in Darwin in 1977.

It was a defining moment as the ANMM's shipwrights fixed the tarpaulin, huddling beneath the low canopy as they tied up the ropes. The author imagined the conditions as Lu and his crew assembled this makeshift shelter out on the open sea, having risked everything on a voyage into the unknown. It brought home the terrifying reality of their escape and validated the ANMM's rationale for restoring *Tu Do*. As the issue of unauthorized boat arrivals continues to dominate political debate in Australia—encapsulated in the rhetoric around "stopping the boats"—and stirs the full gamut of responses in the community, from compassion and support to resentment and xenophobia, *Tu Do* stands as testament to the courage and hope exhibited by Lu, his family, and their fellow passengers.[4] It offers a distinctly Australian perspective on

Figure 2.1. The Lu family on board the restored *Tu Do* at the ANMM, 2005. (L-R) Mo, Dzung, Dao, Tuyet, and Quoc Lu. Photographer: Andrew Frolows. Courtesy of ANMM.

a global story, allowing the ANMM to personalize the Vietnamese exodus and provide visitors with a compelling, tangible insight into the nature of refugee journeys.

Interpreting Tu Do

Over the past two decades the ANMM has developed a range of interpretive and educational programs based around *Tu Do* and the Lu family, including the photography project "Intertwined Journeys" in 2010, which looked beyond the 1977 arrival story to showcase contemporary portraits of the family. These portraits included Dao Lu in her tailoring business on Queensland's Gold Coast and Mo Lu with his own young family in Brisbane. It was imperative that the Lus not remain frozen in time, that they be pictured as perennial boat people captured in black and white in 1977. The project demonstrated the ANMM's commitment to documenting living history, to extending the focus past the boat voyage to consider agency, settlement, and cultural preservation within communities and across generations.

However, there are also opportunities to expand interpretation beyond the Lu family and to use *Tu Do* to explore the stories of refugees and asylum seekers in a global framework. Planning is under way for programs that position the vessel as a stimulus for oral history projects and multidisciplinary artistic collaborations, programs that have the capacity to generate intercultural and intergenerational dialogue, and interrogate the notion of the boat as a site of both refuge and trauma. This corresponds with a broader ANMM strategy to reach across the Pacific, to uncover comparative experiences of Vietnamese refugees in the United States and Canada, and to highlight transnational perspectives on the story.

It is a story that continues to attract media attention as a new wave of seaborne asylum seekers makes the perilous voyage to Australia. Media portrayals of these asylum seekers rarely focus on the individual, which has the effect of dehumanizing them.[5] In contrast, the ANMM has tried to personalize and contextualize the plight of boat people using *Tu Do,* thereby facilitating cross-cultural understanding of the courage and desperation that have motivated so many refugee journeys. The fishing boat called "freedom" remains an evocative vehicle for the ANMM to examine historical and contemporary immigration debates that are a central part of Australia's history.

Case Study 2: Illuminating Australia's Waves of Migration

The concept of bridging the historical and the contemporary was also essential to the ANMM's award-winning rooftop digital projection, "Waves of Migration," which is the focus of the second case study.⁶ The show was inspired by two lines from the second verse of Australia's national anthem, "Advance Australia Fair," which reference its history as a migrant nation: "For those who've come across the seas / We've boundless plains to share." This section discusses the ANMM's use of historic collections, new technology, and personal stories to create a dramatic digital representation of migration by boat on a scale never before seen at an Australian museum.

The ANMM has one of the most distinctive façades of any museum in the world and its soaring roofline, evoking sails and waves, is an iconic feature of Sydney's Darling Harbour. The installation of new digital projection technology in late 2012 provided an exciting opportunity to use the façade of the ANMM as an extension of the gallery space, literally bringing the inside out. The objective was to put a spotlight on current issues, and there are few issues with more currency than immigration.

In recent years Australians have been confronted daily with media images of dilapidated refugee boats overcrowded with families clutching the remnants of uprooted lives. We have witnessed contested political debates about refugee policy, border protection, and the offshore processing of asylum seekers. In the midst of this discourse, we can sometimes lose sight of the fact that much of Australia's history and national identity has been influenced by the migration of people from across the seas. One of the roles of the ANMM is to provide historical context to contemporary debates, and to give a voice and a presence to those who have peopled Australia's maritime history. The ANMM achieves this through its exhibitions, research, education and public programs, and collecting activities.

Since the late 1980s the ANMM has been assembling a diverse collection that spans the many waves of Australia's immigration history. These objects encompass a fascinating array of personal stories, from British convicts and free settlers to Jewish refugees and displaced persons from war-torn Europe; from Japanese war brides and Ten Pound Poms to Indochinese boat people and seaborne asylum seekers from Iraq and Afghanistan.⁷ For its inaugural digital projection in January 2013, the ANMM wanted to weave together this rich tapestry of migration stories and to encourage audiences to reflect on the current divisive immigration debate by demonstrating the historical continuity of migration by sea.

The Narrative

"Waves of Migration" opens with an indigenous fisherman in a bark canoe, to acknowledge that indigenous Australians are the only ones to have witnessed all the waves of migration to the country. It then follows the journey of a single migrant boat, changing its form across oceans and cultures, and through the passage of time. The thought-provoking eight-minute show is accompanied by a soundtrack that vividly captures the universal emotions associated with migration—hope and fear, courage and adventure, grief and triumph.

The boat emerges as HMS *Endeavour* departing England in 1768 under the command of Lieutenant James Cook to observe the Transit of Venus and search for the legendary Great South Land (Australia). It transforms into the British First Fleet convict transport *Charlotte* and then a clipper ship carrying Chinese migrants to the Australian goldfields in the 1850s, before struggling to make its way through a sea of early twentieth century, White Australia Policy paperwork.

The boat transitions into a post–World War II ocean liner passing through a ruined European landscape, transporting displaced persons and assisted migrants to new lives in Australia. It contracts into a small fishing boat loaded with refugees escaping the aftermath of the Vietnam War, before devolving into a decrepit Indonesian fishing vessel carrying Afghan asylum seekers on the last leg of their voyage to Australia. The boat then reemerges in the present day as the ANMM's HMB *Endeavour* replica and arrives in Sydney's Darling Harbour alongside the Museum.

"Waves of Migration" employs a cyclical storytelling device that emphasizes the cyclical nature of Australia's migration history. It asserts that the country's history and identity as an island nation have been, and continue to be, shaped by immigration. The show was supported by a dedicated Web site (http://waves.anmm.gov.au) with links to the ANMM's collection, as well as opportunities for people to share their own migration stories through social media channels. It launched on Australia Day in 2013 to significant media and public attention as audiences in Sydney and online engaged with this "shining reminder of Australia's rich migration heritage" (Calixto 2013) and the compelling personal stories presented within it.[8]

Personalizing the Projection

A major curatorial challenge for "Waves of Migration" was to balance the scale and spectacle of digital projection with the more intimate, human dimensions of immigration, and to explore the emotional possibilities of this new storytelling medium through the use of personal stories and objects from the ANMM's collection.

One of the most poignant scenes in the show centers on a house door key in the collection that belonged to Jewish refugee Valerie Lederer (see figure 2.2). The scene portrays Lederer on board SS *Orama* in 1939 as she recalls locking the door to her family's home in Nazi-occupied Austria before escaping prior to the outbreak of World War II. Even after finding safety in Australia, she continued to carry the key in her purse, providing a powerful reflection of the migrant's enduring loss and longing for home.

Figure 2.2. "Waves of Migration": Digital projection on the roof of the ANMM, 2013. Photographer: Andrew Frolows. Courtesy of ANMM.

Another moving scene tells the story of sixteen-year-old asylum seeker Hedayat Osyan, who in 2009 was forced to leave his mother and two siblings in Afghanistan in order to escape persecution by the Taliban. Osyan is depicted at the bow of an Indonesian people-smuggler boat as the sky fills with memories of his difficult journey to Australia via Malaysia and Indonesia; his journey ended with a rescue at sea by the Royal Australian Navy and transfer to the offshore Australian territory of Christmas Island. After three months in detention he was granted a permanent visa and resettled in Sydney in 2010. Osyan arrived with only a few personal possessions, including an embroidered Hazara handkerchief made by his sister, which he later donated to the ANMM. Osyan's story was profiled widely in the media with the launch of "Waves of Migration," presenting a valuable human dimension to one of the most polarizing debates in contemporary Australian society, and validating the ANMM's efforts to provide context to these debates.

The show illuminated the historical parallels between the many waves of migration by boat in Australia's history–from the early European settlers to the asylum seekers who continue to embark on dangerously overcrowded boats in the hope of a better future. "Waves of Migration" bridged the historical and the contemporary, the personal and the universal, to highlight the long sea voyage as a defining and unifying narrative of the migrant story. The use of digital projection technology allowed the ANMM to represent histories, memories, and emotions of migration by boat in an innovative, accessible format for both physical and virtual audiences.

Case Study 3: Gina's Journey

The final case study expands on the concept of representing emotions by discussing the ANMM's program of commissioning contemporary art to capture those intangible aspects of the migration experience that are often difficult to convey through objects, such as the trauma of displacement, the pain of losing a homeland, and the enduring attachment to home. It assesses the power of art to give material form to memory within the museum context, following Elizabeth Edwards's (2010) analysis of the materiality of photographs as memory texts, and Andrea Witcomb's (2013) survey of the materiality of Holocaust art as forms of testimony and enactments of memory. This relates to a larger museological shift toward art as object, identified in the work of Eureka Henrich (2011: 77), and Chiara O'Reilly and Nina Parish (2013). This shift provides museums with an engaging and effective means of representing migration, memory, and trauma in the absence of objects, while also playing an important role in empowering the marginalized to tell their stories. This section examines how migration by boat is narrated and visualized in a series of naïve, yet deeply personal, artworks that the ANMM commissioned from Gina Sinozich in 2003.

Homelands Lost and Found

Like many post-war refugees, Sinozich abandoned her homeland for a country she knew little about. In 1957 she and her family arrived in Australia from Istria, Croatia, part of the former Yugoslavia. It was only in 2000, when she was seventy years old, that Sinozich completed her first painting. Her husband Eugen had been diagnosed with dementia and she recognized the urgent need to record her memories of their life together and their family's passage to Australia on SS *Neptunia*.

Sinozich's first painting was on a discarded council sign that she found on the side of the road. This inspired the beginning of a prolific output that now sees her work represented in major collecting institutions across Australia and New Zealand. With no formal training, she has developed her own unique style–instinctive, honest, and intensely personal. As she says, "I want to do what I feel inside. I am not Sidney Nolan or Arthur Boyd.... I do it my own way" (Rousset 2007*)*. Referencing the strong tradition of naïve art in her homeland, Sinozich's work gives compelling tangible form to the migration memories in her mind and navigates the complex emotional terrain between homelands lost and found.

From Istria to Australia

After World War II Croatia was absorbed into the communist republic of Yugoslavia. Life was difficult and food was scarce, with daily queues for bread and milk. Sinozich's mother was jailed for two months after one of her sons fled the country. Sinozich wanted a more secure future for her own children, Michael and Jenny.

In the heartfelt painting *Our Story* Sinozich depicts herself and her family at the bow of the *Neptunia* (see figure 2.3). They are balanced over the edge of a waterfall, at the point of no return. Behind them are the lightness of Istria and an idyllic village of red rooftops, flowering trees, and a cherished little church on top of the hill. Before them is the darkness of Australia, empty, unpopulated, and unknown. In the lower left corner, she describes, in her distinctive hand, her family's escape.

In April 1956 Sinozich and her children slipped across the Italian border under the cover of visiting her mother in Trieste. She could not risk telling anyone, even close family, that they were leaving. In the painting she expresses her grief at deceiving her youngest brother Riko who had visited her children daily and who was devastated when he discovered the family gone. She writes, "He ask me how long we will be away. Now this was the hardest

Figure 2.3. Gina Sinozich with her painting, *Our Story*, 2005. Photographer: Andrew Frolows. Courtesy of ANMM.

thing for me. My heart broke to pieces. Lump in my throat and tears in my eyes. I mumble 2 weeks. I knew we will not be back" (Sinozich 2003).

As with all of Sinozich's work, *Our Story* is multilayered, with a whimsical child-like simplicity that belies its emotional intensity. Although it does not adhere to any rules of perspective, scale, or representation, it clearly conveys what she feels—anticipation and fear, suspended between the nostalgic and the unknown, between a Croatia that is certain and an Australia that cannot even be imagined. And resonating beyond this visual representation is the pain captured in her written words.

In an attempt to reconcile her guilt, Sinozich created the poignant *Our Precious Things We Left Behind*. Here she illustrates, on a rain-swept wharf in Rijeka, an imagined farewell to loved ones—her best friend, brother, mother, and mother-in-law. She says, "I know in my heart it was raining," and the tears and pouring rain in the painting symbolize the "cleaning out" of her insides (Sinozich, personal interview 2014).

On arrival in Italy Sinozich applied for political asylum and was sent to a hostel in Udine sheltering three thousand other refugees. Her husband arrived several months later, having escaped on foot and walking at night to avoid discovery. It was sixteen months before they were given the choice of resettlement in Australia or Canada. Sinozich and her husband chose Australia, a new country that they believed would offer greater opportunities for their children. The family departed from Genoa on *Neptunia* in July 1957. In the aptly titled *We Are Sailing from the Known to the Unknown*, *Neptunia* is visualized as steaming down under from Croatia to Australia. Uluru, two Aboriginal people, and a kangaroo encapsulate all that Sinozich knew about Australia.

One of the highlights of the ocean passage is depicted in *The Dining Room*, full of vivid color and activity, with elegant waiters in white jackets and bow ties serving pasta and wine to the passengers. Conversely, the perils of ocean travel are represented in *We Are in the Sea Storm of the Indian Ocean*. Seasick passengers in orange lifejackets roll around on the deck of *Neptunia* as the vessel pitches about in wild seas. Sinozich herself suffered terrible seasickness during a terrifying storm that lasted four days.

The vibrant *We Arrive in Melbourne* shows passengers waving and embracing as *Neptunia* docks safely in Victoria following a month at sea. The ship's captain says farewell to the passengers as they disembark to a waiting train that will take them to the Bonegilla migrant hostel near Wodonga. The Sinozich family would spend several weeks at the hostel before settling in Sydney. They are distinguished by their brown suitcases inscribed "Sinozich Genova to Melbourne."

The suitcases also appear in the modest but moving painting *Three Suitcases*. In the center the six words "All our possession [*sic*] arrive in Melbourne" are a powerful reminder of how much the family was forced to leave behind.

Sinozich refers to her work as recycled memory, as painting from memory the pictures in her mind. Through her practice, she gives tangible form to history, effectively recreating her lost family albums and lost homeland through art.

Narrative, Memory, and Trauma

Sinozich's work is characterized by a strong narrative content, and what cultural theorist Mieke Bal has termed "narrative memories," which are defined as, "affectively colored, surrounded by an emotional aura that, precisely, makes them memorable" (Bal, Crewe, and Spitzer 1999: viii). But her life has also been dominated by "traumatic memories," which for Bal need to be "legitimized and narratively integrated in order to lose their hold over the subject who suffered the traumatizing event in the past" (Bal, Crewe, and Spitzer 1999: viii).

In 2004 Sinozich decided to return to Croatia for the first time since her escape in 1956. News footage of the 2003 U.S. invasion of Iraq had recalled her own childhood experiences of the Nazi invasion of Istria, and she felt compelled to revisit the traumatic memories of her early life. In response to the visit Sinozich produced an intimate series of textile works that give three-dimensional form to the stories in her paintings. The collection includes miniature replicas of clothing she remembered from her childhood: a green dress her aunt made for her as a child, a school uniform representing her desire to become a teacher, a beloved pair of shoes her brother Tomi bought for her when she was fifteen. Without any mementos of her childhood or homeland, she was inspired to create tactile pieces embodying a sense of history and home.

Sinozich also produced three large-scale embroidered works on Croatian linen that explored her family's experiences of World War II. Her use of Croatian linen signifies a powerful connection between the lost dowry from a distant homeland and an artistic canvas in the new homeland. Within its threads Sinozich weaves together personal memories and family histories in an intriguing dialogue between homelands lost and found. She describes her emotional visit to the site where her husband Eugen had faced a Nazi firing squad, and her joy at uncovering the army records of Eugen and her brother Riko in Croatia. During this trip Sinozich was able to reunite with Riko and mend the rift caused by her secret departure almost fifty years earlier. She had finally come home and come to terms with her past.

Sinozich's work is significant because it is rare for an older first-generation migrant to articulate her own story through art. More commonly these stories are explored by children or grandchildren negotiating issues of cultural heritage, identity, and belonging. Her work gives tangible, visual form to the sea passage and the elusive concepts of memory and emotion in a museum environment. It has been used in a variety of contexts at the ANMM, most recently the second showing of the "Waves of Migration" digital projection in 2014, illustrating the complexities of the migrant experience while also retaining accessibility and impact for audiences in its very naivety. The ANMM's Sinozich commission represents a compelling intersection between artistic practice and museology, one that enables the artist to reclaim history, memory, and lost homelands, and in the process create a powerful new evocation of home.

Conclusion

Migration by boat remains one of the enduring themes in Australia's history and pivotal to the collecting, research, and interpretive activities of the ANMM. This chapter has examined three recent ANMM programs that look beyond the traditional exhibition framework to respond to the challenges of representing migration by boat in the changing political climate of the past decade, drawing powerful connections between objects, memory, and lived experience to amplify personal stories within broader narratives of forced migration. By embracing the interpretive potential of the Vietnamese refugee boat *Tu Do,* the "Waves of Migration" digital projection, and contemporary art created by Gina Sinozich, the ANMM has been able to personalize, contextualize, and visualize the experiences of refugees and asylum seekers against a landscape of often-dehumanizing political and public debates. This is particularly critical as a new wave of seaborne asylum seekers arrives on Australia's shores, reminding us that the history of migration by boat is living and evolving, and that the Australian National Maritime Museum plays a vital role in representing this history as it unfolds.

Kim Tao is curator of Post-Federation Immigration at the Australian National Maritime Museum. She has won a number of national and international awards for her curatorial projects, which focus on migration in the Australian context. Tao has a bachelor of arts and a master of arts in museum studies from the University of Sydney. Her research interests include migration, memory, and material culture in museums, and histories of child migration. In 2008 Tao was awarded a Churchill Fellowship to study partnerships between museums and culturally diverse communities in the United Kingdom, Canada, and the United States. She has presented conference papers in Australia and overseas, and has written articles for *Signals,* exhibition catalogues including *Bodgies, Westies & Homies* (2006) and *Rituals & Traditions* (2008), and chapters for *100 Stories from the Australian National Maritime Museum* (2012) and *Migrating Heritage: Experiences of Cultural Networks and Cultural Dialogue in Europe* (2014).

Notes

This chapter is derived in part from an article published in *Third Text* 135, vol 29, no 4, 2016.
1. See also Szekeres 2011.
2. According to Australian government figures for 2012–13, "Historically, boat arrivals only made up a small proportion of asylum applicants—estimates vary, but it is likely that between 96 and 99 percent of asylum applicants arrived by air. More recently the proportions of Irregular Maritime Arrival (IMA) and non-IMA (that is air arrival) asylum seekers have shifted due to the increase in boat arrivals. However, boat arrivals still only comprise about half of Australia's onshore asylum seekers. Although the proportion of asylum seekers arriving by boat has increased significantly in the last few years, and boat arrivals continue to be the focus of much public and political attention, they are in fact more likely to be recognized as refugees than those who have arrived by air. … The number of people arriving unauthorized by boat in Australia, is small in comparison to the numbers arriving in other parts of the world such as Europe. Similarly, the number of asylum claims lodged in Australia is small in comparison to the USA, Canada, and Europe." See Parliament of Australia n.d.
3. The White Australia Policy is the colloquial term for the Immigration Restriction Act 1901, which aimed "to place certain restrictions on immigration and to provide for the removal from the Commonwealth of prohibited immigrants," namely those from Asia and the Pacific Islands. See Australian Government Department of Immigration and Border Protection n.d.
4. The current Coalition government's "stopping the boats" policy is known as Operation Sovereign Borders, "a military-led response to combat people smuggling and to protect our borders," which includes the controversial practice of turning back asylum seeker boats where it is safe to do so. See Liberal Party of Australia 2013.
5. For a detailed discussion of media representations see Goodnow, Lohman, and Marfleet (2008).
6. "Waves of Migration" won a silver MUSE Award for public outreach from the American Alliance of Museums in May 2013, "Waves of Migration," ANMM, http://waves.anmm.gov.au.
7. Ten Pound Poms refers to the British migrants that traveled to Australia under an assisted passage migration scheme between 1945 and 1972 and paid a government-subsidized fare of ten pounds.
8. Australia Day marks the anniversary of the arrival of the First Fleet on January 26, 1788, to establish the first permanent British settlement at Sydney Cove, New South Wales.

Bibliography

Australian Government Department of Immigration and Border Protection. n.d. "Fact Sheet 8: Abolition of the White Australia Policy." http://www.immi.gov.au/media/fact-sheets/08abolition.htm.

Australian National Maritime Museum (ANMM). 2011. "Collection Development Policy." Sydney: Australian National Maritime Museum.
Bal, Mieke, Jonathan Crewe, and Leo Spitzer, eds. 1999. *Acts of Memory: Cultural Recall in the Present.* Hanover, NH: University Press of New England.
Calixto, Julia. 2013. "Sea Migration Stories to Light up Sydney." http://www.sbs.com.au/news/article/2013/01/26/sea-migration-stories-light-sydney.
Edwards, Elizabeth. 2010. "Photographs and History: Emotion and Materiality." In *Museum Materialities: Objects, Engagements, Interpretations,* edited by Sandra H. Dudley, 21–38. London/New York: Routledge.
Goodnow, Katherine, Jack Lohman, and Philip Marfleet. 2008. *Museums, the Media and Refugees: Stories of Crisis, Control and Compassion.* New York: Berghahn Books.
Henrich, Eureka. 2011. "Suitcases and Stories: Objects of Migration in Museum Exhibitions." *International Journal of the Inclusive Museum* 3, no. 4: 71–82.
Jakubowicz, Andrew. 2004. "Vietnamese in Australia: A Generation of Settlement and Adaptation." *Multicultural Research Library.* http://www.multiculturalaustralia.edu.au/library/media/Document/id/731.
Liberal Party of Australia. 2013. "Media Release: Operation Sovereign Borders, 26 July 2013." http://www.liberal.org.au/latest-news/2013/07/26/operation-sovereign-borders.
Marr, David, and Marian Wilkinson. 2003. *Dark Victory.* Crows Nest, NSW: Allen & Unwin.
McShane, Ian. 2001. "Challenging or Conventional? Migration History in Australian Museums." In *National Museums: Negotiating Histories: Conference Proceedings,* edited by Darryl McIntyre and Kirsten Wehner, 122–33. Canberra: National Museum of Australia.
O'Reilly, Chiara, and Nina Parish. 2013. "How Objects Are Being Used to Collect and Tell Migrant Stories in Museums." Paper presented at *Suitcases, Boats and Bridges: Telling Migrant Stories in Australian Museums,* Australian National Maritime Museum, Sydney, August 2.
Parliament of Australia. n.d. "Asylum Seekers and Refugees: What Are the Facts?" http://www.aph.gov.au/About_Parliament/Parliamentary_Departments/Parliamentary_Library/pubs/BN/2012-2013/AsylumFacts.
Rousset, Olivia. [Director]. 2007. *The Passion of Gina Sinozich.* [Film.] Clovelly, NSW: Vagabond Films.
Sinozich, Gina. 2003. *Our Story.* Sydney, ANMM Collection.
Szekeres, Viv. 2011. "Museums and Multiculturalism: Too Vague to Understand, Too Important to Ignore." In *Understanding Museums: Australian Museums and Museology,* edited by Des Griffin and Leon Paroissien. Canberra: National Museum of Australia. http://nma.gov.au/research/understanding-museums/VSzekeres_2011.html.
Witcomb, Andrea. 2013. "Testimony, Memory, and Art at the Jewish Holocaust Museum, Melbourne, Australia." In *Museums and Communities: Curators, Collections and Collaboration,* edited by Viv Golding and Wayne Modest, 260–74. London: Bloomsbury.

3
Nước/Water
Oceanic Spatiality and the Vietnamese Diaspora

Vinh Nguyen

In the Vietnamese language, the word for water—*nước*—is the same as that for "a country, a homeland, a nation." According to Huỳnh Sanh Thông, the "most significant derivation from the meaning of *nước* as 'water' is the concept of people who have gathered near a body of water to grow rice for one another, founding a stable community, sharing rain and drought, plenty and famine, peace and war" (Thông 1996: 142). Water, as both an experience and an idea, has played a central role in the imagining of Vietnamese collective cultural identity. From Vietnam's inception as a civilization, it helped to define a distinct consciousness of peoplehood. Keith Weller Taylor, in his seminal study *The Birth of Vietnam,* locates the notion that "sovereign power came from the sea" as a "basic psychological truth of ancient Vietnamese society" in various myths and legends, especially the founding myth of Lạc Long Quân, a water god regarded as the progenitor of the Vietnamese people (Taylor 1983: 6). He writes, "The idea of an aquatic spirit's [*sic*] being the source of political power and legitimacy, which attended the formation of the Vietnamese people in prehistoric times, is the earliest hint of the concept of the Vietnamese as a distinct and self-conscious people" (Taylor 1983: 7). Water's enduring importance can be traced to numerous cultural practices of identification and collectivity, including the engravings on heritage Đong Sơn drums, traditional water puppetry, and the centrality of the Red River, Perfume River, and Mekong Delta to Vietnamese settlement and civilization, just to name a few.[1] Yet, its symbolic association with community and belonging, acquired through centuries of Vietnamese history, takes on different significations in the wake of the War in Vietnam, when hundreds of thousands of people took to boats to flee the ruins of war and the incoming communist regime. On the open seas, many of these asylum seekers lost their lives as a result of storms, starvation, disease, and pirate attacks.

This mass migration—in successive waves—captured the world's attention and gave rise to a new cultural lexicon: the *boat people*. For the Vietnamese diaspora, water at once signals a cultural identity and separation from that identity, a home(land) as well as the violent rift from, and loss of, that home. My chapter dwells on this paradox, focusing on the concept of water as a way to think through the intricacies of nation, diaspora, and home. I suggest that the historical context of the Vietnamese boat people allows us to rethink the dialectical tension between continuity and rupture—one of the central issues in diaspora studies—as we contemplate the embodied experiences and memories of those who were displaced by way of water. Analyzing Vietnamese diasporic literary representations of boat journeys, I examine the kinds of subjectivities and collectivities forged through shared loss, that are built on both intense affective fear and unusual intimacies, on deep tenderness and jagged brutality, on longing and desire. My analysis is concerned with the ties, attachments, and relations not circumscribed by terrestrial nationalism but instead facilitated by what I call *oceanic spatiality*—the waterscape of the boat and of the sea.

I contend that Vietnamese diasporic cultural producers employ and explore these aqueous spaces as critical tropes to represent, imagine, and negotiate the painful and productive interplay between history, memory, and identity. The boat on water becomes an image, an affect, a vehicle for writers and artists to make sense of what it means to be subjects of war and to understand the work of having to reconstruct a life and identity in its wake. While I heed Hester Blum's caution that "the sea is not metaphor" (Blum 2010: 670), that it is limiting to engage bodies of water purely as a metaphorical space of mobility and connection rather than an experienced reality, and I acknowledge Philip E. Steinberg's (2013) important point about the partiality of our human encounter with the sea, I assert that metaphors *arise* from and through histories of lived and embodied contact, and that contact, however partial or filtered through the inadequate human lens, is powerful in shaping the epistemologies and discourses available to us as we approach the natural world. It is within discursive, metaphorical representations that we can come to some, if limited, understanding of the material and the historical—the textures of the extra-textual, meta-intellectual—sea, to reach for the edges of human experience.

For these cultural producers, the sea is a metaphor that reveals the complexities, contradictions, and ironies of exile and migration. It endures like stubborn memories that are sometimes buried in silence and defy comprehension, that are often difficult to recall and impossible to forget. The sea itself *is* memory. But the sea is also beyond a metaphor, because it is, at the same time, material—experiences acquired first-hand or inherited that are lived and felt as realities. And so scenes of water populate Vietnamese diasporic cultural productions; the sea and the boat become sites of return to re(-)member and (re)imagine personal and collective histories and identities that undulate on water, in excess of total recollection and containment. In this chapter, I focus on two short stories—Linh Dinh's "A Floating Community" (Dinh 2004) and Nam Le's "The Boat" (Le 2008)—that productively take up the notion of oceanic spatiality. In aesthetically different ways, both stories demonstrate how the sea and the boat provide means of cultural contemplation and creation. I focus on them not only because they describe refugee boat journeys, but also because they consciously comment on and discursively generate knowledge of the Vietnamese diaspora. Rather than re-present the past, Dinh and Le's short pieces engender, through narrative, the past as that which is not yet complete, as an important resource for the present and the future. Literary representations are not only a way of reflecting on migration experiences but crucially determine *how we think about* and *materially experience* those experiences. My discussion explores how representations of migration by boat extend the significance of water to understandings of Vietnamese diasporic identity, and how such understandings can begin to conceptualize the relationship between water and something we might call refugee space.

To Thirst: The Boat People

Many Vietnamese in diaspora refer to April 30, 1975, as the day of *mât nuóc*: to lose one's country, to be without the life source of water. On that day, communist tanks rolled into Saigon, the capital city, ending three decades of warfare. As North Vietnamese troops approached, many residents scrambled to flee the city. After runways at the international airport had been bombed and the last overloaded helicopters had lifted off from the rooftop of the American embassy, people desperately took to boats to escape. Most of these early boat refugees did not have to endure prolonged journeys because they quickly reached neighboring ports or naval ships waiting not far from shore.

The second wave of refugees—and the first of boat people—did not fare as well. Beginning in 1977 and lasting until 1979, the number of people fleeing Vietnam rapidly increased, due mainly to the Hanoi government's targeted persecution of particular groups of people (ethnic Chinese and those with ties to Americans and the deposed South Vietnamese regime) as well as its massive overhaul of society, making life untenable for many. These societal restructurings included, for example, changes to the economy such as a new currency system and state seizure of businesses and industries; the forced relocation of people to rural "new economic zones"; political repression, social ostracization, and public executions; and the incarceration of those associated with the former government in "reeducation" camps.[2] In the span of three years more than a quarter of a million people fled the country.

The majority of them left clandestinely, through organized smuggling operations, some of which were headed by corrupt officials. Some did not make it far as they were caught by guards and returned or killed on the spot. Those who made it out to sea, often on small boats crammed beyond capacity with hundreds of people, had to contend with stormy conditions, illness, lack of food and water, engine failures, and pirate attacks. It is estimated that "two-thirds of the boats were attacked by pirates, each boat an average of more than two times" (Takaki 1993: 414). Of the 277,500 people who escaped Vietnam, "at least 30,000 to 40,000 perished at sea" (Wolf and Lowman 1990: 103). Survivors landed on neighboring territories such as Malaysia, Thailand, Indonesia, Hong Kong, and the Philippines, where they were housed in refugee camps (figure 3.1). However, many of these countries quickly began to feel compassion fatigue and instead of welcoming the boats and its refugees, they refused entry, sending them back out to sea, where the refugees anchored and awaited rescue. Their plight caught the international community's attention, resulting in the first Geneva Conference in 1979.

Initiated by the United Nations, the conference outlined the Orderly Departure Program (ODP), designed to facilitate sanctioned departures from Vietnam and the resettlement of Vietnamese asylum seekers already in camps. Because of the program's successful implementation, people leaving by boat decreased to low numbers throughout much of the 1980s. However, in 1987 and 1988 figures began to rise once again, mainly due to backlogs, red tape, and the eventual breakdown of the ODP. A second wave of boat people occurred late in the decade. In 1989 alone roughly seventy thousand people arrived on foreign shores seeking asylum (Robinson 2000: 193). A second Geneva Conference was held and a Comprehensive Plan of Action (CPA) was put in place to contain the mounting crisis. In total, close to 2 million refugees left Vietnam between 1975 and 1992, and a significant number of these were boat people. My cursory description of events here does not begin to touch on the complex historical forces at play in the Vietnamese boat people phenomenon. My intention, however, is to sketch out a rough and basic understanding in order to build some background information for my readings of cultural texts to follow and, in doing so, to also signal that the boat people were an important part of the beginnings of a late twentieth-century transnational Vietnamese diaspora formed in the aftermath of war.[3]

Nước/Water | 69

Figure 3.1. Vietnamese refugee boat people arriving in Hong Kong in 1979. Photographed by Terry Fincher/The Fincher Files 2015. Courtesy of Jayne Fincher.

Oceanic Spatiality, Refugee Space

The sea has been the backdrop for some of Western modernity's defining moments: the age of exploration that facilitated the expansion of European colonialism and global capitalism, the Middle Passage that brought African slaves across the Atlantic, the multiple routes that indentured laborers navigated to the Americas, and the refugee crises of the twentieth and twenty-first centuries, just to name a few.[4] These examples demonstrate that the sea has a history, or, in the words of Derek Walcott "The sea is History" (1986: 364). The sea indexes the major and minor events that have shaped what we erroneously think of as the world occurring exclusively on land. Through the case of the Vietnamese boat people, I want to suggest that the sea is also a *refugee space*–that is, to the motley crew of seafaring figures such as the sailor, the slave, and the indentured laborer, we can add the refugee escaping persecution. This, however, is not to create a false equivalence between these disparate histories or to suggest that they are necessarily discrete, but to highlight the sea as a space that both facilitates and bears the traces of various human movements—one of them being that of asylum seekers.[5]

As the surface through which refugees move as well as the material reality that shapes their lives, the sea forms one dimension of oceanic spatiality. For the boat people, the sea often functioned as the first place of refuge, even as it induced great uncertainty and fear. Here, the sea is not merely a physical setting, but rather a crucible, a place and an experience that destroys and produces, that molds and transforms. Recently, scholars in the emerging field of oceanic studies have turned to the sea as a "proprioceptive point of inquiry" that can "make possible other ways of understanding affiliation, citizenship, mobility, rights, and sovereignty, all of which have been read in recent critical history as overdetermined by nationalism" (Blum 2010: 671). For them, the sea promises an alternative frame, a space–physical and psychological– beyond the confines of terrestrial nationalism that enables the reconsideration of human history, social relations, and political forms of organization. Iain Chambers emphatically writes, "Contemplating undulating seascapes can lead to rethinking ideas of time, space, and change" (Chambers 2010: 679). The sea is one chronotope–a time-space–of analysis and epistemology that can be critically employed to illuminate asylum seeking in the age of transnationalism and globalization.

Another dimension of oceanic spatiality is the scale of the boat, the physical vessel tasked with carrying refugees to a different future, to safety and freedom. The boat is a locus of various investments, principally those of faith and hope. Paraphrasing Michel Foucault's description of the ship as the heterotopia par excellence, Trinh T. Minh-Ha asserts, "The boat is either a dream or a nightmare. Or rather both, a no place, a place without a place that exists by itself, is closed in on itself and at the same time is given over to the infinity of the sea.... It has also been a reserve of the imagination. It is said that in a civilization without boats dreams dry up, espionage takes the place of adventure, and the police take the place of pirates. Hope is alive when there is a boat, even a small boat" (Trinh 1989). The floating boat holds out hope—the assurance of life itself. Yet, as Trinh reminds us, it is also a nightmare: the location of death and suffering, of grief. The chronotope of the boat, like the sea, is an experience that produces the refugee, as well as a locale where such experiences occur.

"In diaspora discourses," Christopher Lee writes, "ships are not only discussed as the material means for migration but also function as a discursive figure signifying the relationship between migration and subject formation" (Lee 2015: 147). Theorists like Paul Gilroy and Vijay Mishra have written about the ship as a society, a radical space of movement, negotiation, and world building. According to Gilroy, the ship is "a living, micro-cultural, micro-political system in motion," enabling the circulation of bodies, texts, ideas, and memories in the production of Black Atlantic diaspora networks (Gilroy 1993: 4). Mishra's work on the "old" Indian diasporas of indentured laborers demonstrates how the ship re-created but also altered social and cultural relations among those who left the homeland (Mishra 1996). Similarly, I suggest, the refugee boat can and should be analyzed as a world, one that records and reveals the textures of experience and the affective relations that form the nexus of diaspora and diasporic subjectivity.

The sea and the boat, water and vessel, forms an analytical configuration that allows for examinations of refugee migration on water. Oceanic spatiality connects these two time-spaces in creative relation, providing us with "oceanographic" coordinates for contemplation and critical inquiry. It refers to both material places as well as intellectual constructs, and to the ways in which they are mutually constitutive. I suggest that it is within these spatialities that alternate epistemologies and narratives surface and circulate, especially those that are illegible within the logics of terrestrial nationalism and normative historiography In the boat on water, there exists potential for different rememberings, for impossible tellings, for becomings. I turn now to two literary examples from Vietnamese writers living in diaspora to further elaborate on the idea of oceanic spatiality. My aim is to gesture to the wider prominence of the sea and boat journeys within Vietnamese diasporic attempts to represent, and make sense of, displacement and its lasting legacies.

Home/Water: Linh Dinh's "A Floating Community"

Linh Dinh's speculative postcard story recounts the discovery of a small floating community off the coast of Guam in the year 2049. It begins, "On eleven rotting boats, lashed together by ropes, were ninety-nine individuals of indeterminate nationality" (Dinh 2004: 59). The narrative then offers one possibility, among others, that they are remnants of the Vietnamese boat people before going on to describe a culture and collective identity based on and around water: "they had survived on flying fish and rain water. Most of them had never seen land. (The ones who had seen land were considered schizophrenic by the others; the hieroglyphs for 'land' and 'schizophrenic' were the same.) The sea, as the final resting place of their ancestors, was revered as holy and toxic. God dwelled in the lowest depths and was referred to as 'The Biggest Lamprey'" (Dinh 2004: 59). For this community, the sea is a place of vexed rooting—a source of subsistence and imagination as well as of danger and existential caprice. Here, the ocean is reconfigured as home rather than transit; or, water becomes a home *in* transit, a drifting home moored in motion. Correspondingly, cultural identity is carved through life on, with, and in the movement of water.

Furthermore, water is conceived as the catalyst and source for human life and civilization. Dinh tells us that their creation myth begins with the phrase: "In the beginning, this monotonous earth did not bobble ..." (Dinh 2004: 59). The community's origin story reverses conventional narratives in which an orderly world was created from extensive chaos or watery abyss. Here, life begins at the moment of water, with the bouncing motion of the boat. The monotony of the earth is also its homogeneity, broken by the oncoming water, not to destroy life but to give it shape. In the story, the sea is the space of creation as well as its method, one that allows for being, and being differently. For these boat people, motion constitutes the self rather than disrupts it. In presenting a world centered on water instead of land, Dinh delineates an alternative trajectory of social formation and identity that resonates with a contemporary Vietnamese diaspora that had its formative moments on water.

Read as an allegory for the postwar Vietnamese diaspora—one that remains deeply connected to the homeland in its dispersal, that metamorphoses through recourse to an established symbol of cultural essence—Dinh's story illuminates the diasporic process of transformation, a process that is not oppositional to constancy and purity, but utilizes the very grammar of origins to declare difference. The "indeterminacy" of the floating community speaks to experiences of in-between, of hybridity and creolization, that often arise from the disturbances of displacement—what Stuart Hall points out as, the "critical points of deep and significant *difference* which constitute 'what we really are'; or rather—since history has intervened—'what we have become'" (Hall 1990: 225 his emphasis). Indeterminacy here does not presuppose only a loss or a lack, but also a critical emergence. Dinh's concisely wrought thesis expresses the idea that the Vietnamese diaspora is fundamentally distinct from Vietnam, and yet the defining characteristic that distinguishes diaspora from motherland is inextricably shared between the two. The common link—water—is both the materiality and the cultural lexicon that allows Vietnamese formations abroad to simultaneously be the same and different from Vietnam, to feel connected to but also separate from it. "Floating" Vietnamese diasporic communities, thus, are not drifting toward a land of origins—many of the members have never seen this land, this signifier of splitness—but are instead moving out of descent, in the Foucauldian sense, to a becoming filled with the "accidents" of war and history.

While the allegorical story describes a culture seemingly isolated and adrift in a forgotten corner of the world, Dinh's account of the Vietnamese diaspora is, in many ways, one of reconciliation. Yoking together incongruent diasporic tensions—continuity and rupture, home and away, stasis and movement—through the trope of water, Dinh demonstrates a way of working with and holding migrant contradictions. The various conflicting demands of memory and oblivion, of authenticity and assimilation, of survival and everyday living, that structure Vietnamese refugee and diasporic lives are not neatly resolved in the narrative, but are allowed space to coexist within the element of water. Dinh's story gestures to the possibility of complexly lived life that neither makes definitive claims to nor denies the processes that make it possible. The common, often-cited wordplay in diaspora studies—the words *root* and *route*—reveals its core concerns with movement, place, and identity. It also tells us that these two concepts are not so much binary opposites but are instead dialectically related in a way that suggests their mutual imbrication, their doubling in divergence. Dinh's enigmatic piece blurs the tenuous distinctions between movement and sedentariness in its depiction of home as simultaneously "a place of safety and of terror" (Brah 1996: 177).

Isabelle Thuy Pelaud (2005) writes that a critical "transgression of essentialist assumptions and rejection of more common refugee narratives" can be found in Dinh's work (Pelaud 2005: 45). As a refugee narrative with an unconventional form, "A Floating Community" dwells in ambiguity, indirection, and symbolic representation to speak of Vietnam and its diaspora. Eschewing a confessional, often didactic auto/biographical or ethnographic aesthetic that is common to Vietnamese diasporic cultural productions, Dinh sidesteps the predominant theme of loss in his account of boat migration. In its place, getting "lost" becomes a means to begin anew without necessarily completely starting over. In referencing the Vietnamese boat exodus as a possible point of embarkment and estrangement in his story, Dinh consciously performs a diasporic process of generative indeterminacy in the act of writing. "A Floating Community" is about the Vietnamese in diaspora, and it is not about them; the diasporic writer always writes about Vietnam, and he never writes about it. As the story shows, the production of art can be fluid like water and expansive like the sea, especially for those producers who have experienced the discontinuities of migration. The oceanic spatiality in Dinh's story illustrates that water can become a home place, that community and culture are built not on departures or arrivals, but in transit; or rather, transit becomes the foundation for the formation of an identity, one that is not necessarily temporary or ephemeral, but rather substantial and steady in its flow.

Embodied Ethics: Nam Le's "The Boat"

Nam Le's titular story, "The Boat," from his short fiction collection *The Boat* (2008) describes, with painstaking realism, the emotional, psychological, and embodied experience of a refugee boat passage. The specificity of the Vietnamese context in Le's story stands in sharp contrast to Dinh's allegorical piece; yet, both authors characterize the boat as a dangerous space that reverberates with promise, grief, and strange, unexpected intimacies. Le's narrative takes place in the span of thirteen days on the open seas, and is told from the perspective of Mai, a young woman making the escape journey alone, as she forms a deep bond with Truong, a taciturn boy who inherits and embodies, in his small frame, the hard and cruel legacies of war. The story begins with an oncoming storm, and with it, the threat of death and destruction. It ends with an image of the six-year-old central character's limp, lifeless body being flung from the back, "as far behind the boat as possible so he would be out of sight when the sharks attacked" (Le 2008: 272).

Between the storm and Truong's death that bookend the narrative, Le sketches the raw details of life within the asylum-seeking boat moving across water. He writes, "Inside the hold, the stench was incredible, almost eye-watering. The smell of urine and human waste, sweat and vomit. The black space full of people, bodies upon bodies, eyes and eyes and eyes ... here she [Mai] could hardly breathe, let alone move. Later she counted at least two hundred people, squashed into a space meant for fifteen" (Le 2008: 247). The compression of both space and bodies inside the boat creates contact as it constricts—refugees are pressed up and against each other, sharing physicality as well as an undetermined fate. In the boat, life and death sit in intense, delicate suspension, straddling an intimate point of existence. This precarious, suspended condition manifests itself most forcefully in the child refugee figure of Truong. He is described as "a skinny child with an unusually bony frame and a head too big for his body. His eyes, black and preternaturally calm, were too big for his head. He spoke in a watery voice—rarely—and, as far as Mai could tell, never smiled. He was like an old man crushed into the rude shape of a boy" (Le 2008: 235). Yet "an electric flurry" raced "through the concavities of his back, stomach and chest. His body furious with life" (Le 2008: 235). Truong is both enigmatically fragile and full of affective intensities; he lives out what it means to exist on a refugee boat. His bodily experience of the journey—the innocence and weariness, the calm and turbulence—elicits a desire in Mai to touch, to affect and be affected, to connect with a deeper part of his self: "she'd grasped that nothing—nothing—was more important than her trying to see whatever it was he was seeing behind his dark, flat eyes" (Le 2008: 235).

Through the escapees' complicated inhabitation of the boat, the story presents an understanding of the refugee boat as a contained structural entity that facilitates a "shared consciousness" of death, fear, and surrender among the passengers huddled in its hold (Le 2008: 232). Inside the boat's belly, time merges "with memory, until it seem[s] as though everything that had ever happened had happened on the boat" (Le 2008: 251). The story opens up a consideration of the temporal and spatially bound form of the boat as a place—a site of time, sociality, and experience—not unlike other spaces of social organization and collectivity. The boat is, in short, a world that forces a frightening psychic communion between its temporary dwellers, defining a gathering of people attuned to the precarity of life and the imminence of death.

In this awareness of danger, there is also a kind of terrifying—and simultaneously comforting—physical intimacy that occurs. Crammed into the hatch of the boat, bodies collide, "thighs and ribs and arms and heads—jammed this way and that with each groaning tilt, writhing toward space as though impelling the boat to heave to, back into the wind" (Le 2008: 230). Le continues, "the contact of flesh pressed against her [Mai] on every side, the human warmth, feeling every square inch of skin against her body. ... She stayed in that human cocoon, heaving and rolling, concentrating, until it [the storm] was over" (Le 2008: 231–32). In this metaphor, the boat becomes a "human cocoon," melding refugee bodies together physically as well as psychically. It is both protective, by way of containment and shared tactile contact, and reproductive, in its suggestion of birth and renewed life outside the womb of the cocoon. Ultimately, however, it is unable to keep alive its most vulnerable passengers; and so, while the possibility of community, connection, and contact is presented, Le makes it clear that nothing is guaranteed inside the boat's unforgiving belly.

Yet, the feeling body occupying the boat, one that is able to, indeed must, exist beyond itself, is foregrounded in this oceanic space as a figure of ethical reckoning. In his reading of the story, Donald Goellnicht offers bodily sensation as a response to questions of authenticity, ethical representation, and responsible behavior that Le's collection raises. For Goellnicht, it is in the attention to, and meticulous meditation on, how bodies feel, endure, and respond to others on the sea that Nam Le's narrative grapples with the difficulties and (im)possibilities of remembering and telling. The sea thus brings into relief how individuals relate, how they interact and feel together, and how moral quandaries are confronted and worked through. He writes, "In existing beyond the law of nation–states, as a space of potential freedom, the sea is paradoxically a site of 'natural law' (Darwinian survival of the fittest) and human lawlessness. It is precisely in such a space, where the stakes are at their highest, a matter of life and death, of vulnerability and interdependence, that ethical behavior between human beings is tested to the limits" (Goellnicht 2012: 218).

Following Goellnicht's analysis, Mai's dedication to Trung, her love for a boy not her own, her willingness to put her body on the line for his protection, and the care with which she ushers Trung's mother away from his lifeless body becomes a measure of ethics within an experience that has no preestablished guide for conduct and existence. Mai's embodied experience, and that of numerous others on the boat, is another dimension of oceanic spatiality. The corporeal body in the boat, in Le's story, becomes a vantage point from which to contemplate and come to terms with what is for many a trauma beyond words and representation. "The Boat" posits that a story of trauma and diaspora, one that is often difficult for both first-hand and secondary witnesses to recount, can be told with trust in and through what the body experiences—its corporal knowledge.

Conclusion: Movements of Resistance

Dinh and Le mobilize water and the boat as critical tropes to narrate and shape understandings of Vietnamese diasporic refugee experiences. Their stories demonstrate that literary representation constitutes another coordinate in the configuration I have elaborated as oceanic spatiality, a site from which the memories and histories of those who have fled war can be (re)invoked, (re)invented, and (re)examined. Deploying very different approaches, these two writers provide glimpses of insight into the dimensions and dynamics of the Vietnamese diaspora. Such refugee dimensionality, I suggest, critically addresses conventional, mainstream representations that often depoliticize, dehistoricize, and gloss over the crucial subjective textures that make up refugee lives during, before, and after the migration event. In such a context, Dinh and Le's stories are political acts, presenting alternative versions of reality, and the possibility of apprehending refugees more complexly.

In the final minutes of her experimental film *Surname Viet Given Name Nam,* Trinh T. Minh-Ha provocatively asserts that the mass exodus from Vietnam after the War represents a "silent popular movement of resistance … that continues to raise problems of conscience for the international community" (Trinh 1989). Trinh interprets the migration of the boat people through its causes—both pretext and conviction—and in doing so opens up political agency, one that is so often lacking in humanitarian, sociological, and journalistic discourses on and about refugees. Her employment of the term *movement* refers to the physical scattering of Vietnamese people while resignifying their fleeing as a collective political struggle, a pointed and purposeful act of refuge-seeking that is also one of resistance. For Trinh, to step foot on a precarious boat and launch oneself onto the sea is not simply to become homeless, helpless, and aimless, but also to make a political statement, a claim that gets at the heart of a global, communal sense of action and ethics.

Yet, this statement is "silent" because the refugee is illegible—as viable and legitimate—in a contemporary political imaginary organized by the frames of nation–state, citizenship, and rights. They are, in the words of Peter Nyers, who borrows from Liisa Malkki, "speechless emissaries," whose lives get appropriated for the advancement of various state-sponsored agendas, whose stories are deployed to enact further forms of epistemological and material violence (Nyers 2006).[6] Like the two writers discussed in this essay, Trinh, however, utilizes the boat migration experience to illuminate the multifaceted dimensions of diaspora and to further a political project. Whether it is a commentary on the constitutive conditions of the Vietnamese diaspora or a depiction of the intersubjective relations and affective communities formed in movement, at stake in these cultural texts is a redefinition of historical events and social experiences that have rarely taken into account the complex subjectivities of Vietnamese refuge seekers. The sea and the boat, as sites of oceanic spatiality, enable Dinh and Le to (re)examine and reconstruct definitive moments in Vietnamese/diaspora history in which identities, relationships, and belongings are determined "not by blood but by water" (lê 2004: 3).

Vinh Nguyen is assistant professor of diaspora literatures in English and East Asian Studies at Renison University College, University of Waterloo. He received his doctorate in English and Cultural Studies at McMaster University, where he held a Vanier Canada Graduate Scholarship. He specializes in Asian diasporic literature and culture and refugee studies. His writing can be found in *Canadian Literature, Life Writing, ARIEL,* and *MELUS.*

Notes

1. For a good example of the last point see Osborne 2000.
2. For an account of life and the reeducation camps in post-"liberation" Vietnam see Nguyen 1982.
3. For more-comprehensive discussions of the Vietnamese boat people see Chan 2006 and Cargill and Huynh 2000.
4. See Mack 2011.
5. Refer to other contexts of boat migrations such as the recent rise in African and Middle Eastern migrants arriving in Europe through the Mediterranean, the Cuban boat people during the 1980s, and the Komagata Maru incident in Canada at the turn of the century, just to name a few.
6. See, in particular, Yến Lê Espiritu (2006), who points out that the figure of the "good," successful Vietnamese refugee becomes the featured evidence in revi-

sionist accounts of the War in Vietnam and America's role in Southeast Asia, as well as the human rationale for current and future U.S. military and neo-imperial projects.

Bibliography

Blum, Hester. 2010. "The Prospect of Oceanic Studies." *Publications of the Modern Language Association of America* 125, no. 3: 670–77.
Brah, Avtar. 1996. *Cartographies of Diaspora: Contesting Identities*. London/New York: Routledge.
Cargill, Mary Terrell, and Jade Quang Huynh. 2000. *Voices of Vietnamese Boat People: Nineteen Narratives of Escape and Survival*. Jefferson, NC, and London: McFarland & Company.
Chambers, Iain. 2010. "Maritime Criticism and Theoretical Shipwrecks." *PMLA: Publications of the Modern Language Association of America* 125, no. 3: 678–84.
Chan, Sucheng. 2006. *The Vietnamese 1.5 Generation: Stories of War, Revolution, Flight, and New Beginnings*. Philadelphia: Temple University Press.
Dinh, Linh. 2004. "A Floating Community." In *Blood and Soap: Stories*. New York: Seven Stories Press.
Espiritu, Yến Lê. 2006. "The 'We-Win-Even-If-We-Lose' Syndrome: U.S Press Coverage of the Twenty-Fifth Anniversary of the 'Fall of Saigon,'" *American Quarterly* 58, no. 2: 329–52.
Gilroy, Paul. 1993. *The Black Atlantic: Double Consciousness and Modernity*. Cambridge, MA: Harvard University Press.
Goellnicht, Donald. 2012. "'Ethnic Literature's Hot': Asian American Literature, Refugee Cosmopolitanism, and Nam Le's *The Boat*." *Journal of Asian American Studies* 15, no. 2: 197–224.
Hall, Stuart. 1990. "Cultural Identity and Diaspora." in *Identity: Community, Culture, Difference,* ed. Jonathan Rutherford. London: Lawrence and Wishart, 222–37.
Huỳnh, Sanh Thông. 1996. "Live By Water, Die For Water: Metaphors of Vietnamese Culture and History." *Vietnam Review* 1.133: 121–53.
Le, Nam. 2008. *The Boat*. Toronto: Bond Street Books.
lê, thi diem thúy. 2004. *The Gangster We Are All Looking For*. New York: Anchor Books.
Lee, Christopher. 2015. "Mobility and Metaphor: Theorizing the (In)human in Asian/Diaspora." *Verge: Studies in Global Asia* 1. no. 1: 138–161.
Mack, John. 2011. *The Sea: A Cultural History*. London: Reaktion Books.
Mishra, Vijay. 1996. "The Diasporic Imaginary: Theorizing the Indian Diaspora." *Textual Practice* 10, no. 3: 421–47.
Nguyen Ngoc Ngan with E.E. Richey. 1982. *The Will of Heaven: A Story of One Vietnamese and the End of His World*. New York: E. P. Dutton.
Nyers, Peter. 2006. *Rethinking Refugees: Beyond States of Emergency*. London/New York: Routledge.
Osborne, Milton. 2000. *The Mekong: Turbulent Past, Uncertain Future*. New York: Grove Press.
Pelaud, Isabelle Thuy. 2005. "Entering Linh Dinh's Fake House: Literature of Displacement." *Amerasia* 31, no. 2: 37–49.

Robinson, Courtland W. 2000. *Terms of Refuge: The Indochinese Exodus and the International Response.* London and New York: Zed Books.
Steinberg, Philip E. 2013. "Of Other Seas: Metaphors and Materialities in Maritime Regions." *Atlantic Studies* 10, no. 2: 156–69.
Takaki, Ronald. 1993. *A Different Mirror: A History of Multicultural America.* Boston: Back Bay Books.
Taylor, Keith Weller. 1983. *The Birth of Vietnam.* Berkeley and Los Angeles: University of California Press.
Trinh T. Minh-Ha. 1989. *Surname Viet Given Name Nam.* [VHS]. New York: Women Make Movies.
Walcott, Derek. 1986. *Collected Poems 1948–1984.* New York: Farrar, Straus, & Giroux.
Wolf, Daniel, and Shep Lowman. 1990. "Toward a New Consensus of the Vietnamese Boat People." *SAIS Review* 10, no. 2: 101–19.

Section II

The Artist and the Illegal Migrant

Figure S.2. *The Refugee Ship* (M/S Anton foldt lastet med flygtninge) 2010. Artist and Photographer: Jens Galschiot. Courtesy of www.aidoh.dk.

4

Imagining Europe's Borders
Commemorative Art on Migrant Tragedies

Karina Horsti

Mediated images of boats full of migrants, migrants surviving shipwrecks, and bodies on beaches have become iconic ways to represent undocumented migration in Europe since the 1990s. While undocumented migration by boat in the southern European sea borders makes only a very small percentage of irregular migration, it is the most mediatized and dramatized representation of migration.[1] The 1990s are marked as the period when the European Union (EU) began tightening and militarizing its borders, particularly in a phenomenon that the activists call Fortress Europe. European human rights activists estimate that more than twenty thousand people died at Europe's borders between 1993 and 2015 (United for Intercultural Action 2015) and almost four thousand in the year 2015 alone (International Organization for Migration 2015). Increased reinforcement of external EU borders is connected to the Schengen process that has diminished the control at the nation–state border of twenty-six participating countries. In addition, European countries and the EU have extended border management beyond the actual border to neighboring countries. This means exporting border violence outside of Europe in the form of locating detention camps outside of the EU and making agreements with countries such as Libya and Morocco. Moreover, the European Agency for the Management of Operational Cooperation at the External Borders of the Member States of the European Union (Frontex), has patrolled the seashores of the African continent in order to prevent migrant boats from leaving toward Europe.[2]

This chapter draws on theorization of the border and the practice of bordering in connection to two publicly displayed art works that touch on undocumented migration by boat in the context of European southern sea borders. The notion of the border is examined by following Étienne Balibar's (2002) thinking on European citizenship and difference and Edward Casey's (2011) work on place and space. Both of these philosophers point to the constructed nature of borders and to the ways in which borders have become increasingly dispersed within contemporary globalized societies. Moreover, the chapter examines critical potential of art in the intersection of European border regimes and mediatized societies.

The first artwork, *At Crossroads* by Kalliopi Lemos, was exhibited at the Brandenburg Gate in Berlin during the twentieth anniversary of the fall of the Berlin Wall in 2009. This installation of damaged migrant boats collected from the shores of the Greek island Chios and situated at the financial center of Europe in Berlin reminds the celebrating public that exclusions and borderings of a different kind exist in Europe. Moreover, the work visualizes and reterritorializes the so-called border zone to the imagined center of Europe. The second is the *Porta d'Europa (Gateway to Europe)* a memorial monument by Mimmo Paladino, which was created on the Italian island of Lampedusa in 2008. In the form of a gate, this permanent artwork rises from the rugged landscape by the sea to commemorate the migrants who died in their attempted crossing from North Africa to EU territory. The gate evokes visual imagination of a wall within which the gate offers an opening—making visible the border that exists, but is invisible for (most) Europeans. Both works leave the spectator with questions about humanity and humanitarianism, and the ethical treatment of people who fall in liminal spaces between categories.

European Undocumented Migration by Boat

Undocumented migration, which refers to unauthorized entry, residence, or work, became a policy concern across Europe at the turn of the twenty-first century. Simultaneous to the abolition of internal borders between Schengen countries, migration of so-called third country nationals became tighter (Düvell 2011; Triandafyllidou 2010) as did cooperation among the police, customs, and judiciary, particularly through the border control agency Frontex, which was created in 2004 as a "compensatory measure" to Schengen (Vaughan-Williams 2008: 66). Therefore, the recent accelerated bordering of Europe is constitutive of the integration of Europe itself. The dark side of this integration reflects how restrictions in border and migration control have resulted in more-dangerous means of travel, such as migration by small and overcrowded fishing boats through rough seas, along dangerous routes.

For centuries the Mediterranean has been a region of crossover mobility and cultural hybridity, similar to *la frontera,* or the United States–Mexico border. Bordering practices and militarization of the border that have accelerated after North American Free Trade Agreement (NAFTA) of 1994 and 9/11 terrorist attacks in 2001 produce death and suffering of migrants. The U.S. government imagines and constructs the United States–Mexico edge as a linear border. However, it is more like a boundary, and the recognition of the historical–and, as Edward Casey (2011: 385) points out, the most likely future–condition of *la frontera* as a boundary and a borderland would be the most ethical attitude toward the current situation. Casey (2011: 393) argues, "Ultimately, once it [the constructed and imagined border] has outlived its political or economic or symbolic usefulness, every border is destined to become a boundary and to return to an abiding state of nature." The word *boundary* in Casey's (2011) theoretical framework is a more porous and relaxed circumstance than a border. It allows movement and exchange. Boundary is a permeable edge that does not resist crossing from either direction.

The conditions of mobility in the Mediterranean region have changed in the past thirty years, mainly because of structural shifts in the politics and economics in the region. For instance, northern Mediterranean countries gained economic growth and political stability after joining the EU, which eventually shifted emigration patterns in these countries into that of immigration. Moreover, many Arab countries in the region, particularly Libya, became destinations for Sub-Saharan and Asian labor migrants in the 1990s, partly because of Gaddafi's pan-African migration policies (de Haas 2011: 59–63.) Another chapter in the Mediterranean migration by boat began from political upheavals in the North African countries in 2010 and the NATO strikes to Libya that followed in 2011, which generated record numbers of migrants crossing the sea to Europe by boat, as well as an increasing number of migrant deaths at sea. Sub-Saharan migrant workers were no longer welcome in Libya (Council of Europe 2012; Frontex 2012.) Futhermore, human rights violations in countries like Eritrea and armed conflicts in Iraq, Afghanistan, and Syria have continued to be major reasons for increasing numbers of undocumented migrants in the 2010s. In 2015, the numbers of asylum seekers in Europe rose compared to the previous years, particularly in the smugglers' sea route from Turkey to Greece. People avoided registration in Greece that is suffering from austerity measures and they continued to North European countries through Western Balkans.

Shipwrecks of migrant boats have created controversies between European states and other agents, such as the Council of Europe and the European Parliament. There have been several deaths at sea in which the responsibility of rescue has been unclear. The media and the Council of Europe have brought public attention to large shipwrecks and have pressured states and other stakeholders into taking responsibility (Council of Europe 2012). While unauthorized migration by boat has been visible in the media coverage since the 1990s, only a small percentage of irregular migrants come to Europe this way. For example, in Italy 60–70 percent of irregular migrants overstay their legal permits (Clandestino Project 2009: 74).

Ideas about borders in the Mediterranean are constantly being symbolically constructed in the mediatized coverage of migrations by boat. Images of arriving boats and detained migrants construct an imagined border zone where the European frontier ends. Similarly, the mediatization of policing and Frontex operations construct a sense of European border that is securitized and guarded against migrants who become defined as unwanted, and sometimes dangerous, strangers (Horsti 2008). This circulation of meanings and images assists in defining the concept of a European border, which again legitimates control practices and immigration policies in locations beyond the borderlands (Balibar 2002: 87–88). Thus, mediatization of boat migration and Frontex operations construct an imagined geography of European identity. With this term I refer to Brian Osborne's (2001) concept of geography of identity that he developed in the context of the nation–state. According to Osborne (2001: 1) "Peoples' identification with distinctive places is essential for the cultivation of an awareness—an 'a-where-ness'—of national identity." In addition to landscapes, memorials, and notable buildings that Osborne refers to, such imaginings are also constructed through mediation.

The bordering of Europe has required an increasing investment. Frontex's budget has grown over twentyfold since its establishment in 2004, from six million euros to 143 euros in 2015. The directorate general for Home Affairs of the European Commission used nearly half of its Solidarity and Management of Migration Flows Programme to pay for activities, equipment, and technological infrastructure for border control and just 17 percent toward asylum procedures and the reception of refugees (Amnesty International 2014).

Moreover, this investment reaches beyond Europe since the EU and individual countries have externalized border control to neighboring countries in order to prevent migrants from reaching Europe. Cooperation arrangements with Libya, Morocco, and Turkey have turned these countries into a European buffer zone. (Amnesty International 2014; Mezzadra and Neilson 2012: 68; Vaughan-Williams 2008: 67). The bordering practices are not unanimously agreed on in Europe, but cause constant struggles and negotiations between countries. The North tends to criticize the South not only for the low human rights standards inherent in their migration controls, but also for being too lax with policies such as the regularization of migrants and registering of asylum seekers. These relocations of borders reflect a double border character of colonial empires where there is a boundary between the metropolis and subjected territory on the one hand, and a boundary between the empire and the rest of the world on the other hand (Balibar 2006: 4). In

Europe there is no one linear border, but rather there are multiple heterogenous bordering practices that are aimed to control elasticity and the porousness of boundary regions.

Migrants in European territory often live in a precarious situation, particularly those who struggle without papers or with temporary permits. Human rights organizations report inhumane conditions in detention centers in the southern countries and hardship among those who move north. Migrants are marked as different by culture, economics, ethnicity, and race in everyday situations. The border produces an optic that differentiates migrants into those who might integrate and those who remain external (Mezzadra and Neilson 2012: 68). Following Balibar (2002: 75), Kartik Varada Raj (2006: 517) argues that migrants embody borders and the borders follow them in their daily lives. Therefore, migrants are forced into liminal spaces, as he expresses: "This violence not only finds its expression in overt violence—beatings, arrest, detention of migrants—but also pervades the social realm in the most quotidian of instances, such that certain classes of people are made to inhabit an everyday limbo of precarity and indeterminancy in which they have to *be* borders" (Raj 2006: 517; italics in the original).

These examples signify how borders are dispersed across societies—both within and outside Europe—in ways that Étienne Balibar (2003: 9) at the turn of the century termed "a barely hidden apartheid." In European societies, noncitizens who originate both from the global South live in different kinds of precarious situations in which their right of belonging is under constant suspicion, reflected, for instance, in differentiated treatment in health care, housing, and jobs. Moreover, while Eastern European Roma are citizens of the EU they often fall into liminal spaces and are treated as noncitizens. This process of differentiation has only accelerated after Balibar's analysis.

Contemporary Art in the Intersection of Place, Space, and Commemoration

Within this context, two artists—Kalliopi Lemos and Mimmo Paladino—displayed their public art works that speak volumes about contemporary migration experience and bordering practices in Europe. While irregular migration and bordering are highly mediatized in Europe and artists have worked with the themes,[3] a cultural amnesia regarding migrant tragedies has existed at the level of public acknowledgment, particularly at the European level. Attention to commemoration of migrant death has emerged gradually in the 2000s, specifically in connection to large shipwrecks such as the October 3, 2013, accident near Lampedusa in which 369 migrants died. This cultural amnesia is one motivation behind the two artworks: they aim to bring awareness to migrant tragedies and commemorate those who have suffered.

Moreover, images of both artworks have been circulated across mainstream and social media, and through these mediations they reconstruct the "geography of European identity." I decided to examine these two artworks in particular for two reasons: their rare commemorative aspect and their critical intervention to the notion of the border. Below I examine Lemos's and Paladino's works in the intersection of European border regimes and mediatized societies and focus on theoretizations of the border, particularly on the ways in which borders can be understood to have been territorially and socially dispersed. My writing on art is based on my cultural studies–oriented scholarship in media and migration research. This research offers a ground for thinking critically about art but also for examining the cultural, social, and political contexts of the creative process. Nevertheless, for me art always has multiple meanings and openings that can never be explained or reduced into a particular politics or discourse.

In both cases, the sculptures are displayed in public spaces–in a city square in the case of Berlin and in an empty space away from town center in the case of Lampedusa. Thus, a short discussion of spatial aesthetics and politics is necessary. Space and place are crucial for contemporary art in general. Boundaries between art and the everyday are often blurred by exhibiting work outside museums or gallery spaces and by signifying found and everyday objects as art (Papastergiadis 2010: 15). Both works are exhibited outside the museum context, and are read as part of the landscape and the community that surround them. For instance, the location is a crucial dimension of Kalliopi Lemos's installation. She searched for a specific location that symbolizes a crossroads and designed her installation accordingly (Lemos 2010). While the social, cultural, and historical contexts–the time and space–of an artwork are always crucial for the artist and the audience, they are particularly important for publicly displayed art. In his discussion on spatial aesthetics, Nikos Papastergiadis (2010: 90) argues, "To understand the meaning of this [contemporary] art, historians and critics need to recognize the significance of spatial elements. The art historian is now compelled to track not just the history, but also the geography of the artwork." Following this line of thought, the geography of the artwork should be seen as being entangled with the "geography of identity"–that is, the social, cultural, and political contexts in which the art is created and exhibited. Moreover, mediatizations of migrant death and suffering, witnessing *through* media exposure, have urged artists to "do something" and to create awareness to the issue that is both political and humanitarian. Furthermore, both displays went through public decision-making processes prior to their installation. These contexts are constitutive of the artwork and its reception, but, in addition, the artworks themselves construct the landscape, community, culture, and societies in which they are exhibited and interpreted (Gibbons 2007). In particular, permanent artworks become linked to identities through practices such as commemorative or ritual performances (Osborne 2001: 5). In addition to the spatial dimensions of these two artworks, it is crucial to discuss the role of contemporary art in commemoration. Building on Pierre Nora's notion of a memory site, *lieu de mémoire,* Joan Gibbons (2007: 71) argues that an artwork itself can be a site, or *lieu,* of memory. The artwork is a memory site within a site—the place where it is exhibited.

The tradition of commemorative art in Western Europe has gone through changes that reflect trends in contemporary art more broadly. First, memorialization of war has shifted from remembering "heroes" to remembering victims, particularly after World War II (Gibbons 2007; Huyssen 2000). Holocaust memorialization has crucially shaped the ways in which societies remember trauma (Huyssen 2000: 23). Moreover, recognition of the diversity of those who suffered in Holocaust has expanded to include other populations such as those in the gay community and the Roma (van Baar 2011). Because of this focus on victims and the tradition of public commemoration, in times of catastrophe people feel the need to commemorate even if the victims were not known to them.

Second, public commemoration is currently taking more participative, creative, and performative forms that engage people of individualized societies and that draw from therapeutic imaginaries (Kantola 2014: 4; Till 2008). Different types of memorial performances and anti-monuments highlight the experiential and site-specificity of remembering that counters and criticizes permanent monuments (Gibbons 2007: 94). These practices are aligned with a broader shift in public art in general toward a more participatory, community specific, and experiential art, what Nicholas Bourriaud (1998) has called "relational aesthetics." This mode in contemporary art is "taking as its theoretical horizon the realm of human interactions and its social context, rather than the assertion of an independent and private space" (Bourriaud 1998: 14). Public commemoration is what a civilized Western nation and people do, a socially acceptable practice that assists society to move on after tragedy. The artworks analyzed in this chapter deliberatively commemorate migrant victims; these artworks, therefore, need to be understood in connection to these broader trajectories.

Third, commemorative practice and monuments are commodified and spectacularized as any cultural production today since "there is no pure space outside of commodity culture" (Huyssen 2000: 29). Places and heritage are being marketed in the context of entertainment and tourism; this seems macabre in connection to migrant tragedies, but it nevertheless mediatizes places and narratives draw in tourists. Moreover, in the context of mediatized societies where "everything is mediated" (Livingstone 2009), people experience the world through the lenses of mobile devices. Lemos's and Paladino's works also circulate as backgrounds of tourist photos and become interpreted in different kinds of off-site situations.

At Crossroads by Kalliopi Lemos in Berlin, Germany

At Crossroads (fig 4.1.) is an installation of nine abandoned wooden boats that undocumented migrants used for travel from Turkey to Greece. The boats had been left on the shores of the Greek island Chios where the artist Kalliopi Lemos (born 1951) found them and collected them in 2003. The boats are displayed upside down in a metal structure that rises to fourteen meters. *At Crossroads* is among a series of three publicly displayed installations in which Lemos used broken migrant boats in 2006–9. The work discussed here was presented at the Brandenburg Gate at the heart of Berlin, Germany, October 12–30, 2009, during the twentieth-anniversary festivities of the fall of the Berlin Wall. The installation was part of Lemos's exhibition at the Akedemie der Kunste, a major art institution.

The object of boat is crucial for the installation, and it refers to both separation and connection. Scholars concerned with theories about borders and border crossings often stress that edges are zones that differentiate and separate one thing from another, but that in addition edges are points of connection and crossing (Balibar 2002; Casey 2011: 384). As Étienne Balibar (2002: 77) defines edges, they are "lines or zones, strips of land, which are places of separation and contact or confrontation, areas of blockage and passage." Therefore, in this artwork the boat signifies the ambiguous nature of borders

Figure 4.1. *At Crossroads* by Kalliopi Lemos, Brandenburg Gate, Berlin, 12–30 October 2009. © Kalliopi Lemos, courtesy of the artist.

and boundaries and their ability to both connect and separate places and people. By presenting the physical migrant boats in the power center of the EU and a site of Cold War divide, the installation suggests several connections and divisions: the one between the EU and the global South, the one between the West and the East, and the one between past and the present.

As an object, the boat is bursting with meaning. It is an ancient symbol of voyage, transition, and separation found in many mythologies: for instance, in the Finnish epic *Kalevala* a wooden boat carries a mother across the Tuonela River to her dead son in the underworld. In the more recent collective memory of Europeans, the sea and a passenger ship represent migration to the New World away from war and poverty. However, in the collective memory of European migration, large ships are symbols of industrial achievement. In mediatized representations of irregular migration today, the hypervisibility of the wooden fishing boat constructs an antimodern Other who leaves without knowing the risks. While several ethnographic researchers (see Carling 2007; de Haas 2011; Ifekwunigwe 2013) document that migrants have made a conscious decision to take dangerous routes because that route is the only alternative, and that these journeys are just one risk among many others, media representation often depict migration by boat as an irrational act (Horsti 2008).

For Kalliopi Lemos, the boats represent and witness migrant experiences. When she discovered the remains of the boats, she saw them as "relics of human suffering" (Lemos 2010). Thus, in her installations the boat signifies a migrant body that expresses wounds of suffering. The boat becomes a witness to the tragedy of migration and border violence. By collecting the boats from the shores of the sea, Lemos herself witnesses the tragedy, and through her work she mediates that tragedy to the audience. Finally, the audiences become aware of the issue through this mediated witnessing of the tragedy.

These human relics did not only remind Lemos of the perils of boat migration in general, but also of her own grandparents who were forced to leave the city of İzmir (now part of Turkey) during the Greco-Turkish war in 1919–22. By connecting her own private memories to the present and making a parallel between the past migrations with the present, her work powerfully adds dimensions of a more universal understanding of forced migration. Lemos explains how transition and transformation that are so deeply attached to the symbol of the boat are widely shared, and therefore the boat can be seen as a symbol of humanity. She explains how this meaning appears in her work: "Boats can be seen as the carriers of memories, as metaphors for our journey through life's different stages or as symbolizing birth or fertility. I have used the boat to suggest a life carrier, a womb, the container of life as well as the passage through which we enter the world and through which we leave this life. The boats carry our experiences, our sufferings and different stages of existence" (Lemos 2010).

Boats carry items and hopes and are able to move people and things from one place to another. However, Lemos presents the boats in an unnatural position. In this work the boats are turned upside down, in a way that for her empties their contents, "symbolising the end of hope and the end of life" (Lemos 2010). An upside-down boat refers to death widely across Mediterranean cultures. Nevertheless, this position of the boat can also protect the people who seek refuge underneath. In any case, the hierarchical positioning of the boats points to inequalities of movement, protection, and the capacity to hope.

Location of the broken boats in the capital of the most powerful EU member state offers another dimension to the notion of border. In European imagination, the border is associated with the South–a deterritorialization that moves the border violence out of sight and mind of Northern Europeans. Militarization of external borders is a joint European decision but the people in the southern European countries are left to deal with the practicalities of unauthorized crossings. The installation brings the border–and the violence of its production–to the financial and political center of Europe in a way that forces Northern Europeans to become aware of the issue. Seeing damaged boats as meaningful artifacts at the most prestigious site of the city, therefore, domesticates the otherwise distanced violence of bordering.

The timing of Lemos's installation, the festivities in remembrance of the fall of the Berlin Wall that divided the city and Europe during the Cold War, brings yet another dimension to her work. The installation was viewed during a celebration of borderless Europe, and therefore presentation of the boats strongly points to the existing borderings and the violence that European migration control produces. The presentation permeates the celebratory atmosphere by reminding the public that borders of a different kind exist in Europe. Simply put, the damaged boats as relics of suffering, and the hierarchical positioning of the boats, make visible how borders treat people unequally. To my understanding, the damaged wood and the unnatural positioning of the boats refer to wounds and suffering and to the ways in which border (violence) sticks to certain bodies. Migrants carry the burden of bordering practices in their daily lives as they are often marked as the Other. The installation makes visible the borders that seems invisible to more privileged, white Europeans.

At Crossroads presented in this particular place, at this particular time, exemplifies the ways in which borders multiply and then disperse into societies. They are vacillating as a matter of experience both beyond and within Europe (Balibar 2002: 89). In a similar way, Saskia Sassen (2009) argues, "Today, it is becoming evident that even as national territories remain bounded by traditional geographic borderlines, globalization is causing novel types of 'borderings' to multiply" (Sassen 2009: 567). This is particularly true in the European context where the relaxation of internal borders coexists with the militarization of external borders. Dispersement of dissymmetrical bordering practices within and outside Europe target irregular migrants. This exemplifies what Sassen means by bordering, or the condition in which traditional borders now coexist with a variety of other bordering dynamics and capabilities (Sassen 2009: 568).

Porta d'Europa by Mimmo Paladino in Lampedusa, Italy

Porta d'Europa/Gateway to Europe (fig 4.2) memorial rises to five meters in height from the deserted landscape of the southernmost point of Italy, the small island of Lampedusa. The Italian artist Mimmo Paladino (born 1948) who is associated with the Italian transavantgarde art movement of the 1980s, designed and decorated the *Porta d'Europa* that was opened on June 26, 2008, to commemorate migrants who lost their lives at sea. Paladino himself was not so keen on creating a memorial sculpture but rather "to tell a story" that touches people (Boltzoni 2008). He takes a humanist position and wishes that the work "explains something of forced exodus, something that everyone can comprehend" (as quoted in the Italian *La Repubblica*, Boltzoni, 2008). To my understanding, the position of the sculpture in the landscape shapes the story. In the form of an open gate the sculpture faces the Mediterranean toward the shore of Tunisia. Through the gate, one sees turquoise water and

Figure 4.2. *Porta di Lampedusa–Porta d'Europa–Gateway to Europe* by Mimmo Paladino, Lampedusa. © Karina Horsti.

boats that pass by. Or the sculpture can also be viewed from the sea as a landmark, almost like a lighthouse. It is made of yellowish ceramic that reflects the light of sun and moon. The sculpture has ceramic objects attached to its surface: broken cups, hats, and shoes. These objects seem like they once belonged to someone but now remain to evoke memories of them. While being ceramic sculptures, these objects seem like found objects lying on a surface that resembles sand. Comparable to Kalliopi Lemos's found boats, these objects signify migrants' lives and histories, particularly of those migrants who did not survive but whose belongings drifted to the shore.

The form of a gate suggests that there is a wall or a fence into which the gate offers an opening. In so doing, this sculpture inspires European spectators to imagine a wall that, for them, remains invisible. This is much different from the mediated images of crowded migrant boats or floating corpses, which definitively express border violence. Thus, the European gaze of Mediterranean has a double character. For most Europeans, the Mediterranean and visions of the sea signifies beauty and leisure activities. From this viewpoint, the border is invisible or inconsequential. It is the irregular migrants who are stuck between categories, and it is their movements that make the border visible. This edge is not a symmetrical one, but one that changes depending on *who* is moving. The border is felt by undocumented migrants and, even more, it transforms them to unwelcomed and sometimes dangerous strangers—or, as Raj (2006), argues, into those who embody borders. *Porta d'Europa* brings the border violence into the realm of European awareness and makes this transformative border imaginable for Western audiences.

Paladino's sculpture is framed as a memorial monument to commemorate migrants who died at sea while trying to reach Europe. An Italian poet, Arnoldo Mosca Mondadori, initiated the creation of this sculpture with a nongovernmental development organization called Amani. Paladino donated his time, and a tourist organization in Palermo, Sicily, donated 35,000 euros. The monument was therefore initiated by people and organizations that are not specifically local islanders. The memorial sculpture is a product of a nationwide search for a specific site of commemoration of migrant tragedies. Italian cultural, religious, and humanitarian agents were perplexed because of a lack of public memorialization of tragedies that nevertheless have been visible in mainstream media for years. The director of Amani, Gian Marco Elia, explains that he and his colleagues were shocked to find out that there was no memorial, "not even a simple plaque," in Sicily to commemorate the almost three hundred migrants who had drowned in a shipwreck in Porto Palo in 1996, known as the Christmas massacre (Boltzoni 2008). The commemorative aspect of Paladino's sculpture is important for visitors and locals because it assists them in finding a way to manage the recurring confrontation of migrant deaths and unfinished burials. The mayor of Lampedusa, Giusi Nicolini, has publicly demanded support from Italy and the EU to give proper identification, funeral, and burial to the bodies that have been discovered after shipwrecks. In a statement the Amani group said, "The fundamental significance of this work is to consign to memory this last two-decade period in which we have seen thousands of migrants perish at sea in an inhumane way in an attempt to reach Europe ... often without burial and therefore without pity" ("Africans Remembered" 2008).

The commemorative significance of the sculpture also reaches beyond the local context. The monument and the whole island of Lampedusa is becoming—and being constructed as—a *lieu de mémoire* (Nora 1989), a memory site that invites different kinds of remembering in relation to migration tragedies. On the one hand, *Porta d'Europa* is a fairly traditional commemorative monument. It honors the victims but does not blame anyone for the tragedy. As a permanent structure it transforms the meaning of the landscape and the community. It suggests an identity of openness for Lampedusans: this is the community that self-identifies as opening the gate. However, the sculpture is located in a rather remote corner of the island and therefore one encounters it accidentally and only from the sea. Moreover, the sculpture is not mentioned as a point of interest in tourist maps or other promotional material of the island. As such, the monument does not necessarily engage people to shared activity or encourage intersubjective encounters that are the new tradition of public commemorative art inspired by relational aesthetics (Bourriaud 1998; Gibbons 2007). On the other hand, however, its existence and particularly its globalized existence through mediation draws in commemorative performances of different kinds. The monumental sculpture reinforces global and local imaginations of Lampedusa as the *lieu de mémoire*, the memory site of irregular migration. It reinforces the island's reputation as a wounded place (Till 2008: 108) that represents the pain of others and difficult social pasts. According to Karen Till, wounded places invite particular attention and create a specific atmosphere where mourning, healing, and commemoration can take place.

Moreover, in a mediated society, some performances of remembering migrant tragedies are remediated in news throughout Italy and globally. Therefore, these memory performances can extend beyond the wounded place itself. For instance, film star and UNHCR Goodwill ambassador Angelina Jolie drew global attention to Lampedusa by visiting the *Porta d'Europa* monument in 2011. Her speech at the site is circulated on YouTube and images of it are reprinted in various celebrity sites. In addition, Pope Francis paid his first visit outside of Rome to Lampedusa in 2013 where he celebrated a mass near a yard of abandoned migrant boats. In the ceremony he held a cross made of wood taken from a migrant boat.

The arrival of migrants has made the island known to global audiences and media attention has shaped Lampedusa into a (mediated) manifestation of the European border. However, through cultural activism, including

Paladino's memorial sculpture, the island's public position as the border is rearticulated. Commemoration aims to turn the articulation of Lampedusa from a borderized island (Cuttitta 2014), or the border control zone, into a humanitarian space where migrant suffering is honored and where migrant death is worth public grief (Butler 2009).

Acts of commemoration are problematic in that they primarily take place among privileged Europeans and these rituals too can be mobilized for politics that result more border related death. The opening ceremony of *Porta d'Europa* itself illustrates how a commemoration procession from the town square to the monument includes almost only white Europeans (Ilacqua 2008). Migrants are kept under surveillance at a detention center on the island or they have been transferred to other centers in Italy, and therefore they could not participate in the commemorative procession. This struggle over who is allowed to participate was also noticeable after a major shipwreck on October 3, 2013, in which 369 victims were found. Eritrean survivors were not allowed to attend the funeral held in Sicily, whereas the Eritrean ambassador—thus, the representative of the regime the migrants had fled—was invited (Zerai and Estefanos 2013). The survivors protested and finally held an alternative memorial ceremony. The controversies around remembering exemplify how commemoration and grieving are not necessarily recognized as human rights in the regimes that control migration. Paolo Cuttitta (2014) said, "The *Porta d'Europa* is not meant to be a monument to human rights, to humaneness according to law, but rather a monument to humaneness per se, to humaneness even beyond the law" (Cuttitta 2014: 214). In this case, the question of human rights remains: Can human respect for the dead be extended to those who survived? The symbol of a gate is ambiguous because it offers an opening, but just a small, conditioned, and differentiating opening in a wall that can be imagined to continue around Europe.

Conclusions

The two public art works discussed in this chapter critically illuminate the inequalities and violence of European bordering practices. They force European spectators and governance to consider morality in relation to irregular migration. Both works powerfully visualize borders in a critical way: they create an awareness of border violence and make the invisibilities of bordering practices more visible. Kalliopi Lemos's *At Crossroads* reterritorializes the border zone into the political and economic center of Europe, and critically reminds European publics how borders are heterogenous and arbitrary. Mimmo Paladino's *Porta d'Europa,* in the form of a gate facing Tunisia, suggests an imagination of the border and its violence to spectators who otherwise might ignore them. These works exemplify how contemporary art can shape the political by expanding the ways of seeing and experiencing borders "through its own internal process of extending the language of resistance and representation" (Papastegiadis 2010: 19).

The artworks transform these spaces into sites of commemoration for people who witness migrant suffering and death, also through media coverage. Although Kalliopi Lemos's work was temporary, it appeared at a time when migrant tragedies were a pressing issue in the public domain. After all, public commemoration of migrant tragedies had been scarce in European public spheres at the time. European institutions have rather forgotten the histories and tragedies of irregular migration to Europe. Nevertheless, recent negotiations over commemoration in Lampedusa exemplify how collective memory is always contested and political and how official memorial monuments can become sites of power struggles. The critical question of course is what these types of commemorative art works can offer for migrants and their descendants. Will Lampedusa become such a wounded place (Till 2008) that could offer a space and atmosphere for therapeutic imaginaries? And whose therapy would this be? Migrant tragedies are not in the past but very much in the present, which makes commemorative practices even more political and complex. Contemporary art creates openings for moral meditation, but also spaces for conflict and negotiation. These two artworks recognize the complexity and injustice that often takes place near borders as well as bordering practices in ways that have the critical potential to rethink the migration regimes and border violence in Europe.

Dr. Karina Horsti is Academy of Finland Research Fellow at the Department of Social Sciences and Philosophy, University of Jyväskylä, where she also teaches in the master's program in cultural policy. She has been a visiting fellow at the Department of Media, Culture, and Communication, New York University (2009, 2011–12) and at the Department of Media and Communications, London School of Economics and Political Science (2016). Her current research examines remembering of forced migration in cultural productions in Europe. Horsti's research interests focus on qualitative and critical studies on media and culture in the contexts of migration, cultural diversity, and humanitarian action. Horsti's work has appeared in journals such as *International Journal of Cultural Studies*; *Communication, Culture & Critique*; and *Journalism: Theory, Practice and Criticism*. She is the coeditor of *National Conversations: Public Service Media and Cultural Diversity in Europe* (2014).

Notes

1. The term *migrant* used throughout this chapter covers all people who have reached Europe for different reasons and by different means. This chapter, however, fo-

cuses on irregular or undocumented migration, which refers to unauthorized border crossing or residence. However, after unauthorized crossing, many migrants may seek asylum and eventually obtain a refugee status. Many are registered as refugees even before the crossing. Some might find work or begin studies and gain a permit to stay.
2. The Schengen Agreement was implemented in seven countries in 1995 and has grown to cover twenty-six countries. People who cross the external border can move to other Schengen countries without documentation. Frontex is the EU agency that coordinates and assists national agents in border control and asylum processing.
3. There are also other European artists whose works concern European borders or irregular migration by boat. Serbian feminist artist Tanja Ostojić's several works have criticized European borders, particularly from a gender perspective, British artist Isaac Julien's audio-visual installation "WESTERN UNION: Small Boats" (2007) concerns irregular migration at southern European sea borders, as did Finnish Maaria Wirkkala's installation "Landing Prohibited" (2007) in the Venice Biennale and Germany-based Finnish artist HMJokinen's installation "On That Third of October" (2014) in a bomb bunker in Hamburg. In addition, Catalan designer Antonio Miro exhibited migrant boats on the catwalk in his 2007–8 fall–winter collection show in Barcelona fashion week.

Bibliography

"Africans Remembered: A Memorial for Europe's Lost Migrants." 2008. *Spiegel Online,* June 17. http://www.spiegel.de/international/europe/africans-remembered-a-memorial-for-europe-s-lost-migrants-a-560218.html.
Amnesty International. 2014. *The Human Cost of Fortress Europe. Human Rights Violations against Migrants and Refugees at Europe's BGorders.* London: Amnesty International. https://frantic.s3.amazonaws.com/amnesty-fi/2014/07/EUR-050012014_-Fortress-Europe_complete_web.pdf.
Balibar, Étienne. 2002. *Politics and the Other Scene.* London: Verso.
——2003. *We, the People of Europe: Reflections on Transnational Citizenship.* Princeton, NJ: Princeton University Press.
——2006. "Strangers as Enemies: Further Reflections on the Aporias of Transnational Citizenship." *Globalization Working Papers Series.* Hamilton, ON: McMaster University.
Boltzoni, Attilio. 2008. "La porta che guarda l'Africa in ricordo di chi non è mai arrivato." *La Repubblica,* June 26.
Bourriaud, Nicolas. 1998. *Relational Aesthetics.* Dijon, France: Les Presses du Réel.
Butler, Judith. 2009. *Frames of War: When Is Life Grievable?* London: Verso.
Carling, Jørgen 2007. "Migration Control and Migrant Fatalities at the Spanish–African Borders." *International Migration Review* 41, no. 2: 316–43.
Casey, Edward. 2011. "Borders versus Boundary at La Frontera." *Environment and Planning D: Society and Space* 29, no.1: 384–98.
Clandestino Project. 2009. "CLANDESTINO Project Final Report." http://cordis.europa.eu/documents/documentlibrary/126625701EN6.pdf.

Council of Europe. 2012. Lives Lost in the Mediterranean Sea: Who Is Responsible? http://assembly.coe.int/committeedocs/2012/20120329_mig_rpt.en.pdf.
Cuttitta, Paolo. 2014. "'Borderizing' the Island. Setting and Narratives of the Lampedusa 'Border Play.'" *ACME: An International E-Journal for Critical Geographies* 13, no. 2: 196–219.
de Haas, Hein. 2011. "Mediterranean Migration Futures: Patterns, Drivers and Scenarios." *Global Environmental Change* 21, no.1: 59–69.
Düvell, Franck. 2011. "Irregular Immigration, Economics and Politics." CESifo DICE Report. http://www.compas.ox.ac.uk/fileadmin/files/People/staff_publications/Duvell/1210202.pdf.
Frontex. 2012. "Annual Risk Analysis 2012." http://frontex.europa.eu/assets/Attachment_Featured/Annual_Risk_Analysis_2012.pdf.
Gibbons, Joan. 2007. *Contemporary Art and Memory: Images of Recollection and Remembrance*. London: I. B.Tauris.
Horsti, Karina. 2008. "Europeanisation of Public Debate: Swedish and Finnish News on African Migration to Spain." *Javnost–Public* 15, no. 4: 41–54.
Huyssen, Andreas. 2000. "Present Pasts: Media, Politics, Amnesia." *Public Culture* 12, no. 1: 21–38.
Ifekwunigwe, Jayne. 2013. "'Voting with Their Feet:' Senegalese Youth, Clandestine Boat Migration, and the Gendered Politics of Protest." *African and Black Diaspora: An International Journal* 6, no. 2: 218–35.
Ilacqua, Fabio. 2009. *Lampedusa: Porta d'Europa*. [Video]. Amani for Africa, Milan. http://www.amaniforafrica.it/?p=1301.
Kantola, Anu. 2014. "The Therapeutic Imaginary in Memory Work: Mediating the Finnish Civil War in Tampere." *Memory Studies* 7, no. 1: 92–107.
Lemos, Kalliopi. 2010. "A Discussion with Kalliopi Lemos" by Alexandra Koroxenidis. In *Kalliopi Lemos: Crossings—A sculptural trilogy about migration*, edited by Johannes Odenthal and Elina Kountouri. Göttingen: Steidl.
Livingstone, Sonia. 2009. "On the Mediation of Everything: ICA Presidential Address 2008." *Journal of Communication* 59, no. 1: 1–18.
Mezzadra, Sandro, and Brett Neilson. 2012. "Between inclusion and exclusion: On the topology of global space and borders." *Theory, Culture & Society* 29, no. 4–5: 58–75.
Nora, Pierre. 1989. "Between Memory and History: Les lieux de mémoire." *Representations* 26: 7–26.
Osborne, Brian. 2001. "Landscapes, Memory, Monuments, and Commemoration: Putting Identity in Its Place." *Canadian Ethnic Studies* 33, no. 3: 39–77.
Papastergiadis, Nikos. 2010. *Spatial Aesthetics, Art, Place, and the Everyday*. Amsterdam: Institute of Network Cultures.
Raj, Kartik Varada. 2006. "Paradoxes on the Borders of Europe." *International Feminist Journal of Politics* 8, no. 2: 512–34.
Sassen, Saskia. 2009. "Bordering Capabilities versus Borders: Implications for National Borders." *Michigan Journal of International Law* 30, no. 3: 567–97.
Till, Karen. 2008. "Artistic and Activist Memory-Work: Approaching Place-Based Practice." *Memory Studies* 1, no. 1: 99–113.
Triandafyllidou, Anna. 2010. "Irregular Migration in Europe in the early 21st Century." In *Irregular Migration in Europe: Myths and realities*, edited by Anna Triandafyllidou, 1–21. Surrey, UK: Ashgate.

United Against Racism. 2012. "List of Deaths." http://www.unitedagainstracism.org/pdfs/listofdeaths.pdf.
van Baar, Huub 2011. "Cultural Policy and the Governmentalization of Holocaust Remembrance in Europe: Romani Memory between Denial and Recognition." *International Journal of Cultural Policy* 17, no. 1: 1–17.
Vaughan-Willams, Nick. 2008. "Borderwork beyond Inside/Outside? Frontex, the Citizen–Detective and the War on Terror." *Space and Polity* 12, no. 1: 63–79.
Zerai, Mussie, and Meron Estefanos. 2013. "Commemoration-:Gimmick for Convenience of Politicians." *European External Policy Advisors News,* October 25. http://www.eepa.be/wcm/320-eepa-news-and-activities/3425-dead-eritrean-refugees-remembered.html

5

"Washed Clean"

The Forgotten Journeys of "Irregular Maritime Arrivals" in J. M. Coetzee's Estralia

Jennifer Rutherford

J. M. Coetzee's allegorical novel *The Childhood of Jesus* (Coetzee 2013) is as slippery as a fish, and requires an act of interpretation that slips (with the novel) between ideas, places, and realities. In the novel a man and a boy arrive at the city of Novilla where resettlement awaits them at the hands of a benevolent and seemingly providential state. Novilla appears to offer everything that human kindness could bestow—a reception center for new arrivals, a room to house them, access to work, financial assistance, and even free education—but this benevolence is as evasive as it is pervasive. There is something about this allegorical world that is *like* Australia. This is not to suggest that *The Childhood of Jesus* is a novel *about* Australia. It is not. Nor is it a novel *about* Australia's infamous immigration policy; there is no simple key to this allegory. But as a syncretic, polysemous, and extended metaphor, the novel creates a shadowland in which the shadowed effects of Australia's contemporary refugee policy flicker momentarily into view. Coetzee creates a cosmos of being in absentia, a place riddled with holes in which we find, amongst other lost possibilities of being, the maritime refugees of today, stateless, faceless, and "washed clean" of their past. In this chapter I suggest that Coetzee's allegory makes visible the hidden logic in play in policies of detention, deterrence, pushback, and excision deployed by the Australian government against asylum seekers arriving on Australian shores by boat. Beyond a pragmatic attempt to limit the economic costs of settlement and rhetorical attempts to garner populist nationalist support, such strategies reveal a will *to hole*. *The Childhood of Jesus* makes visible this practice of *holing* pursued by successive Australian governments.

Holing

What do I mean by *holing?* As a transitive verb *to hole* has two meanings: (1) to make a hole in and (2) to drive or hit into a hole. Unlike holing up which is to take refuge like an animal in a hole, holing means to put holes into something or to put or propel something into a hole. One holes a ball in games of sport or holes a garment, but here I suggest another more oblique meaning for the verb to hole in which holing (the act of propelling an object into a hole) is fused with the verb's aim—a hole. As a noun, hole has many meanings including: an opening through something; an area where something is missing; a hollowed out place; a cave, a pit, a burrow; a wretched or dreary place; a prison cell; an awkward position or circumstance; having a score below zero; and being in a position of owing money.[1] To be in a hole implies failure. Criminality, debt, logical inconsistency, insolvency, or bad form can all end in a hole. Failures of style, status, or good marks can also put one in a hole. If we fuse the various meanings of the noun hole with the verb to hole, the act of holing assumes a social dimension, especially when applied to someone rather than to something. It connotes propelling or projecting a subject into a negative space. To hole someone is to excise them from the social into a state of unbeing in which they are absented and symbolically negated. To be holed is not to die as such, but to die socially. Holing is not simply synonymous with casting out; one can be present but holed.

    Let me give a concrete historical example to demonstrate how one might use holing to capture a particular kind of powerful social act that one finds across diverse cultures and historical epochs. Zombification as practiced socially in Haiti provides an illustration. In its traditional Haitian form, zombification is a supreme sanction enacted on those who have profoundly offended social law (Wade 1988: 60). Ethnographers Wade Davis (1985) and Zora Neal Hurston (2009) have argued that secret societies (Bizango) that formed the basis of the revolutionary slave movement in Haiti continued postrevolution as an underground social system of governance. Bizango functions as an institution of policing and justice, a role it has filled in the void of a stable and competent state. The Bizango, as Katherine Smith (2010: 80) argues, have the capability "not only to inflict mystical death, but also to implement fates even worse, like transforming humans into mindless chattel." Haitian zombies are lawbreakers who have been buried in a trance induced by a poison that gives the appearance of death, then raised from the grave, displaced far from their homes, and set to work in perpetuity as semicomatose slaves. Once zombified, the victim is permanently exiled from society, dead to all prior relations, and bound over to toil endlessly, which casts them back into the abjection of the slave condition. Wade provides tragic examples of zombies who have returned to their former homes but been denied recognition by their families. Able to be seen but invisible, able to speak but not to be heard, they are present but holed. Zombies are cast into the grave and from there disinterred to live as invisible nonbeings amongst the living. Disinterred into the past, they become its walking exemplars. Zombies are the Thing that haunts Haiti: the fear of a return to the slave condition. In this sense, zombification is both an act of sanction and a performance of it. This extreme example of subjects who are desubjectivized, deprived of all rights, cast out of life, and yet still present and living serves as an example of what I mean by holing.

The policies and practices developed by the Australian state in response to relatively small numbers of the world's stateless people arriving on Australian shores in search of asylum are another contemporary example of holing. These policies demonstrate an escalating will to hole. From early attempts to detain asylum seekers in closed camps in the most isolated regions of Australia and to deny them access to telephones, news reports, or contact with families, to the most recent policy initiative known as Sovereign Borders that involves secreting boats carrying asylum seekers to unknown destinations, successive Australian governments have used the power of the state to hole asylum seekers semantically, spatially, juridicially, and discursively (Mares 2002). Australia's treatment of 'Irregular Maritime Arrivals' (IMAs is the acronym used by Australian governments for asylum seekers arriving by boat) has been at the center of national political debate for well over a decade but tossed around on the waves of political rhetoric, refugees remain barely visible barely conceivable.

The logic of propulsion and dematerialization in play in policies developed by the world's rich nations to invisibilize the world's stateless peoples is not new. In Hannah Arendt's thesis, the fusion of the "rights of man" with the idea of citizenship in the French and American revolutions left the stateless–rightless. As such, the totalitarian regimes of the twentieth century were able to dehumanize them. By denationalizing minority groups during the interbellum, totalitarian regimes made real the semantic holes their rhetoric consigned them to. "The official SS *Schwarze Korps,* stated explicitly in 1938 that if the world was not yet convinced that the Jews were the scum of the earth, it soon would be when unidentifiable beggars, without nationality, without money, and without passports crossed their frontiers" (Arendt 1994: 269). Arendt identified statelessness as "the newest mass phenomenon in contemporary history" and stateless persons, as "the most symptomatic group in contemporary politics." History has borne out her assessment: "Once they had left their homeland they remained homeless, once they had left their state they became stateless; once they had been deprived of their human rights they were rightless, the scum of the earth.... [E]very politic event since the end of the first world war inevitably added a new category to those who live outside the pale of the law, while none of the categories, no matter how the original constellation changed, could ever be renormalized" (Arendt 1958: 269).

The UN Refugee Agency estimates there are up to 45 million internally displaced people, asylum seekers, returnees and stateless people in need of refuge. In UNHCR's former top policy adviser Jeff Crisp's (2013) assessment, the overwhelming response of the rich West has been to adopt strategies of deterrence and enforcement, including interceptions and pushbacks, transfers and offshore processing, militarized border controls, antismuggling operations, surveillance, detention, and dissuasive information campaigns aimed at deterring stateless people from seeking asylum. The Australian state has played a leading role in designing and implementing such strategies, at times attaining world infamy for its treatment of asylum seekers arriving by boat.

Legal Black Holes: The Excision of Australia's Boat People

The policy of mandatory detention for all citizens without valid visas was introduced by the Keating Labor government in 1992 (Migration Reform Act 1992 sec. 13), and this power to detain was extended by the Howard Liberal Coalition government to include the right of immigration officials to board and control the vessels of IMAs, even when such vessels were on the high seas (Border Protection Legislation Amendment Act 1999). In the incident known as the Tampa Affair, the Howard government refused to allow a Norwegian freighter carrying 433 rescued asylum seekers to enter Australian waters and deployed forty-five Special Air Service commandos to board and control the ship in contravention of international law. A suite of legislation was passed retrospectively to provide legal legitimacy to these actions and to allow the government to eject persons from Australian territory. In a further set of policies known as the Pacific Solution, introduced by the Howard government in 2001, asylum seekers were detained and processed offshore in camps in Papua New Guinea and Nauru. Although both onshore and offshore Australian detention camps are prison-like in their conditions, including a lack of privacy, room searches, frequent musters, and the use of numbers to refer to IMAs (Human Rights and Equal Opportunity Commission 2001; McLoughlin and Warin 2008: 261–62); offshore camps are reported to be exceedingly horrific in their treatment of detainees. In its 2012 visit to Nauru, Amnesty International reported "a toxic mix of uncertainty, unlawful detention and inhumane conditions that are creating an increasingly volatile situation, with the Australian Government failing spectacularly in its duty of care to asylum seekers" ("What We Found on Nauru" 2012). Both Amnesty International and the United Nations were refused entry into Nauru detention center in 2014, and conditions in these camps remain veiled in secrecy.

A key part of the Pacific Solution involved excising specific parts of Australian territory from its migration zone, including Christmas Island, Ashmore Island, Cartier Island, and the Cocos Islands (Migration Amendment [Excision from Migration Zone] Act 2001; Migration Amendment Act [Excision from Migration Zone] [Consequential Provisions] 2001). These are the most common landing sites for boats carrying asylum seekers. IMAs who arrived or were intercepted in these areas became legally defined as *offshore entry persons* and were excluded from rights under international and domestic law and thus had no right to apply for asylum in Australia or to access Australian courts (Crock, Saul, and Dastyari 2006: 117). In 2013 the Gillard Labor government recast IMAs as "unauthorised maritime arrivals" and excluded them from all rights obtained by all other migrants and asylum seekers in the event that they landed on the mainland (Migration Amendment [Unauthorised Maritime Arrivals and Other Measures] Act 2013). Many commentators have seen this as an excision of the mainland itself from the migration zone (e.g., Coorey and Flitton 2012). Whereas the earlier policy had excised territory, this policy effectively excised an entire group. The government also sought to further contain asylum seekers offshore by resettling those found to be genuine refugees perforce in Papua New Guinea, thus permanently removing them from any access to Australian territory or to Australian legal rights.

Following its election in September 2013, the Abbott Liberal Coalition government introduced a new policy, Sovereign Borders, which militarized the government's response to IMAs. Sovereign Borders is characterized by a new language of warfare and a new policy of secrecy. Introducing this new military rhetoric, Abbott argued that asylum seeker arrivals constitute a national emergency necessitating the nation to be put on a war-footing. While in opposition, Abbott had maintained a strenuous attack on all aspects of the Gillard Labor government's refugee policy, but once in power he mandated secrecy: "We are in a fierce contest with these people smugglers. And if we were at war, we wouldn't be giving out information that is of use to the enemy just because we might have an idle curiosity about it ourselves" ("Sorry, Mr Abbott, There Is No War" 2014). Under Sovereign Borders, the government routinely refuses to provide information on the location, condition, or existence of IMAs on the grounds that it relates to operational or on-water matters A new rhetoric has also been introduced in which IMAs are referred to as successful people smuggling ventures. In July 2014 a boat carrying more than 150 Tamils was intercepted at sea. The asylum seekers were transferred to a customs vessel and then held for over a month in locked rooms without windows and with no idea of where they were or where the government was taking them. As the *Sydney Morning Herald* reports on a document served to the Australian High Court, "They have no freedom of movement, can only leave their rooms in the presence of guards, and do not know who the guards are, the document says. It also reveals that their possessions, including any mobile phones, were seized when they were detained, and asserts they are being denied "reasonable access to legal advice" (Gordon, 2014).

Social theorist Andrew Jakubowic (2013: 6) argues that such policies are extraordinarily destructive to the humans concerned and exceedingly irrational given that there is no valid reason for such excessive brutalization either of the people concerned or of public values of compassion and empathy. Albeit extraordinarily destructive, there is a rational logic afoot here and one that is contiguous with Australia's history. The nation has its origin in a penal colony distinguished by an era of excessive and lawless brutality and a colonial frontier distinguished by acts of land theft and massacre. Cultural ingenuity was required to transform these grim realities into a national mythos, but the nation remains haunted by all it has erased from memory. Despite a national apology to "the stolen generation," (indigenous Australians taken from their families), the overturning of the legal doctrine of *terra nullius,* and the recognition of indigenous land rights, much of the rich content of the past has been erased through acts of willed silence. Most recently, the so-called history wars in Australia were an attempt by politicians and conservative historians to wash clean the record of past atrocities. Prime Minister John Howard (1996–2007) played a leading role in decrying what historian Geoffrey Blainey (1993) coined "black-arm-band history" (in his view, the overly melancholic and apologetic accounts of Australia's colonial atrocities). In the 1996 Sir Robert Menzies Lecture, Howard warned of the need "to ensure that our history as a nation is not written definitively by those who take the view that Australians should apologise for most of it. This 'black arm band' view of our past reflects a belief that most Australian history since 1788 has been little more than a disgraceful story of imperialism, exploitation, racism, sexism and other forms of discrimination. I take a very different view. I believe that the balance sheet of our history is one of heroic achievement (Howard 1996).

Albeit irrational, the governance of IMAs reveals a familiar logic, well rehearsed in the camps of the frontier and the forced exclusions of the White Australia Policy. Asylum seekers are "matter out of place," to borrow Mary Douglas's (2002: 44–50) acute phrase. By removing them from sight, by creating excised zones (legal black holes) in which they are cast out of international law, by erasing their faces from public visibility and ultimately by silencing even the sign of the call they make on "us," the heroic nation is able to sustain the illusion that it is complete unto itself. This double vision has been core to Australian culture since its foundation as a penal colony on the colonial frontier. As irrational as it might be to brutalize refugees in exodus from wars in the Middle East in which Australians are fighting, it is an irrationality that has long been the nation's fellow traveler. It is this double vision that flickers into view in the hole-ridden world of J. M. Coetzee's Novilla.

Washed Clean

Critics have puzzled over the allegorical dimensions of J. M. Coetzee's most-recent novel *The Childhood of Jesus,* declaring it puzzling, elliptical, and bizarre. Jason Farago (2013) argues that Coetzee has never published a book as bizarre as *The Childhood of Jesus,* and finds it the most perplexing of all Coetzee's novels. Roger Bellin ("Roger Bellin on *The Childhood of Jesus*" 2013) suggests it is "stranger than any reader could wish or anticipate." Benjamin Markovits (2013) finds it an odd book. Unsure of where it leaves the reader, he writes, "The whole novel is a kind of escape act, an elaborate rope trick. Coetzee has tied himself up in a number of narrative problems and has to find a way to wriggle out of them. The world he describes isn't real; the main characters have no relation to each other; their quest is implausible." Curiously, none of these reviewers raise the possibility that *The Childhood of Jesus* is a work conceived in response to, and in dialogue with, the writer's new locus: Australia. Peter Craven (2013), discussing Susan Sontag's view that Coetzee's Australian novels are a "descent" into meta-fiction, writes, "It's not hard to see how the lack of the bloody hand of history makes some readers think that the later Coetzee lacks, in Hopkins' phrase, 'the roll, the rise, the carol, the creation.'" But such comments seem more in tune with the sanitized mythos of Australia as a land of untroubled history than with the Australian novels themselves, many of which puzzle over the problem of history in Australia.

Slow Man (Coetzee 2005) grapples with the question of historical amnesia in Australia. Its protagonist, Paul Rayment, devotes his solitary and dispassionate life to collecting photographs from Australia's colonial past, as if these images could gainsay a culture barely cognizant of its own historical emergence. Rayment is intrigued with the magic of the darkroom and its sudden manifestations of luminance and life, but he remains a being occluded to himself. The photographs at the center of his collection are by Antoine Fauchery, a French colonial photographer who has intrigued many scholars, not least because of the mystery surrounding his missing photographs purported to record a colonial atrocity (the sacking of the Summer Palace in the Second Opium War).[2] But Coetzee's imagined Fauchery captures an Australian past in photographs that are of Coetzee's invention. Within the space of the novel, the lost images of the past are returned to "us" in works that record a past that never happened. And, this, only to be stolen and digitally remastered to recreate a new history of the past in which migrant faces appear where heroic colonial "diggers" had been (Coetzee 2005).

In *Diary of a Bad Year* (Coetzee 2007), Coetzee creates a contemporary anatomist of melancholia. Unlike Robert Burton (who begins his *Anatomy of Melancholy* [2001] with a utopia), Coetzee's anatomist is unable to springboard from pessimism into utopian fantasies of a new rule-bound order. Despite its complex literary structure and global themes, this novel is placed. The thoughts, essays, dramas, and desires of its protagonists unfold in John Howard's Australia, as Howard assumes the mantle of Pauline Hanson,[3] beating his chest in a war cry against the territorial incursion of criminal refugees. Coetzee's Australia is melancholic *and* territorial, and his characters are boundary riders. Alan polices his territorial rights over his girlfriend Anya while Juan and the Magpie (an iconic Australian bird of dominance and territorial incursion) stare each other down over the boundary of the windowsill.

Unlike these earlier Australian novels, *The Childhood of Jesus* (Coetzee 2013) unfolds in an uncolored and timeless space of indeterminate history. The novel could be unfolding anywhere—the characters appear to be living in a German-speaking Spanish town called Novilla and speak in a barely acquired Spanish (which we read in English). The philosopher Raimond Gaita (2013) points out this is not a language we know, but one stripped of the deep history of language—a timeless, passionless language with no irony, no tone, no memory. The history of Western intellectual culture haunts these pages, which reverberate with references to Plato, Wittgenstein, Voltaire, and Cervantes, amongst others, but the past remains unanchored and ghostly as if the novel takes place in the afterlife or the after-thought of our world.

Leo Robson (2013) suggests, "[I]t is tempting to see Novilla not as a reconfigured version of the feudal or industrial or post-industrial city but as an outpost of the republic of letters with its own customs, laws and logic—Novel-land." I would argue Novilla is exactly the opposite. It is a postfictional city devoid of irony in which all the passions that drive literary characters (desire, hunger, taste, rivalry, distinction, ambivalence) have been erased. Novilla's citizens enjoy debating the ideal form of various objects, but in this republic (without letters) real subjects are untroubled by interiority. They are, in the language of the novel, "washed clean" of their past. Perplexingly empty, Novilla's inhabitants are subjects without lack. Untroubled by the yawning chasm between need and desire that is intrinsic to being human, they are humans without holes dwelling in the timeless state of a society where all needs are met and where desire is foreclosed as the wellspring of action. It does not follow, however, that *The Childhood of Jesus* is a novel that has no bearing on history.

The novel begins with a man, Simón, and child, David, arriving in the city of Novilla in search of refuge. The man's first words are direct: "Good day. We are new arrivals. I am looking for employment. Also for a place to live.

I have a child with me" (Coetzee 2013: 7). Resettlement awaits them at the hands of a benevolent and seemingly providential state. A sign on the door reads, "Welcome newcomers" (Coetzee 2013: 21). The nun-like woman who receives them explains, "People arrived needing help, and we help them. We help them and their lives improve. None of that is invisible. None of it requires blind faith. We do our job, and everything turns out well. It is as simple as that" (Coetzee 2013: 39).

After two days in Novilla, Simón has endured hard physical labor but he and the child have eaten only a few slices of bread and margarine, washed themselves in tepid water without soap, and slept in the only comfort on offer—a shelter of cast-off debris. They have arrived at Novilla by sea and via an intermediary way station—a camp named Belstar. We know little of this camp. It is somewhere in the desert, the first destination of those who arrive by sea in search of a new life. Simón and the child David have been living in a tent for six weeks and they are lucky—others stay in the camp for months. At Belstar they are given new names and treated to the bare exigencies a new life requires: cast-off clothes, language classes, and bad food. Of those who arrive at Novilla by sea, there is an additional requirement: they must arrive "washed clean" of their past.

Reviewers have asked, What does this obscure parable have to do with Jesus or with his childhood? Certainly Jesus is never mentioned in the novel, although, like David, the infant Jesus was a child of enigmatic provenance, his parents outcasts in search of those elementary human needs: shelter, food, and security. Simón, like Joseph, is a man called on to stand in as surrogate father for a child of mysterious provenance. As the novel unfolds, a woman will be also called on to be his mother, as if by an act of divine will. Why her? We do not know. But this child could be any wandering child, displaced and in search of refuge. His name encodes his migrant state: David, the wandering star.

Simón and David enter into a world where all needs seem to be met, but where the world shrinks to its surface, where memory erases its own tracks, where desire short-circuits into a happy acceptance of satiety, where love conquers desire and friendship love, where progress moves only forward and the benevolent state has no shadow albeit one that Simón feels in every cell of his body. Kafka hovers in these pages. As Walter H. Sokel (1999: 838) writes, "Franz Kafka sensed ... a profound discrepancy between the appearance of solidity and a reality of alienation and vague but persistent menace. He felt a hopeless split between what seemed to be solid ground under his feet and the suspicion that things were really not holding together very well and might fly apart at any moment. But he also felt that he alone was cursed to feel this, while all others, and his parents above all, could blithely ignore all threats." Like Kafka's K, Simón is alone in his presentiment of all that is missing, all that lies below the smoothed out surfaces of the place he dwells in. He is haunted by shadows, by the presentiment of alienation, of emotional deprivation, and of the barbarity lurking in the goodness of those around him, as all around him blithely ignore his questions and his insistence that the "thing in itself" is an ideal stripped of history and therefore of being. Simón states, "I have not let go of the idea of history, the idea of change without beginning or end. Ideas cannot be washed out of us, not even by time. Ideas are everywhere. The universe is instinct with them. Without them there would be no universe, for there would be no being" (Coetzee 2013: 136). But Novilla allows no tear, no tears, no tissue, no time. Before long, its promise of a new life is something David and his surrogate parents flee from, as the authorities decree that David must be cured of his distinction, his oddity, by an extended sojourn in a new camp. Soon Simón, David, and his surrogate mother Inés are once more mobile, itinerant, and in search of Estrellita, a township somewhere down the highway, a place we know they will never find or at least not in the form of its imagining. As Brian Castro writes in *Looking for Estrellita,* a meditation on migrancy, loss, and literature, "Estrellita: you could make words of her. A letter. Lettres. Littera. Something read; dropped from the bed. Both beautiful and profane" (Castro 1999: 15). Somewhere in the empty space between two mythical stars (Belstar, or the beautiful star, and Estrellita, or the little star), these wandering stars are, like Castro's narrator, lost subjects in search of an object that will never be found.

Anthony Uhlmann (2013) writes astutely in the *Sydney Review of Books*:

> Coetzee seems to be a writer who values the external: his works enter into a dialogue with what is outside, though what is outside his works are not only real world problems, but other works, other books. *Foe* (1986), for example, refers to *Robinson Crusoe* (1719) and *The Master of Petersburg* refers to Dostoevsky's *Demons* (1872).... And when Coetzee refers to other writers in his books, he never really refers to them, even when he names them. Rather, he offers deliberately distorted images of them—so that his character Foe is not Daniel Defoe but an idea of the writer, and his Dostoevsky is not the historical author but an idea of the writer. Yet perhaps this deliberate distortion is a kind of dialogue: a doubleness that enables meaning to emerge.

In this sense, *The Childhood of Jesus* is in dialogue with an external world (of places, authors, ideas, histories), but this external world is itself a fictional allegory of the text. Like all allegories, the text requires interpretation but the symbolic surplus that builds outside the frame of the novel resists literal capture. The novel is not about *anything* per se, but it is *like* many things. Coetzee reveals this in the novel when Simón, perplexed by David's enigmatic character, looks into the child's eyes and momentarily glimpses something: "For the briefest moment he sees something there. He has no name for it. *It is like*–that is what occurs to him in the moment. Like a fish that wriggles loose as you try and grasp it. But not like a fish–no, like *like a fish*. Or like

like like a fish. Then the moment is over, and he is simply standing in silence, staring" (Coetzee 2013: 220; all italics as found in original).

The Childhood of Jesus is *like* this. Novilla is not Australia any more than Estrellita is "Estralia," although when innkeeper Señora Robles quips, "I don't think you will find much life in Estrellita. I have friends who moved there, and they say it is the most boring place in the world" (Coetzee 2013: 315), we glimpse something familiar, something *like* Australia, as it manifests in the migrant's lament. Such likenesses proliferate in an endlessly digressing chain of similitude that extends far beyond Australia but that also resonates with being like *like* Australia. Not least amongst these likenesses is the haunting sense of a culture that creates holes by banishing the hole that makes us human.

The novel unfolds in such a hole—in the space between camps, words, pages, numbers, and stars. David is a child troubled by holes that only he can see: "*What if I fall?* He keeps asking" (Coetzee 2013: 290). His universe is a world of holes where the space between two things is a space he is always at risk of falling into: "[I]s it like when the numbers open up and you fall?" (Coetzee 2013: 265). David sees with the eye of God, or rather, he sees *like* God. Or like *like like* God. The synthetic order of symbols and numbers that creates similitude out of singularity is something he cannot see, because he sees singularity and, therefore, *like God* he sees the spaces between each and every one. Trying to grasp how David sees, Simón conjectures, "What if we are wrong and he is right? What if between one and two there is no bridge at all, only empty space? And what if we, who so confidently take the step, are in fact falling through space, only we don't know it because we insist on keeping our blindfold on? What if the boy is the only one among us with eyes to see?" (Coetzee 2013: 291). Falling into the space between things this child is stateless in every sense of the word. His belonging has no place in Novilla. Falling outside the categories of being and belonging, he will be assigned by the state to a new place of containment, to a new camp. And what the reader catches a glimpse of at this moment of consignment is something *like* the invisible holes where unseeable and nameless subjects are consigned in Australia today.

Rather than the retreat of the writer into a late style of formal experimentation, this novel marks a deepening engagement with Coetzee's new place where, to recall Australian anthropologist W. E. H Stanner's (2009) famous words, "[A] cult of forgetfulness is practiced on a national scale" (Stanner 1969: 67). A place where people, ideas, and events fall into the space between words, a place riddled with holes.

To reiterate: The novel is not an explicit commentary on Australia's asylum policy. Coetzee has never written explicitly on any political matter and, as his critics have often complained, he has consistently refused to make explicit political comments. But, as in Kafka's parables of modern power, the mutable, indeterminate and endlessly digressing meaning of this allegory assumes historical weight in an interrogation of power and the forms it has taken in modernity, in camps, gulags, perverted bureaucracies, and totalitarian regimes *and* in the place in which Coetzee now writes.

Like the camp dwellers of Australia's penal and colonial past, today's irregular maritime arrivals are subjects *subject to* the benevolence of an Australian state, its rhetoric of criminality, and its policies of arbitrary detention, just as in the mythical Novilla new arrivals dwell within a contradictory logic that is *like* the bipolar logic of the refugee discourse of the rich West—benevolence *and* disposability, settlement *and* incarceration. Novilla is not Australia but it is like like *like like* Australia's hidden other. One visible, the other invisible; one disgraced, the other valorized And this distorted, doubled Australia is shot through with the imaginings of other writers, notably Murnane's fictionalized Nueva Australia (the socialist colony started in Paraguay led by the racist rhetorician William Lane) and Castro's (1999) Estrellita, the lost object of the migrant's journey. *The Childhood of Jesus* navigates a passage *like* that made by today's irregular maritime arrivals. And the unfound Estrellita is *like* another mythical place—*Estralia*—a migrant country, a country of forgotten journeys and lost histories. These journeys across the sea lead to *Estralia,* the forgotten interior history of Australia. There, incarcerated in camps, in zones excised from the national territory, unnamed inhabitants dwell in limbo, stripped of all but the barest exigencies of life, thrown out of time and space, and washed of their past. These subjects, emptied of their histories are the ideal form of a nation born, as Bentham argued, from the excrement of Europe.[4] They are boat people, the ideal type of an interior and elided history. To borrow a phrase from *The Childhood of Jesus,* they are the ideal type of excrement, "the pooness of poo" (Coetzee 2013: 159), and as such they star in the daily drama of a nation washing itself clean.

Jennifer Rutherford is Director of the J.M. Coetzee Centre for Creative Practice and Research Professor in Sociology and Literature at the University of Adelaide. Her published works include *Zombies* (Routledge 2013); *Halfway House; The Poetics of Australian Spaces* coedited with Barbara Holloway (UWA Press 2010); *The Gauche Intruder: Freud, Lacan and the White Australian Imaginary* (MUP 2001); and the acclaimed television documentary *Ordinary People* (Film Australia 2001). Trained in psychoanalysis at the École de la Cause freudienne, she writes in the fields of psychoanalytic and social theory, literary cultures, and race relations. She has held research and teaching positions in English, Cultural Studies, Sociology, and Australian Studies at the Universities of Sydney, Melbourne, and Macquarie, and at the Australian National University. She has formerly held positions as the Director of the Hawke EU Centre for Mobilities, Migrations and Cultural Transformations and Deputy Director of the Hawke Research Institute at the University of South Australia. In 2012 she directed a National summit on Asylum. Her forthcoming book, *Melancholy Migrations: Journeying with the Negative* is coauthored with novelist Brian Castro).

Notes

I am indebted to Louis Everuss for his research on Australian asylum policy used in this chapter and to Rita Horanyi for her research assistance and editing of this chapter.
1. "Hole," *Merriam-Webster,* http://www.merriam-webster.com/dictionary/hole
2. For further analysis of the mystery surrounding Fauchery's work, see, e.g., Thiriez 1998: 6; Rutherford and Castro forthcoming.
3. Pauline Hanson was the leader of the extreme nationalist party One Nation, which gained sudden electoral support in 1996 following Hanson's election to federal parliament.
4. For a discussion of Bentham's views on Australia and excrement, see Hughes 2003.

Bibliography

Arendt, Hannah. 1958. "The Decline of the Nation–State and the End of the Rights of Man." In *The Origins of Totalitarianism.* New York: Meridian Books.

Bellin, Roger. 2013. "A Strange Allegory: JM Coetzee's *The Childhood of Jesus.*" Los Angeles Review of Books.

Blainey, Geoffrey. 1993. "Drawing up a Balance Sheet of Our History." *Quadrant* 37, no. 7–8 (July–August): 10–15.

Burton. 2001. *Anatomy of Melancholy,* edited Jackson Holbrook. New York Review of Books.

Campbell, Angus. 2014. *Operation Sovereign Borders: Initial Reflections and Future Outlook.* Australian Customs and Border Protection Service. http://newsroom.cust oms.gov.au/channels/transcripts-operation-sovereign-borders/releases/transc ript-operation-sovereign-borders-initial-reflections-and-future-outlook

Castro, Brian. 1999. *Looking for Estrellita.* Brisbane: University of Queensland Press.

Coetzee, J. M. 2005. *Slow Man.* London: Vintage.

———. 2007. *Diary of a Bad Year.* London: Harvill Secker.

———. 2013. *The Childhood of Jesus.* London: Harvill Secker.

Coorey, Philip., and Flitton, Daniel. 2012. "Mainland Removed from Zone for Asylum Seekers." *Sydney Morning Herald,* October 31.

Craven, Peter. 2013. "Avauncular Question Marks." *Sydney Review of Books,* March 22. http://www.sydneyreviewofbooks.com/avuncular-question-marks/

Crisp, Jeff. 2013. "Keynote Address to the National Asylum Summit, Adelaide 2013." In *National Asylum Summit Report,* Jennifer Rutherfrd and Louis Everuss, Adelaide: Hawke Research Institute.

Crock, Mary., Ben. Saul, and Azadeh. Dastyari. 2006. *Future Seekers II.* Sydney: The Federation Press.

Davis, Wade. 1985. *Passage of Darkness*. Chapel Hill, NC, and London: The University of North Carolina Press.

Douglas, Mary. 2002. *Purity and Danger*. London/New York: Routledge Classics.

Dudley, Michael. 2003. "Contradictory Australian national policies on self harm and suicide: the case of asylum seekers in mandatory detention." *Australasian Psychiatry*, 11, no. 1: 102–8.

Farago, Jason. 2013. "J. M. Coetzee's Stunning New Novel Shows What Happens When a Nobel Winner Gets Really Weird." *New Republic*, September 13. http://www.newrepublic.com/article/114658/jm-coetzees-childhood-jesus-reviewed-jason-farago

Gaita, Raimond. 2013. "Rai Gaita Interview Transcript." *The Monthly*, April. http://www.themonthly.com.au/book-club/2013/april/transcript

Gordon, Michael. 2014. "High-Seas Prison for 150 Tamils." *Sydney Morning Herald*, July 17.

Howard, John. 1996. "The Liberal Tradition: The Beliefs and Values Which Guide the Liberal Government." Sir Robert Menzies Lecture Trust. http://menzieslecture.org/1996.html

Hughes, Robert. 2003. *The Fatal Shore: A History of the Transportation of Convicts to Australia, 1787–1868*. London: Vintage Books

Human Rights and Equal Opportunity Commission (HREOC). 2001. "A Report on Visits to Immigration Detention Facilities by the Human Rights Commissioner." Australian Human Rights and Equal Opportunity Commission, Canberra. https://www.humanrights.gov.au/publications/report-visits-immigration-detention-facilities-human-rights-commissioner-2001.

Hurston, Zora Neal. 2009. *Tell My Horse: Voodoo and Life in Haiti and Jamaica*. New York: Harper Perennial Modern Classics.

Jakubowic, Andrew. 2013. *National Asylum Summit Report*. Adelaide: Hawke Research Institute.

Mares, Peter. 2002. *Borderline: Australia's response to refugees and asylum seekers in the wake of the Tampa*. Sydney: UNSW Press.

Markovits, Benjamin. 2013. "The Childhood of Jesus by J. M. Coetzee – review." *The Guardian*, March 2. http://www.theguardian.com/books/2013/mar/02/childhood-of-jesus-jm-coetzee-review

McLoughlin, Pauline., and Megan. Warin. 2008. "Corrosive Places, Inhuman Spaces: Mental Mental Health in Australian Immigration Detention." *Health & Place* 14, no. 2: 254–64.

Robson, Leo. 2013. "Reviewed: *The Childhood of Jesus* by JM Coetzee and *Harvest* by Jim Crace." *New Statesmen*, March 7. http://www.newstatesman.com/culture/2013/03/reviewed-childhood-jesus-j-m-coetzee-and-harvest-jim-crace

"Roger Bellin on *The Childhood of Jesus*." 2013. *Los Angeles Review of Books*, November 6. https://lareviewofbooks.org/review/magical-child-troubled-child-on-jm-coetzees-the-childhood-of-jesus

Rutherford, Jennifer, Forthcoming. "The Missing Suitcase." In Jennifer Rutherford and Brian Castro, *Melancholy Migrations: Journeying with the Negative*. Artarmon, NSW: Giramondo.

Smith, Katherine. 2010. "Lansetkod: Memory, Mimicry, Masculinity." In *Kanaval: Vodou, Politics and Revolution on the Streets of Haiti,* photography and oral history by L. Gordon. London: Soul Jazz Records.
Sokel, Walter. 1999. "Kafka as a Jew." *New Literary History* 30, no. 4: 835–37.
"Sorry, Mr Abbott, There Is No War." 2014. Editorial. *The Age,* January 11. http://www.theage.com.au/comment/the-age-editorial/sorry-mr-abbott-there-is-no-war-20140110-30min.html
Stanner, William Edward Hanley. 1969. *After the Dreaming: Black and White Australians: The Boyer Lectures.* Sydney: ABC Press.
http://trove.nla.gov.au/work/20638870?q&sort=holdings+desc&_=1451624241202&versionId=9811027
Thiriez, Régine. 1998. *Barbarian Lens: Western Photographers of the Qianlong Emperor's European Palaces.* Amsterdam: Gordon and Breach.
Uhlmann, Anthony. 2013. "Signs for the Soul." *Sydney Review of Books,* July 9. http://www.sydneyreviewofbooks.com/signs-for-the-soul//
"What We Found on Nauru." 2012. Amnesty International. December 17. http://www.amnesty.org.au/refugees/comments/30726/

6

Unstable Vessels

Small Boats as Emblems of Deaths Foretold and as Harbingers of Better Futures in Figurations of Irregular Migration across the Strait of Gibraltar

David Álvarez

Small boats bulk large in cross-Mediterranean irregular migration as well as in the discourses and cultural forms and practices that thematize it. In "Léxico de la Emigración" [Emigration lexicon] Inés D'Ors lists twenty different types of vessel–most of them of modest proportions–that irregular migrants use in order to cross from the Mediterranean's southern coasts to its northern shores (D'Ors 2002: 64–68).[1] At the sea's westernmost end, two types of small craft have predominated in clandestine migrant crossings of its heavily patrolled waters: the *patera* and a fast inflatable vessel generically referred to by the brand name Zodiac.[2] In everyday parlance, the names of these two vessels have come to stand in for the various kinds of small-scale craft that are used in illegalized South to North traversals of the Strait of Gibraltar. They also, as Mohamed Abrighach has noted (2006: 135), have come to metonymically signify irregular migration from Morocco to Spain as such.

In this chapter I will first explain the significance of the Strait of Gibraltar in the context of irregular migration across the Mediterranean, one of a trio of geopolitical sites in which the global South and North brusquely abut each other and across which migrants plot and pursue their extralegal itineraries.[3] In so doing, I will explain the function that small craft play in attempts to breach the external frontiers of the European Union (EU). I will also assess some of the ways in which small boats are figured in anti-immigrant imaginaries. Finally, I will examine the figuration of the *patera* in a novel originally published in French in 1999 by the Moroccan painter and writer Mahi Binebine entitled *Cannibales: Traversée dans l'enfer de Gibraltar* (*Cannibals: Crossing the Hell of Gibraltar,* translated as *Welcome to Paradise*; 2003), and in a performance piece by the Belgian artist Francis Alÿs, called "Don't Cross the Bridge Before You Get to the River" (Alÿs 2008) both of which take the Strait as their principal setting.

Binebine's novel and Alÿs's performance are two notable examples of a multigenre and transnational body of work that first emerged in Morocco and that empathetically probes the nature of what Julia Kristeva (1988: 25) has called "the cosmopolitanism of the flayed" (my translation).[4] Boats are key figures in this corpus of written and visual production; in this chapter I show how figurations of the small vessels that are used in surreptitious traversals of the Strait implicitly contest the priorities of current cross-Mediterranean mobility regimes. I argue that counter-representations of Mediterranean crossings such as those by Binebine and Alÿs partly function as critiques of the ways in which the EU's immigration policies and practices strip migrants of rights, oblige them to endanger their lives, and, if they survive their furtive travels, thrust them into an illegalized limbo on the margins of politically constituted communities.

At the same time, however, while Binebine's novel and Alÿs's performance share a critical thrust, they do not do so to identical effect. In the case of *Cannibales,* the novel's critique is blunted by the totalizing pessimism that permeates the text and that is forcefully condensed in its depiction of the boat that fails to transport the characters to a new life in Europe. Conversely, in the case of Alÿs's installation the boat is represented in a manner akin to the way in which Giorgio Agamben (1996) reads the refugee as symbol in his short essay, "Beyond Human Rights." Agamben accords the "seemingly marginal figure" of the refugee considerable politico-symbolic power because of the way in which "it unhinges the old trinity of State-nation-territory" (Agamben 1996: 162) and can thereby give rise to more-inclusive categories of collective belonging than those that attach to the territorially bounded and multiply-bordered nation–state. Analogously, Alÿs's performance refigures the ostensibly negligible figure of the small boat in such a way as to call in question dominant constructions of national identity and mobility rights. Moreover, it does so in a utopian register that contrasts instructively with the overwhelming despair that pervades Binebine's text.

As my differing assessments of Binebine's and Alÿs's works suggest, in the realm of figuration small boats are unstable vessels, carriers of varied and sometimes contradictory meanings. Moreover, both in dominant and in counter-dominant discourses of clandestine migration, such boats possess a power of signification out of all proportion to their small size and to their fragile material properties. The overarching subject of this chapter is the precise manner in which these boats convey meaning. Before unpacking their significance, however, I turn to an account of the abrogation of the freedom of movement across the external frontiers of post-Schengen Europe.

Dire Metaphors: The Strait of Gibraltar as a New Berlin Wall and as the "Biggest Abyss in the World"

In the aftermath of the fall of the Berlin Wall, the EU simultaneously liberalized its internal borders and fortified its external frontiers (Harding 2012: vi–xi). One consequence of this double and reciprocal move was that the Strait of Gibraltar (see figure 6.1) was transformed into a heavily patrolled moat surrounding one of the main entrances to an increasingly forbidding Fortress Europe (Carr 2012: 21–24). For migrants on the coasts of North Africa, the Strait—which is the narrowest waterway between Europe and Africa, and one of the world's busiest maritime channels—was both the only place

Figure 6.1. The Moroccan coast and the Strait of Gibraltar from the south end of the Rock of Gibraltar. Despite the Strait's seeming placidity, it is one of the world's busiest maritime channels. May 31st, 2014. Photographer: David Álvarez. Courtesy of David Álvarez.

from which the European coastline could be tantalizingly espied with the naked eye (at its narrowest, the channel is only about eight miles wide) and the terminus of the first and terrestrial part of a journey that might have begun as far away as Bangladesh. Conversely, xenophobic and racist currents within Spain and other European countries came to regard the Strait as an Achilles's heel at the farthest extremity of Europe. Thus, the funnel through which Atlantic waters replenish the Mediterranean became one of the main loci of the many hopes, fantasies, and fears that both engendered and were generated by the phenomenon of seaborne irregular migration from North Africa to southern Europe.

In the early 1990s, when the EU started implementing the new and much more restrictive external border regimes stipulated by the Schengen Accords, it was the Spanish coastline's ostensible accessibility by small boat that prompted Moroccans to hazard the crossing; eventually other Africans and Asians followed suit.[5] Faced with the prospect of entrenched authoritarian rule and of long-term unemployment at home, and in part prompted by newly available televised images of the prosperous life apparently enjoyed by millions in neighboring Europe, increasing numbers of Moroccans began to head north.[6] They were soon followed by postcolonial Sub-Saharan Africans and Asians whose income level and nationality also made them ineligible for visas that would enable them to enter Europe legally and who took to boarding repurposed fishing boats and other small craft in an effort to gain access to the EU under cover of darkness.

Over the course of a decade, and in pursuit of the fervent dream of remaking their constricted lives within the internally borderless space of the EU, thousands of men, women, and teenagers placed their trust in the hands of small boat owners and trafficking mafias who made large profits from their passage.[7] They also placed their lives in the hands of pilots who in many cases were ill equipped to navigate the Strait's notoriously treacherous waters, which are bedeviled by powerful winds and currents that can quickly transform the placid conditions enjoyed by pleasure craft into raging tempests. Moreover, even if they were successful in reaching the Strait's northern shore, these often-inexperienced helmsmen would have to exercise extreme care so as not to run aground on the rocks and shoals that pose navigational hazards along much of Spain's southernmost coast.

As the above account suggests, clandestine maritime crossings of the Strait have always been exceedingly dangerous for all those who were willing to leave behind the tenuous security of their lives on land for the even greater insecurity of a fraught crossing by sea. Despite this fact, xenophobic sectors of Spanish and European society regarded the unarmed, exhausted, often hypothermic, and frequently terrified migrants themselves as threatening, and the small craft on which they are ferried across the channel became emblems of a putative social, existential, and civilizational "threat." As Francesca Falk notes in her analysis of the iconology of illegalized immigration, in Europe "cramped boats have become an icon of threatened borders" (Falk 2010: 86), an image keyed chiefly on fears of invasion and of infection.

Thus, for Spaniards and other Europeans fearful of being "invaded," "swamped," or even "reconquered" by "Moors" and by other unwanted travelers, the Strait of Gibraltar symbolized the uncomfortable proximity of Europe's alleged civilizational Others (Taras 2012: 68–108).[8] Concomitantly, the *patera* and the Zodiac became key symbols of the unwanted and anxiety-inducing nearness of the worlds of Islam and of Third World underdevelopment. Furthermore, the instrumental conflation of clandestine migration with drug trafficking and more recently with Islamist terrorism (Carr 2012: 33, 35, 113) served as partial justification for the erection and ongoing fortification of a figurative kind of new Berlin Wall along the Strait zone (Goytisolo 1992), a notable instance of the process of distributing and administering fear in pursuit of a politics of securitization (Huysmans 2006).

As Matthew Carr has noted, however, "'[I]nvasion' narratives were often based on hypotheses and fantasies rather than on actual numbers" (Carr 2012: 22). Moreover, the majority of irregular migrants have usually arrived in Europe by land or by air, rather than by boat. Writing in 2007 Spanish journalist Eduardo del Campo noted that, according to most estimates, only about 5 percent of clandestine migrants arrived in Spain on *pateras* (del Campo 2007: 16). The figures are also low in comparison to the number of Libyan refugees who sought refuge in Tunisia after the 2011 uprising against the Qaddafi regime, an event that led to numerous clandestine crossings of the Strait of Sicily.[9] Nevertheless, of the relatively small number of migrants who undertook covert nocturnal crossings of the Strait, a considerable proportion drowned or nearly drowned, despite the short distance involved.

Nobody knows for certain how many migrants have lost their lives in attempting to enter the EU by boat, but by the end of the 1990s Jeremy Harding could note that "a figure in the thousands" was probable for the Strait alone (2000: 103).[10] Although the invocation of such statistics can risk reducing the drowned and disappeared to what Achille Mbembe calls "meaningless corporealities" inscribed in a register of "undifferentiated generality" (Mbembe 2003: 35), at the same time the figures convey a sense of the magnitude of the problem, one that liberal-democratic polities and modernizing autocracies alike attempt to minimize and manage, rather than resolve.

What was theEU's response to this unprecedented conversion of its south-westernmost maritime border into a mass watery grave, a situation that prompted Mahi Binebine to dub the Strait "the biggest abyss in the world" (Binebine 2001: 130)? Notwithstanding its official professions of humanitarianism, the EU created and deployed a massive surveillance system the main purpose of which was "to seal Europe's borders against its unwanted immigrants" (Carr 2012: 5).[11] Known by its Spanish acronym SIVE (Sistema

Integrado de Vigilancia Exterior), the Integrated System of External Surveillance and Security was predicated in part on fears and anxieties provoked by images of overcrowded *pateras* and shadowy Zodiacs in the Spanish mass media. Despite their small size and relatively small numbers, the small boats that ply the Strait's clandestine routes were often figured as physical and metaphorical vehicles for (imagined) assaults on the integrity of the European body politic. Furthermore, the immigrants they carried were regarded as potential assaulters of the physical and social security of individual Europeans.[12]

Although the SIVE eventually had the desired effect of substantially reducing the passage of undocumented migrants across the Strait, it hardly constituted an integral solution to the problem of clandestine migration. Instead, its main effect was to push migratory routes eastwards toward the Sea of Alborán and the Sicilian Channel, which both lengthened the distance of the traversal and increased the dangers involved in traveling from one coast to another. Migratory routes were also pushed southward to the passage between Northwest Africa and Spain's Canary Islands, where the dangers that regularly attach to clandestine migration were exacerbated by the chief means of conveyance, long dugout canoes called *cayucos* that are can easily capsize out in the open sea (Carr 2012: 48). Moreover, before immigrant routes relocated to other channels, the need to avoid the SIVE's radars, helicopters, and fast motor launches became a major cause of "accidents" and of deaths. As the Spanish journalist Juan José Téllez put it at the time, "More sensors, more TV cameras, more security, more corpses" (Téllez 2001: 100).

In a macabre reminder of the death toll that irregular migration occasions, the drowned to whom Téllez refers have periodically washed up ashore on Spanish and Italian beaches. This grim reality is captured in the opening scenes of Chus Gutiérrez's feature film *Retorno a Hansala* (2008; Return to Hansala), which is named after a hamlet in Morocco's interior that was home to one of the first groups of *harragas* to drown in trying to reach the shores of southern Spain. Immediately plunging the viewer into a migrant's point of view, the film opens to the sound of a man gasping for air as he tries—and fails—to swim ashore, a scene followed by footage of an early morning Spanish jogger stopped in his tracks by the sight of several young men lying dead on the beach.

As this scene implies, in Europe the tragedies of clandestine cross-Mediterranean migration typically obtrude on public consciousness only when migrants disturb the recreational pursuits of beachgoers as corpses (or as fugitives running away from shore), or when large-scale capsizes take place and the migrants are rescued by coast guards. As Francesca Falk observes, "[I]t is usually the survivors that are depicted in the media, not the dead or dying or the actual sinking of a boat" (Falk 2010: 85).

It is in part because survivors are typically rescued by the law-enforcement agencies of EU countries that the EU can frame the part it plays in clandestine migration in humanitarian terms (Feldman 2011). The SIVE's Web site, for instance, informs readers that "the SIVE can locate distant boats, which enables us to identify and quickly respond to the needs of the victims of this new modality of human trafficking [i.e., irregular migration] (http://www.guardiacivil.es/es/prensa/especiales/sive/introduccion.html). In the same paragraph, which is flanked by images of the SIVE's patrol boats, the Web site's home page goes on to explain that the surveillance system "enables us not only to deter trafficking mafias but also to save many human lives." From the standpoint of migrants traveling on small boats, however, the SIVE's function is not primarily humanitarian, thankful though they are to be rescued when the vessels on which they are traveling capsize. Rather, the SIVE is a powerful instrument in a battery of laws, mechanisms, and practices that are designed to bar them at all costs from entering the space that they have risked their lives to get to. Yet clandestine migrants keep on trying to breach Europe's borders, since as the narrator of Salim Jay's text *Tu ne traverseras pas le détroit* (You will not cross the strait) observes, "[T]he barrier that will scare us off has yet to be invented" (Jay 2001: 11; my translation).

Jay's book is one among a sizable number of literary texts that fictively document the subjective dimensions of the experiences of undocumented migrants. It is usually the case that clandestine migrants are represented in the mass media and in political discourse as nameless and faceless people who lack any narrative capacity or authority and who are simply acted on and buffeted about by force majeure. Sometimes, however, the selfhood and agency of migrants is eclipsed not just by institutional actors that have a vested influence in reducing them to an anonymous throng, but by those sincerely concerned about their plight, as Liisa Malkki (1996) has argued. The sort of imposed speechlessness and dehistoricization that Malkki analyzes can also mark the work of sympathetic theorists such as Agamben (1996), whose reflections on the refugee that I quote above construct the latter as a singular, monolithic, dehistoricized entity.

A useful corrective to the sort of abstract language that robs refugees and other migrants of their variegated and specific humanity is provided by imaginative literature that explores the interiority of individuals in relation to the objectivity of their lived circumstances. Unlike terse news reports that at best typically limit themselves to listing a migrant's approximate age, gender, and country or region of origin, novels and other literary forms bring clandestine immigrants out of the shadows by giving them names and the attributes of personhood, by presenting readers with fleshed-out images of their circumstances, and by endowing them with narratives about their pasts. Moreover, as in life, so too in literature do migrants often try to escape their lot by means of small boats, emblems of their precarious present and of their desperate hope for a better future.

Boats as Emblems of a Death Foretold: Mahi Binebine's *Cannibales*

On the rare occasions in which the faces of migrants heave into public view, they typically do so within the framework of brief reports about their interception and detention (either at sea or once ashore), or in human-interest stories about their rescue by security forces, or in barely contextualized pieces about the capsizing of the flimsy craft in which they make their fateful crossings. They tend to emerge, in other words, into a context in which they are framed as law-breakers, or as recipients of humanitarian charity, or as helpless victims of naturalized disasters that lack systemic causes.

Literary writing by Moroccan authors and others tells a different story. For instance, in such novels as Youssef Amghar's 2004 *Il était parti dans la nuit* [He had left in the middle of the night] and Youssouf Amine Elalamy's 2001 *Les clandestins* [The clandestine migrants, translated as *Seadrinkers*), the complex subjectivity and social situation of migrants constitutes the stories' principal thematic focus and ethical center of gravity. Furthermore, fictional immigrants either tell their own stories or are commemorated by someone to whom they mattered. In both cases, the endangered and the drowned get a hearing. They speak, address themselves to others, and articulate their subjectivity.[13] In addition, they are heard, spoken about, and recognized as subjects by their peers. As a result, and in the words of the Spanish picaresque novel *El Lazarillo de Tormes,* the stories they tell bring to readers' attentions exceptional matters "perhaps never before heard or seen," in order that they "not be buried in the grave of oblivion" (Applebaum 2001: 3).

One of the most powerful fictional attempts to rescue the story of clandestine migration across the Strait from "the grave of oblivion" is Mahi Binebine's novel *Cannibales* (1999), translated into English as *Welcome to Paradise* (2003). In flight from a variety of wretched situations described by a young narrator named Azzouz ("Aziz" in the English-language version) who is himself among their number, the novel's main characters find themselves on an isolated Moroccan beach at night waiting for a smuggler to seize upon the best moment to ferry them across the Strait on a small boat. The intersecting forms of lack that hollow out the characters' existence—lack of material resources, of access to services, of meaningful citizenship, and of any realistic hope for a positive change in their circumstances—stand in sharp contrast to the ostensible plenitude of life in Europe, which they conceive of as replete with material prosperity and with boundless possibilities for self-improvement, fulfillment, and gratification. However, the novel's representation of Europe suggests that the images the characters entertain of the nearby yet faraway continent are not just fantastical, but auto-cannibalizing. Their burning faith in those images, and their desire for the life that the images appear to reveal, ineluctably devours them.

One portent of the deadly fate that befalls the majority of the characters, save for the narrator and his cousin, who are inadvertently left behind when the boat is finally launched, is the image of the *patera* itself, which for the bulk of the novel lies upside down on a deserted strand while the characters wait for the smuggler to decide when to cross over to the other side. At the end of the second chapter, the characters agree to shelter the only woman among them under the boat in hopes that her baby—whose loud wails might betray their presence on the beach to the police—will fall asleep. In the passage with which the chapter concludes, the narrator Azzouz offers this reflection:

> For me this image of the upturned boat on the sand prompted strange thoughts, images without beginning or end, a parade of fantasies I couldn't get out of my head. Yes, that boat covering living souls made me think of a giant coffin, a bottomless box open to the shades below. I saw Earth pregnant with a mother nursing her child, life and death joined in the same, lonely silence. I saw the sand breathing, the night conspiring. Mother and baby warm and dry, their hearts at peace, huddled together in the dark pit of a stomach, where the roar of the sea sounded, as in a shell. Were they still alive? Had they tasted the first fruits of that bliss my grandfather used to speak of, that ineffable peace on the banks of everlasting night? Whatever the truth of it, for hours on end and until the first barking of the dogs, no one heard them so much as twitch. (Binebine 2003: 14–15).

In its representation of the *patera,* this passage departs from dominant connotations of the craft as a means and vector for the invasion and infection of the European body politic. Instead, this *patera,* which the characters themselves have repositioned for their own purposes, is in part depicted as a refuge from the world's unremitting harshness—one in which a young mother can afford her baby girl a brief respite from the elements and from the fraught unpredictability of the journey on which they have embarked. Just as the child is temporarily safe in her mother's embrace, so too are mother and child safe in the space that the upturned boat provides, at least while it is still beached. Moreover, in the middle of a surreptitious odyssey marked by despair and by the fear of death, the boat constitutes a temporary haven in which a familial bond is reaffirmed and life—in however fragile a state—persists.

At the same time, however, this boat is evidently also a place of potentially claustrophobic confinement, one whose coffin-like appearance prefigures the fate that awaits mother and child on the open sea. As Azzouz evokes it in his reflection, the small boat on the beach is characterized by an ambiguous duality: it is at once a tomb-like space and a place of shelter. This analogy applies to the novel as a whole, which simultaneously creates a lyrical space in which the humanity of clandestine migrants as concrete individuals is foregrounded and rendered audible and visible, and that nevertheless resolutely forecloses the possibility of any hopeful outcome for any of its characters.

Concrete, individual humanity in this passage is embodied in the young mother, Nuara, and in her baby, for whom the boat serves as a transitory sanctuary. Yet once that same boat is mobilized to transport the mother, her child, and the other migrants across the Strait, it looms distantly on the horizon as a mere "black dot," which "melted slowly into the darkness" (Binebine 2003: 176). In the next and final chapter, at a Tangiers café Azzouz sees a TV report on a capsizing in the Strait, and recognizes in the faces and bodies of the drowned victims the fellow members of the makeshift community that had assembled on a remote strip of coastline in hopes of attaining a better life. Ultimately, the ambiguity that characterizes Azzouz's thoughts about the boat in the passage quoted above gives way to a much starker representation. When the boat proves to be a weak vessel, unable to withstand the assault of the waves and of the wind, the consoling metaphors of birth, life, and physical security that Azzouz evokes in the earlier passage yield to an image of all-enveloping extinction.

In the end, the only refuge that mother and her child find from the world's harshness is oblivion in the waters of the Strait, into which they silently plunge, never to be seen or heard again. In consigning mother and child to this blank narrative fate, and in never again mentioning the boat that conveys them to their doom, the novel eerily reproduces the manner in which so many migrants have disappeared without a trace. Nevertheless, by the time the mother drowns, *Cannibales* has limned her subjectivity and social situation, and has thus represented her as amounting to much more than the mute, passive, and anonymous victims that appear in television news reports or newspaper notices.

Boats as Harbingers of Better Futures: Francis Älys's "Don't Cross the Bridge before You Get to the River"

As is the case with literature, art that thematizes clandestine migration also seeks to counter the ways in which migrant lives and deaths are rendered invisible and inaudible. But whereas in literary texts small boats are chiefly represented as instruments of deaths foretold,[14] other cultural forms and practices do not just implicitly denounce migration policies and "the normative schemes of intelligibility" (Butler 2004: 146) that underpin them. Instead, they announce different and more-hopeful possibilities, which are sometimes figured through the means of transportation on which migrants travel, or via representations of the routes along which they do so.[15]

One notable example of such a counter-representation is Belgian artist Francis Alÿs's project, "Don't Cross the Bridge before You Get to the River" (Alÿs 2008). For this installation event, Alÿs arranged for scores of Spanish and Moroccan children to walk out into the Strait from their respective shores—specifically from beaches in Tarifa, Spain, and Tangiers, Morocco—while clutching toy boats in their right hands. In the eight-minute-long video of the event, two frames containing footage of the Spanish and Moroccan coasts on the left and on the right respectively are horizontally juxtaposed to take up the entire screen.[16] After a few seconds of watching seawater lapping up against the two cameras and of seeing the Strait's mountainous coasts appear to bob up and down in the far background, we start hearing children's voices faintly. Simultaneously, in both frames we see children entering the picture in the distance. Their talk increases in volume and their presence on both screens gets larger and closer until at around minute 1:45 the cameras plunge under water and the following legend appears in Spanish (in the left frame), in Arabic (in the right frame), and in English (at the bottom of both frames): "The Strait of Gibraltar is 7.7 nautical miles wide / and separates Europe from Africa. / If a line of kids/leaves Europe towards Morocco/ and a line of kids leaves Africa toward Spain / will the two lines meet / in the chimera of the horizon?" (Alÿs 2008).

Putatively, then, the project's intention was for the children to meet on each other's shores or perhaps somewhere in the middle of the Strait—"the chimera of the horizon"—although strictly speaking along the Strait's north/south axis there is no horizon, simply two opposing coastlines. However, since doing so would obviously constitute a physical let alone political impossibility, the entire operation seemed to announce itself as gestural and chimerical from the start.[17] Nevertheless, it is precisely because of its playful and even whimsical character that Alÿs's project can be read in part as a critique of both the exclusionary mobility regime that is operative in the Strait and of that regime's xenophobic underpinnings.

For one thing, the searching innocence of children can lay bare the absurdity of a world arranged according to needlessly exclusionary and repressive adult norms. Furthermore, the toy boats that these children from the Strait's facing shores availed themselves of evince the playfulness that children everywhere have in common. This project implies that there is no good reason why the two sides of the Strait should be implacably divided in the world that these children will inherit, even though present attempts to free the Strait from the straitjacket of repressive national and supranational borders are likely to founder.

Thus, although the two lines of kids never did meet in reality and although in the film we must perforce see them wading out into the Strait's waters in separate lines and on separate screens, "Don't Cross the Bridge before you Get to the River" continuously foregrounds commonalities. Thus, for instance, the separateness of the twin frames and of the sundered reality they frame is partly bridged by the single intermingled soundscape that children's voices, breaking waves, splashing water, and seagulls' cries jointly create. A bridge is also tentatively tendered between the two groups of children (and figuratively between the two shores of the Strait) by the many similarities between the two landscapes, seascapes, and bodyscapes that are simultaneously depicted in both frames. At the same time, however, the scenes depicted in either frame are never identical and differences of topography and culture also remain intermittently visible, if deemphasized. (Two examples are the greater height of the mountains that line Morocco's northernmost coast, and the fact that whereas the line of Spanish children includes boys and girls, their Moroccan counterparts are exclusively male.)

In the course of the event, the children entered the sea separately but as equals, at least in visual terms. In their parallel and mirror image movements across the Strait, they momentarily suspended a series of binary terms that operate to keep the two shores of the Strait politically, juridically, and existentially apart–for example, North/South, Developed/Underdeveloped, Rich/Poor. Furthermore, in attempting to construct a kind of human bridge across the heavily patrolled moat of the Strait, the children performed a desire to ignore or to subvert the kinds of borders and barriers that separate Europe on the one hand and Africa on the other. They did so whilst holding aloft "boats" fashioned out of repurposed shoes (flip-flops, beach sandals, Moroccan slippers) to which small sails had been affixed, an image that calls to mind the moment when emigrants set foot aboard fragile watercraft in an effort to breach the political/existential borders that are imposed on them.

Although the specific reasons for clandestine migration change from year to year and from place to place, underlying and animating all of its manifestations everywhere is what in his comments on Alÿs's piece T.J. Demos dubs an "intolerable reality" against which Alÿs latches on to utopia as "a critical force" and as a "creative proposal for an imaginative alternative, expressing the power of what could be, and what might yet be" (Demos 2010). Nearly thirty years after the first drowned *harragas* started washing up on the shores of southern Spain, the Mediterranean continues to be a dangerous and often deadly setting for migrants in desperately dire straits, including many children and the need to imagine alternatives to "an intolerable reality" is as pressing as ever. Despite its critical utopian thrust, Alÿs's project ends on an image that recalls the Strait's late-twentieth-century identity as a maritime mass grave: the scenes of children playing in the Mediterranean's warm waters against a backdrop of blazing sky give way to footage of seawater and algae against a background of aqueous silence. The last image we see is of two little shoe-boats adrift and forlorn on the Strait's swirling and indifferent waters.

In English, as well as in the Romance languages, the geographical denotation *strait* carries connotations of both narrowness and distress. In Arabic, however, the Strait has historically been known by a different name, Bab az-

Zakat (or the door/gateway of charity). The openness and generosity of that designation is akin to that of the name that a northern Moroccan nongovernmental organization (NGO) that fights for the rights of clandestine migrants has given itself, Asociación Pateras de la Vida (Pateras for Life Association). Although small boats that ply the Mediterranean's clandestine migratory routes continue to be associated with despair and with death, and thus with conditions that need urgently to be denounced, the Moroccan NGO's name life-affirmingly refigures the charged keyword *patera* in order to prefigure a time in which the Azzouz's and Nuara's of our world will be free to stay at home or to exercise their right to mobility as they see fit.

David Álvarez is professor of English and an affiliate of the Middle Eastern Studies Program at Grand Valley State University in Grand Rapids, Michigan, where he teaches comparative topics in contemporary international literatures. Author of articles on Caribbean and South African literature, he has also published essays on colonialism in his native Gibraltar as well as on irregular migration from Morocco to Europe. He is currently at work on a book-length study of figurations of clandestine Mediterranean crossings in Moroccan and Spanish literature, photography, and film.

Notes

1. No single term adequately captures the many permutations of status and identity that people who undertake covert journeys across national borders can undergo. Following Koser (2007: 54–69), in this chapter I will chiefly rely on the terms *irregular migrant* and *migrant,* although on occasion I will also invoke such commonly used alternatives as *clandestine migrant* and *undocumented migrant.* I will also sometimes employ the North African vernacular word for such migrants, *harragas* (Arabic for the ones who burn), an appellation that alludes to the practice among migrants of incinerating their identity documents so that if detained they will not be immediately deported to their countries of origin. (See Arab and Souvannavong 2009.)
2. Originally, *patera* referred solely to a small boat with a flat bottom propelled either by oars or by an outboard motor, that is used for duck hunting in Spain. For a discussion of the ways in which the meaning of the word has changed, see Abrighach (2006: 131–39).
3. The other two main sites are the United States–Mexico border and the border region between continental Australia and the islands around it.
4. As Pieprzak (2007: 104) and Abderrezak (2009: 462) note respectively, "a new terrain in Moroccan literature" has emerged that centers on clandestine migration and that "resonates with other national literatures" from countries that border the Mediterranean. Furthermore, musicians, filmmakers, photographers, and other artists from those countries and elsewhere have also thematized clandestine migration.

5. For a critical overview of the implementation of the Schengen Accords, see Carr (2012: 25–28, 64–83).
6. Moroccan photographer Yto Barrada, whose photo-essay *A Life Full of Holes: The Strait Project*, explores the nature and impact of clandestine migration across the Strait, attributes the yearning to migrate in part to the simultaneous reinforcement of the EU's external borders and the introduction of satellite television in Morocco (Barrada 2005).
7. Harding (2000: 24) notes that because of the EU's institutional inhospitality toward irregular migrants, "being smuggled to sanctuary has become the only option," even for those among them with a well-founded fear of persecution.
8. For an analysis of these tropes in Spanish literature and culture, see Flesler (2008: 55–96). A more recent product of the xenophobic imagination than the tropes examined by Flesler is *Le Camp des Saints*, a 1973 novel by the French writer, Jean Raspail (translated as *The Camp of the Saints*, 1995), that evokes lurid images of countless starving Indians boarding ships in Calcutta harbor, entering the Mediterranean via the Strait of Gibraltar, and overrunning an enervated France.
9. Since the 2011 Arab Revolts, the Strait of Sicily has become the main conduit for seaborne irregular migration across the Mediterranean.
10. Carr (2012: 4) notes that in contrast to the many thousands of migrants who have died trying to breach Europe's borders since 1988, 125 people were killed trying to cross the Berlin Wall throughout its entire history.
11. It also increased the establishment of detention centers around the region, and increased the reinforcement of the land borders between Morocco and Spain's North African cities of Ceuta and Melilla.
12. See Fassin (2005: 380–81) for a discussion of three kinds of security—public, social, and "racial"—that are often perceived to be threatened by "asylum seekers and by aliens in general" (Fassin 2005: 381).
13. Few irregular migrants have ready access to a life lived openly and publicly, let alone access to the publishing industry. Thus, for reality-based portrayals of their journeys and of their transformation into outcasts on the margins of nation–states, as well as in the interstices between them, it is to nonautobiographical novels by sympathetic middle class writers that curious readers must chiefly turn. For a notable exception, see Nini (2002).
14. The title of Mohamed Teriah's novel, *Les "Harragas" où Les Barques de la Mort* tersely condenses this idea.
15. For instance, for her "The Mapping Journey Project" Franco-Moroccan artist Bouchra Khalili (2011) asked irregular migrants to trace their own clandestine itineraries on maps in order to produce a counter-geography of migration at odds with the cartography of officialdom.
16. Interested readers can access the video at http://francisalys.com/dont-cross-the-bridge-before-you-get-to-the-river/,
17. After the cameras reemerge from under the water at minute 2:35, visually the remainder of the film largely consists of looping footage of the children wading into the sea, diving into the water, resurfacing, playing with their boats, and running across the sand. Shot from a variety angles, the scenes jostle for our attention, and convey a festive air accompanied by splashing sounds and scored by moments of unsettling silence.

Bibliography

Abderrezak, Hakim. 2009. "Burning the Sea: Clandestine Migration across the Strait of Gibraltar in Francophone Moroccan 'Illiterature.'" *Contemporary French and Francophone Studies* 13, no. 4: 461–69.

Abrighach, Mohamed. 2006. *La inmigración marroquí y subsahariana en la narrativa española actual (ética, estética e interculturalismo)*. Agadir, Morocco: ORMES, Facultad de Letras y Ciencias Humanas.

Agamben, Giorgio. 1996. "Beyond Human Rights." In *Radical Thought in Italy: A Potential Politics,* edited by Paolo Virno and Michael Hardt, 158–64. Minneapolis: University of Minnesota Press.

Alÿs, Francis. 2008. "Don't Cross the Bridge before You Get to the River." http://francisalys.com/dont-cross-the-bridge-before-you-get-to-the-river/

Amghar, Youssef. 2004. *Il était parti dans la nuit*. Paris: L'Harmattan.

Anonymous. [1554]. *Lazarillo de Tormes*. Translated by Stanley Applebaum. Mineola, NY: Dover, 2001.

Arab, Chadia, and Juan David Sempere Souvannavong. 2009. "Les jeunes *harragas* maghrébins se dirigeant vers L'Espagne: des rêveurs aux brûleurs de frontières." *Migrations Société*: 191–206.

Barrada, Yto. 2006. "Morocco Unbound. An Interview with Yto Barrada." Open Democracy, May 16. https://www.opendemocracy.net/arts-photography/barrada_3551.jsp

Binebine, Mahi. 2001. "Interview." *Banipal: Magazine of Modern Arab Literature* 10–11: 130–31.

———. 1999. *Cannibales*. Paris: Fayard. Translated by Lulu Norman as *Welcome to Paradise* (London: Granta, 2003).

Butler, Judith. 2004. *Precarious Life*. New York: Verso.

Carr, Matthew. 2012. *Fortress Europe: Dispatches from a Gated Continent*. New York: The New Press.

del Campo Cortés, Eduardo. *Odiseas*. 2007. *Al otro lado de la frontera: historias de la inmigración en España*. Sevilla, Spain: Fundación José Manuel Lara.

Demos, T. J. 2010. "Rights of Passage. Migration." Mark Godfrey, T. J. Demos, Eyal Weizman, Ayesha Hameed." *Tate, Etc.* www.tate.org.uk/context-comment/articles/rights-passage.

D'Ors, Inés. 2002. "Léxico de la emigración" [Emigration lexicon]. In *La inmigración en la literatura española contemporánea,* edited by Irene Andrés-Suárez, Marco Kunz, and Inés d'Ors, 21–105. Madrid: Editorial Verbum.

Elalamy, Youssouf. 2001. *Les clandestins*. Casablanca, Morocco: Eddif. Translated by John Liechty as *Seadrinkers* (Lanham, MD: Lexington Books, 2008).

Falk, Francesca. 2010. "Invasion, Infection, Invisibility: An Iconology of Illegalized Immigration." In *Images of Illegalized Immigration: Towards a Critical Iconology of Politics,* edited by Christine Bischoff, Francesca Falk, and Sylvia Kafesy, 83–100. Bielefeld, Germany: Transcript Verlag.

Fassin, Didier. 2005. "Compassion and Repression: The Moral Economy of Immigration Policies in France." *Cultural Anthropology* 20, no. 3: 362–87.

Feldman, Greg. 2011. "Europe's Border Control with a Humanitarian Face." *Middle East Report* 41: 14–17.

Flesler, Daniela. 2008. *The Return of the Moor: Spanish Responses to Contemporary Moroccan Immigration*. West Lafayette, IN: Purdue University Press.
Goytisolo, Juan. 1992. "Constructing Europe's New Wall: From Berlin to the Strait." *Middle East Report* 178: 17–19.
Gutiérrez, Chus. 2008. *Retorno a Hansala* [Film]. Sevilla: Maestranza Films, 2008.
Harding, Jeremy. 2000. *The Uninvited: Refugees at the Rich Man's Gate*. London: Profile Books.
——. 2012. *Border Vigils: Keeping Migrants Out of the Rich World*. New York: Verso.
Huysmans, Jeff. 2006. *The Politics of Insecurity: Fear, Migration and Asylum in the EU*. London: Routledge.
Jay, Salim. 2001. *Tu ne traverseras pas le détroit*. Paris: Mille et une nuits.
Khalili, Bouchra. 2011. "The Mapping Journey Project, 2008-2011." http://www.sharjahart.org/projects/projects-by-date/2011/the-mapping-journey-project-khalili
Koser, Khalid. 2007. *International Migration: A Very Short Introduction*. Oxford: OUP.
Kristeva, Julia. 1988. *Étrangers à nous-mêmes*. Paris: Fayard.
Malkki, Liisa, H. 1996. "Speechless Emissaries: Refugees, Humanitarianism, and Dehistoricization." *Cultural Anthropology* 11, no. 3: 377–404.
Mbembe, Achille. 2003. "Necropolitics." *Public Culture* 15, no. 1: 11–40.
Nini, Rachid. 2002. *Diario de un ilegal*. Madrid: Ediciones del oriente y del mediterráneo.
Pieprzak, Katarzyna. 2007. "Bodies on the Beach: Youssef Elalamy and Moroccan Landscapes of the Clandestine." In *Land and Landscape in Francographic Literature: Remapping Uncertain Territories*, edited by Magali Compan and Katarzyna Pieprzak, 104–22. Newcastle, UK: Cambridge Scholars.
Raspail, Jean. 1973. *Le camp des saints*. Paris: Éditions Robert Laffont. Translated by Norman Shapiro as *The Camp of the Saints* (Petoskey, MI: Social Contract Press, 1995).
Sistema Integrado de Vigilancia Exterior (SIVE). "Introducción." http://www.guardiacivil.es/es/prensa/especiales/sive/introduccion.html
Taras, Raymond. 2012. *Xenophobia and Islamophobia in Europe*. Edinburgh: Edinburgh University Press.
Teriah, Mohamed. 2002. *Les "harragas" ou les barques de la mort*. Casablanca: Afrique Orient.
Téllez, Juan José. 2001. *Moros en la costa*. Madrid. Editorial Debate.

Section III

Media, Politics, and Representation

Figure S.3. Melbourne refugee and asylum seeker rights rally to protest the Rudd Labour Government new proposal for assessment and resettlement of asylum seekers in Papua New Guinea, Saturday July 27, 2013. Photographer: John Englart. Courtesy of Flickr.com.

7

Memorializing Boat Tragedies in the Mediterranean

The Case of the *Katër i Radës*

Daniele Salerno

On March 28, 1997 (Good Friday that year) the Albanian boat *Katër i Radës* left Vlorë Harbor. On board were approximately 120 people who were fleeing the civil disorder (some might call it civil war) that was caused by economic crisis. Like the hundreds of thousands of Albanians who fled their country after the fall of the communist regime in 1990, the migrants intended to cross the Strait of Otranto that divides that part of the Balkan Peninsula from Italy. Their goal was to land on the Italian coast between Otranto (the easternmost point of Italy, just seventy-two kilometers from the westernmost point of Albania) and Brindisi. The Italian military corvette *Sibilla* that was patrolling the strait interrupted their crossing. This military action was conducted under the *bandiere bianche* (white flags) operation organized by the Italian government in agreement with the Albanian state just three days earlier. The operation was intended to allow the Italian navy to patrol the entire strait, including the Albanian Sea, to prevent people from landing in Italy and to send boats back to Albania. The rules of engagement included harassment procedures and the active disruption of navigation. In one of the naval maneuvers, *Sibilla* hit *Katër,* causing it to sink. In total, eighty-one people died and thirty-four survived. Of the dead, only fifty-seven bodies were found.

Due to the number of victims and the political responsibility of a Western government, the sinking of the *Katër* represents a turning point in the recent history of migrations (post 1989) in Europe, which is marked by a gradual militarization of the southern European seaboard.[1] Since then, innumerable shipwrecks have turned the Mediterranean into a mass grave where, it is estimated, twenty thousand migrants have died in the past two decades in attempts to cross it. Recently, for this reason, public debate has arisen concerning how to memorialize migrant boat tragedies in the Mediterranean, and how to publicly mourn victims.

The purpose and contribution of this chapter is to question the discursive and semiotic processes concerning the memorialization of sea tragedies in the context of boat migrations in the Mediterranean. The analysis of the different discursive practices and genres (public debates, commemorations, media representations, monumentalization, and art intervention) through which the *Katër* tragedy has been memorialized, serve as an exemplary case for questioning the memorialization of sea tragedies in the Mediterranean context. I argue that the *Katër* case study can offer insight into the social dynamics and symbolic efficacy of the memorialization practices of boat migration. To this aim, I will focus on how the *Katër* tragedy has been memorialized in the town of Otranto. In particular, among other events, the wreckage of the boat was transformed into a monument that was placed in the town harbor. In order to examine this context, different texts and practices will be analyzed from the period in the beginning of 2011, twenty years after the beginning of Albanian arrivals and when this new historical phase of migrations was addressed in public discourse, to the unveiling of the monument in the beginning of 2012. First, I will examine how public debate and interpretations of the *Katër* sinking emerged in the local press in particular. I will then focus on the transformation of the wreckage into a monument by the Greek artist Costas Varotsos, and how this affected the way the narratives circulated in public space. Adopting the approach of cultural semiotics (Eco 2014; Lotman 2005), I argue that the process of inclusion of the *Katër* story in the local semiotic space of Otranto implied a process of deep transformation concerning the narration of this event. In this transformation some aspects of the historical context of the sinking, and even the very identity of the victims seems to have been removed from collective awareness in order to adapt to local narratives (in particular those linked to "hospitality" framing). Following Judith Butler (2009), I contend that, by eliminating the possibility of reconstructing the actual story of the sinking, the memorialization practices did not create the social conditions for the public mourning of the eighty-one victims, and did not fully recognize them as individual lives that matter and are worthy of being mourned.

The Albanian Diaspora and the Italian Response: From 1990 to the *Katër i Radës*

In the twentieth century the liminality of the Adriatic Sea has played different roles in the relationship between Albania and Italy. Both border and bridge, the sea has been crossed for trading, invading, colonizing, migrating, and escaping from conflict or poverty. Both countries concluded their nation-building processes relatively late with respect to other European nations, between the end of the nineteenth and the beginning of the twentieth century. Fascist Italy occupied Albania in 1939 establishing a protectorate. After the war, while Italy joined the Atlantic alliance, Albania adhered to the Warsaw Pact. The dictator Enver Hoxha ruled Albania from 1946 to 1985. After 1978 he sealed Albania off from both the communist and Atlantic axes in an autarkic policy. In those forty years, the seventy kilometers of the Strait of Otranto widened further, representing an insurmountable barrier. Even if Italians from Salento (the southern part of Apulia region, the so-called heel of the Italian boot) could still see the Albanian coast, and Albanians could receive signals from Italian national and local media (despite risking jail if caught watching or listening to Italian channels), the two sides of the Adriatic appeared farther apart than ever before. Eventually, when the regime fell in 1990, Albania figured as the poorest country in Europe and hundreds of thousands migrated in the following years. At the end of the 1990s, out of a population of 3 million, more than 1 million Albanians were estimated to have left the country. Most headed to Greece and Italy, primarily in three major phases: spring and summer 1991, immediately after the fall of the regime; spring 1997, after civil disorder caused by a financial crisis (the phase to which the *Katër* episode belongs); and between 1998 and 1999, during the Kosovo War, when Albania itself saw the arrival of 500,000 war refugees from the ethnic Albanian areas of the former Yugoslavia.

From the other side of the Adriatic, political and media responses to the Albanian arrivals morphed quickly from welcoming to hostile. With the first arrivals in spring 1991, Italian authorities modified and relaxed laws on immigration in order to help Albanians settle in Italy. This preferential treatment caused migrants of other nationalities, particularly from North Africa, to protest (Pittau and Devole 2008). Albanians did not fit the social process of "othering" to which migrants from North Africa were submitted during the 1980s. Their "whiteness," juxtaposed to the "blackness" of North Africans, and their often fluent Italian (learned from radio and television as well as the postcolonial legacy that unites the two countries; see Duncan 2008; Comberiati 2013) helped in constructing a perception of Albanians as more familiar. In addition, their arrivals were framed in the media within narratives of liberation and "Western victory" over the communist dictatorships. Albanians were initially defined as *refugees,* as victims of illiberal regimes that deserved help and hospitality. This phase ended very quickly, in particular with the arrival in Bari on August 8, 1991, of the *Vlorë* with twenty thousand people on board. This event is still today ingrained in Italian cultural memory, with its iconic and traumatic images, both of the boat and of the local stadium transformed into a camp (which Giorgio Agamben [1998: 98–99] compared to concentration camps). As witnessed in the media narratives at the time, the social construction of Albanians as a threat was realized through the *topos* of the invasion, or human flood (Gariglio, Pogliano, and Zanini 2010), both labels widely used in media representations of migrations by boat.

In the year of the *Katër* tragedy, Albanians were no longer refugees, but illegal or clandestine migrants in Italian law. The visual portrayals of Albanians in the media shifted from close-up portraits of individuals landing on Italian territory, to large groups with frequent images of overcrowded boats from a distance. This visual and narrative pattern annihilates migrant individual identities and frames the phenomenon "as a potential threat that sets in place mechanisms of security and border control" (Bleiker et al. 2013: 399). The migrants no longer exist as individuals with their own life stories, but are "a collective force endangering welfare provisions, everyday security of citizens, the moral fabric of society, etc." (Huysmans 2006: 56). The media representations, narrative framing and visual rhetoric are consistent with a national-security oriented response that sees migrants as a "collective dangerous force" (Huysmans 2006: 56). Different discursive domains, from legal and military, to media, journalism, and popular culture, are therefore shaped in this way. This also affects, I argue, the very conditions in which shipwrecks are memorialized. In particular, we can consider the fact that journalists, who are frequently the first agents of collective memory (gathering testimonies from survivors), are often not allowed access to immigration detention centers (and are also not allowed to be present on patrol boats). The elimination of individual narratives therefore also creates the elimination of the possibility of remembering individual deaths. The loss of a life can go unnoticed, unrecorded, forgotten, and then unmourned as actually happened and still happens today.[2] The sinking of the *Katër* occurred within these historical, cultural, and social dynamics, in the full deployment of securitization practices, and still represents a dramatic turning point in the recent history of migrations in Italy. The *Katër* was in fact the first boat to be submitted to pushback sea military operations, and the first that sank in a de facto naval blockade against migration flows. However, unlike the innumerable shipwrecks that have followed, the *Katër* tragedy is a somewhat peculiar case because it has been narrated in various venues.

Translating the *Katër*'s Meaning

The *Katër* was kept in the harbor of Brindisi from its recovery until the end of the trial,[3] and later put at the disposal of the Albanian state, which did not claim it. Although the survivors' and victims' relatives asked for the boat to be returned to Albania in order to construct a monument to the victims in the city of Vlorë, it seems that neither the Italian government nor the Albanian state wanted to bear the conspicuous costs of its transport. When the wreckage was about to be demolished on the magistrate's order, the municipality of Otranto decided to claim the wreckage, saving it from destruction. The mayor of Otranto's request came after pressure from local associations. Particular pressure came from *Integra,* a nonprofit organization (NPO) based in Lecce, that works for the integration of migrants into Italian society and is led by a young Albanian woman who arrived in Italy in 1992. The court accepted and gave the boat to the town in order to build, in the mayor's words, "a monument for the massacre's victims, to be a lasting testimony so that such tragedies will not occur again" (Buffa 2012: 120).

The magistrate's permission marks the beginning of public debate on the meaning of the *Katër* story for the local community and in collective memory, as well as on the physical and symbolical collocation of the wreckage in the urban landscape. I interpret these debates as part of the translation processes of the *Katër* into the Otranto semiotic space, which we can call (following Youri Lotman) its semiosphere. As Lotman (2005: 208) admits, it is difficult to formally define the category of semiosphere. However, we can conceptualize it as the ensemble of different languages, codes, and narrations that, as a whole, constitute a recognizable, homogeneous and individual semiotic space delimited by boundaries that limit penetration or filter the movement of the "external to the internal" (Lotman 2005: 210). We can consider Otranto's peculiar semiosphere as the intertextually connected ensemble of local narrations and practices that allow people living in that territory to define themselves as part of a recognized political community with its own history, memory, territory, and identity. This implies that what is outside and alien needs to be translated into the internal systems of narrations and values, through discursive "filtering and transformative processing" (Lotman 2005: 210), in order to find their proper place and become intertextually connected to the local cultural context. If "the implanting of a fact into the collective memory ... is like a translation from one language into another" (Lotman and Uspensky 1978: 214), then the *Katër* story also needed to be shaped through different discursive genres (historical, commemorative, monumental, artistic, etc.) and interpretative practices in order to enter the local collective memory. The "continual process of rewriting and selecting information," as Umberto Eco (2014: 79) argues, deeply affects the semantic system of what is translated, with the creation of new meaning and even the erasure of different aspects.

News reports in August 2011 suggest that the translation of *Katër* into the Otranto semiotic space happened through different discursive devices. The story of the sinking was remembered in the commemoration of the twentieth anniversary of the *Vlorë* landing in Bari (Anonymous 2011a). However, in addition, it was often referred to in reports on the new phase of arrivals from North African and Middle Eastern countries, marked almost daily by shipwrecks and deaths.[4] A number of newspapers and national magazines wrote about the story of the *Katër,* calling it *la strage del venerdì santo* (the Good Friday massacre), and spoke of the political desire to preserve the wreckage in order to "host in Otranto a monument in memory of all the victims of the sea" (Anonymous 2011a). I argue here that it is specifically the concept of "hospitality," with its related semantic and social practices, which helps rewrite and reshape the memory of the *Katër* and locate it in Otranto's semiophere.

Katër *through Commemorative and Tourist Practices*

As extensively analyzed by Émile Benveniste (1973) on an etymological and linguistic basis and, more recently, in the seminal philosophical reflection of Jacques Derrida (2000) on Kant's *Perpetual Peace,* we can see that the very word *hospitality* is part of the rich family of words that derive from the Latin *hostis* to which also the word *hostility* belongs. The discursive and cultural practices through which the stranger is othered can be gathered under the labels of *hospitality* and *hostility.* Boundaries are constructed and regulated as spaces of transition or rejection. Who and what are allowed to cross these boundaries and enter the space of the community, of the semiosphere, and who and what are not? In this sense the act of hosting the wreckage, is actually a boundary-producing act (Campbell 1998) that by recognizing "strangeness" allows something or someone to enter the community.

The dialectics between hostility and hospitality play a pivotal role in Otranto, and regulate the processes of inclusion of the *Katër* into the local cultural memory. In fact, the story of the sinking of this boat has been shaped, readapted, and rewritten in order to meet the shifting narratives on which Otranto and its community base their collective identity. Otranto's collective identity is particularly focused on the peculiar geopolitical position of the town, defined as the Peoples' Crossroads. Otranto's seascape is in fact always on the threshold of being disrupted by the arrival of the uninvited from the sea (while the invited guests, tourists, come mainly from the more secure space of land). These Others could be migrants, castaways, asylum seekers who flee war, or invaders and enemies. Otranto's foundation myths are modeled on these figures, as epitomized in different mythical, historical, and religious local narratives. First, there is the myth of Porto Badisco, where Aeneas fleeing the Trojan War is said to have landed for the first time on the Italian peninsula, thus starting the history of Roman civilization. Second, there is the invasion of the Ottomans, who killed the eight hundred people that refused to convert to Islam, whose skulls are displayed and worshipped as town martyrs in the cathedral. Affectively, Otranto is in this sense on the cusp between a sort of borderphilia, epitomized by the value of hospitality, and a borderphobia, embodied by the martyrs' skulls and in which hostility toward those who come from the sea is made evident. Such narrative configurations are commodified and offered to visitors, playing an important role in tourism promotion. Through the myth of Aeneas and the religious tales of the martyrs, Otranto builds its territorial identity and touristic image on the very idea of its marine boundary, as well as on the dichotomy between who and what is hostile (the invasion of the enemy or the "clandestine" migrants) and who and what deserves hospitality (the asylum seeker and refugee).

Some weeks before the physical arrival of the wreckage (December 14, 2011), pictures of the boat and the story of its sinking had already circulated in news reports and in the public domain. The passage of twenty years since the first phase of Albanian arrivals was commemorated by an event named, "Landings and Shipwrecks: Narrating the Exodus 1991–2001," which took place November 18–19, 2011 (Puricella 2011), in which the town remembered the generous welcoming of Albanians by Otranto. The picture of the *Katër*'s rudder was used as the logo of the event, and some specific activities were dedicated to the story of the 1997 sinking. These cultural activities framed the story within the narration of welcoming and generosity. When the ship arrived, news reports described the wreckage as "the boat of all migrants" landing in Otranto, in a "safe haven" as the "natural crossroads of peoples" (quoting verbatim the press release from the municipality; Longo 2011: 35). The municipality commissioned the transformation of the wreckage into a monument to the Greek internationally renowned artist Costas Varotsos. They also invited eight young artists from different Mediterranean countries to attend a weeklong workshop on the theme of migration. The municipality intended to unveil both the boat and the works of the eight young artists during winter holiday, for the benefit of the "locals and of the many tourists that will come for Christmas and New Year's Eve" (Longo 2011: 35). The workshop and the unveiling of the monument was later scheduled for December 29 (but the unveiling was pushed back to the end of January 2012), with a concert in memory of the *Katër* the following day. These events were to be part of "L'alba dei popoli" (Peoples' dawn), activities that the municipality organizes at the end of every year to promote Otranto as a "point where peoples and cultures meet" in the Mediterranean (Anonymous 2011b: 29).

The reception of the *Katër* in Otranto was framed within the idea of *hosting* and *welcoming* in order to include the ship in the (self-) representation of the territory and of its community. The story was refashioned to celebrate and remember the generosity of local population (the "race to host people" coming suddenly from the sea) (Paiano 2011: 7). This version is consistent with the repertoire of local stories that are offered to tourists in order to depict a positive representation of local identity. This discursive dynamic, interpreted as a filtering device, brings about an important erasure of the historical context of the Good Friday massacre. The political responsibility of Italy and the Italian government for the tragedy that occurred after the decision to push boats back out to sea using military force was erased. This element, emerging from the semantic field of hostility, does not fit into the welcoming narration, the celebration of local hospitality, and tourism promotion. I argue that it was downplayed and even removed from media narration for this reason. In numerous local news reports the boat just "sank," without any reference to what provoked the sinking. As a reporter in the *Nuovo Quotidiano di Puglia* stated, the "only truth is that the Albanian boat sank, bringing down with it 81 migrants" (Longo 2011: 35). But even this truth faded once the *Katër* was transformed into an art installation and rendered part of the local cultural heritage.

Rewriting the Katër *through the Artistic and Monumental Practices*

By carrying imprints of what happened, the wreckage embodies and witnesses the story of the sinking, but cannot speak for itself. During the trial, the imprints were read by magistrates and investigators as evidence with which to reconstruct the narrative scene of a crime. In a similar manner, memorial practices and genres must translate the imprints in order to acquire a testimonial and monumental nature.[5] The boat needed to undergo a semiotic process that transformed the imprints and material remains of the past into a physical support for narrations that will be remembered and transmitted (Violi 2012: 39). The boat was cleaned and treated, the keel was cut off, and Varotsos inserted shards of glass into the body of the ship (see figures 7.1, 7.2, and 7.3), which was then put on a concrete base.

Figure 7.1. *L'approdo. Opera all'umanità migrante* (side view). Photographer: Daniele Salerno, Otranto, February 12 2012. Courtesy of Daniele Salerno.

Figure 7.2. *L'approdo. Opera all'umanità migrante* (front view). Photographer: Daniele Salerno, Otranto, February 12 2012. Courtesy of Daniele Salerno.

Figure 7.3. *L'approdo. Opera all'umanità migrante* (from a distance). Photographer: Daniele Salerno, Otranto, February 12 2012. Courtesy of Daniele Salerno.

The use of spiky glass is a very important element for understanding the process of rewriting of the sinking's story through the artistic genre and the artist's idiosyncratic style. Varotsos is internationally renowned for installations based on the use of glass. His most famous work is *Dromeas* (The runner), an impressive twelve-meter-high statue in Athens made of jagged shards of glass that celebrates the marathon and the Olympics. What is peculiar in Varotsos's style is that glass is not used to give this hard and fragile material the sense of harmony, smoothness, and softness as traditionally appreciated in the use of marble or other materials in the classical statuary genre. On the contrary, the artist uses glass to produce discontinuities and the effects of motion. The sharp edges and the points affect the viewer by transmitting a sense of fragility and precariousness from the glass, as do the threat of the acuminated shards. The shards of glass inserted into the body of *Katër* are intended to represent seawater and waves. Their disposition and direction symbolically give form to the natural forces that can threaten a boat, when violent seawaters, in particular, endanger the overcrowded and fragile boats migrants most often travel in.[6] I would argue that this choice fosters a naturalization of the event. In fact, the glass seems to conceal the imprints of the human action that caused the sinking, and the sinking is thus memorialized as natural violence. This is reflected in an interpretation communicated to the local press by the artist himself on the day of the unveiling (January 29, 2012):

> It is as if it is in the middle of the storm and the sea was exploded on it. *Katër i Radës* is the symbol of the Europe of today that is about to implode. Also my Greece and our Italy are in the middle of the storm, as this boat was that night in 1997. Maybe that tragedy wanted to warn us of the deviation from the united Europe's objectives. We were not able to change direction in time.... [T]he wound is still open on both sides of the Otranto strait. The mourning, on one side, the guilt, on the other, both to be healed. (Colluto 2012)

Varotsos's comments were also published in *La Repubblica Bari*: "The offer of transforming *Katër i Radës* into an art work came at a moment in which my country, Greece, is in a storm.... The storm being unleashed ... reminds us who we are, who Greek People are, the Italian People are.... [T]he boat had to arrive in some way to its destination though the adversities" (Varotsos 2012).

The artist describes a storm, symbolically represented by the glass, suggesting it was the cause of the sinking. Overall, he makes very few, if any, references to Albania and the Albanian people. Indeed, Greece and the Greek people are victimized and put in the place of Albanians through a comparison, between the Albanian financial crisis (which caused the civil war and the second phase of the Albanian diaspora in the 1990s) and the Greek financial crisis. The storm represented in the installation becomes a metaphor for the political and financial storm that was unleashed in Europe, and in particular in Italy and Greece. Furthermore, when Varotsos says, "[W]e were not able to change direction in time" (Varotsos 2012), he is distributing blame, by fostering an inaccurate version of the story. In fact, Varotsos's narration not only suggests that the boat sank by storm, but is also implying that the boat sank just because it did not succeed in tacking in time. The narrations in the public discourse refer to the boat as a trace of a past event, but they do not seem to strictly focus on the *Katër,* and instead take multiple directions. The wreckage, after its transformation into a monument/installation, lends itself as support for other narrations, which also partially eliminate the story of the sinking and of its victims. The lexical choices of the Italian newspapers in this period followed the same idea. Newspaper reports talked about how the *Katër* entered into a "collision with our Navy," and also ironically, that the monument dedicated to this ship would be hosted in the harbor as a "symbol of welcoming and solidarity among peoples" (Anonymous 2012). Again, in order to fit the "welcoming narrative," the institutional and public narrations suppressed the historical context.

Varotsos's intervention and public interpretations of his work were fostered by recent development in the global practices of remembrance in which the distinction between different media and genres of memory (monument, memorial, museum, etc.) "have become blurred" (Arnold-de Simine 2012: 19). In this context much more emphasis is put on emotional investment, instead of on historical knowledge, through the adoption of specific representational strategies of art.[7] In the case of the *Katër,* the object's functions seems to lie in-between an art installation, a monument and a memorial. The interpretative openness and ambiguity of aesthetic intervention (its being an art installation), has not been counterbalanced by an adequate policy of display (its being a memorial and monument), which could have provided historical background information capable of anchoring the artistic form and affective effects in more precise historical content. This has so far prevented the elaboration of a clear narration of the historical events. The name given to the installation/monument "L'approdo. Opera all'umanità migrante" [The landing. Art work for the migrant humanity] also seems to do this work. The name was in fact intended to represent the object, not as a marker of the memory of a peculiar event (the *Katër* sinking and commemorating the death of eighty-one Albanians crossing the sea), but as a tribute that Otranto pays to all migrants who die crossing the sea. The victims' relatives and survivors were disappointed by the eraser of the specificity of their loss, and rejected the invitation to assist the unveiling of the monument (even if they were present at the inauguration). The inauguration occurred without any words from the victims' relatives or survivors.[8] The victims' narratives and even their visual representations were practically absent. There were only a handful of exceptions (for example Cristante 2012: 1), the most important of which was the public Italian channel, *Raitre,* that dedicated a two-minute long report to the issue almost a month after the inauguration (February 26, 2012), in which a victim's mother and pictures of the dead were finally shown.

Overall, I would argue that the morphology of the installation, the name of the memorial as well as its interpretation and reception (as seen in the news reports) function to erase the specificities of the event, particularly the fact that the loss of individual human lives was caused by the Italian government's choice to reject Albanian arrivals through military securitization of the border. In addition, there was a clear suppression of the historical victims of this event, Albanians fleeing violence in their country in 1997 that was substituted by a "typological victim" that the community intended to commemorate: the Migrant Dead at Sea. By eliminating a historically accurate reconstruction of the story of the sinking, the installation and its reception are symptoms of a rewriting of the event, rather than a memorialization, which includes the obvious erasure of the Italian government's responsibility for the sinking and the death of the eighty-one Albanian refugees.

Conclusion

It is almost a truism to say that to remember is a moral duty. Forgetfulness would condemn societies to repeat the tragedies of the past, and would kill the victims a second time, while remembering honors the debt to the dead by hoping to make the promise of "never again" possible. These statements constitute the basis for the moral duty embedded in the age of commemoration and memory after the Holocaust (Williams 2007), in which the process of remembering and forgetting are thought of as processes in opposition. Actually, remembering, both at the individual and collective level, implies a process of filtering the narratives to be remembered. Some aspects of remembered events are marginalized, while others are semantically exalted. Paradoxically, processes of remembering also produce forgetfulness, as shown by the example of the *Katër*. Different discursive devices eliminated eighty-one people's stories, who drowned while attempting to find refuge. In this way, processes of remembering can support and strengthen *topoi* and forms of representation that contribute to framing immigration as a "war at home," where migrants and refugees are positioned "less as victims and more as a threat to national security" (Mannik 2012: 274). What I contend is that memorialization practices can shape narratives by reiterating this "war at home" framing and its correlated forms of representation, quite the opposite of the "never again" mantra. In particular, this can happen when the historical, political, and social cause of shipwrecks in boat migrations are not thoroughly addressed or, as in the case of *Katër,* are even removed from collective awareness. According to Judith Butler, the "war at home" position frames discourse by producing a tacit differentiation "between those populations on whom my life and existence depend, and those populations who represent a direct threat to my life and existence" and those that "are worth defending, valuing, and grieving when they are lost, and those that are not quite lives, not quite valuable, recognizable or, indeed, mournable" (Butler 2009: 42–43). There is indeed a strong nexus between the securitization of migration, media portrayal, and the difficulty of elaborating a memory politics capable of recognizing the "memorability" and "grievability" of the lives lost in migration tragedies at sea, as the translation of *Katër* shows. The possibility of challenging this system of representations is precisely what is at stake in the politics and aesthetics of memorials of shipwrecks in the Mediterranean. Such practices can challenge the current tendency to depict migrants as a collective force that endangers us, therefore allowing the general public to see people who migrate by boats as individual with lives that matter.

Even if, as a whole, the memorialization of the *Katër* in Otranto was not effective in producing such a disruption, there is another example in which the conditions of grievability seem to be reestablished that grew out of the correlated events. Two Albanian artists, Arta Ngucaj and Arben Beqiraj (known with the collective name Scaf Scaf) attended the week-long workshop on the theme of migration in Otranto. Ngucaj and Beqiraj collected the images

Figure 7.4. Victim's relative touching the picture of his beloved on the *Infin che 'l mar fu sovra noi richiuso* by Scaf Scaf (Arta Ngucaj and Arben Beqiraj), Otranto, January 29 2012. Courtesy of Arta Ngucaj and Arben Beqiraj.

of the victims and printed them on panels that they displayed not far from the wreckage on the day of the unveiling with the epigraphic title *Infin che 'l mar fu sovra noi richiuso* ("Until the sea above us closed again"), from Dante's *Inferno,* canto 26.

These pictures show us, in contrast, what was removed in the construction of the public memory of the *Katër* tragedy: the narration of the lives of the victims. These pictures hold the potential to "instantiate grievability" (Butler 2009: 97) by allowing such stories to assume the perceptual and semiotic form of individual lives that matter. This happens through the display of the faces and names of the victims that allow one to individualize them and to activate affective responses. This response is entirely different from the language of fear and threat that support politics of security such as the one that provoked the *Katër* tragedy. The visual disposition clearly draws on a funerary *genre* typical of the southern nations of the Mediterranean. Photographs are shaped in an oval form, which is the same style used on headstones or photo pendants, and the names and dates of birth are listed. The date of the tragedy, which is the same date of death for each person, is repeated on every panel under the pictures. This display singularizes each life and story lost in the shipwrecks, by using both the iconic function of the image and the individualizing function of the name. Therefore, it disrupts the construction of the indistinguishable "horde," "mass," "wave" or "flood" of people, which is typical of the media representation of migration by boat, which in turn the securitization of borders is based on.

Apulia was indeed a workshop for the securitization of the European southern sea boarders in the 1990s. Such policy has recently been questioned and is now under revision. In particular on October 18, 2013, after the so-called Lampedusa tragedy (the sinking not far from Lampedusa island of two boats on October 3 and 11, which claimed the lives of three hundred and sixty-six people), the Italian government decided to use the Navy in an extensive rescue operation, named *Mare Nostrum* (from the Latin, our sea).[9] In doing so the Italian military force has assumed a humanitarian role and appeased its role of defense of "our coasts" from an external "invader." However, processes of mourning, commemoration, and memorialization often are regulated by "war at home" framing, and securitization approaches. The most emblematic example is the contradictory treatment of migrants after the tragedy of Lampedusa. While the government proclaimed national mourning, and public ceremonies were held across the country and attended by State leaders, the survivors were charged by magistrates with clandestine immigration according to the Italian penal law. The migrants were again treated as a threat, instead of as victims.

Nevertheless, a change in the public narration of these events seems evident in recent public debates,[10] fostered also by the highly symbolic ceremony for migrants who die at sea, performed by the Pope in Lampedusa in

July 2013. There have been proposals submitted to the Italian Parliament requiring the establishment of forensic procedures for identifying victims, as well as granting burial to each victim with their name on a headstone. Moreover, different voices in the public sphere have requested that October 3 be dedicated to refugees that die crossing the sea.

The *Katër* memorialization could be a lesson from which to learn for the future. It shares the symbolical process of migrant expulsion with the Lampedusa tragedy national mourning, through the removal of victims' and survivors' life stories from the public space. On one hand, the *Katër* shows how the memory of tragedies at sea can be actually (ab)used in the construction of local and national identities, as well as in accordance to national ideologies. Through the reconstruction of the *Katër*'s story, the Italian people in Salento region did not imagine the lives and deaths of the victims, but rather imagine and celebrate their "own generosity" (Ahmed 2001: 364). On the other hand, the *Katër* and the national mourning for Lampedusa reveal that security discourses strongly affect memory practices, and that memory practices can support securitization approaches, by easing the responsibility for such events. The mere duty of remembrance is not sufficient if memorial practices are not addressed more critically. On the contrary, they can transform "never again" into just "again."

Daniele Salerno is a postdoctoral research fellow at University of Bologna. He is a member of the Centre for the Interdisciplinary Study of Cultural Memory and Traumas (TraMe), and of the Interdisciplinary Research Group on Race and Racisms (InteRGRace-University of Padua). He received his doctorate in Semiotics in 2009, with a dissertation on security and terrorism discourse concerning the 'war on terror'. He was appointed as visiting scholar at the School of Advanced Study at University of London and as honorary research assistant at University College of London.

Notes

I am very grateful to Chiara Gius and Lynda Mannik for their sensible and useful comments and feedbacks on a previous version of this work. I wish to thank also Daniela Crocetti for the editing of the text.
1. Apulia, the region that was the most impacted by arrivals in the 1990s, was in this sense a national and international workshop for Italian and European migration policies, for the securitization of borders, and for the management of population flows (see Ravenda 2011). Such policies are currently regulated at the European level by the Frontex agency, polemically called also Fortress Europe.
2. Some journalists, for example Fabrizio Gatti (2005), succeeded in entering immigrant detention centers by pretending to be irregular migrants. Currently, different projects try to counter this semiotic regime of invisibility; for example, see

Forensic Oceanography 2013; and documentaries as *Mare chiuso* (2012) by Andrea Segre and Stefano Liberti and *Come un uomo sulla terra* (2008) by Andrea Segre, Dagmawi Yimer and Riccardo Biadene (on the function of documentaries in these contexts see Demaria 2012). Moreover, very recently migrants have begun to record their crossing with mobile phones. Such footage is sometimes published online and broadcasted on television.

3. On June 28, 2011, the court of appeal in Lecce condemned the *Sibilla* Italian captain and the Albanian man that was in charge of the *Katër* at the moment of the collision. The sentences were upheld by the supreme court in May 2014. For a reconstruction of the event, the work of Alessandro Leogrande (2011) is pivotal.

4. For example, on November 27, 2011, the front page of one of the most important local newspapers, *Nuovo Quotidiano di Puglia,* was dedicated to new arrivals from the Middle East and North Africa, and to the tragedies that were occurring again in the Mediterranean. On page 5 the stories of these new dramatic arrivals are linked to tragedies of the past. The story of the *Katër* is remembered as one of "the biggest tragedies in Salento." The article is titled, "In '97 in Otranto, the massacre of the newborns" (Iaia 2011: 5). The journalist draws again on biblical language, after the use of the expression "Good Friday massacre." The *Katër*'s story was evoked several times on the local and national newspapers in the context of new migrations by boat. The phase provoked by post–Arab Spring conflicts in North Africa and the Middle East was marked by many shipwrecks. The *Katër*'s story is used as term of comparison for narrating the new tragedies at sea with a colligation of different historic events and periods (Wagner-Pacifici 2010: 1372–74). In this context, the press works as an "easily accessible storehouse of memory" (Zelizer and Tenenboim-Weinblatt 2013: 7), by retrieving and recategorizing information and events under a same narrative.

5. Here I connect notions of *imprint, trace,* and *narrative* drawing on the indexical theory developed by Umberto Eco (1976), and very recently reworked by Patrizia Violi (2012) for analyzing trauma sites. They argue that the physical imprints of past events require a double semiotic process of interpretation. In our case, first, we recognize that a gash on a boat indicates that it was hit by something (trace recognition); second, we reconstruct what happened (narrative content). A narrative and an adequate policy of display is necessary to link the material remains to the narration of their past when memorial practices involve objects that witness the event.

6. Italians call the rickety boats used by migrants *carrette del mare,* literally sea carts, but meant to be understood as old unsafe boats or clunkers.

7. This tension is epitomized, for example in Holocaust commemorative sites in Berlin and in general in memory museums (Arnold-de Simine 2012). The Holocaust Manhmal, the memorial to murdered Jews of Europe in the centers of Berlin, is composed of 2,711 stelas and fosters an aesthetic, affective, and corporeal approach open to multiple uses and interpretations. In particular, it also provokes very controversial behaviors for a memorial dedicated to 6 million dead such as entertainment, play, and tourism. Similarly, the Libeskind's Jewish Museum adopts representational strategies that emphasize an emotional impact through the architectonic space. However, in both cases the aesthetics is "complemented by more didactically-oriented documentation centres" and "counter-balanced by

historical background information" (Arnold-de Simine 2012: 20) that make the visitor aware both of the constructedness of memory (the forms of representation of the event) and of history (what is represented).
8. This aspect was ignored by the Italian press and reported only on two news Web sites, *Stranieri in Italia* and *L'albanese d'Italia* (Biçoku 2012), Web sites for foreigners and migrants living in Italy.
9. According to the Italian navy official and as confirmed by UNHCR (2014), from January to August 2014 124,000 people tried to cross the Mediterranean, of which 108,000 landed in Italy. In that period, it is estimated that 1,900 perished in the attempt. The search and rescue *Mare Nostrum* operation ended on October 31, 2014. It was superseded by the EU operation *Triton* (conducted by the EU Agency for the external borders, FRONTEX).
10. In Italy, between 2013 and 2014 media coverage of landings and rescue operations changed. Migrants were more visible, clearly shown, and their life stories were narrated more often. This reflected the attempt of Italian authorities to spread a (neo)humanitarian image of the military force in the management of population flows. But it was also the result of a outburst of protests in immigration detention centers, where some migrants sewed their lips shut to represent the condition of silence to which they were subjected. In 2015, the image of the three-year-old boy, Alan Kurdi, altered opinions in Italian media coverage from what was previously described as the "refugee crisis" to a more humanitarian view.

Bibliography

Agamben, Giorgio. 1998. *Homo Sacer. Sovereign Power and Bare Life*. Stanford, CA: Stanford University Press.
Ahmed, Sarah. 2001. "The Organization of Hate." *Law and Critique* 12, no. 3: 345–65.
Anonymous. 2011a. "Otranto un dolore da ricordare." *Famiglia Cristiana*, August 7. http://www.famigliacristiana.it/articolo/otranto-una-tragedia-da-non-dimentica re_070811112942.aspx.
——. 2011b. "In ricordo della *Katër i Radës*." *Il Paese Nuovo*, December 30.
——. 2012. "Immigrazione: Otranto, motovedetta albanese diventa monumento." *Ansamed*, January 27. http://www.ansa.it/ansamed/it/notizie/stati/albania/2012/01/27/visualizza_new.html_70180214.html.
Arnold-de Simine, Silke. 2012. "Memory Museum and Museum Text. Intermediality in Daniel Libeskind's Jewish Museum and W. G. Sebald's *Austerlitz.*" *Theory, Culture & Society* 29, no. 1 (January): 14–35.
Benveniste, Émile. 1973. *Indo-European Language and Society*. London: Faber & Faber.
Biçoku, Keti. 2012. "L'ultimo approdo della Katër i Radës, monumento all'umanità migrante." *Stranieri in Italia*, January 30. http://www.stranieriinitalia.it/nuovi_cit tadini-l_ultimo_approdo_della_kater_i_rades_monumento_all_umanita_mig rante_14524.html.
Bleiker, Roland, David Campbell, Emma Hutchinson, and Xzarina Nicholson. 2013. "The Visual Dehumanisation of Refugees." *Australian Journal of Political Science* 48, no. 4 (December): 398–416.

Buffa, Mario. 2012. "Relazione per l'inaugurazione dell'anno giudiziario 2012." Lecce: Corte di Appello di Lecce.
Butler, Judith. 2009. *Frames of War. When Is Life Grievable.* London–New York: Verso.
Campbell, David. 1998. *Writing Security: United States Foreign Policy and the Politics of Identity.* Minneapolis: Minnesota University Press.
Colluto, Tiziana. 2012. "Rivive la nave '*Katër i Radës*,' da relitto di una tragedia a opera all'umanità migrante." *Il Fatto quotidiano,* January 29. http://www.ilfatto quotidiano.it/2012/01/29/rivive-nave-kater-rades-relitto-tragedia-opera-alluman ita-migrante/187484/.
Comberiati, Daniele. 2013. "Modalità di rappresentazione del colonialismo italiano in Albania." *Incontri. Rivista europea di studi italiani* 28, no. 1 (January): 25–33.
Connerton, Paul. 2009. *How Modernity Forgets.* Cambridge: Cambridge University Press.
Cristante, Stefano. 2012. "Dalla tragedia al monumento." *Nuovo Quotidiano di Puglia,* February 10.
Demaria, Cristina. 2012. *Il trauma, l'archivio, il testimone. La semiotica, il documentario e la rappresentazione del reale.* Bologna: Bononia University Press.
Derrida, Jacques. 2000. "Hostipitality." *Angelaki: Journal of the Theoretical Humanities* 5, no. 3 (June): 3–18.
Duncan, Derek. 2008. "Italy's Postcolonial Cinema and Its Histories of Representation." *Italian Studies* 65, no. 2 (July): 195–211.
Eco, Umberto. 1976. *A Theory of Semiotics.* Bloomington: Indiana University Press.
———. 2014. *From the Tree to the Labyrinth.* Cambridge, MA, and London: Harvard University Press.
Forensic Oceanography. 2013. "Addendum to the Report on the Left-to-Die Boat." International Federation for Human Rights. http://www.forensic-architecture.org/forensic-oceanography-addendum-report-left-die-boat/.
Gariglio, Luigi, Andrea Pogliano, and Riccardo Zanini (eds.). 2010. *Facce da straniero. 30 anni di fotografia e giornalismo sull'immigrazione in Italia.* Milan: Mondadori.
Gatti, Fabrizio. 2005. "Io clandestino a Lampedusa." *L'Espresso,* October 7. http://espr esso.repubblica.it/palazzo/2005/10/07/news/io-clandestino-a-lampedusa-1.594.
Huysmans, Jef. 2006. *The Politics of Insecurity. Fear, Migration and Asylum in the EU.* London: Routledge.
Iaia, Massimiliano. 2011. "Nel '97 a Otranto la strage dei neonati." *Nuovo Quotidiano di Puglia,* November 27.
Leogrande, Alessandro. 2011. *Il naufragio. Morte nel Mediterraneo.* Milan: Feltrinelli.
Longo, Barbara. 2011. "La nave di tutti i migranti." *Nuovo Quotidiano di Puglia,* December 10.
Lotman, Youri. 2005. "On the Semiosphere." *Sign Systems Studies* 33, no. 1 (January): 205–29.
Lotman, Youri, and Boris Uspensky. 1978. "On the Semiotic Mechanism of Culture." *New Literary History* 9, no. 2 (Spring): 211–32.
Mannik, Lynda. 2012. "Public and Private Photographs of Refugees: The Problem of Representation." *Visual Studies* 27, no. 3 (October): 262–76.
Paiano, Ennio. 2011. "Da Valona a Otranto. L'esodo travolse la città." *Nuovo Quotidiano di Puglia,* March 11.

Pittau, Franco, and Rando Devole. 2008. "Ondate migratorie degli albanesi e atteggiamenti della popolazione." In *Gli albanesi in Italia. Conseguenze economiche e sociali dell'immigrazione,* edited by Rando Devole, Franco Pittau, Antonio Ricci, and Giuliana Urso. Rome: Idos.

Puricella, Anna. 2011. "Otranto ricorda il grande esodo." *La Repubblica Bari,* November 18.

Ravenda, Andrea. 2011. *Alì fuori dalla legge: migrazione, biopolitica e stato di eccezione in Italia.* Verona: Ombre corte.

United Nations High Commissioner for Refugees (UNHCR). 2014. "Three Boat Tragedies in Five Days on the Mediterranean–Scores Feared Dead." http://www.unhcr.org/cgi-bin/texis/vtx/search?page=search&docid=53fc5e491c3&query=mare nostrum.

Varotsos, Costas. 2012. "La nave della tragedia diventa un monumento." *La Repubblica Bari,* January 29. http://bari.repubblica.it/cronaca/2012/01/29/news/kater-28979083/.

Violi, Patrizia. 2012. "Trauma Site Museums and Politics of Memory: Tuol Sleng, Villa Grimaldi and the Bologna Ustica Museum." *Theory, Culture & Society* 29, no. 1 (January): 36–75.

Wagner-Pacifici, Robin. 2010. "Theorizing the Restlessness of Events." *American Journal of Sociology* 115, no. 5 (March): 1351–86.

Williams, Paul. 2007. *Memorial Museums. The Global Rush to Commemorate Atrocities.* Oxford, UK and New York: Berg.

Zelizer, Barbie, and Keren Tenenboim-Weinblat. 2013. "Journalism's Memory Work." In *Journalism and Memory,* edited by Barbie Zelizer and Keren Tenenboim-Weinblat. London: Palgrave Macmillan.

8

"Where Are Our Sons?"

Tunisian Families and the Repoliticization of Deadly Migration across the Mediterranean Sea

Federico Oliveri

They are gone, far away, where it's dangerous.
They are gone, the sea below, the sky and the rain above them.
They are gone, where the wave decided they should go.
Where the death is present and news gets lost.
They are gone, as they were still young.
They are gone, on a boat in the sea.
They are gone, where the lives end.
They are gone, where the fishes eat.
They are gone, where the mothers cry.
   Balti-Samir Loussif, *Mchaou*, Tunisian pop-rap song, 2010.

So far migrant deaths in the Mediterranean Sea have not produced any real change in the dominant paradigm of immigration controls. The management of the European Union's (EU's) maritime border continues to oscillate between securitarian and humanitarian approaches: authorities select the people to be admitted or rejected through flexible legal rules, legitimized by recurrent "states of emergency" reacting to an almost enduring "migrant crisis." European public opinion goes monotonously in a circle, moving from indifference to daily updates of the death toll, to empathy for the dramatic shipwrecks that periodically occur. Yet, hostility against "illegal migrants," represented as "invaders" or as a "burden" on public budgets, has spread extensively, especially during the economic crisis. At the same time, causal links between border controls, unauthorized migrations by boat, and deaths at sea have been systematically repressed in the European debate. Political responsibilities for missing people thus remains generally hidden, are given to "smugglers" or even to migrants themselves, according to a victim-blaming frame. Within this context, no alternative policies seem to be available, except the reinforcement of controls.

There are multiple reasons for this worrying impasse. In this chapter, I will stress the key role played by the subtle, yet powerful, mechanisms of depoliticization that affect migration, disappearance, and death at the Euro-Mediterranean border. These mechanisms work on many levels: They deprive migrants of their identity and autonomous subjectivity, and even of their humanity. They represent deaths at the maritime border as almost natural accidents. They present border technologies of control and selection as neutral tools of security risk management. And, they normalize structural inequality in life opportunities and mobility that detrimentally affects non-European people. Depoliticization inhibits solidarity with the migrants and their families, and protects the dominant migration and border policies from being substantially questioned, especially in terms of their consistency with human rights and democratic principles. A rather paradoxical situation emerges, in which hyperemotional debates on "human tsunami" or "biblical exodus" coexist with the lack of any truly political debate on the roots, the consequences, and the remedies of recurrent "migrant-deaths crises."

The focus of my analysis will be on some emergent actors and strategies in reaction to mass deaths at the Euro-Mediterranean border in the aftermath of the Tunisian Revolution. Since the summer of 2011, mothers, fathers, uncles, sisters, and brothers of about five hundred Tunisian migrants who disappeared during the journey to Italy are still demanding the truth about what happened to their relatives after they left the country by boat between September 2010 and September 2012. Many families of missing migrants decided to self-organize and are now gathered in an association called "La terre pour tous," or "The Earth for everyone." This mobilization offers a significant case study for the repoliticization of deadly migrations by boat across the Mediterranean.

In this chapter I will show how the families of missing Tunisian migrants challenged the dominant Euro-Mediterranean migration regime and its systematic depoliticization from the point of view of the people concerned. I assume that the critical potential of this perspective is necessarily different, and under certain aspects more powerful, than that of militant researchers, and of human rights and no-border activists. My key argument is that a durable change in European public opinion and immigration politics can take place only if the people who have personally experienced, or might experience in the future, the deadly consequences of crossing the Euro-Mediterranean border become politically active—that is, autonomously visible, audible, and engaged in the public sphere. This may allow them to translate their private pain and grievances into generalizable claims for human rights and democratic accountability. This double-sided process, including the political subjectivization of usually marginalized people and the repoliticization of previously ignored issues raised by them, may finally generate new solidarity between migrants, their families, and European citizens in the host nations.

The campaign "From one shore to another: lives which matter" was launched by Tunisian families with the fundamental support of the Italian feminist collective "2511" (*leventicinqueundici*).[1] This campaign perfectly embodies the two sides of the repoliticization process and provides, therefore, an ideal case study. Moreover, it is the first mobilization of this kind to be developed both in the country of origin and the country of destination of the missing migrants. This chapter is divided into three parts. In the first part, I will explain why images and narratives of death at the border are not sufficient per se to provoke indignation and political change: I argue that only direct encounters with those whom I call "politicized suffering others," such as the self-organized families of missing Tunisians, may help to overcome indifference toward or even hostility against the thousands of migrants who have died since the end of 1990s in the Mediterranean Sea. In the second part, I will conceptualize the mobilization as a process of "political subjectivization" (Rancière 2004: 304) of the families involved and, indirectly, of their missing relatives on behalf of which they were acting and speaking (Edkins 2011: 488). In the third part, I will analyze how discourses and practices of Tunisian families repoliticize deaths and unauthorized migrations by boat across the Euro-Mediterranean border. Here, I will focus on four controversial topics raised with special intensity during the campaign: the identity of missing people and their motivations to migrate, the causes and responsibilities of their death or disappearance, border technologies and information applied to migration by boat, and mobility inequality dividing people on the two shores of the Mediterranean.

My analytical frame largely draws on contemporary critical studies on citizenship, borders, and migrations, which I let freely interact and resonate with the voices and acts of Tunisian families. This approach is the result of a specific methodological preference for a "militant investigation" that "engages with the power asymmetries that make migrants into subjects of migration knowledge production" (De Genova, Mezzadra, and Pickles 2014: 10). This kind of research aims not to substitute the perspective of "the subaltern" with that of the researcher (Oliveri 2014), but instead to focus on "the identification or creation of spaces of engagement and proximity. Sites of shared struggle and precarity" between the researchers and "the researched" (De Genova, Mezzadra, and Pickles 2014: 10).

Against this background, my analysis relies on the intersection of multiple sources: (1) public petitions, press releases, videos, banners, and other documents produced by the families of missing Tunisians and by their supporters; (2) interviews I conducted in the summer of 2014 with a relative of a disappeared migrant who coordinates the newly established association of the families, and with a Tunisian human rights activist; (3) news and reportages published by Tunisian, Italian, and French newspapers, often including interviews with relatives of missing migrants or with survivors; and (4) the few official statistics and documents available on Tunisian migrants who disappeared between 2011 and 2012.

The documents produced by the families themselves, or those with the families as protagonists, are accessible on the Web site Storie Migranti,[2] on the blog of the "2511" collective, on the blog *Fortress Europe*[3] and on some dedicated Facebook pages.[4] Articles concerning the campaign and the story of the disappeared Tunisian migrants have been published by mainstream French and Italian newspapers, such as *Libération, la Repubblica,* and *Il Corriere della Sera*; by Tunisian national and local newspapers; and by some French and Tunisian specialized collectives of independent journalists[5]. In addition, articles are accessible on the Web. The most detailed official information available on the case of missing Tunisian migrants has been produced so far by the Italian government, as a result of inquiries by two members of parliament (MPs).[6]

Questioning Indifference for Migrant Deaths at the Euro-Mediterranean Border

Impressive Yet Underestimated Data

In the neoliberal globalization, borders are far from being obsolete. On the contrary, they proliferate and deeply shape human mobilities, and are continuously reshaped by migrants and their autonomous struggles (Mezzadra and Neilson 2013: 1–25). States and supranational institutions try to manage demands for free movement and better life opportunities within the dominant logics of labor markets and public security. While formally claiming to respect human dignity and fundamental rights, these procedures of selecting and stratifying the world population produce dangerous and often lethal borders, especially for the most vulnerable people, such as unauthorized migrants, asylum seekers, women, and children.[7]

Available unofficial data reveal that, during the past two decades, the "external borders" of the EU have become the deadliest frontier in the world.[8] Reported fatalities document not only an increase in the absolute number, but also an increase of the mortality rate—that is, a higher percentage of unauthorized migrants who have disappeared. These data are still underestimated, as they do not include those who are simply missing—for example when no shipwreck has been attested nor bodies found. Since 2000 more than thirty thousand people have died or disappeared trying to reach Europe according to the Migrants' Files, which is the most comprehensive database on migrant fatalities ever assembled by collecting and crosschecking data from news, official archives, and reports from nongovernmental organizations (NGO).[9] It states also that at least thirteen thousand migrants have died or disappeared since 2000 while crossing the central Mediterranean, with the peaks of 1,674 people during 2011, 2,447 people during 2014, and 2,901 during 2015.[10] These numbers attest to the extreme dangers of this specific route.

There are many reasons explaining these trends. In the past few years, the number of people trying to enter Europe without authorization via the central Mediterranean has generally risen because of the increasing controls on other maritime routes and a stronger militarization at land borders. This has often led to migrants choosing longer and more dangerous routes, which predictably corresponds to higher death rates. Moreover, since 2011 the overall number of asylum seekers has risen because of recurrent political instabilities in North Africa and the Middle East, namely in Syria, and more specifically after the end of the Ghaddafi regime in Libya. Detected unauthorized arrivals on this route amounted to 4,500 migrants in 2010. They increased to over 64,300 in 2011, in connection with the Tunisian Revolution and the NATO war in Libya: in particular, of the migrants arrived in 2011, 27,982 were Tunisians (Frontex 2012: 14). Then, arrivals dropped to 15,900 people in 2012, in correspondence with the consolidation of the new regimes in North Africa, rising again in 2013 and 2014 to 40 304 and 170,000 people respectively (Frontex 2014, 2015), in connection with escalating civil war in Syria and political unrests in Libya. As for 2015, migrant maritime arrivals in Europe reached the unprecedented peak of 1,000,064.[11]

Widening Solidarity through Political Subjectivization

Daily additions to the numbers of missing people, those who drowned in the Mediterranean, are simply too monotonous to enter into the mainstream news. Similarly, no one cares about the boats used by migrants to cross the sea, abandoned and amassed in the ever-growing ships' graveyard on Lampedusa (see Figure 8.1), which is periodically destroyed.

Only when dramatic shipwrecks occur do headlines and photos make front-page news reports and stimulate public authorities to take action. This happened after the sinking of a boat near Lampedusa,[12] on October 3, 2013, when 366 migrants who had departed from Libya died, 20 went missing, and 155 survived; and after the deadliest shipwreck in the Mediterranean Sea after World War II on April 19, 2015, when about 900 people drowned and only 28 survived.

Social indifference or even intolerance concerning migrant deaths at the European borders raises two kinds of issue. The first issue concerns the pain

Figure 8.1. Cemetery of migrant boats in Lampedusa. Photographer: Sara Prestianni, September 3 2011. Courtesy of Sara Prestianni.

of those who migrate by boat, despite being made highly visible through images of overcrowded ships or dead bodies on the shores, and despite being made accessible through many accounts of highly dangerous migrations, continues to receive little recognition in European public opinion. The second issue concerns challenges to this lack of responsiveness and changes to current migration policies so that unauthorized migrants may fully and effectively access human rights.[13]

Boundaries of empathy and responsibility, especially in relation to distant suffering people, have always puzzled philosophers, social scientists, and artists (Ginzburg 1994: 49–50) in search of strategies for widening the scope of human solidarity—that is, to increase "our sensitivity to the particular details of the pain and humiliation of other, unfamiliar sorts of people" (Rorty 1989: xvi). The contemporary rise of a global information and communication society may have reduced spatial and temporal distances. Nevertheless, moral distances remain effective and have even increased, along with widespreading borders and growing global inequalities.

We should be aware that repeated exposure to images and stories of pain is not enough to stimulate identification with others, feed a sense of injustice, and promote political change. On one side, the dominant culture of spectatorship tends to blur the divide between reality and fiction, and to neutralize the moral force of photographs and visions of atrocities (Sontag 2003: 105), where citizens often remain cruel voyeurs instead of becoming active and sensitive participants. On the other side, contemporary global wars seem to have almost normalized the killing of innocent people as "collateral damages" (Zolo 2010: 34). Moreover, scenes of the hardships of others may even irritate, produce insecurity, and infuse the desire to withhold compassion. According to Zygmund Bauman, this may have to do with the current generalized insecurity as an effect of neoliberal globalization: "We are each individually anxious about the ease with which we ourselves could become *collateral casualties* and be turned into *waste*, and immigrants embody—visibly, tangibly, in the flesh—the inarticulate yet hurtful and painful presentiment of their own *disposability*. It is this notion of disposability that deepens our sense of *vulnerability* and *fear,* as we do not want to see our own faces amongst those relegated to the trash heap" (Bauman 2004: 56; emphasis added). In the end, the problem is not that we see too few or too many suffering bodies on TV, on the Web, or in newspapers, but that "[w]e do see too many *nameless* bodies, too many bodies incapable of *returning the gaze* that we direct at them, too many bodies that are an *object of speech* without themselves having a chance to speak.... The *visual* [becomes] the lot of multitudes and the *verbal* the privilege of the few" (Rancière 2009: 96, emphasis added). If this is true, images and narratives of the pain suffered by other people may become a vehicle for solidarity and political change (Clohesy 2013: 58–60) only if they are politically framed through direct encounters and interactions with politicized suffering others. A sense of injustice cannot develop toward an idealized Other, imagined as powerless and as a passive victim in need of our help, nor toward Others who are represented as the enemy, or as a threat to our lives and properties, but toward those concrete Others who struggle to speak and act autonomously, and to be treated as our equals. Through unexpected acts of "political subjectivization" (Rancière 2004: 304), previously silenced people ask disturbing questions and raise unexpected claims that modify the existing boundaries of the political. By rejecting the subaltern and fixed place assigned to them, emerging political subjectivities problematize the circumstances, the causes, and the implications of their sorrow as a matter of justice.

Against this theoretical background, the mobilization of Tunisian families concerning the truth about the fate of their missing relatives can be addressed as a case study on repoliticizing border deaths and migration by boat. In the case of migrant deaths, there are only two actors who can play the role of politicized suffering others, producing narratives and performances that can break the monotony of daily updates of losses through their political subjectivization and the politicization of their experiences. These two actors are the survivors and the relatives of missing people.

In the current circumstances, there is limited room for survivors to collectively organize, take the public scene, and address the issue of lethal borders. They are affected by more-urgent problems, such as being without documents and regular jobs, incarcerated, marginalized, exploited, or threatened by expulsion, even if migrant communities already established in Europe may eventually support them.

As I will show below, the 2011 Tunisian Revolution provided instead a favorable context for the families of missing migrants to become political subjects (Sossi 2013: 154–56) and let the experience of their relatives, and thus of all those who cross the Mediterranean by boat, acquire a political status. On the one side, by asking the truth about what happened to their sons, Tunisian families provoked fundamental questions about who or what can be political: their discourses and conducts challenged the supposed impossibility of second-class citizens, especially women, to act and speak autonomously, while fearlessly and noisily defeating the silence of public authorities. On the other side, by claiming the right to grieve their losses, those families raised key political issues on "whose lives are considered valuable, whose lives are mourned, and whose lives are considered ungrievable" (Butler 2009: 38).

How Families of Missing Tunisians Became Political Subjects

The Campaign

The campaign "From one shore to another: lives which matter." was launched in the summer of 2011 by the families of about 250 young people who left Tunisia on five different boats, respectively on March 14, 29, and 30, and May 5, 2011. The support provided by Federica Sossi and Martina Tazzioli, two militant researchers and members of the "2511" Italian feminist collective, was crucial at the beginning of the mobilization as they encouraged the mothers to build an informal network and to give a collective meaning to their individual sorrow. By the end of 2012, relatives of other missing migrants had joined their campaign: their sons and brothers had left by boat on September 10, 2010, April 28, 2012, and September 21, 2012. Except for the shipwreck on September 6, 2012, none of the shipwrecks have been officially documented. In the case of this uniquely reported incident, with fifty-six survivors and seventy-nine disappeared people, no official truth has been established. In all cases, no official information was provided directly to the families by Tunisian authorities: precise details of the boats and the dates when migrants left Tunisia were collected by the families themselves through autonomous inquires.

Lacking definitive and reliable proof concerning what really happened during and after the sea journey, many families recognized, or believed that they had recognized, their sons in some of the videos shown by Italian and French newscasts, and in some Italian newspapers, reporting on disembarkations of undocumented migrants at Lampedusa or on internments in immigration camps. A few relatives received SMS or calls from the migrants during the journey, announcing that they had been rescued or that Italian shores were close. This is why many families strongly believed that their sons were still alive, eventually detained in some administrative center for undocumented migrants or in some prison, registered under fake names and identities. This enduring hope may also explain why the recurring question addressed by the mothers to Tunisian and Italian authorities is, "Where are our sons?"

Both governments, especially the Tunisian government, were accused by the families of not really investigating disappearances and of giving incomplete or even contradictory information. Between 2011 and 2014, dozens of Tunisian relatives organized marches and sit-ins almost monthly in Tunis, especially in front of the Ministry of Social Affairs, which is in charge of immigration issues, and in front of the Italian embassy. They met with representatives of both governments, visited a few Italian immigration detention centers, published two open petitions, and created videos depicting themselves during their sit-ins and press conferences. The videos clearly expressed their claims and desires to public authorities. Through these initiatives, they did not just ask for generic support: they rather suggested specific strategies for investigations, such as fingerprint exchanges between Italian and Tunisian institutions (Tunisian Families 2011).

On December 17, 2011, a year after the self-immolation by fire of Mohammed Bouazizi, which strongly contributed to the start of the Tunisian Revolution, two sit-ins were organized in Milan and Parma. These initiatives were promoted by the collective "2511" and by a Tunisian NGO based in Italy called Giuseppe Verdi, in solidarity with the families of the missing migrants, who were initially unable to get visas and search for their relatives in Italy. The following day, the International Migrants Day, families of disappeared Tunisians gathered in the Place des Droits de l'Homme in Tunis city center in order to inform other citizens about the campaign and to get further public support.

Between the end of January and April 2012, a delegation of families traveled throughout Italy, visiting many immigration detention centers, meeting authorities, and stimulating solidarity. Arci and Asgi, two Italian NGOs with a strong focus on migrant human rights, made a judicial complaint to the attorney of Rome for the official opening of a file on the disappeared Tunisians. Due to a lack of response from the authorities, three mothers tried to kill themselves in Tunisia. Among them, Jannette Rhimi set fire to herself on April 12, 2012, and suffered serious burns (Smith 2012). This act of extreme protest should be understood within the Tunisian context, in which self-immolation by fire has been spreading since the first case of Mohammed Bouazizi. It is considered a last resort for citizens who believe they have no other alternative in terms of being heard by public authorities, including the formally democratic mechanisms established after the 2011 Revolution (Rivera 2012: 62).

On June 5, 2012, about forty mothers of missing migrants, joined by a few men, organized a large sit-in in front of the Italian embassy in Tunis. They blocked the street while holding up photographic portraits of their sons, on crumpled paper or framed in gold, as they did in all their public demonstrations. Determined to receive attention and clear answers to their demand for the truth, the mothers fearlessly pointed the pictures toward the embassy that was protected by the police who erected a roll of barbed wire around its entrance. Under the sympathetic look of the neighbors, who watched the scene from their balconies, a sort of nonviolent, yet angry siege, of the palace took place with some mothers wearing the Tunisian flag (see Figure 8.2), and oth-

Figure 8.2. Mother of a missing migrant wearing the Tunisian flag during a sit-in at the Italian embassy in Tunis. Photographer: Sara Prestianni. June 4 2012. Courtesy of Sara Prestianni.

ers waving banners. All were demanding rights for migrants (Fouteau 2012). Similar scenes have become rather usual in Tunis since then, continuing to stimulate solidarity and awareness in the rest of the population.

On September 10, 2012, three days after a shipwreck near the Italian island of Lampione, the families of twelve disappeared migrants organized a general strike in El Fahs, a village sixty kilometers south of Tunis. Economic activities were blocked, as was the principal road of the town, and the local police offices were burned down in protest against the silence and the misinformation of the authorities. At first, neither national nor local governments communicated any news to the families about the incident. Later, local authorities published an incorrect list of those who survived (Mourad 2012). The families of El Fahs were among the protagonists of two large sit-ins at the Italian embassy in Tunis, on January 11, 2013 and on September 6, 2013, a year after the shipwreck. In February 2013, after two years of "vague answers, formalistic commitments, and no clarity on whether the fingerprint exchange has indeed been performed" (Tunisian Families 2013), the families addressed a second petition asking the European Union to form a special inquiry commission, with the participation of Italian and Tunisian government representatives and one family representative, for each missing boat. In particular, the families wanted to investigate the fingerprints and information in European databases, and to get access to further data concerning "the localization of the boats at the moment when we received phone calls from our sons and daughters while they were traveling and all the information that migration control instruments have gathered in the days indicated" (Tunisian Families 2013). They also asked to compare news videos with the pictures of their sons, and to have access to news images in TV archives of the days preceding and following the departure of their relatives. Finally, they asked for the right to recover the bodies of those who died in the shipwrecks.

In July 2013 the mothers asked the mayor of Lampedusa, Giusi Nicolini, to support these claims. The mayor answered and called all concerned authorities to

> take this sorrow seriously
> ... As the mayoress of Lampedusa, the island which saves the life of many people forced to undertake these "journeys of hope," or that has mercy upon the corpses returned by the sea, *I feel the duty to consider your demand for truth*; and to give you my small aid, as small as my island and my voice. You are great, like your sorrow, your perseverance, your strength to refuse silence and resignation. ... I hope I will be able to stand by you, and be your *sister* on your way (Nicolini 2013; emphasis added).

As this answer clearly shows that families of missing Tunisian migrants have become recognized and legitimate political subjects in the debate on migrations in the Euro-Mediterranean area. This public recognition depends on their human qualities, such as their courage, determination, and perseverance, but is also intimately related to the political and innovative nature of their mobilization.

A Double Rupture in the Given Political Script

The campaign launched by the families of missing Tunisian migrants is a truly political campaign: it has produced, at the same time, the political subjectivization of the people involved and the politicization of the issues raised by them. This is made clear if we consider politics not as something already given and regulated, but as the result of continuous conflict about who, in a particular time and space, is qualified to say and to do what, and why. Through their self-organized initiatives and autonomous discourses, the families of missing Tunisian migrants produced significant ruptures and innovations in the given political script. Of course, it is not the first time that Tunisian (and Moroccan) families of missing migrants have gone in search of their relatives, or that committees of parents have asked the government to provide news about their children.[14] The difference between those initiatives and the ongoing mobilization is that the latter enacted a double rupture in the current political space. The first rupture concerned the end of impotent isolation that has so far affected the relatives of missing migrants; through their mobilization, the families succeeded in translating a private issue, the sorrow for the disappearance of their relatives, into a public issue calling all the authorities concerned, including the European ones, to recognize their political responsibilities. The second rupture concerned the Euro-Mediterranean border that aims to prevent unwanted migrations from Africa. During their campaign, the families succeeded in conducting their search of the disappeared relatives directly in Europe, physically and symbolically reconnecting the two shores of the Mediterranean.

The double political rupture enacted by the families of missing migrants is strictly related to the new context produced by the Tunisian Revolution. On one hand, the experience of the collective mobilizations and resistance against police and military, which produced the fall of Ben Ali's regime in January 2011, let many people stop complaining and gathering "as small groups around kitchen tables, as has gone on for decades, but occupy the streets and the squares" (Balaton-Chrimes 2011), enacting instead new forms of activist citizenship and grassroots self-organization. On the other hand, under the previous authoritarian regime it would have been impossible to even raise the issue of irregular migration, and to travel to Europe and tell the story of disappeared Tunisian migrants, as this would have discredited the international image of the country in the government's eyes (Soltani 2014, interview). As a result, maybe for the first time in the history of contemporary Tunisia unauthorized migrations and migration policies are not taboo any more (Boukadida 2014, interview).

How Families of Missing Tunisians Repoliticized Border Deaths

For years migration by boat and migrant deaths at the Euro-Mediterranean border have been systematically depoliticized, as attested indirectly by the lack of solidarity toward the victims and the general impasse in changing the paradigm of immigration control despite its evident failure. While primarily interested in knowing the truth about their relatives, families of missing Tunisians contested de facto many mechanisms of depoliticization, such as the deindividualization and the irregularization of migrants, the naturalization of their death, the neutralization of border technologies, and the normalization of inequality between people on the two shores of the sea.

Repoliticizing Identity against Deindividualization and Irregularization

There is very little information available about the majority of those who die in the Mediterranean, except in general terms such as age and sex and, in certain cases, the country of origin or departure. More importantly, we do not know their names, we cannot imagine their faces, or grasp their personal reasons for leaving. Loss of identity is the seemingly natural consequence of collective deaths or disappearances during migration by boat: the large majority of the bodies found floating in the sea or on the Mediterranean shores after a shipwreck have no personal documents, will not be identified by local authorities, and therefore end up in unnamed, numerated, or collective burials. Once deprived of their identities, people are deindividualized and dehumanized and this inhibits empathy and responsibility for them, which contributes to the depoliticization of their deaths.

These trends were partially stopped by the families of missing Tunisians, who spelled the names of their sons, showed their faces through identification cards, and pictures carried in public protests (see Figure 8.3) and official meetings. They hoped someone might recognize the face of their relatives and confirm that they were alive in Europe or elsewhere. Giving their assumed dead family members back their names and faces is a first step toward the repoliticization of the issue. This allows the relatives of migrants to claim fundamental rights, concerning both the missing people and themselves, such as the rights to be identified (Grant 2011), to be properly buried, and to have their lives and deaths commemorated (Rygiel 2014: 65).

The key role of Tunisian families was recognized by the mayor of Lampedusa: "Without the struggle of these women, [it would happen that] those men who disappeared in the void would have *never existed for us*. We must answer these women, since, thanks to them, these men have never ceased to exist" (Nicolini 2013; emphasis added). The demand to count migrant deaths as people rather than as numbers, or as the object of governmental practices, can disrupt the dominant biopolitical regime, and help to overcome the emotional barriers that protect European consciousness from feeling compassion and enforcing active solidarity. The right to be counted among humans includes not only those who died, but also those who live on the other shore of the Mediterranean Sea and who eventually plan to travel to Europe.

Identity of missing Tunisians was repoliticized by their families and in regard to the legitimacy of their decision to exit the country without authorization, and become *harraga* (Arabic for those who burn the borders) in order to be free to move. All those who left were male and generally aged between eighteen and twenty-eight, nevertheless there were also many adolescents among them. The choice to exit after the Revolution, profiting from the lack of border controls, disclosed once again the authoritarian nature of the previous regime with whom the European states have been cooperating for years in an effort to stop migrations through the "irregularization" of human mobility. Young Tunisian migrants enacted their right to choose where to live, in continuity with the spirit of the Revolution in which they actively participated: they reinterpreted freedom as the freedom of movement, and dignity as the possibility to shape their lives according to their aspirations.

Figure 8.3. Mothers of missing migrants during a sit-in at the Italian embassy in Tunis. Photographer: Jana Favata, January 11 2013. Courtesy of Jana Favata.

This was true for the many who came from the poorest neighborhoods of Tunis or from some depressed towns in the center south of the country, but also for the few who were highly educated and were looking for jobs equated to their skills (Dhaouadi 2012).

Repoliticizing Deaths at the Border against Naturalization

While media mention shipwrecks, they tend to present migrant deaths as tragic fatalities and accidents, reinforcing security and humanitarian discourses that suggest that lethal migration by boat may only be stopped by more-efficient border controls, and systems of search and rescue. This naturalization of deaths at the border includes an emphasis on sea conditions, on the bad condition of vessels, on the criminality and unscrupulousness of *passeurs*,[15] or on the migrants themselves who are depicted as victims of misery in search of an imaginary Europe, the land of well-being, or represented as childishly unaware of the risks they take (Albahari 2006: 2). The main result of this naturalization of border-related deaths is the removal of political responsibilities.

Families of missing Tunisians contested this mechanism of depoliticization, first by stressing the lack of alternatives their sons face when deciding to leave and in accepting the risks of the journey: "They left crossing the Mediterranean *in the only way allowed to them,* namely on small boats" (Tunisian Families 2013; emphasis added). At the same time, Tunisian families denounced the political responsibilities of sending and receiving countries whose immigration policies and border management practices impeded the free circulation of people, and which criminalize unauthorized migrants by holding them in administrative detention centers or in prison (Tunisian Families 2011). They were determined in identifying the EU as the main actor responsible for the dominant Euro-Mediterranean migration regime, in particular as they openly contested the granting of the Nobel Prize to the EU in December 2012 (Leventicinqueundici 2012).

The abolition of internal borders within the Schengen Area of free movement, and the connected strengthening of external borders, have produced in the past two decades a highly complex Euro-Mediterranean migration regime. This regime is essentially driven by the logic of deterritorialization and the externalization of border management (Casas, Cobarrubias, and Pickles 2010: 75–76), in connection with securitization and militarization of migration issues, especially in the aftermath of September 11 (Huysman 2006). The Euro-Mediterranean migration regime functions through multiple and overlapping mechanisms, more or less linked to the rise of migrant deaths, such as the criminalization of emigration, visa obligation, carrier sanctions, development and police cooperation, readmission agreements, discouragement of rescue by private boats, and jurisdictional conflicts on sea law (Cuttitta and Vassallo Paleologo 2006). Holding governments accountable for this deadly migration regime, Tunisian families contest the ultimate sovereign "right to make live and to let die" (Foucault 2003: 241) and denounce the incongruence of this power with the democratic state responsibility to respect and protect *every* human life. They also uncover those "sovereignty games" through which the European states put extraterritorial border policies into practice in order to avoid responsibility under human rights law (Gammeltoft-Hansen 2011).

Significantly, on July 10, 2014, in Rome, families of missing migrants, within a group of activists, jurists, and members of migrant associations, announced the intention to constitute an "international opinion tribunal" paying "justice to the new *desaparecidos*" at the European borders.[16] "We suggest to call such a tribunal with the aim: to offer to families of disappeared migrants an opportunity for witnessing and being represented; to help establishing responsibilities and omissions of individuals, governments and international agencies; to offer a tool for filing judicial complains to national, European and international courts. We want to ascertain the truth, punish those who are responsible, do justice to the victims and their relatives" (Comitato Giustizia 2014).

Repoliticizing Knowledge of Borders against Technical Neutralization

During their unfruitful research, families of the missing Tunisians disclosed the paradox of migrants dying or disappearing in the most densely traveled and controlled maritime areas in the world, like the Mediterranean (Tunisian Families 2013). They polemically assumed that surveillance mechanisms should include the protection of human life at sea. This is why in their second appeal to public authorities, conveniently titled "We Demand Your Knowledges," the families asked for access to information concerning their relatives and their travels by boat, especially fingerprints and data on monitoring maritime mobility. They claimed fundamental rights, formally recognized and protected by democratic states, such as the right to know—that is, to receive and have access to information concerning relatives, and to interact with accountable institutions that use biometrics and other new technologies in respect of human dignity and life. Through this claim the families repoliticized those knowledges by openly suggesting that they are not neutral: they are essentially oriented to the security of borders rather than of people, aimed at distinguishing insiders from outsiders, authorized and unauthorized mobilities, and at deterring unwanted migrants.

Digital fingerprints are by far the most well used devices to mark entry into the EU of certain categories of migrants. Since January 2003 European Dactyloscopy (EURODAC) has functioned as the principal continental fingerprint database for identifying asylum seekers and unauthorized border-crossers. Through digital fingerprints the EU's borders have been spatially and temporally dispersed within and beyond European territory (Walters 2002). By asking to have access to the personal identities of missing people detected through fingerprint exchanges and confrontations, Tunisian families tacitly denounced the fact that practices of digitally scanning physiological characteristics of individuals are used to anchor bordering functions into the human body, fixing identities as the basis for prediction and prevention of unauthorized mobility (van der Ploeg 2006): those technologies dehumanize people, especially migrants, by transforming their physical presence and movement into faceless digital data.

Current maritime surveillance detects possible "threats" out of thousands of vessels that cross the Mediterranean annually, with the help of optical and thermal cameras; sea-, air- and land-borne radars; vessel tracking technologies; and satellites. Surveillance means are key factors in the Euro-Mediterranean border management, with the aim of detecting migrants before they enter EU waters, meaning that the EU's neighboring countries are still responsible to intercept or rescue them. Tunisian families asked to use these technologies not for blocking unwanted movements of people, but for documenting what happens at sea, including violations of human rights law. Anticipating this alternative approach, they developed a sort of life-oriented "counter-mapping" (De Genova, Mezzadra, and Pickles 2014: 11–12), gathering information on when their relatives left, from where, where they were headed, on which boats, how many people were in each boat, the phone numbers they called from during their trip, the time of their phone calls, the phone company used, and so on (Tunisian Families 2013).

Moreover, the development of "biometric border technologies" (Amoore, Marmura, and Salter 2008) is problematic given the lack of legal mechanisms at the Euro-Mediterranean level that are able to monitor the enforcement of human rights concerning data protection and other sensitive issues related to the balance between privacy, life protection and public security. Tunisian families contributed to the democratization of border knowledge by asking for the institutionalization of commissions of inquiry at national and European levels, in which they, and others, could participate on equal terms. Once established, these commissions would make migrants, at least indirectly through their relatives, into subjects of border knowledge production, instead of being exclusively its target.[17]

Repoliticizing Inequality in Global Mobility against Normalization

Developing their campaign on the two shores of the Mediterranean, the families of missing Tunisians personally experienced how unequal rights of mobility are in contemporary global society, and how the access to this right has a direct link with the value of certain people. "We are mothers, fathers, sisters and brothers in the *same* way as in Europe. But only six of us obtained a visa to go to Italy and try to understand what happened to hundreds of missing young people. For European policies, our love and our pain do not have the *same value* that would be recognized to family members of European young people in a *similar* situation" (Tunisian Families 2013; emphasis added).

Demanding equal respect on the basis of parental feelings of love and pain, Tunisian families succeeded in highlighting the roots of a contemporary, global hierarchy of mobility (Bauman 1998)–that is, the unequally distributed possibility of people with different passports to move from one country to another. Human lives outside of Europe and other privileged regions of the world are simply less valuable than others. Against this "global apartheid" (Balibar 2004), which stratifies world populations according to class, race, and gender-based criteria, Tunisian families stressed on many occasions that all lives count. This was declared in the solemn proclamation that "Earth belongs to everyone," as it was written on a banner during a sit-in in Milan in January 2012, in front of the Tunisian embassy. There is no possible recognition of the equal value of everyone's lives without the recognition of the freedom to move. This is a direct consequence of the common ownership of the planet by humans, and not by states and their governments, which select and stratify the world population according to the interests of labor markets and the concerns for security of powerful countries and not of people.

Conclusion

Repoliticizing migration by boat across the Mediterranean is a ponderous yet unavoidable task for all those who refuse to be the silent accomplices of deaths at the southern European border. The families of missing Tunisian migrants who decided to self-organize and who are now gathered in an association called "La terre pour tous," or "The Earth for everyone," play a significant role in this struggle.

Changes in Euro-Mediterranean public opinion and immigration politics will be extremely difficult to achieve. Nevertheless, they would be impossible without the political subjectivization and the active involvement of the people most directly concerned, such as the migrants themselves and the families of those who died or disappeared. The voices and the bodies of Tunisian families, with their pain and anger, their hope and obstinacy, their consistency in showing visual evidence of their missing relatives will hopefully encourage European citizens to recognize all migrants as part of a larger "we," and the Mediterranean as an area of justice, peace, well-being, and free circulation.

Federico Oliveri is a research associate to the Sciences for Peace Interdisciplinary Centre at the University of Pisa and editor-in-chief of the online journal *Scienza e Pace*. He is the coauthor of several books, including *Migrants and their Descendants. A Guide to Policies Ensuring Well-being for All in a Plural Society* (2012). He has also published extensively in journals such as *Citizenship Studies, openDemocracy,* and *ACME–International Journal for Critical Geographies*. His main research interests are racism, migration, citizenship, and social movement studies, with a special focus on migrant struggles in contemporary Europe.

Notes

1. The collective "2511," which is no longer active, was constituted on November 25, 2009. On that day, Italian feminists with different backgrounds met in Milan during an antiracist sit-in, on the International Day for the Elimination of Violence against Women, to protest abuses suffered by women detained in centers for irregular migrants. After the sit-in was repressed by the police, they decided to build a collective focused on, among other issues, the links between institutional racism, gender, and migration. This explains the support provided to the mobilization of the mothers of missing Tunisian migrants.
2. Storie Migranti (http://www.storiemigranti.org/) is a Web archive of migrant stories where the narratives of first-hand experiences of migration are collected and made available to the public as written narratives, transcriptions of interviews, or audio interviews.
3. *Fortress Europe* (http://fortresseurope.blogspot.it/) is the blog of journalist and writer Gabriele Del Grande who has since 2006 documented journeys and deaths of migrants across European borders. The blog has a section devoted to stories of missing Tunisian migrants, significantly called "Lampedusa's Spoon River" (Del Grande 2011).
4. There are three regularly updated Facebook pages publishing news on missing Tunisian migrants: "Association la Terre pour Tous," administrated by the president of the association founded by the families of missing Tunisian migrants; "Haraga: scomparsi in Italia," administrated by a political collective called "Parti Tunisien"; and "X i dispersi in mare 2011," administrated by Rebecca Kraiem, president of the Tunisian association "Giuseppe Verdi" based in Parma, Italy.
5. Three reportages on the missing Tunisian migrants have been published by independent media collectives such as *Nawaat.org, Basta!,* and *Mediapart. Nawaat.org* (http://nawaat.org/portail) is a Tunisian blog aiming to give voice to activist citizens inside and outside the country. *Basta!* (www.bastamag.net) is a participative information Web site on social issues, aiming to publicize community and individual actions, social claims, and solidarity movements, primarily through images and videos. *Mediapart* (http://www.mediapart.fr) is an online investigative and opinion journal.
6. So far the Italian government has answered two MP's inquiries concerning the fate of missing Tunisian migrants, on July 11, 2012, and September 30, 2013, providing information on the exchange of fingerprints with the Tunisian government. According to the Italian government, only five fingerprints gathered after January

2011 correspond with those of supposed missing Tunisian migrants. Nevertheless, the identities of these fingerprints remain unknown.
7. I use the term *migrant* as a comprehensive notion, encompassing all the different kinds of people who travel across international borders, irrespective of their legal status and their personal motivations for moving. This choice of term is the result of my preference for a critical epistemology of migration that considers differentiations among migrants as politically, socially, legally, and culturally constructed, and thus as a field of conflict and negotiation.
8. Estimates of the death toll at the United States–Mexico border range from 3,861 to 5,607 between 1993 and 2008 (Himenez 2009: 8). At the Australian maritime border, about 1,972 deaths have been reported between January 2000 and August 2015, according to the Border Crossing Observatory (http://artsonline.monash.edu.au/thebordercrossingobservatory). On how to conceptualize, map, and assess "border-related deaths," see Weber and Pickering (2011). On specific problems related to the documentation of deaths at borders, see Brian (2014).
9. Launched in 2013 by a group of European journalists, the Migrants' Files is the first source on the deaths and disappearances of migrants. This data is collected by United for Intercultural Action, a nonprofit network of 550 organizations across Europe; and by the already mentioned blog *Fortress Europe*. The Migrants' Files are regularly updated and can be found at http://www.themigrantsfiles.com/. Mostly based on press reports, these data are problematic because shipwrecks may remain unknown, and changes in the number of reported deaths may also reflect changes in media attention. In order to have more-reliable data, a new methodology has been recently developed by creating an aggregated data set based on local death registries (Spijkerboer 2012).
10. Updated figures for 2015 have been provided by the Missing Migrants Project (http://missingmigrants.iom.int/), promoted by the International Organization for Migration (IOM), which is currently the only global database sharing key data on deceased and missing migrants around the world, using statistical information from governments and sources from other agencies, as well as NGOs and media. These figures present deaths in the Mediterranean by month, by migrants' region of origin, and by route.
11. These estimates, regularly updated by the Missing Migrants Project, are based on data from governments and IOM field offices (http://migration.iom.int/europe/).
12. Lampedusa is an Italian island twenty square kilometers large in the Strait of Sicily, 113 kilometers from Tunisia and 176 kilometers from Sicily. Since the early 2000s, for many reasons related to the construction of the Euro-Mediterranean migration regime, the island has become the worldwide symbol of the "fortress Europe," alternatively staging humanitarian and securitarian versions of the "border spectacle" (Cuttitta 2012).
13. In the past few years, many reports have been published by European institutions and international NGOs concerning violations of human rights affecting migrants at European borders, especially in the Mediterranean. See European Union Agency for Fundamental Rights and Council of Europe (2014); and Amnesty International (2014).
14. The movement of families of missing Tunisian migrants is not the first of this kind. Since the 1980s mothers of migrants who disappeared while traveling to

the United States from Central America are mobilized in order to know what happened to their children. All these families share similar experience, such as the anguish of not knowing what happened to their relatives, and the silence of public authorities. They also enacted incredibly similar practices of struggle. For Central American mothers, too, the symbol of the search is the photo of their disappeared son or daughter. Holding these pictures, the mothers move from one town to another, along the migratory route, hold sit-ins in the parks and squares of the cities, give press conferences, meet with police and migration authorities, visit migrant shelters, jails, hospitals, and morgues. More can be found at http://caravanamadres.wordpress.com/english. As for the Euro-Mediterranean area, the first organized movements of the families of missing migrants saw the light in Morocco, such as the "Association des familles des victimes de l'immigration clandestine" (association of families of the victims of irregular migration) founded in 2001.
15. I do not use here the word *smugglers* as it carries a negative moral connotation. Using instead the word *passeurs,* I intend to signal the essentially noncoerced nature of this kind of mobility by boat, in opposition to trafficking.
16. The integral text of the petition launched by the committee, "Giustizia per i nuovi desaparecidos," can be found at http://habeshia.blogspot.it.
17. On August 14, 2014, the Tunisian government finally agreed to constitute an interministerial commission of inquiry on missing migrants, according to the demand of the families (Soltani, interview).

Bibliography

Personal Interviews

Boukadida, Syrine. July 14, 2014. Interview through e-mail [member of the Tunisian association "Article 13" dealing with migrant rights, especially the right to free movement].

Soltani, Imed. August 16, 2014. Interview on Skype [brother of a missing migrant, president of the association La Terre pour tous].

Other Sources

Albahari, Maurizio. 2006. "Death and the Modern State: Making Borders and Sovereignty at the Southern Edges of Europe." Working Paper 137, Center for Comparative Immigration Studies, University of California, San Diego.

Amoore, Louise, Stephen Marmura, and Mark B. Salter. 2008. "Editorial: Smart Borders and Mobilities: Spaces, Zones, Enclosures." *Surveillance & Society,* 5(2): 96–101.

Amnesty International. 2014. *The Human Cot of Fortress Europe. Human Rights Violations Against Migrants and Refugees at Europe's Borders.* London: Amnesty International. http://www.amnesty.org/en/library/info/EUR05/001/2014/en.

Balaton-Chrimes, Samantha. 2011. "The Might of Power Facing Up to the Violence of Strength–An Arendtian View of Politics and Revolution." openDemo-

cracy, February 2. https://www.opendemocracy.net/samantha-balaton-chrimes/might-of-power-facing-up-to-violence-of-strength-arendtian-view-of-politics.
Balibar, Étienne. 2004. *We, the People of Europe? Reflections on Transnational Citizenship.* Princeton, NJ, and Oxford: Princeton University Press.
Bauman, Zygmunt. 1998. *Globalization: The Human Consequences.* New York: Columbia University Press.
———. 2004. *Wasted Lives.* Cambridge: Polity Press.
Brian, Tara. 2014. "Death at the Border: The Challenge of Documenting Lives Lost in Border Regions." *Migration Policy Practice,* December 2013–January 2014.
Butler, Judith. 2009. *Frames of War: When Is Life Grievable?* London: Verso.
Casas, Maribel, Sebastian Cobarrubias, and John Pickles. 2010. "Stretching Borders Beyond Sovereign Territories? Mapping EU and Spain's Border Externalization Policies." *Geopolítica(s),* 2(1): 71–90.
Clohesy, Anthony M. 2013. *Politics of Empathy: Ethics, Solidarity, Recognition.* New York: Routledge.
Comitato Giustizia. 2014. "Giustizia per I nuovi desaparecidos." Online petition. http://habeshia.blogspot.it/
Cuttitta, Paolo. 2012. *Lo spettacolo del confine. Lampedusa tra produzione e messa in scena della frontiera.* Milan and Udine: Mimesis.
Cuttitta, Paolo, and Fulvio Vassallo Paleologo (eds.). 2006. *Migrazioni, frontiere, diritti.* Naples: Edizioni Scientifiche.
De Genova, Nicholas, Sandro Mezzadra, and John Pickles (eds.). 2014. "New Keywords: Migration and Borders." *Cultural Studies.* doi:10.1080/09502386.2014.891630
Del Grande, Gabriele. 2011. "Lampedusa's Spoon River." *Fortress Europe* (blog). http://fortresseurope.blogspot.it/2011/11/lampedusas-spoon-river.html.
Dhaouadi, Meriem. 2012. "Looking for Dignity Elsewhere: Tunisian Youth Fleeing the Birthplace of the Arab Spring." openDemocracy, September 9. https://www.opendemocracy.net/meriem-dhaouadi/looking-for-dignity-elsewhere-tunisian-youth-fleeing-birthplace-of-arab-spring.
Edkins, Jenny. 2011. *Missing: Persons and Politics.* Ithaca, NY: Cornell University Press.
European Union Agency for Fundamental Rights and Council of Europe. 2014. *Handbook on European Law Relating to Asylum, Borders and Immigration.* Luxembourg: Publications Office of the European Union. http://fra.europa.eu/sites/default/files/handbook-law-asylum-migration-borders-2nded_en.pdf.
Foucault, Michel. 2003. *"Society Must Be Defended." Lectures at the Collège de France, 1975–1976.* New York: Picador.
Fouteau, Carine. 2012. "The Tunisian Mothers Searching the Sons Who Vanished Crossing the Med." Mediapart.fr, June 8. http://www.mediapart.fr/content/tunisian-mothers-searching-sons-who-vanished-crossing-med/
Frontex. 2012. *Annual Risk Analysis 2012.* Warsaw: Frontex.
———. 2014. *Annual Risk Analysis 2014.* Warsaw: Frontex.
———. 2015. *Annual Risk Analysis 2015.* Warsaw: Frontex.
Gammeltoft-Hansen, Thomas. 2011. *Access to Asylum: International refugee law and the globalization of migration control.* Cambridge: Cambridge University Press.
Ginzburg, Carlo. 1994. "Killing a Chinese Mandarin: The Moral Implications of Distance." *Critical Inquiry* 21 (Autumn).

Grant, Stefanie. 2011. "Irregular Migration and Frontier Deaths: Acknowledging a Right to Identity." In *Are Human Rights for Migrants?*, edited by Marie-Benedicte Dembour and Tobias Kelly. London: Routledge.

Himenez, Maria. 2009. "Humanitarian Crisis: Migrant Deaths and the US–Mexico Border." ACLU of San Diego and Imperial Counties, Mexico's National Commission of Human Rights.

Huysman, Jef. 2006. *The Politics of Insecurity. Fear, Migration and Asylum in the EU.* London/New York: Routledge.

Leventicinqueundici. 2012. "La pace della UE non è la nostra." http://leventicinqueundici.noblogs.org/?p=1333.

Mezzadra, Sandro, and Brett Neilson. 2013. *Border as Method, or, the Multiplication of Labor.* Durham, NC: Duke University Press.

Mourad, S. 2012. "Tunisie: Des parents de victimes du drame de Lampedusa incendient les postes de police et de la garde nationale d'El Fahs." *Tunisie numérique*, 11 September. http://www.tunisienumerique.com/tunisie-des-parents-de-victimes-du-drame-de-lampedusa-incendient-les-postes-de-police-et-de-la-garde-nationale-del-fahs/143389.

Nicolini, Giusi. 2013. "Let's Take This Sorrow Seriously." http://www.storiemigranti.org/spip.php?article1056.

Oliveri, Federico. 2014. "Acts of Citizenship against Neoliberalism: The New Cycle of Migrant Struggles in Italy." In *Multicultural Challenges and Sustainable Democracy in Europe and East Asia*, edited by Nam-Kook Kim. London and New York: Palgrave Macmillan.

Rancière, Jacques. 2004. "Who Is the Subject of the Rights of Man?" *South Atlantic Quarterly* 103, no. 2–3: 297–310.

———. 2009. *The Emancipated Spectator.* London and New York: Verso.

Rivera, Annamaria. 2012. *Il fuoco della rivolta: torce umane dal Maghreb all'Europa.* Bari, Italy: Edizioni Dedalo.

Rygiel, Kim. 2014. "In Life through Death: Transgressive Citizenship at the Border." In *Routledge Handbook of Global Citizenship Studies*, edited by Engin F. Isin and Peter Nyers. New York: Routledge.

Rorty, Richard. 1989. *Contingency, Irony, and Solidarity.* Cambridge: Cambridge University Press.

Smith, Winston. 2012. "The Case of the Missing Tunisian Migrants: From One Shore to Another, Lives Which Matter." Nawaat.org, July 24. http://nawaat.org/portail/2012/07/24/the-case-of-the-missing-tunisian-migrants-from-one-shore-to-another-lives-which-matter/.

Sontag, Susan. 2003. *Regarding the Pain of Others.* New York: Picador/Farrar, Straus and Giroux.

Sossi, Federica. 2013. "Struggles in Migration. The Phantoms of Truths." In *Spaces in Migration. Postcards of a Revolution*, edited by Glenda Garelli, Federica Sossi, and Martina Tazzioli. London: Pavement Books.

Spijkerboer, Thomas. 2012. "Moving Migrants, States and Rights: Human Rights and Migrant Deaths." *Social Science Research Network*, June. http://papers.ssrn.com/sol3/papers.cfm?abstract_id=2097748.

Tassel, Fabrice. 2013. "Tunisie: disparus entre paradis et enfer." *Libération.fr*, 13 September. http://www.liberation.fr/monde/2013/09/13/tunisie-disparus-entre-paradis-et-enfer_931783.

Tunisian Families. 2011. "Petition for Missing Tunisian Migrants." http://www.storiemigranti.org/spip.php?article995.
———. 2013. "We Demand Your Knowledges. A Petition by the Mothers and the Families of Missing Tunisian Migrants." http://www.storiemigranti.org/spip.php?article1047.
van der Ploeg, Irma. 2006. "Borderline Identities: The Enrollment of Bodies in the Technological Reconstruction of Borders." In *Surveillance and Security: Technological Politics and Power in Everyday Life,* edited by Torin Monaham. New York: Routledge.
Walters, William. 2002. "Mapping Schengenland: denaturalizing the border." *Environment and Planning D: Society and Space* 20: 561–80.
Weber, Leanne, and Sharon Pickering. 2011. *Globalization and Borders: Death at the Global Frontier.* London: Palgrave Macmillan.
Weiler, Nolwenn. 2013. "Un millier de jeunes Tunisiens ont disparu aux frontières de l'Europe." *Basta!,* March 28. http://www.bastamag.net/Un-millier-de-jeunes-Tunisiens-ont/.
Zolo, Danilo. 2010. *Tramonto globale: la fame, il patibolo, la guerra.* Florence: Florence University Press.

9
Mysterious Refugees
Social Drama Ensues

Lynda Mannik

On July 12, 1987, Canadian media was ignited with the news that 173 men (all Indian nationals), one woman (from Turkey), and approximately six crew members had landed off the tip of Nova Scotia on a small freighter called *Amelie*. The male passengers were mostly between the ages of eighteen and thirty-five. Media reports claimed most were Sikhs, and that some were members of the All India Sikh Youth Federation.[1] All of the passengers claimed to be escaping persecution in their homeland, which was a result of anti-Sikh massacres that began in Punjab in 1984. They landed in Canada at approximately 3:00 A.M. on a Sunday. The area had been under heavy fog for four days. This group managed to get onto the shore near Charlesville, a tiny fishing village (population seventy-seven), and then walked through a bog for two kilometers up to the main highway. They continued along the main, and only, road through Charlesville shouting, "Hello, hello! ... Refugees! ... Refugees!" Simply announcing oneself as a refugee at a border crossing, usually in airports, is a common way to enter a country as an asylum seeker, but arrivals by boat are considered to be different, and the timing and size of this group definitely shocked the residents of this sleeping village. Still, some occupants came out to help the *Amelie*'s passengers. They gave them water, tea, muffins, and sandwiches, while others remained hiding in their homes in fear. One woman immediately called the Royal Canadian Mounted Police (RCMP) and within a couple of hours this group had been whisked away and relocated in a gymnasium at CFB (Canadian Forces Base) Stadacona in Halifax, where they were kept under detention and in isolation, from the press and the public, for sixteen days.

All media representatives were barred from initial immigration hearings, nor were they allowed to speak with the passengers until they were released from custody in late August. Nevertheless, portrayals of the voyage, comments about the identity of the men, comments about their status as refugees, their possible deportation, their past association with terrorists groups, and their ability to possibly commit terrorist acts in Canada all abounded in media reports. In fact, the profusion of news reports published in local as well as national newspapers created a dynamic and extremely controversial media extravaganza, as described by one of the journalists present (Jeff 2010, personal interview). Arrivals of refugees by boat often have this effect on the nations they arrive in. However, the responses to this event were notable. Within the first week there were over 150 articles printed in Canada's top national newspapers. As Mark Allen Peterson (2003: 241) explains, sometimes, specific events take over communications ecologies for a period to actively engage large numbers of people. In this way, they take on the status of a "social drama." This chapter will position the *Amelie*'s arrival as a "social drama" according the Victor Turner's (1974) categories with an emphasis on a detailed discussion of the public performances that followed and that were described in media reports. It will highlight the fluidity between media and performativity in descriptions of enacted responses to show how news images and reports can set in motion individual and collective action, which in turn may shift and influence identities.

Migration by Boat as Social Drama

Much previous work has attempted to understand the symbolic importance of news images and the ritualistic ways they are used to promote ideological values (Coman 2008; Coonfield and Huxford 2009; Cottle 2006; Ettema 1990; McDevitt, Briziarelli, and Klocke 2013). As part of this project, Turner's categories concerning social dramas have become an important component of analyses undertaken by communication studies and cultural studies scholars. Anthropologist Mark Peterson claims that even though many scholars have used Turner's notions of ritual to explain how media consumers are affected by media texts, few have captured the anthropological sense of the ritualized and transformative nature of social dramas in Turner's work (2003: 241). Social dramas are significant because they are one of the central processes by which societies create themselves, and also how citizens come to know how to act concerning political events. They are political processes that produce shared meanings and they are emergent, like social life itself. In print media, visual accoutrements such as photographs and headlines are intended as accessories that visually accentuate and facilitate shared interpretations of textual narratives.

Victor Turner designed a formulaic approach to social dramas that outlined four specific stages starting with a breach or crisis that initiates an antistructure in which the values and norms of a society are put on critical display. The declared crisis breaks open social values where hidden contradictions lie, and eventually leads to a messy process of change. However, as Peterson explains, few scholars have adequately taken up the challenge to "capture the anthropological sense of ritual as a social practice, a form of *action,* through which persons are made" (Peterson 2003: 241). News stories evolve as producers of social dramas that also always act as consumers of their own productions. They feed off themselves while narrating all four stages of a social drama for public consumption, including the final stage where the reintegration of "the disturbed social group" takes place (Turner 1974: 41). Media saturation creates a social environment that can dominate the everyday discourses of a society—discourses that inevitably create social meaning. Nevertheless, social dramas are not always effective in altering or fixing social cleavages because the reactions of individual social actors are often random and self-serving.

In general, media portrayals of refugees have been regarded as dehumanizing and dehistoricizing, and they fit well into Simon Cottle's (2006) model of mediatized rituals. As a type of refugee, so-called boat people[2] are represented in the most negative light, and frequently are positioned as the instigators of "mediatized public crises" that move past media scandals to produce "disruptive effects" (Cottle 2006: 424). The people involved are considered the least deserving and the most threatening because they have deviated from what are deemed to be the appropriate channels of entry. Their entry onshore is generally described as a criminal assault on the nation they arrive in. Terms related to water metaphors are commonly used in the press about the movements of refugees; however, these terms are used profusely in commentary about the arrival of refugees in boats, which in turn, remains extremely hypocritical and overtly biased in favor of state agendas. Objectifying terms such as *flow, tide, flood, and wave* are the most common. Michael Pugh claims that refugees who chose this type of movement are repeatedly associated with natural disasters. Words such as *engulfed, swamped, flooded, washed away, and inundated* are used to describe the effect they have on the national spaces they arrive in (Pugh 2004: 54). This stereotypical language manifests in commonly seen photographs of large groups crowded together on the deck of the ship or hanging over the edge. Ironically, refugees, who often have no choice but to travel by boat, incur far greater risks, yet media text and images are, most often, intended to embody fear and create anxiety for their readers.

The media's use of visual symbols to elicit drama and emotional responses is central to understanding the performative nature of media, both in its production and its reception. Although symbols and metaphors are embedded in all visual and textual aspects of news reports, arrivals of refugees by boat can be considered exceptional events where representations are intended to enact power, and power relations in dramatic ritualized form. They also directly call for public responses to the national importance of immigration, and the central question, "Who gets in?" In this chapter I will discuss the metaphoric and more-explicit messages in both text and image, but focus on an anthropological emphasis that looks at the physicality of social dramas as performative acts. What did people do after they read and looked at news reports? I will emphasize the body/mind connections within social dramas as well as links between the symbolic and the performative by describing the physical, emotional, and verbal responses of politicians and various members of the Canadian public. Following Peterson's suggestion, I will explain how social dramas as a form of social action can be responsible for forming and changing identities; a social process whereby "people co-construct their social and personal identities through physical and mental activities" (Peterson 2003: 242). In a Canadian context, the arrival of refugees by boat provides an apt example because they have always been events that inspire a great deal of controversy and media exposure.

The research for this chapter covers a wide berth, but focuses primarily on print media: Canada's top three national newspapers—the *Toronto Star,* the *Globe and Mail,* and *the Ottawa Citizen;* several local newspapers—the *Montreal Gazette* and Halifax's *Chronicle Herald;* and *Maclean's Magazine. Maclean's* was chosen because it is Canada's only weekly news magazine and because it focuses on current affairs from politics to popular culture. As of this writing it has approximately 2.4 million readers, and boosts professional investigative reporting from leading Canadian journalists. The *Toronto Star* is Canada's highest-circulation newspaper and has been in existence since 1892. The *Star* has been criticized for its open liberal support in the Canadian context, yet has long been considered an important voice of Canadian nationalism. Its principal competitor, the *Globe and Mail,* is also a nationally distributed newspaper based in Toronto with a weekly readership of approximately 1 million. These sources were scoured for articles, photographs, letters to the editors, and even cartoons, between July 13 and October 30, 1987 inclusively. I also performed a more lax search for articles on the event in question that were published between 1987 and 2013.

The Breach and Ensuing Crisis

The first stage of Turner's social drama model is constituted by a breach of social order in the form of breaking laws or other violations of norms, and this breach reveals underlying conflicts in a social system (Turner 1974: 38).

Interestingly, in this example, as stated above, the *Amelie*'s arrival constitutes the breach in terms of national security, but not in terms of local interests for some of Charlesville's residents who welcomed this group with open arms, as well as water, tea and sandwiches. Internationally, and in particular in North America, these types of events are immediately recognized and portrayed in the media as crises. In general, as Sara Ahmed explains, this type of breach sets off "border anxiety" linked to an "ontology of insecurity" (Ahmed 2004: 119). Yet, in this case, even reports that circulated on the first day in national newspapers referenced it both as a crisis of securitization, and simultaneously as a moment where regional, all-inclusive hospitality was expressed.[3] The contradictory representations of this arrival reveal the deep conflicts in Canadian society in terms of multicultural policy and national ideology, which solely emphasize tolerance, hospitality, and acceptance.

In the second stage, "[o]vert conflict and antagonism arise as sides are taken and as factions are formed resulting in the widening of the breach to include more and more members of the social group" (Peterson 2003: 243). This is the messy part where the drama moves into a full-blown crisis, and where the voices of Canadian politicians and members of the Canadian public expose tensions and conflicts, which deepens and further exposes narratives about racial prejudice. The day after the *Amelie* arrived, July 14, was the first full day of media coverage, and published representations of this event can be considered the opening act. The hospitality this group received in Charlesville was soon forgotten and conflicts concerning the meaning of this "crisis" were developed through the voices of sets of main actors who were identified both in direct quotations and in photographs. Included in the cast were Charlesville's residents who are depicted as exclusively hospitable and caring; the captain, Rolf Nygren, and his crew, and their devious involvement with international refugee smuggling rings; immigration officials and politicians who are forcefully trying to secure Canada's borders and stop this crisis; various Canadian Sikh community members who are sympathetic to the plight of this group and willing to support them financially and emotionally; and of course, the *Amelie*'s passengers, who were repeatedly described as "human cargo" or "the 174," and possible terrorists. News reports emphasized passionate struggles over human rights versus the rights of Canadian citizens with a focus on the identities of the *Amelie*'s passengers as the deciding factor as to whether they should be allowed into Canada or receive humanitarian aid. Fear of impending danger was also fueled by comments about another boat filled with refugees that was supposedly on its way, and second, through comments about the ballooning refugee problem in general, which could mean that arrivals by boat would become far more common.[4]

Immediately after the *Amelie*'s passengers were secured in CFB Stadacona in Halifax, all journalists were notified that any information surrounding this event was classified, and that they would not be allowed to interview anyone who was involved. However, on July 14 reporters were allowed to enter the hot, stuffy gymnasium where all 173 men were being detained.[5] As described by one reporter in the *Toronto Star,* each person had a gray blanket and pillow with DND (Department of National Defence) stamped on it. There were no chairs, only neat rows of mats on the floor. The men kept their shoes beside them and wet clothing lined the bars along the gymnasium walls. Police patrolled inside and outside the gym; outside they carried batons the size of baseball bats (Dutton 1987). Reporters were allowed in the gym for five minutes only, under strict instructions that they were not allowed to talk to anyone or they would be escorted out and their cameras seized. They were allowed to take photographs as they walked around the perimeter, and that was the express reason why they had been allowed in. This photographic experience was mediated by government officials who obviously wanted the Canadian public to see how this group was being detained, yet did not want personal accounts of their plight exposed.

Needless to say, the resulting visual portrayal or visual performance of the *Amelie*'s' passengers in detention fulfilled government intentions, and objectified this group on several levels. Their secure living conditions were captured from various angles to expose the bad treatment these men are being afforded. They had not been offered proper beds; they had no privacy and few personal items, and were expected to live for weeks in cramped spaces. Although viewers cannot see the police circling the gym, it is obvious that they are in positions where surveillance and control are optimized, and viewers are also put into the position of authoritative surveyors (see figure 9.1). The objectivity that photojournalists strive for was negated and directed in some ways by immigration officials, who obviously wanted the public to see how these men were being treated in order to prove state securitization.

In the following days, news reports explained in detail the responses of two primary groups, Canadian politicians and the Canadian public. The initial published comments from leading Canadian politicians are controversial and emotionally charged. They definitely gave the impression that all were shocked by this event. In one article in the *Globe and Mail,* Brian Mulroney, then prime minister, is quoted as saying, "[F]air and reasonable action will be taken, that is the kind of country we are" (Sallot, 1987). However, on the same day in an article in the *Toronto Star* titled, "Mulroney Rules Out Special Treatment," Marc Lortie, Mulroney's press secretary, told reporters that Mulroney was determined Canadians would not be pushed around, or be perceived as being pushed around (O'Donnell 1987). Lortie added, "[D]id you notice in his exchange with the reporters here that he did not mention the words *tolerance or civility* with regard to these new circumstances" (O'Donnell 1987). John Turner, then Liberal leader, stated, "[I]t is just another manipulative commercial effort to bypass our legislative process of receiving refugees" (O'Donnell 1987). Bouchard, the immigration minister, is quoted

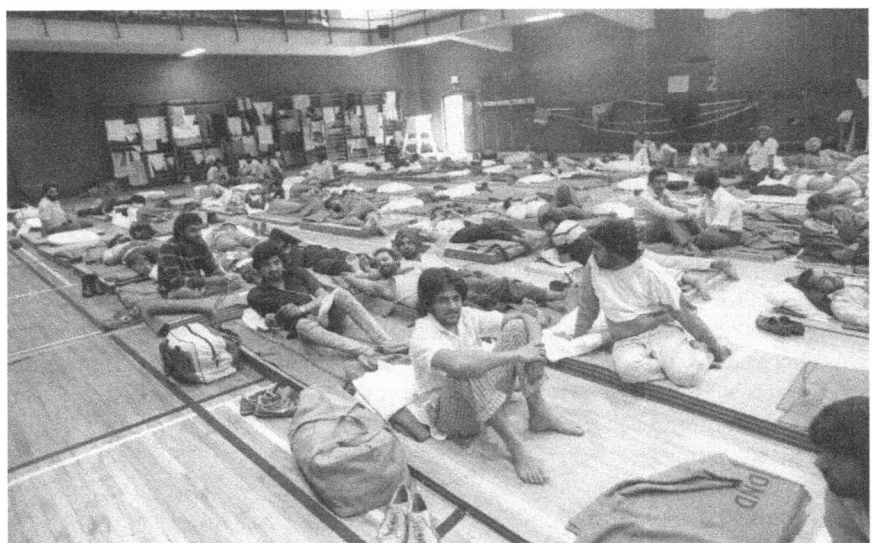

Figure 9.1. "173 men and one woman are being held at the Canadian Forces Base Stadacona," *The Globe and Mail*, Photographer: Edward Regan, July 14, 1987: A2. (Courtesy of The Globe and Mail).

as begrudgingly stating, "[E]ven if they are not genuine refugees they cannot be deported under current federal laws.... I'm stuck with the same laws as last year!" (Toulin 1987). Comments from a variety of government sources emphasized that this group would not be treated in the same way as the Tamils who had arrived the previous year,[6] and that they would definitely not be granted temporary admission. Overall, the litany of initial derogatory quotes from Canadian politicians are particularly disturbing because it is through politicians' comments that citizens come to know how they should act in regards to social dramas. According to Colin Hay (1996), the most important instrument of crisis management is language. State officials are responsible for defining the appropriate strategies for a resolution; they must take the lead in responding to it, but also in identifying, defining and constituting the crisis in the first place (Hay 1996: 255). I would argue that the photos taken in the detention center, combined with politicians' comments, set the tone for the primarily discriminatory public response that ensued.

Generally speaking, Canadian public responses, across the country, were volatile, determined, and creative. Public performances of discrimination in oral, written, and physical form lasted for weeks. National press reports depicted the mainstream Canadian public as 99 percent in favor of immediately sending the *Amelie*'s passengers back. It is noted in the *Globe and Mail* that hundreds of angry calls were made to a variety of media administrators and government officials. In Etobicoke, for example, MPs were getting a hundred calls a week, all saying that the government should deport this group. In a lengthy article in the *Toronto Star* titled, "Frustration, Racism Mark Irate Calls over East Indians," it is made blatantly clear that Metropolitan Toronto MPs are inundated (the specific term used is *flooded*) with calls from residents all in favor of sending this group home (Edwards 1987). Callers were described as displaying an "ugly undercurrent of racism." (Edwards 1987). During an open-line radio talk show in Montreal, 80 percent of callers wanted to "talk about the Sikhs" and most "wanted the refugees to go home" (Anonymous 1987a). On a similar show in Vancouver, callers claimed that it was a well-known fact that Sikhs who wore turbans had a higher rate of communicable diseases and that this group looked like "rabbits in a warren" (Harper 1987), which I assume is in reference to the detention photos taken on July 14.

Discriminatory comments abounded in letters to the editors of both of Canada's leading newspapers. Up until August 7 (three weeks after this group's arrival) 90 percent of the letters to the editor published in the *Toronto Star* and the *Globe and Mail* expressed anger and a defiant "No" as to whether the *Amelie*'s passengers should be allowed to stay in Canada. It was assumed that if they were allowed to stay in Canada, a flood of similar incidents would follow. As stated in one letter, "When tankers carrying thousands of refugees appear off both coasts we will rue the day our government did not take immediate action to halt this travesty of an immigration policy" (Anonymous 1987b).[7] Group petitions were also organized. One example took place in Vancouver where the Citizens for Foreign Aid Reform collected 2,700 signatures from citizens who demanded tighter immigration laws (Anonymous 1987a). There are also two reports in local newspapers of several letters and cassette tapes sent from Germany and England. All were addressed to the Lord Mayor of Charlesville, were described as "hate mail," and confiscated by local authorities. A petition was signed by eighty residents in the area "calling for the municipality to turn over the tapes to the people of Charlesville" (Medel 1987a) who believed they had a right to the information contained within.

Physical performances were staged by individuals and by groups. Outside of CFB Stadacona military base, there were daily traffic jams for weeks with long lines of people slowing down, hanging out of their cars, and yelling, "Send them all back." One reporter defined this scene as a "total circus" where "Taunts, racist jokes and redneck remarks have replaced bran muffins, peanut butter sandwiches and *Kool-Aid* the immigrants were served 12 days ago in Charlesville" (Story 1987a). He also described homemade placards reading "Deport AND Prosecute" (Story 1987a). In total, there were three interesting reports of individualized physical acts of discrimination against the *Amelie*'s passengers. One involved a lawyer in Vancouver who gathered together $2,500 with a group of friends to pay for ads in two national newspapers that demanded tougher immigration laws. Horst describes himself as "a common Canadian" (Anonymous 1987a). The second involved three university students who paid $250 to have an airplane fly over downtown Toronto with a banner that read, "Immigrants ... Front Door Only" (Janigan Mackenzie, and Gessell 1987). And finally, a photograph published in the *Globe and Mail* depicts Allan Docherty of Erskine, Alberta, standing in front of his automobile repair shop with an angry face. In the background looms a large hand-painted banner that spans the length of the garage with the bold message, "Send Refugees Back C.O.D." The caption reads, "Allan Docherty, or Erskine Atla., says he is not a red neck or a bigot, but he wants the 174 Asians returned to India at their own expense. He thinks they should go through proper channels if they want to stay in Canada" (Martin 1987). If the old adage "actions speak louder than words" carries any weight, then these acts, and the fact that descriptions of them were published in print media news reports, makes them notable.

Redress

According to Turner, in the third stage of a social drama, members of a society attempt to make use of formal and informal mechanisms to limit the contagious spread of the breach (Turner 1974: 39). It is also the stage where liminal features become most obvious and cultural performances are perhaps most striking as members of a society try to make meaning out of the crisis. Mihai Coman reminds us that at this stage it is the media's responsibility to present a range of perspectives emphasizing "the fears and aspirations of the entire social body" (Coman 2008: 108) to allow for shifts in social orders. However, sometimes something dark emerges, as suggested by Ian Maxwell (Maxwell 2008: 60). In this section I will discuss the performative dimensions of the redressive and liminal phase, and again highlight bodily performance alongside intellectual debate. Efforts to contain and understand the crisis–the arrival of refugees on a ship–happened on three levels.

The first begins almost immediately with a barrage of quotes from government officials emphatically assuring the public that they have everything under control. In securing the nation, they had seized the ship, put the smugglers in jail, were investigating international smuggling rings, and had locked the newcomers in a detention facility under heavy guard. Another boat was possibly arriving, but they knew about that, and were conscientiously patrolling the waters. They were also investigating international smuggling rings that were at the root of this crisis. Politicians' comments repeatedly justify the isolation and heavily guarded detention of the *Amelie*'s passengers, and the fact that they were not allowed legal counsel or any public contact due to fears of connections with terrorist groups in India. They reiterated two primary solutions: (1) The Canadian government should never have allowed the *Amelie* to land in the first place. (2) And the government must fix refugee policies immediately so that this type of crisis will never happen again and the power to send boats back is clarified.

The second act of redress as portrayed in news media was in direct response to politicians' actions and comments. It focused on how the Sikh community in Canada was trying to limit the breach against human rights laws for refugees. On July 14, the day that the photos of the passengers were published nationwide, the Sikh community started expressing concerns about the fact that the *Amelie*'s passengers are virtually under house arrest. They also stressed that they were collectively willing to take care of this group through monetary means, jobs, shelter, and legal aid. As stated earlier, due to heavy security no one had been allowed in to see this group and the men's treatment was known only through the afore-mentioned photos. Two days later, Mendel Green, a prominent immigration lawyer from Toronto, was hired by the Sikh community to bring the unjust treatment of these men to the forefront. Initially he was not granted access and was quoted in the media as declaring it unconstitutional that this group is hidden away and not allowed legal representation, religious guidance, or even a phone call. Within a few days, the cry of discrimination deepens; Green and other lawyers are quoted as acknowledging that this group's treatment does violate the Charter of Rights and Freedoms in Canada (Martin 1987). Amnesty International calls CFB Stadacona "Canada's first refugee camp" (Ward 1987). This escalates into the demand for a stop to unjust treatment on July 17 when the president of the Canadian Federation of Sikh Society was quoted as saying that the government's treatment the *Amelie*'s passengers is akin to "an authorized version of the KKK" (Wilson 1987). On July 20 a petition signed by 1,500 Sikhs from Montreal demands the release of this group (Buckie 1987). Later that week, Carmencita Hernandez, representing the Coalition for a Just Refugee and Immigration Policy that comprises ninety churches, labor groups, and immigrant groups, visited the United Nations High Commissioner for Refugees (UNHCR) in Geneva to ask for mediation (Stefaniuk 1987). There were also several reports of one "non-Sikh teacher" who is offering a $5,000 bond to sponsor one of the *Amelie*'s passengers. Ann Griffiths, a teacher of English as a second language in Ontario, says she is willing to offer help because of fond memories she has of one student, a boy named Ranit Singh, who was delightful. His family offered her hospitality in their home (Stefaniuk 1987). Members of Canada's Sikh community, one lawyer, human rights activists, and a few individual citizens are represented as members of the public who are willing to fight for justice and stop this breach of international human rights.

Clearly, negative comments from politicians who were responsible for the authorization of the unfair treatment of this group spawned action, anger, and, consequently, the acknowledgment that prejudice against refugees exists. Tensions, made evident in print media, were addressed by the Sikh community in Canada who took the lead in identifying racist acts and in assuming financial responsibility for upholding Canadian humanitarianism. In terms of redress, there are no comments from politicians regarding racist attitudes that need to be stopped. There were no actions taken, or even comments made, about the need to stop or address aggressive and discriminatory protests, including those still taking place outside CFB Stadacona. In published news media there were also no comments or quotes from politicians stating how they planned to address issues of humanitarianism in terms of refugee policy. The sole focus was on the importance of tightening up immigration policy in Canada, so that no more boats filled with refugees could land on Canadian shores.

The third act of redress is perhaps the most curious. It evolves when Charlesville, Nova Scotia, a small, almost completely isolated fishing village (population 77), is turned into an international tourist site, which then becomes a physical point of contact between Charlesville's residents and the rest of the world. Prior to the arrival of the *Amelie,* Charlesville was literally not on any maps of Canada, or even of Nova Scotia. In a personal interview, one Charlesville resident clearly stated, "[T]he arrival of the *Amelie* literally put Charlesville on the map. I mean literally on the map!" (Jack 2010, personal interview 2010). Over the summer of 1987, more than five hundred tourists stopped in Charlesville, some from as far away as Texas (Hatfield 1987) and including several celebrities, such as hockey star Ken Dryden (Medel 1987b). According to news reports, residents were thrilled. They opened their hearts and homes in the same hospitable way that they had welcomed *Amelie*'s passengers. They conducted tours of the coastline, showed home videos they had made while this group was in their village, and told stories about what had happened that day (Hatfield 1987). In marking Charlesville as a destination, several residents altered lawn ornaments depicting small, black children fishing to "resemble Sikhs by painting beards and fashioning turbans out of towels" (Brazao 1987) (see figure 9.2). They also put small Canadian flags in the hands of these figures. Annie Huskins had four of these figures seated on her front steps. She said, "[N]othing exciting ever happens in Charlesville.... This is not meant as a racial slur.... We just decided to have some fun with it" (Brazao 1987). The heavy tourist traffic over the whole summer prompted residents to begin talking about capitalizing on the event by erecting a monument or building a museum, and possibly a boardwalk at the landing site that could facilitate boat tours (Medel 1987b).

Turning Charlesville into a tourist site, as an act of redress, limits the perceived crisis in several ways. One, it creates an opportunity for a heightened sense of national identity, much needed in an isolated village. It allowed Charlesville's residents to feel like they were part of an important national

Figure 9.2. "Refugees Remembered," *The Toronto Star,* Photographer: Dale Brazao, July 28, 1987: A8 (Courtesy of GetStock.com).

moment and, therefore, to establish themselves as worthy citizens in Canadian history. For many of them it never was a crisis: it was simply an opportunity to express regional hospitality, something they would have done for anyone. In reference to both the tourists and the Sikhs that visited Charlesville, Hilda Allen (age eighty-three) said, "The Lord says you never know when you might be entertaining an angel" (Hatfield 1987). For Canadians living outside Charlesville and some international tourists, it allowed them an opportunity to survey the place where the "breach" took place. In reference to 9/11, Ahmed talks about how this type of event, known as a crisis of security, spawns action in two ways: (1) It justifies the politicians' calls for a return to tighter policies. (2) And it invites citizens to police national boundaries–to look out for suspicious others (Ahmed 2004: 76). Perhaps this is what they were doing, or perhaps they were simply performing a type of "rubbernecking ... when people slow down their cars at the scene of an accident to stare out of [morbid] curiosity and then drive away" (Lippard 1999: 118, as seen in Pezzullo 2009: 101). Moreover, perhaps the summer of 1987 in Charlesville could be described as a fleeting performance of "dark tourism," where unexpected events of violence, suffering, or disasters become spur-of-the-moment attractions that draw in the curious (Foote 1997). Either way, turning a perceived crisis into a tourist attraction dilutes signs of immediate dangers.

The Final Stage: Reintegration and Shifts in Identity

According to Turner, a social drama is complete when "reintegration of the disturbed social group" occurs, or when there is recognition of an "irreparable schism between contesting parties" (Turner 1974: 41). In this case, several journalists did provide concluding commentary that either explains or suggests how social identities were altered. Ideally, it would be imagined, that in terms of this type of social drama, and at this stage in a multicultural society such as Canada, the newcomers or outsiders would be brought in, and there would be a focus on traditions and values (hopefully of humanitarianism) and national norms (hopefully tolerance) that would emphasize inclusion. Yet, it was not that simple, and I would argue that the news media's lack of follow-up articles about the *Amelie*'s passengers and their integration into Canadian society, even years later, leaves the door open for doubts and suspicions.

On August 2, 1987, one reporter from the *Toronto Star*, Louise Brown, summed up this frenzied media event in her article titled, "Our Nation: Is It Guilty of Racism?" After providing an overview of several historical moments in Canada's history, when blatant acts of racism toward refugees occurred, she summarized this event by saying, "When they first arrived the migrants were served tea and sandwiches by the people of Charlesville, Nova

Scotia, but as their unusual arrival sank into Canadian consciousness feelings changed, rumours spread about terrorism, murder and political conspiracy and suddenly frightened Canadians called newspapers, radio talk shows and politicians saying 'send them back'" (Brown 1987). In conclusion, Brown states, "[I]f we see ourselves playing a role in the international refugee scene we should stop treating the irregular arrival of a group of people as a huge circus! Our actions are not the actions of a country that says one of its fundamental concepts is multiculturalism!" (Brown 1987). Interestingly Brown refers to a collective "we," but does not identify the Canadian print media as ringmaster, production manager, and crew of this circus. Nevertheless, Brown does address the issue of racism in Canada, which was also brought forward by the Sikh community initially. Therefore, in some ways this group is vindicated and given more power–the power to speak out for justice as Canadian citizens through this social drama. In effect, the Sikh communities in Canada were almost solely responsible for the reintegration of the *Amelie*'s passengers into Canadian society because they paid for immigration lawyers, offered jobs and accommodation, and paid the hefty government bonds required for their release.[8] Through their actions, including financial assistance, they defended humanitarianism, protected this group, and brought them into Canadian society. In the end, the *Amelie*'s passengers were embraced and taken care of by Sikh communities, which were portrayed in the media as generous, caring, and unconditionally compassionate.

Although Charlesville's residents had been initially portrayed as hospitable, generous, and caring, their identities were quickly turned into that of hosts to a bourgeoning tourist industry, which was in some ways also self-affirming, and possibly offered monetary gain. According to media reports, as mentioned above, Charlesville's resident were marked as a group that would be changed forever. They had been put on the map, and could now consider themselves members of a community that was of national historic importance. I spent some time in Charlesville in 2010 talking with the individuals who had participated in helping the *Amelie*'s passengers when they first arrived. They said that the momentum for a museum or boardwalk quickly died out due to lack of funds. In the end, there was one large painted mural installed in the tourist office. Some still had clear memories, and many had large collections of newspaper clippings and certain souvenirs, which they viewed as valuable. They did feel that their lives had been changed because of this event, mostly in the sense that a connection to the rest of the world had been gleaned through an international media spotlight, and because they had been exposed to another culture, even if that lasted only for a few hours. The experience opened their eyes to immigration and multicultural issues and marked the place where they lived as part of Canada's multicultural community, something that they could not claim before this event. However, overall, life had not changed much. Tourists who visited that first summer did not return, and Charlesville returned to a quiet, mostly isolated fishing village on the edge of Nova Scotia.

Issues related to reintegration were debated through politicians' comments focused on tightening up immigration policies. Government officials were portrayed as using this event as an excuse to push Bill C-55 and a new Bill C-84 quickly into law. Bill C-84 was described in news reports as "ominous," and if put into effect would permit the Minister of Immigration "to turn away ships that are in or approaching Canadian waters if he reasonably believes them to have unauthorized immigrants aboard" (Angus and Hathaway 1987). As I stated earlier, comparably speaking there have been few arrival of refugees on Canadian shores. However, historically there have been two incidents when ships carrying refugees were turned away. One, interestingly, was the *Komagata Maru* in 1914, when 376 Indians, mostly Sikhs, arrived on the shores of Vancouver Island. They were claiming refugee status, yet were never allowed to come ashore. Canada's racist immigration policies associated with this incident have been documented by Hugh Johnston (1989), and Kazimi (2004). The second was the *St. Louis* in 1939, which was carrying approximately one thousand Jewish refugees. Both of these instances have been heralded as dark moments in Canadian history. In 1987 the media was swift to discredit Bill C-84, yet also provided a series of detailed debates concerning why it should or should not be implemented. In the end, both bills were stalled until the summer of 1988; due to heavy criticism concerning their disregard for human rights, neither came to fruition (Green 1989: 135). In 2007 an immigration spokesperson was quoted in the press as saying, "Essentially, if the *Amelie* was to arrive today under the same circumstances as 20 years ago, more or less the same thing would happen. Should they be found to not represent a risk or danger to the public, in theory they could be granted temporary work permits" (Keller 2007). This is an interesting comment in terms of ideas about representation and power.

The *Amelie*'s passengers or "the 174" were given multiple personas throughout this social drama that ranged from angels to terrorists, or even to illegal invaders! They were treated and viewed as nonhuman and as objects of desire. This dichotomy has been well documented in various histories of othering,[9] and, more specifically, can be associated with histories of othering in relation to refugees, "boat people," and Sikhs. In late August 1987, there were several published articles that explained the persecution these men endured in India in their own words, including printed quotes from leaders within the group. One man clearly stated, "We are not [immigration] queue-jumpers. We're not immigrants. We're refugees fleeing persecution" (Malarek 1987). The same individual also said, "If the media gives the right story we will win the sympathy of Canadians at large. We will win their support. We simply want to tell them what has happened to us, to our families, to our people" (Malarek 1987). Over the years since the *Amelie*'s arrival there have been occasional articles reminiscing and updating the public about this event. In 2007 an article written by James Keller circulated in several newspapers across the country. It is typical in that it provides a brief overview of the story: hungry and thirsty refugees crammed together on a freighter for three weeks, Charlesville's residents bring them peanut butter sandwiches and Kool-Aid when they land, and the federal government's initial call to tighten the system evaporates (Keller 2007). There has yet to be a published explanation of the fate of this group and how, or if, they integrated into Canadian society. They have obviously integrated, and assumingly are well, have families and are prosperous, but for the Canadian public, this still remains a mystery.

Lynda Mannik is a lecturer in Cultural Anthropology at York University. Her research interests include race, ethnicities, and multiculturalism; refugee and asylum seeker migration; photography and memory; journalism and media studies. She is the author of *Photography, Memory and Refugee Identity: The Voyage of the SS Walnut, 1948* (University of British Columbia Press, 2012); *Reclaiming Canadian Bodies: Representation and Visual Media* (Wilfrid Laurier Press, 2015); and *Canadian Indian Cowboys: Rodeo, Representation and the RCMP at the Royal Easter Show, 1939* (University of Calgary Press, 2006). She has also published in *Visual Studies, Journalism Studies*, and *Memory Studies*.

Notes

This research has been supported by the Social Sciences and Humanities Research Council of Canada (SSHRC) through the Postdoctoral Fellowship Program.

1. Canadian government documents concerning this voyage are still under restricted access even for researchers, but one later news report stated specifically that there were 165 Sikhs, 4 Muslims, 4 Hindus, and one female Turkish national (Story 1987b).
2. The term *boat people* became popular in the 1970s in reference to refugees fleeing Vietnam on small, crowded boats. Although considered to be a derogatory term, it is still used frequently, particular in media and popular culture venues, to describe any refugees or asylum seekers that are migrating by boat.
3. See an earlier article for a detailed account of the different ways local newspaper and national newspapers portrayed these sentiments (Mannik 2014).
4. As I have stated elsewhere, it is common in Canadian media to find sensationalized reports of one or more additional boats that about to arrive days after the original event. For example, after the *Amelie*'s arrival, details about the origins of a second boat abound for 3 days (Mannik 2014: 79).
5. The sole woman from Turkey seems to have disappeared and was not mentioned in the press after the first day.
6. In August 1986 two lifeboats holding 151 Tamils from Sri Lanka were found floating just outside Newfoundland. Initially they claimed to have been adrift for five days and would not say how they had made it across the Atlantic.

7. For a more detailed discussion of letters to the editor concerning the arrival of the *Amelie*, see Mannik (2014: 82–83).
8. The Canadian government required every passenger to pay a performance bond valued between $3,000 and $9,000 prior to their release and these bonds were all paid by various members of Sikh communities in Canada. Controversy ensued over the insistence on bonds based solely on ethnic and religious affiliations (McAndrews and Henteon 1987).
9. Two scholars who have written seminal works on the relationship among desire, fear, and others are Ann Stoler (2002) and Mary Louise Pratt (1992).

Bibliography

Ahmed, Sara. 2004. *The Cultural Politics of Emotion*. London/New York: Routledge.
Anonymous. 1987a. "A Dangerous Backlash." *Maclean's Magazine*, August 10: 13.
———. 1987b. "The Numbers Arriving." *Globe and Mail*, August 6, p. A6.
"Backlog of Paperwork Could Result in Migrants Being Detained Longer." 1987. *Globe and Mail*, July 27.
Brazao, Dale. 1987. "Village Residents Still Trying to Come to Grips with 'Invasion.'" *Toronto Star*, July 28, p. A8.
Brown, Louise. 1987. "Our Nation: Is It Guilty of Racism? East Indians' Case Recalls Some Errors We Made in the Past and Foces Us to Ask Who We Really Are" *Toronto Star*, August 2.
Buckie, Catherine. 1987. "Sikh Petition for Release of Boat People." *Gazette*, Montreal, July 20.
Coman, Mihan. 2008. "Liminality in Media Studies: From Everyday Life to Media Events" In *Victor Turner and Contemporary Cultural Performance*, edited by Graham St. John, 94–108. Oxford: Berghahn Books.
Coonfield, Gordon, and John Huxford. 2009. "News Images as Lived Images: Media Ritual, Cultural Performance, and Public Trauma." *Critical Studies in Media Communication* 26, no. 5: 457–79.
Cottle, Simon. 2006. "Mediatized Rituals: Beyond Manufacturing Consent." *Media, Culture and Society* 28, no. 3: 411–32.
Dutton, Don. 1987. "New Arrivals Silently Greet Parade of Media." *Toronto Star*, July 14, A9.
Foote, K. 1997. *Shadowed Ground: America's Landscapes of Violence and Tragedy*. Austin: University of Texas.
Edwards, Peter. 1987. "Frustration, Racism Mark Irate Calls over East Indians." *Toronto Star*, July 18.
Ettema, James S. 1990. "Press Rites and Rae Relations: A Study of Mass-Mediated Ritual." *Critical Studies in Mass Communication* 7, no. 4: 309–31.
Green, Ian. 1989. *The Charter of Rights*. Lorimer: Toronto.
Harper, T. 1987. "B. C.-bound Migrants Generate a Whiff of Racism." *Toronto Star*, July 31.
Hatfield, Belle. 1987. "Charlesville Big Boom." *Maclean's Magazine*, October 5: 8.
Hay, Colin. 1996. "Discursive Construction of the Winter of Discontent." *Sociology* 30, no. 2: 253–77.

Janigan, Mary, Hilary Mackenzie, and Paul Gessell. 1987. "A Harrowing Story." *Maclean's Magazine,* August 17: 10.
Johnston, Hugh. 1989. *The Voyage of the Komagata Maru, The Sikh Challenge to Canada's Colour Bar.* Vancouver: University of British Columbia Press.
Kazimi, Ali (Director). 2004. *Continuous Journey.* [Film]. In Association with TV Ontario, Toronto, Canada.
Keller, James. 2007. "Sikh Refugees Who Landed on N. S. Beach 20 Years Ago Now Settled across Canada." *National News* (Canadian Press), July 10.
Malarek, Victor. 1987. "Migrants Describe Harrowing 19 Days Spent in Cargo Hold of Leaky Freighter." *Globe and Mail,* August 5.
Mannik, Lynda. 2014. "Remembering Arrivals of Refugees by Boat in a Canadian Context." *Memory Studies* 7, no. 2: 76–91.
Martin, Robert. 1987. "164 Migrants Heading to Toronto and Vancouver When Bonds Paid." *Globe and Mail,* July 24.
Maxwell, Ian. 2008. "The Ritualization of Performance (Studies)." In *Victor Turner and Contemporary Cultural Performance,* edited by Graham St. John. New York and Oxford: Berghahn Book. 2008: 94–108.
McAndrews, Brian and Darcy Henton. 1987. "Sikh Sponsors Feel It's a Duty to Provide Bonds for Migrants." *Toronto Star,* July 30.
McDevitt, M., M. Briziarelli, and B. Klocke. "Social Drama in the Academic-Media Nexus: Journalism's Strategic Response to Deviant Ideas." *Journalism* 14, no. 1: 111–28.
Medel, Brian. 1987a. "Barrington Council opt to leave Charlesville cassettes with RCMP." *Chronicle Herald,* August 27.
———. 1987b. "Migrants Spark Tourism Boom." *Halifax Chronicle* August 27.
O'Donnell Joe. 1987 "Mulroney Rules Out Special Treatment." *Toronto Star,* July 13.
Peterson, Michael A. 2003. *Anthropology of Mass Communication: Media and Myth in the New Millennium.* Oxford: Berghahn Books.
Pezzulla Phaedra C. 2009. '"This Is the Only Tour That Sells": Tourism, Disaster, and National Identity in New Orleans." *Journal of Tourism and Cultural Change* 7, no. 1: 99–114.
Pratt, Mary Louise. 1992. *Imperial Eyes: Travel Writing and Transculturation.* London/ New York: Routledge.
Pugh, Michael. 2004. "Drowning Not Waving: Boat People and Humanitarianism at Sea." *Journal of Refugee Studies* 17, no. 1: 50–69.
Sallot, Jeff. 1987. "PM Praises Freedom, Tolerance in BC Tour." *Globe and Mail,* July 13.
Stefaniuk, Walter. 1987a. "Leaders of Ethnic Groups Seek U.N. Investigation onto Refugees Treatment." *Toronto Star,* July 29.
———. 1987b. "Non-Sikh Teacher Offers $5,000 for Refugee Bond." *Toronto Star,* July 29.
Stoler, Ann. 2002. *Carnal Knowledge and Imperial Power: Race and the Intimate in Colonial Rule.* Los Angeles: University of California Press.
Story, Alan. 1987a. "Racist Taunts Fly as Refugee 'Circus' Angers Residents." *Toronto Star,* July 24.
———. 1987b. "Mystery Surrounds East Indian Migrants." *Toronto Star,* July 29.

Turner, Victor. 1974. *Dramas, fields and metaphors*. Ithaca, NY: Cornell University Press.
———. 1988. "Introduction." In *The Anthropology of Performance*. New York: PAJ Publications. http://erikapaterson08.pbworks.com/f/Antrophology%20of%20performance(2).pdf.
Ward, Olivia. 1987. "Treatment of Migrants Breaks Law, Lawyers Say." *Toronto Star*, July 18.
Wilson, Deborah. 1987. "Detention now 'Racism,' Sikh Leaders Charge Ottawa Officials Likened to Ku Klux Klan; Observer Points to U.S." *Globe and Mail*, July 17.

10

Islands and Images of Flight around Europe's Southern Rim

Trouble in Heterotopia

Helen M. Hintjens

> Islands serve ... as prototypes and microcosmic images of the nation–state.
> Perera 2009: 6.

> If it is genuinely the absolute right of every person to leave his native country, some states must between them have the duty to admit those who do so.
> Dummett 2001: 50.

The main focus of this chapter is to compare media reporting and film related to the flight of refugees to some tiny islands in the Mediterranean. The chapter explores how Europe's small islands are represented in media and in film both as places of refuge and of horror, metaphorical and literal landing points and clearinghouses for human movement between Europe's southern Mediterranean shores, North Africa, and the Middle East. The aim is to shed light on the contradictory images of small islands that can be found in both media and film. Such images represent islands as, at one and the same time, symbolic of safety and protection, and of horror, rejection, isolation, and death.

The combination of utopic and dystopic images is not peculiar to how small islands are imagined. What Foucault characterized as heterotopia can be applied to boats at sea as well, including those vessels that simultaneously bring refugees to safety, and bring them into the direst peril. A contemporary discussion of the notion of heterotopia can be found in Pugliese (2010), a useful source for this chapter. I consider just two examples. One is Lampedusa, and how refugee movements to the island were depicted in the media between 2011 and 2012, at the time of the war with Libya. The second is the island of Linosa, the location of the film *Terraferma* that is briefly analyzed later in this chapter (di Franceschi 2013; Schrader and Winkler, 2013; Crialese 2011).

The context of these examples is the virtual closure of legal avenues of movement for migrants coming into the European Union (EU) by sea. The Libyan civil war, and NATO's armed intervention in Libya in 2011, reinforced a securitization of EU borders that had started before 2001, and was speeded up by the "war on terror." With civil war and flight from Syria, an entire region has become beset by the mass movements of populations, and flight continues out of many parts of the African continent as well. Small islands located along the transit routes to Europe, cannot but become involved in "staving off" the movement of refugees from the south.

So-called boat people, refugees who seek to enter the EU through Lampedusa or other small islands like Lesbos, are in search of safety. Yet in searching for safety, they risk being abandoned by crews, being rammed, or being abandoned to their fate, ignored. If they get in trouble, they may be rescued by a naval vessel or a charity boat, or may not. Lampedusa, an island located some distance south of mainland Italy, is often the destination of boats full of refugees and migrants, leaving from Libya.[1] Lampedusa has also become a mass burial ground, for people and for wrecked boats, making Lampedusa heterotopia incarnate. An even smaller island, Linosa, is the location for the Italian film *Terraferma* (Crialese 2011). In Lampedusa and Linosa, local representations of migrants and refugees, and of others, like tourists, who arrive on the islands' shores, fluctuate between solidarity and rejection. Islanders are divided by conflicting ethical and economic demands placed on them by an era of globalized human movement.

Through an examination of media reports and a full-length feature film, this chapter explores insular paradoxes. Island territories and their populations can be windows to a deeper understanding of wider struggles around meanings, livelihoods, rights, and protection, as well as insecurity and war, in relation to global refugee movements. In a context of securitized border controls and a widening EU perimeter, exclusionary measures are a feature of the European legal system and of the EU imaginary. This is nothing new, perhaps, since from the earliest modern times small islands have been located on the maritime routes of invaders, crusaders, traders, and liberators. Islanders themselves have long feared, and depended on, the depravations of empire, the twists and turns of which have been key for their internal evolution (Gebrewold 2007; Marfleet 2006).

Media reporting of refugees in boats often includes images taken from above, of those in peril, or of those rescued (usually with bright life jackets in the latter case), packed in tightly on the deck of a boat or even a dinghy. Massimo Sestini's photos, for example, show Syrian refugee families rescued at sea, wearing life jackets and body heating blankets, and looking from the air just like brightly packed cargo. Photographs of migrants, arriving half dead or even completely dead at the island jetties, or washed up the beach, have proliferated and can be found across the Internet and other media. Many such images have been analyzed by scholars (Gilligan and Marley 2010). I first consider media reporting, without focusing directly on these images, and then consider the case of the film *Terraferma* (Crialese 2011).

The two island cases presented in this chapter aim to clarify the peculiar mix of horror and hopefulness, creativity and despair that characterize the reporting of "paradisical" island settings gone wrong. Selecting Lampedusa and Linosa as the focus serves to bring attention to paradoxical representations of refugees and boat people, of the island spaces and their locations at the edges of Europe today. By exposing the selective closure of the shore to outsiders, the possibilities open up for reimagining islands as shared public spaces where artists, migrants, islanders, and filmmakers can encounter one another. Islands can be reinvented as places that combine elements of sanctuary with elements of the closed penitentiary, both locking in and locking out. The island, thus imagined, is at once historically a fortress against attacks and somewhere that imagined utopic visions of a better society can be projected onto. The role such small heterotopic places can play is often much more significant than their size or population would imply (Lowenthal, 2007; Hintjens and Newitt 1992).

Fortress Europe as the Wider Context of Media Images

The history of the construction of Fortress Europe in relation to the African continent has been discussed in more detail elsewhere (Basaran 2011: 62–73). Europe's territory is now almost completely closed off to migrants from the poorer Middle East, and from poorer African countries. Fortress Europe is not a purely polemical term, since many EU member states act as if they were under attack from a dangerous alien enemy, erecting legal and even physical barriers around their borders, and policing Europe's southern coastlines through Frontex and national coastguards. Even NATO operations have been extended to include migration policing. Since the 1980s, hardening attitudes and a culture of disbelief have combined to create a massive EU proto-mediaeval city-state, known as Fortress Europe. Not neatly confined to the present borders of the EU, however, the ramparts of this fortress stretch thousands of miles into deserts across the Sahel, cutting across Turkey, Iraq, and the mountainous regions of Syria and the hinterlands of Eastern Europe.

The locking down of an outer perimeter beyond the rim of the EU and its immediate southern border across the trans-Saharan region has not slowed migration. What one author calls the "concentric circles" of EU border controls have shifted well beyond the immediate southern and eastern borders of the EU (Anderson and Armstrong, 2007). Efforts to stem movement through Sahelian and Middle Eastern maritime routes used for centuries for transmigration and trade have resulted in the reversal of human rights norms where migrants are concerned. The results have been more and more rebellions across the new no-man's lands as trans-Saharan and maritime routes of passage are militarized, and as those fleeing hunger, persecution, war, and terror are caught and returned to where they came from. As young men flee Eritrea, and entire families of Syrians try to cross the Mediterranean in dinghies, the profile of migrants and refugees has become more youthful and mixed, with entire families, mothers, small children, and babies on board. Some are rescued, as the movement of decrepit fishing boats across the Mediterranean continues.

The examples in this chapter are centered on the Italian experience. Italy has southern islands closer to the North African mainland than to Italy's southern coast. Lampedusa, one of the southernmost islands, is almost the first dry land those coming by boat from Tunisia or Libya can reach. Located at the very rim of Europe, or in the Atlantic, or in the eastern Mediterranean, these tiny islands are the staging posts of previous eras of trade and warfare.[2]

Nongovernmental organization (NGO) estimates of the numbers of casualties at sea, including drownings and deaths by other means, declined during the 1990s, but increased again from 2003 onward, rising dramatically from 2008 or so around the European perimeter. The "war on terror" has fed into a "proxy war on refugees," with boat people's conditions a reminder of the last period of mass boat-based refugee movement: the Vietnam exodus of the 1970s. The right of *non-refoulement* has been unambiguously violated in the name of border controls, and cruel and degrading treatment has become more or less government policy among some frontier states of the EU, notably Greece (ECRE, 2014; Fekete 2005). Technologies of surveillance-for-exclusion have been stepped up in a widening arc of semipermanent exclusion of those considered "undesirable" (Namh 2006: 238).

During 2011 Italy started to bitterly resent its role as conduit for growing numbers of people, African men in particular, fleeing civil war and violence in Libya especially. Those fleeing civil war in Syria later joined them, crossing the Mediterranean on leaky fishing vessels. Those who undertake such risky journeys weigh up the odds when embarking on such perilous journeys, showing that their choices are very limited. Most cannot go home because of war; if they remain in the camps in the region, they remain close to where the violence continues. They fear being recruited into militias and being forced to fight for one side or another. They then prefer to risk death on the open sea, in a boat even their children can see is not seaworthy, than to remain in the camps. Under cover of darkness, sometimes not knowing where they are supposed to land, locked up and left adrift on the ocean by their captains, thousands of migrants cross the Mediterranean every year in fishing boats, cargo vessels, and rubber dinghies.

Islands in Our Minds: Imagining Heterotopia

The powerfully associative imagery attached to islands suggests they are both safe havens and places of confinement, of liberation but also of horror and imprisonment. Islands as geographical entities, surrounded on all sides by sea or other water, also represent a metaphysical idea of society as a visible unit. Their ambivalent, heterotopic image is pervasive, and veers between mass drownings at sea, desperate efforts to reach the island shore, and promises of arrival and sanctuary, protection and safety on landing. Illusory promises of safety are also common, since migrants can often be deported back to where they embarked in the first place. Paradise is constantly found and lost again, and found again, in such imagery. Thus bodies washed up on beaches, dead or exhausted, are bodies of the hopeful who seek to overcome the barriers of what it is only a small exaggeration to term the "global apartheid" of border controls (Marfleet 2006: 156–57; Muggah and Mogire 2006; Stedman and Tanner 2003).

Thomas More's *Utopia* was famously set on an island created by humans to separate it from the mainland so a perfect society could flourish. Islands are the locus for much past and present scientific research on epidemiology, plant and animal species; they serve as living laboratories for many natural scientists. "The thought or concept of islands has informed literary, scientific, artistic and popular culture" (Royle 2001: 11). It is the boundedness and remoteness of islands that has made them both ideal locations for research that formed the basis for Darwin's theories of the evolution of species, for example, or Margaret Mead's study of human sexuality and maturing. Various novels and other fiction take the island's boundedness as a way to make more visible themes that might be obscured on huge continental land masses (Baldacchino 2007, 2008; Royle 2001: 22–23).

Of course, much fiction and social research around islands is "not about islands at all but about metaphors of islandness" (Lowenthal 2006: 259, reviewing Skinner and Hills 2006). As one review of nissology (i.e., the study of islands) noted, social scientists hesitate to draw the kinds of generalized conclusions that natural scientists do on the basis of studies conducted in islands. The debate is ongoing as to whether "islands are characterised by vulnerability or resilience … victims of change, economically dependent, and at the mercy of unscrupulous neo-colonial manipulation, or ... uniquely resourceful in the face of such threats" (Hay 2006: 21).

The notion of heterotopia is useful for this study since it brings together and juxtaposes intertwined and contradictory qualities of small island life, and the hopes and despairs of the boat people who seek to land at the beach and across the border. Idyllic, romantic visions of remote islands as holiday destinations sit alongside the brutal trope of the internment camp or gulag that may exist within the same space. Such contrasting imagery can also be noted in how small islands were imagined outside Europe, for example in Australia and New Zealand, the Antipodes (Perera, 2009; McMahon 2003). Employing the concept of heterotopia "enables the conceptualisation of absolute difference within the space of simultaneity," as Pugliese puts it, allowing for often bizarre juxtapositions and between images and information about the hopefulness of migrants arriving on islands like Lampedusa and Linosa, and the disillusions of reality once they do land (Pugliese 2010: 106).

As the great human geographer of islands, David Lowenthal, reminded us, islands are used in literature—and in film and other media imagery—as metaphors for the human self, stranded and at sea in the universe. Islands as places of cruelty and isolation, as places of freedom, self-discovery, and realization, serve mainly to illustrate the philosophical and constitutional preferences of authors' imaginations, from William Golding's pessimistic vision in *Lord of the Flies* to the relative optimism of Daniel Defoe's *Robinson Crusoe* and the dream of Thomas More's *Utopia*. "Each of us is at the same time consciously individual, marooned in self-awareness ... yet ... also inseparably bound up with ancestors and descendants. Every atom of our being is shaped by history and prior location and is likewise destined to inhabit innumerable future entities beyond our mortal tenure" (Lowenthal 2007: 219, see also Lowenthal, 1987). Neither a falsely positive picture, nor an entirely gloomy one, can meet the need for realism combined with a politics of hope that needs to endure. Thus heterotopia is a guiding concept for this study because it permits of more than one vision of what islands mean (see the debate between Gilligan and Marley [2010], for example, and Pupavac [2008]).

Dehydration, overexposure, suntan cream, and fish markets all can be found on the beaches of Mediterranean islands like Lampedusa and Linosa. Police and maritime guards patrol these spaces, and lifeguards who keep watch for those swimming for pleasure may also detect those in danger of drowning near the shore. As is explained later, in the film *Terraferma* (Crialese 2011), islanders find themselves behind the beach frontiers, squeezed "between exclusion and inclusion ... the known and the unknown ... the past and the future, utopia and hell, reality and the imagination" (Anderson 2003: 47). First I will consider how migration to Lampedusa was imagined during the period of civil war and NATO intervention in Libya.

Between Libya and Lampedusa: No Innocent Passage?

Article 17 of The United Nations Convention on the Law of the Seas (UNCLOS) states, "Subject to this Convention, ships of all States, whether coastal or land-locked, enjoy the right of innocent passage through the territorial sea." The International Law of the Seas thus protects boats. This provision also clearly protects people in boats or ships, and who find themselves in trouble at sea. Under Article 18, Paragraph 2, it is provided for that boats should move smoothly and expeditiously, except for certain purposes when they may anchor, for example when this is "rendered necessary by force majeure or distress or for the purpose of rendering assistance to persons" (UNCLOS 1994). Furthermore, Article 98 of UNCLOS provides that masters of ships are required: "to render assistance to any person found at sea in danger of being lost," and "(b) to proceed with all possible speed to the rescue of persons in distress, if informed of their need of assistance, in so far as such action may reasonably be expected of him; ships or aircraft in danger or distress."

The European Convention on Human Rights similarly protects not only legal residents, but everyone's right to life. Human rights law and the law of the sea thus converge to give protection to those in trouble at sea. This is supposed to have priority over any security or immigration-based controls by policing agencies like Frontex and the national army, maritime police, or coast guard. Under the provisions of these laws, boats and ships are unambiguously supposed to be locations of safety and security, and should not be loci of fragility and terror, as arguably has become the case in recent years (Tauman 2002). Table 10.1 shows that despite rescues at sea, many lives were lost during this period, taking only a sample of cases that mention Lampedusa explicitly. For some weeks, during the civil war and allied attack on Libya, Lampedusa moved to the epicenter of a "war on migrants" within and around the EU (Rodier 2013). The UNHCR (United Nations High Commission for Refugees 2014) suggests that 1,500 refugees lost their lives fleeing to Europe in 2012 on the Mediterranean route alone. This is likely to be an underestimate based on media reports from different sources, which have produced an estimate that close to 23,000 people have drowned and died in other ways trying to reach the EU, over a period of twenty years or so. The NGO United for Intercultural Action, an EU-wide network of 550 organizations formerly based in Amsterdam, stopped updating the list from October 2012. The list aimed to ensure the visibility of such deaths, something that is more likely without the collection of data in 2013 and 2014. One website reports on the "Fatal Policies of Fortress Europe" and notes, "Most probably 1000s more are never found," even though the "data are collected through ... research [and] information received from 550 network organisations in 48 countries and from local experts, journalists and researchers in the field of migration." Table 10.1 was derived from this list (United Against Racism 2012).[3]

Table 10.1. Recorded deaths at sea near Lampedusa

Date	Number	Details
16/03/12	5 N.N.	found in boat of 57 on way to Lampedusa (I) rescued by Italian authorities in Libyan waters PICUM/LR/jW
16/01/11	33 N.N.	Afghanistan missing, feared drowned when ship sank near Corfu (GR) on way to Italy, 230 survivors Clandestin E/FE/AFP/KI/VK/MNS/BBC
25/03/11	295 N.N.	unknown feared drowned after 2 boats traveling together from Sidi Bilal (LY) sank on way to Italy PUB/Reu/Guardian/ MUGAK/Quotidiano
25/03/11	10 N.N.	Egypt feared drowned after 2 boats traveling together from Sidi Bilal (LY) sank on way to Italy PUB/Reu/TunisieSoir/GuardianUn
27/03/11	308 N.N.	unknown feared drowned, boat of 335 left Libya for Italy has been missing for 2 weeks Quotidiano/LR/Migeurop/Kaosenlared/RAI
04/08/11	100 N.N.	Africa unknown, bodies thrown overboard from LY boat rescued 104 miles from Lampedusa (I) Telegraph/MAS/CDM
06/04/11	37 N.N. (women)	Bangladesh/Chad/Ivory Coast/Nigeria/Somalia/Sudan missing, part of 325 migrants on LY-I boat, sank 39 miles from Lampedusa in Maltesee waters LR/ANSA/Reu/Migreurop/Raz/Mail Online/Irish
06/04/11	177 N.N.	Bangladesh/Chad/Ivory Coast/Nigeria/Somalia/Sudan missing, part of 325 migrants on LY-I boat, sank 39 miles from Lampedusa in Maltese waters LR/ANSA/Reu/Migreurop/Raz/Mail Online/Iris
02/06/11	270 N.N.	West Africa/Pakistan/Bangladesh drowned, 2 found, overcrowded boat capsized 300km from Tripoli (LY) to Lampedusa (I) Migreurop/Mugak/UNHCR/Reu/Universo/RAI/PICUM/MUGAK/Quotidiano
01/08/11	25 N.N. (men)	Sub-Saharan Africa suffocated, traveling on boat with 275 survivors, SOS sent 35 miles from Lampedusa (I) SP/FE/Le Figaro
28/03/11	10 N.N.	Sub-Saharan Africa drowned, boat sank on way to Lampedusa (I) from LY, 6 rescued by Egyptian fishing boats Guardian Un./PerCat/AdnK

Between February and April 2011, as war was raging in Libya, more than thirty thousand migrants landed on Lampedusa, and the island's shoreline become more famous for photos of dead bodies in body bags and coffins in warehouses than it was for the blue sea or warm sun of the tourist brochures and Web sites. Body bags on the beach are of course not the kind of media representation tourist destination islands want. However, since bad news tends to be reported more than good, news of deaths at sea remains a staple for EU media reporting and for press photographers alike.

One of the photos by Javier Bauluz, discussed in a text by Gilligan and Marley, shows the spectacle of an apparently dead body close to a couple of sunbathers.[4] This is the kind of image that at first shocked the European public and later seems to have reinforced a certain indifference to such deaths which seem routine given their frequency (Gilligan and Marley, 2010). During the Libyan war, a boat containing seventy-two Sub-Saharan Africans left Libya heading for Lampedusa. Soon the vessel ran out of fuel, and started drifting back south. People started to die on the boat, but the Italian coast guard ignored requests for help. A NATO warship and several fishing vessels in the area also ignored repeated calls for help. An animated map and blog (now removed from the Internet) showed how only eleven people survived. Nine made it to Europe and to relative safety, where one was later arrested in The Netherlands, and was deported.[5] The terrible journey became the subject of numerous media articles and of a mapping exercise, tracing the movements of the ill-fated boat, to try and determine what happened, why calls for help were ignored, and who was responsible. By coincidence, one of the three survivors of another shipwreck, starred as a migrant woman, heavily pregnant, in the film *Terraferma,* discussed in the next part of the chapter.

There had been deportations from Lampedusa to Libya for years before the civil war in Libya started, and in one example more than a thousand "irregular" migrants were deported to Libya between October 3 and 7, 2004, on military airplanes. As one scholar reported, "It is the last day of August and at the airport of Lampedusa … yet another deportation of 'undocumented' migrants is taking place. The incident appears as wrapped in the mantel of ordinariness that exacerbates even more the violence of the event" (Andrijasevic 2006: 120). This event resonates with the idea of heterotopia as a context where cruelty and dreams interlock in a way that appears banal. By 2011, when war broke out, many who had fled Libya in boats had been returned several times, and were again fleeing to Europe, often for the third, fourth, or fifth time. Without: "access to asylum procedures in Lampedusa," they could be returned again "to Libya, a country that is not their country of origin but of transit and that does not have a functioning asylum system, has not signed the Geneva Convention on Refugees and practices large-scale expulsion of undocumented migrants in which … people … lost their lives" (Andrijasevic 2006: 120).

In 2012, in the case of *Hirsi Jamaa and others v. Italy* (Case No. 27765/09, 23.2.2012), the European Court of Human Rights ruled that the Italian government had clearly violated the principle of nonforcible return prior to asylum applications being lodged, or *non-refoulement.* Italy was accused of ignoring the 1951 Geneva Convention in a court case that involved Eritreans forcibly returned to Libya from Italy in 2009. In this case, the European Court reminded the Italian government that *non-refoulement* was "a cardinal protection principle enshrined in the Convention, to which no reservations are permitted. In many ways, the principle is the logical complement to the right to seek asylum recognized in the Universal Declaration of Human Rights."[6] The judgement of the court also reminded the Italian government that the absolute prohibition of torture requires respect for *non-refoulement*. Summary deportation was strictly prohibited, since "rejection at the frontier, interception and indirect *refoulement*, whether of an individual seeking asylum or in situations of mass influx" was also prohibited (European Court of Human Rights 2012). Since the EU authorities and their North African partners continue to collaborate in mass *refoulement* across borders, legal cases are likely to continue to arise in future.

Some media reports of arrivals in Lampedusa strike a more optimistic note. In an article entitled "By Boat to Lampedusa and a New Life," the emphasis is on Lampedusa as a haven, a place of safety (IRIN 2011).[7] This boat brought people fleeing war in Tripoli, and arrived June 12, 2011. The article reports that, "Migrants are first processed by Italian police at Lampedusa's two centres and are given hot meals, access to showers and beds. A designated ferry then transports migrants from Lampedusa to Sicily several times a week. Next, they are allocated to holding centres in places such as Mineo, Naples or Bari, where it takes 7–30 days to receive a six-month visa" (IRIN 2011). There are also reports that they were issued new shoes and clothes. The island emerges as a place of transition, a stage in their progress toward a new and a better life. Indeed, this story almost appeared too good to be true: obtaining a visa in just thirty days would be far from automatic, as the perhaps the ill-informed journalist suggests.

Coming from eastern Sierra Leone, according to the article, Sonny Johnson, who is interviewed in the same article says that he had a well-paid job in Libya, but that racism had increased with the war, and "I started to get tired in my soul. Then I knew I had to leave, and I decided to try to come by boat," there being no other obvious way out of Tripoli. This sounds like a different Lampedusa, a kinder, more-receptive, and more-generous location, where those seeking refuge are not returned forcibly to a place of former terror, and where grim realities of death, detention, and deportation are not as apparent as outside Europe (Fekete 2005; IRIN 2011).

Refugee movements are likely to continue to rise, and despite the Italian government policy of *Mare Nostrum* involving the Italian navy in operational rescues at sea, the numbers of drownings increased even before 2015. The crisis of boat people heading for Mediterranean islands like Lampedusa is thus far from over (UNHCR 2014). By June 2014 the UNHCR declared openly that the whole asylum and migration situation around the coasts of

North Africa and the southern Mediterranean could no longer continue as it was and proposed processing refugees outside Europe on a massive scale, including in countries such as Egypt, Libya, and Sudan. This model seems to be based on the Australian policy of processing asylum seekers in remote islands like Papua New Guinea, off-shore, a policy that violates many basic rights, including the right to claim asylum and to have legal representation.[8]

Terraferma: Heterotopia on Film

Part of a "new wave" of Italian cinema that questions mainstream approaches to migration, the film *Terraferma* (Schrader and Winkler, 2013; Crialese 2011), meaning dry land or mainland, was Italy's official entry for the Academy Awards Best Foreign Film and Foreign Oscar in 2011. Directed by Emanuele Crialese and set in and around the Sicilian island of Linosa, the film debuted at Venice and won various awards and nominations. The film depicts the contrasting modes of survival of islanders themselves, and is broadly sympathetic to the situation of both islanders and migrants, including those lucky few who arrive on the island's shores (de Franceschi 2013; O'Healy 2010).

It is interesting to note that, culturally speaking, the south of Italy and the islands of Sicily such as Linosa were long considered by Italians (and even by the Romans) as culturally more African than European (Pugliese 2010: 107). According to one source, "[T]he smaller islands of Sicily were nearly all inhabited or at least seen in the Roman times, and with regard to the Middle Ages (12th century) Al Idrisi (1099–1165) mentioned Linosa among the islands, also called in Arabic 'Namusah'" (Maurici 2008). Linosa, like Lampedusa, may be more African than European in terms of history and location, but geopolitically it is inside the EU, and herein lies the central theme of *Terraferma*.

The story revolves around the rescue of–and failure to rescue–people drowning at sea, centering on attitudes and behavior of one intergenerational island family. The old fisherman and his grandson one day rescue a number of migrants, who dive off a dinghy and swam toward their fishing vessel. The last two people to be rescued are a pregnant woman and her young son. When they arrive at night back on the island, most of those they rescue run away into the night, but the pregnant woman and her son remain hidden at the fisherman's family home. This produces a life-changing few days for the family, and is the situation depicted in the film. The daughter of the old fisherman finds the rescue far from ideal, since she knows her whole family can be prosecuted for giving shelter to "illegals," as the authorities make perfectly clear.

The old fisherman's son makes his living from entertaining tourists, and has abandoned fishing altogether. He takes young, beautiful people out on a luxury boat, and their bodies are filmed as they dive off into the blue water, making a sharp contrast with the migrants who also jump off the floating dinghy—not for pleasure, but to stay alive. The film deliberately juxtaposes such images of the desperation and happiness of humanity, contrasting the boats and the humans on them, and their reasons for jumping in the sea. Heterotopia is very much in evidence here. Four boats form the visual pointers in the movie, expressing the polarized realities of island life, and its divided, heterotopic qualities. The old fisherman's vessel is practical and resilient, profoundly linked with the sea and with making a living from it. The migrants' dinghy is hardly a boat, and is barely afloat when it is first sighted. The third boat, a luxury tourist vessel, is not for anything serious, but for pleasure alone. The boat, a ferry, connects the island to the mainland, and is heavily policed by the border police. Tourists come in this way. All these boats meet in the island, expressing its diverse relationship with the sea and with outsiders.

What *Terraferma* depicts in this way is the surreal quality of island life when an imagined holiday paradise overlaps with the nightmare of refugees swimming through the sea, making for the beach, grabbing onto and almost capsizing a small boat at night, being alternately rescued and abandoned to their fate. The grandson of the old fisherman tries to woo a local girl one night, and is terrified when migrants start to swim toward his boat. Afraid they will capsize his small vessel, he pushes them off and leaves the men to drown. The next day some of those he abandoned are washed up on the island's shore and are (somewhat unrealistically) revived by tourists, who are depicted as angels of mercy. They do not sit sunning themselves on the beach in indifference, but care for those who land on the beach. However, soon border guards arrive and those migrants who have just been revived and managed to survive their ordeal are immediately arrested.

As lives intersect, the point of arrival becomes the point of departure, and the two (or three, or four) worlds collide on the beach, and in the boats. In one beautiful scene in the film, the pregnant woman shows on a shining globe of the earth how she traveled from Ethiopia across the desert to reach the shore of Libya and from there to the island across the sea. Within and around the geographical confines of the tiny, mostly barren island of Linosa, most islanders would prefer to turn their backs on the sea and ignore those who travel to seek safety on their shores, but in practice they cannot ignore them, since they arrive and demand their human response.

The four boats in the film—the dinghy, the fishing boat, the pleasure boat, and the ferry—represent microcosmic worlds within the island's overall heterotopic reality. Whereas the dinghy and fishing boat become the scene of a human drama, the pleasure boat is just a jumping-off point for organized fun. The ferry brings tourists and takes them away again, along with goods and mail. The old man and his grandson barely earn their living, and otherwise find themselves in an impossible situation, with the old man doing his best to rescue those in trouble, whilst the grandson fails to do this when he has the chance.

The heavily pregnant woman and her son are given shelter by the old fisherman's daughter and the family. Torn between her sense of responsibility toward the pregnant woman and her fear of being detected helping someone "illegal," and so being fined or punished, the island woman is not kind to the pregnant woman, and does not wish to receive her thanks. Eventually the woman and her son are taken away to the mainland, not on the ferry (where they would be arrested) but in the old fisherman's boat. As the movie depicts it, between the migrants' desperation and their hope of redemption, and the islanders who would like to help them, lies the law, which expressly forbids such help and would like to enforce a tight exclusion from the island, and compulsory return.

The film shows tourism as the main hope economically for the island, since fishing is in decline, and very few fishing boats remain. The constant arrival of boat people, arriving in small, dangerous boats, represents a threat both to tourism and to the business of fishing. At the start of the film we see the locals grappling with utopic expectations of tourists who are disembarking from a ferry, presumably from mainland Sicily, set against the background of the decline of fisheries (de Franceschi 2013). The migrants who later appear in the film resemble the islanders more than the stereotypical tourists, since as refugees, they are also "stuck" between past and present, and have great difficulty moving forward through space and time. Like the islanders, their prospects do not seem good. Symbolically, as de Franceschi suggests, there remains between islanders and the refugees, as between islanders and tourists, a sort of "immovable and reified epistemological apartheid" that keeps them in separate worlds, within the singular and heterotopic island context (Franceschi 2013: 196).

For migrants coming by sea, however, Linosa looks like paradise even more than it does for tourists, for whom it is just a place of temporary pleasure. For refugees the island has become the gateway to the possibility of a new life itself and a safe future. Migrants thus encounter the island as European, although the island is often viewed as less than fully Italian, and less than wholly "white" by mainland Europeans (O'Healy 2010: 22–23). As one tourist brochure advertises it, "A little out-of-the-way with regard to major tourist destinations, Linosa is an island worth visiting and is popular with tourists who enjoy hiking, scuba diving, and walking. In fact it is an island suitable for all visitors, given the accessibility of its coasts and the (warm but windy) climate" (Italy This Way n.d.).

In the film, holiday visitors are always welcome, but migrants are unwanted, and their arrival and residency are illegal; officially they should not remain, and are liable to deportation and detention. If they show a suitable papers, all will be well; others are not considered visitors but interlopers.

In *Terraferma* the pivotal role of the old fisherman is important. He not only does the active rescuing at sea, but also appears to represent an old-fashioned respect for human rights, and for the law of the seas. The old man and his grandson end up defying the authorities, and spirit away the woman and her new baby and her small son to the mainland, taking them in their fishing boat. At one and the same time, the old fisherman and his grandson redeem themselves and become criminals, expressing the heterotopic nature of power and authority in the island. As they help migrants to safety, the family enters into a dance to escape the border police. Eventually, leaving to the mainland becomes the only option for the woman and her small family, as their staying on the island is endangering the entire islander family. The woman and her children are the lucky ones, since they are neither detained nor deported. They are considered "deserving" enough to merit serious attention, and to escape, and move on to a new environment and perhaps safety.

Conclusion: EU Islands and the State of Exception

It is clear under UNCLOS (1994) that "[a] shipmaster's duty to rescue is well established in international law, recognized by both the United Nations Convention on the Law of the Sea and the International Convention for the Safety of Life at Sea." Yet there is ambiguity in what this implies, as Tauman notes, in terms of a corresponding legal duty on the part of coastal states and transit states to grant asylum to those who are seeking asylum (Tauman 2002: 461). The usual approach focuses on return and prevention.

In the Canaries, the UNHCR carried out an investigation a few years ago, speaking with migrants from Africa and from across the globe: from Bolivia, Chad, Colombia, Guinea, Ivory Coast, Liberia, Mali, Mauritania, Morocco, Niger, Nigeria, Senegal, Sudan, and Zambia. Most had arrived on the islands by boat and a small number had traveled by air (UNHCR 2009: 5–6; see also Carrera, 2007). In its report about the situation in the Canaries, UNHCR noted that a policy of containment was being instituted by Spain: "Like many other EU countries, Spain is also using financial incentives to gain the support of countries of origin in its efforts to prevent irregular migration. Spain has established six new embassies in West Africa countries and allocated some 700 million Euros in development aid to the region" (UNHCR 2009: 7).

A state of exception, as defined by Agamben (1998), applies in many of the islands of the Mediterranean. Camps have long existed on such islands and were intended to prevent the escape of exiles and others who are punished by being sent into isolation (think of Alcatraz and Robben Island, but also of Napoleon being sent to Saint Helena). Detention camps in Lampedusa or Malta in recent years thus have their historical roots in earlier militarized settlements across the Mediterranean. Lopasic comments in a similar vein: "The Mediterranean has not only been a connecting link between its different parts, including the islands, but also a barrier," and the site of frequent historical contestations and conflicts (Lopasic 2001: 363). Pugliese also notes that Lampedusa, like Christmas Island, demonstrates "the state of exception" that lies outside the review of the law: "These island gulags arrest the deviant life forms of the Global South that wash up on their respective shores and imprison them within the crisis heterotopia of the immigration detention jail" (Pugliese 2010: 118).

Perhaps reflections on representations in the media and in film suggests that small islands are just like everywhere else. Their boundedness make visible what is a much more general experience of heterotopia in contemporary Europe, and globally. Within the increasingly militarized and concentric rings of border barriers erected by EU states, small islands and those at sea in boats trying to get there are simply a part of business as usual, it could be argued. More widely, in the contemporary global order, for all refugees, hope and despair fuse into one, as they are alternately fleeing, being confined, kept out, and pushed out. This is made more visible than usual through the lens of a focus on two small EU islands (Pugliese 2010: 27), islands crisscrossed permanently by the hopes and the dreams, the nightmares and the fears, of those on the move from war and violence of all kinds.

Islands as far away as the Comoros in the Indian Ocean, the Pacific Australian outpost of Christmas Island, French Tahiti, and the Caribbean islands of France, the Netherlands, and the United Kingdom, are all the loci of similar experiences of hopes, violence, and heterotopic situations to those we have seen in Lampedusa and Linosa, albeit on a smaller scale than in the Mediterranean today. The goal of completely stopping migrants from reaching the outposts of Europe is not realizable, as the case of Lampedusa suggests. This is then very much part of the postmodern condition, which has produced globalized segregation and pressures on "unwanted humanity" with "wasted lives" to move toward the possibilities of a life that is more valued (Duffield 2008; Bauman 2004). There are still some positively utopian proposals around, including one suggestion of an oasis being constructed in the Mediterranean in the form of a floating island, to rescue those lost at sea in international waters (Grausam n.d.).

Since 2005, **Helen Hintjens** has taught in Conflict and Peace Studies and in Human Rights at the ISS (Institute of Social Studies of Erasmus University Rotterdam) located in The Hague. Her publications on Rwanda, the African Great Lakes, and on asylum advocacy have appeared in many journals, including *Development and Change, Ethnicities, Race and Class,* and *Surveillance and Society*. She has completed numerous chapters and articles, as well as edited studies on Gender and Identities, conflict and peace studies, post-colonial relations and small island politics. She most recently coedited *Conflict, Peace, Security and Development: Methodologies and Theorising*, with Dubravka Zarkov (Routledge, 2015).

Notes

1. The best map is produced by the BBC (n.d.).
2. See BBC n.d.
3. United Against Racism, Fascism, Nationalism List of 22.394 documented deaths of asylum seekers, refugees and migrants due to the restrictive policies of Fortress Europe, accessed at: http://www.unitedagainstracism.org/wp-content/uploads/2015/06/Listofdeaths22394June15.pdf [accessed 10 December 2015].
4. See Gilligan and Marley (2010).
5. This was reported in Jack Shenker "Survivor of migrant boat tragedy arrested in Netherlands", *The Guardian,* 29.3.2012, available at: http://www.theguardian.com/world/2012/mar/29/survivor-migrant-boat-arrested-netherlands [accessed 11 December 2015].
6. Hirsi Jamaa and Other v. Italy (Application No 27765/09), Grand Chamber, ECHR. Available at: http://www.unionedirittiumani.it/wp-content/uploads/2012/11/CASE-OF-HIRSI-JAMAA-AND-OTHERS-v.-ITALY.pdf. [accessed 15 December 2015].
7. It was reported in the same newspaper article that a small museum had been created in 2011 at the time of the war, by Lampedusa artists, who turned personal effects of migrants—their "shoes, korans, photos, letters, fuel containers, life jackets," into works of art, surely a creative use of symbols of human pain and suffering. Lampedusa's two processing centers were crowded that summer and as Barbara Molinario, spokesperson for the UNHCR in Lampedusa explained, "Logistically it is difficult when we receive large influxes." When the migrants actually arrived in Lampedusa, the relief resulted in prayers, smiles, and tears: "There is a kind of euphoria," said Johnson, the Sierra Leonean. "We cannot believe we have arrived."
8. See also Sherwood, Smith, Davies, and Grant 2014.

Bibliography

Agamben, Giorgio. 1998. *Homo Sacer: Sovereign Power and Bare Life.* Stanford: Stanford University Press.
Anderson, Marie L. 2003. "Norfolk Island: Pacific Periphery." *Island* 92: 47–53.
Andrijasevic, Rutvica. 2006. "Lampedusa in Focus: Migrants Caught between the Libyan Desert and the Deep Sea." *Feminist Review* 82: 120–25.
Armstrong, Warwick and James Anderson (eds). 2007. *Geopolitics of European Union Enlargement: The Fortress Empire.* London/New York: Routledge.
Baldacchino, Godfrey. 2007. "Introducing a World of Islands." In *A World of Islands: An Island Studies Reader,* edited by Godfrey Baldacchino, 1–29. Charlottetown, Canada and Luqa, Malta: Institute of Island Studies and Agenda.

———. 2008. "Studying Islands: On Whose Terms? Some Epistemological and Methodological Challenges to the Pursuit of Island Studies." *Island Studies Journal*, 3, no. 1: 37–56.

Basaran, Tugba. 2011. *Security, Law and Borders: at the Limits of Liberties*. London/New York: Routledge.

Bauman, Zygmunt. 2004. *Wasted Lives: Modernity and its Outcasts*. Cambridge: Polity Press.

BBC. n.d. "Mapping Mediterrnanean Migration." http://www.bbc.com/news/world-europe-24521614 and https://www.pinterest.com/pin/246572148322508549/.

Carrera, Sergio. 2007. *The EU Border Management Strategy FRONTEX and the Challenges of Irregular Immigration in the Canary Islands*. CEPS (Centre for European Policy Studies) Working Document 261, March, Brussels.

Crialese, Emanuele [Director]. 2011. *Terraferma* [Film]. Producers: Riccardo Tozzi, Marco Chimenz, Giovanni Stabilini, Production companies: Cattleya, Rai Cinema, Babe Films, France 3 Cinema: France-Italy.

de Franceschi, Leonardo. 2013. "L'Attorialita come Luogo di Lotta. Africanie Afrodiscendenti nel Cinema Italiano post-1989." In *L'Africa in Italia: Per una controstoria postcoloniale del cinema Italiano*, edited by L. de Fransceschi, 189–206. Rome: Aracne.

Duffield, Mark. (2008) *Development, Security and Unending War: Governing the World of Peoples*. Cambridge: Polity Press.

Dummett, Michael. 2001. *On Immigration and Refugees*. London/New York: Routledge.

European Court of Human Rights (ECHR). 2012. European Court of Human Rights, Grand Chamber, Application No. 27765/09, judgement at http://hudoc.echr.coe.int/sites/eng/pages/search.aspx?i=001-109231#{"itemid":["001-109231"]}.

European Council on Refugees and Exiles (ECRE). 2014. "European Council on Refugees and Exiles, 12 Refugees Die during Alleged Push-back Operation off Greek island." *Weekly Bulletin*. January 24: 2.

Fekete, Liz. 2005. *The Deportation Machine: Europe, Asylum and Human Rights*. London: Institute of Race Relations.

Gebrewold, Belachew (ed.). 2007. *Africa and Fortress Europe: Threats and Opportunities*. Aldershot–Burlington, VT: Ashgate.

Gilligan, Chris, and Carol Marley. 2010. "Migration and Divisions: Thoughts on (Anti-) Narrativity in Visual Representations of Mobile People." *FQS Forum: Qualitative Research* 11, no. 2 (May). http://www.qualitative-research.net/index.php/fqs/article/view/1476/2981.

Grausam, Michael. n.d. "Offshore Shelter for Refugees in Distress at Sea." http://www.grausam.info/en/projects/offshore-shelter-for-refugees/. Image by Insel-Architektur-Konzept-Piktos-2.

Hay, Peter. 2006. "A Phenomenology of Islands." *Island Studies Journal* 1, no. 1: 19–42.

Hintjens, Helen, and Malyn Newitt (eds.). 1992. *The Political Economy of Small, Tropical Islands: the Importance of Being Small*. Exeter: University of Exeter Press.

IRIN. 2011, June 16. "Libya–Italy: By Boat to Lampedusa and a New Life." http://www.irinnews.org/report/92993/libya-italy-by-boat-to-lampedusa-and-a-new-Life.

Italy This Way. n.d. "Linosa Travel Guide and Tourism." http://www.italythisway.com/places/linosa.php.

Lopasic, A. 2001. "Mediterranean Islands: A Concept." *Coll. Anthropologica* 25, no. 1: 363–70.
Lowenthal, David. 1987. "Social Features." In *Politics, Security and Development in Small States,* edited by C. Clarke and A. Payne, 26–49. London: Allen & Unwin.
——. 2006. "Book Review' of Skinner and Hills." *Island Studies Journal* 1, no. 2: 259–61.
——. 2007. "Islands, Lovers and Others." *Geographical Review* 97, issue 2: 202–229.
Marfleet, Philip. 2006. *Refugees in a Global Era.* Basingstoke: Palgrave Macmillan.
Maurici, F. 2008. "Le isole minori della Sicilia in età Bizantina" [The small islands of Sicily in the Byzantine period]. In *Interconnections in the Central Mediterranean,* edited by B. Bonanno-P. Militello, 69–71. Palermo: Proceedings of the Conference St Julians, KASA – Koine Archaeologica-Sapiente Antichita. Malta: Officina di Studi Medievali.
McMahon, E. 2003. "The Gilded Cage: From Utopia to Monad in Australia's Island Imaginary." In *Islands in History and Representation,* 190–202. London/New York: Routledge.
Muggah, Robert, and Edward Mogire. 2006. "Arms Availability and Refugee Militarization in Africa: Conceptualizing the Issues." In *No Refuge: The Crisis of Refugee Militarization in Africa,* edited by R. Muggah, 1–48. London–New York: Zed-BICC-Small Arms Survey.
Nahm, Sue J. 2006. "From bad to better: reflections on refugee and IDP militarization in Africa." 217–250 in Robert Muggah (ed.) *No Refuge, The Crisis of Refugee Militarization in Africa,* London–New York: Zed Books.
O'Healy, Aine. 2010. "Mediterranean Passages: Abjection and Belonging in Contemporary Italian Cinema." *California Italian Studies* 1, no. 1: Permalink: http://escholarship.org/uc/item/2qh5d59c.
Perera, Suvendrini. 2009. *Australia and the Insular Imagination: Beaches, Borders, Boats, and Bodies.* New York: Palgrave Macmillan.
Pugliese, Joseph. 2010. "Transnational Carceral Archipelagos: Lampedusa and Christmas Island." In *Transmediterranean: Diasporas, histories, Geo-political spaces,* edited by Joseph Pugliese, 105–24. Brussels: Peter Land.
Pupavac, Vanessa. 2008. "Refugee Advocacy, Traumatic Representations and Political Disenchantment." *Government and Opposition* 13, no. 2: 270–92.
Rodier, Claire, Gisti, Migreurop. 2013. "Naufrage de Lampedusa." *Multitudes* 55, no. 2: 20–24.
Royle, Stephen. 2001. "Islands: Dreams and Realities." In *A Geography of Islands: Small Island Insularity,* edited by S. Royle, 1–24. London–New York: Taylor and Francis-Routledge.
Schrader, Sabine, and Daniel Winkler. 2013. "Introduction." In *The Cinemas of Italian Migration: European and Transatlantic Narratives,* edited by S. Schader and D. Winkler, 1–18. Newcastle-upon-Tyne: Cambridge Scholars.
Sherwood, Harriet, Helena Smith, Lizzie Davies, and Harriet Grant. 2014. "Europe Faces 'Colossal Humanitarian Catastrophe' of Refugees Dying at Sea." http://www.theguardian.com/world/2014/jun/02/europe-refugee-crisis-un-africa-processing-centres.
Skinner, J., and M. Hills, eds. 2006 *Managing Island Life: Social, Economic and Political Dimensions of Formality and Informality in 'Island' Communities.* Dundee: University of Abertay Press.

Stedman, S. J., and F. Tanner. 2003. *Refugee Manipulation: War, Politics and Abuse of Human Suffering.* Washington, DC: Brookings Institution Press.

Tauman, Jessica. 2002. "Rescued at Sea but Nowhere to Go: The Cloudy Legal Waters of the Tampa Crisis." *Pacific Rim Law & Policy Journal* 11, no 2: 461–96.

United Against Racism. 2012. "List of Deaths." http://www.unitedagainstracism.org/wp-content/uploads/2015/06/Listofdeaths22394June15.pdf.

United Nations Convention on the Law of the Sea (UNCLOS). 1994. Opened for signature 10 December 1982. Entered into force 16 November 19941833 United Nations Treaty Series 397 electronically available at www.un.org/Depts/los. All relevant information on provisions is contained in a UNHCR (United Nations High Commission for Refugees) report entitled Selected Reference Materials Rescue at Sea, Maritime Interception and Stowaways, November 2006, UNHCR, Geneva. Available at http://www.unhcr.org/4d9486c39.pdf.

United Nations High Commission for Refugees (UNHCR). 2006. *Selected Reference Materials Rescue at Sea, Maritime Interception and Stowaways.* Geneva: UNHCR. http://www.unhcr.org/4d9486c39.pdf.

——. 2009. *Refugee protection and international migration: a review of UNHCR's role in the Canary Islands* (Anna Marie Gallagher, José Riera, Maria Riiskjaer). Spain: PDES, Ref: PDES/2009/01.

——. 2014, April 11. "Italy Rescues 6,000 People Crossing Mediterranean in Four Days." News Stories. http://www.unhcr.org/5347d8fa9.html.

Section IV

Stories of Smuggling, Trauma, and Rescue

Silentio ad Mare (Silence at Sea)
With these thoughts in mind your home is far,
And sickness draws near as hopes run free.
Your safety is like a thread,
Once cut can't be restored.
When the flashing lights appear at sea,
The blankets are drawn and all is still.
For getting caught is not intended.
Heads under hands and not a single breath audible,
The boat at a creak with every wave.
        Excerpt from Alexander Maloof and Rhys Halkidis, 2012.

11

"If We Die, We Die Together"

Risking Death at Sea in Search of Safety

Sue Hoffman

Nazek was in her thirties when I met her. Originally from Iraq, she had traveled from Indonesia to Australia in a smuggler's boat with her husband and two young children in the hope of finding safety. Nazek recalled what she had been thinking as she and her family were about to embark on the dangerous sea voyage. "Good. I'm with my husband and children. If we die, we die together" (Nazek, personal interview 2006–7).

Nazek was one of twenty-two participants I interviewed during research conducted in Indonesia and Australia in 2006 and 2007 for a doctoral thesis about refugee journeys from Iraq to Australia (Hoffman 2010). The thesis was structured to reflect the stages of their journey as the participants traveled from the Middle East, across Southeast Asia, onto the people-smugglers' boats and—for those who made it that far—onto Australian shores. My study also drew from the testimony of thirty-six witnesses at a people-smuggling trial held in Australia who made the same journey.[1] A number of themes emerged from analyzing the data. Central to these was the fear, insecurity, and risk faced by participants and witnesses over a protracted period. For the purposes of this chapter, I draw from that part of the thesis that focused on the boat journeys taken by the refugees, and the relations between them and the people-smugglers who arranged these journeys. I also draw from other sources including a biography of convicted people-smuggler Ali Al Jenabi that adds further insight to the relations between smugglers and their passengers (de Crespigny 2012).

In Australia, people-smugglers have been cast as callous opportunists taking advantage of the vulnerable and desperate with no concern for their well-being or safety. Against prevailing wisdom, I argue against such stereotypes, instead positing that some smugglers have been motivated by compassion as well as profit, and that the characterization of boat passengers as preyed-on victims is misplaced and simplistic.

Between 1999 and 2001 approximately thirteen thousand people tried to reach Australia from Indonesia by boat (Hoffman 2010: 1). Fewer than 170 people a year arrived by boat during 2002 to 2008. There was a marked increase from 2009, such that from 2009 to 2013 there were 51,637 boat arrivals, an average of 10,327 people a year (Phillips 2014: 2). Most of them originated from Afghanistan, Iraq, Sri Lanka and Iran. They recognized the inherent dangers of traveling by smugglers' boats, which are typically wooden and ramshackle. Some sit so low in the water that passengers can trail their hands in the ocean with ease. Stories abound of boats leaking, breaking up, and of boat engines failing. Despite this, refugees on boats that foundered tried again.

Hundreds of refugees have died during these risky voyages. The greatest loss of life in a single incident occurred in 2001 when a boat designated SIEV (suspected illegal entry vessel) X sank in the Indian Ocean, killing 353 people, mainly Iraqi women and children.[2] Since then, there have been other large-scale tragedies. Two main routes have been employed to get from Indonesia to Australia. The primary route from Indonesia to the Australian territory of Christmas Island is a journey of 360 kilometers across the Indian Ocean. A secondary route across the Timor Sea to Ashmore Reef, a group of small Australian-owned islands north of Australia, is much shorter at 90 kilometers, and can be traversed in a day (see Figure 11.1). The monsoon season between October and March affects both routes.

It is worth noting the distinction between people smuggling and people trafficking. Trafficked persons are transported to another country either by force or on a false pretext, such as good employment prospects, and are exploited after the journey ends. By contrast, the people who travel with people-smugglers generally do so by choice. They pay for a service and their association with the smuggler ends when the journey ends (Phillips 2004). Not only the organizers, but also the Indonesian fishermen hired to crew boats to Australia, can be prosecuted under Australian anti-people-smuggling legislation which has been in place since 1999. People-smuggling was only criminalized in Indonesia in 2011 (Brown 2011). I use the term "people-smuggler" or *smuggler* to denote the organizers, not the fishermen they hire.

The boats' crews made no attempt to hide their vessels from authorities as they approached Australia; indeed, the opposite occurred. Every effort was made to attract the attention of Australian authorities with passengers sometimes using their phones to alert authorities of their imminent arrival. From an Australian perspective, "smuggler" is misleading as there was no attempt

Figure 11.1. Southern part of Southeast Asia in relation to Australia. Hand-drawn map. Courtesy of Sue Hoffman.

by the boat crews to smuggle the refugees into Australia. But in Indonesia, and en route to Indonesia, it was a different story.

About the People-Smugglers

Within the Australian context, people-smugglers are associated with leaky boats making the perilous sea crossings between Indonesia and Australia. Former prime minister Kevin Rudd famously (in Australia) labeled them "the absolute scum of the earth" who should "rot in hell" (Rodgers 2009). However, this view is not supported by the data. It is simply wrong to assert that all people-smugglers conform to a single stereotype. While some may be ruthless and driven only by profit with no regard for the extreme harm they may cause, there are also smugglers who have regard for the safety of their customers.

Smugglers operating out of Indonesia did not conform to the traditional idea of organized criminal gangs with hierarchical structures, centralized control, and involvement in a range of criminal activities. Rather, they comprised fluid networks of individuals, operating in countries of origin, transit, and destination (Tailby 2001: 6). Icduygu and Toktas, who conducted research into people-smuggling in Turkey, noted that smuggling operations were more haphazard than trafficking operations, and generally arose in response to local needs (Icduygu and Toktas 2002: 25).This is consistent with other research that concluded smuggling operations can be grassroots affairs (Marfleet 2006: 255). As my research showed, some of the people-smugglers were themselves refugees.

Icduygu and Toktas (2002) also noted that smugglers operating in Turkey tended to deal with migrants (including refugees) from their own countries. The authors pointed to the significance of interpersonal trust in the continuing operation of the syndicates. They also referred to the reciprocal nature of the relationship between the smugglers and the migrants, with the smugglers operating only because the migrants desired the service they provided. Yet this was an unequal relationship, with the balance of power firmly held by the smugglers (Icduygu and Toktas 2002: 44ff). At times trust and empathy were apparent between smugglers and their customers, softening the exploitative nature of smuggling (Icduygu 2005: 13). The latter was evident from reports emanating from Jordan of agents or smugglers encouraging Iraqi refugee women to enter into prostitution to pay for their onward journeys, although other agents were reputed to operate for humanitarian reasons (United Nations High Commissioner for Refugees [UNHCR] 2002: 33).

In my study some participants and all of the witnesses had their trips arranged, or partially arranged, by men registered as refugees with UNHCR. These men became involved with people-smuggling only after they arrived in Indonesia; it was not, at that time, a criminal offense there. They were later charged under Australian law and imprisoned in Australian jails. Each claimed they were helping other refugees reach the safety of Australia. In *Daoed*,[3] it was evident that the Sabi Mandean, who was convicted in relation to SIEV X, took a particular interest in the welfare and well-being of other Mandean refugees. In *Asfoor*, a prosecution witness who had befriended the smuggler to facilitate his arrest by the Australian Federal Police spoke positively about Asfoor's motives. The witness acknowledged that Asfoor appeared to have a genuine concern for the refugees and wanted them to get to Australia where they would be safe.[4] In the case of *Al Jenabi*, the court accepted his primary motivation was to arrange safe passage to Australia for members of his own family.[5] In her book about Al Jenabi's life, which was written in the style of an autobiography and in the first person, de Crespigny recounted his experiences with smugglers and why he became involved in their trade; I will return to de Crespigny later in this chapter (de Crespigny 2012).

The Journey to Indonesia

For many refugees their relationship with smugglers began when they fled their home country. Few Iraqis were issued passports by their own government when Saddam Hussein was in power, and therefore many relied on smugglers to help them escape their homeland. Once out of Iraq, they needed the assistance of smugglers to obtain passports and/or visas because without papers they were unable to travel farther, and feared return to Iraq if caught in a neighboring country without documents. Making contact with smugglers was not difficult, with many obtaining the names and phone numbers of smugglers based in Southeast Asia while they, as potential customers, were still in the Middle East. Others made contact en route.

People-smugglers often waited in the arrivals halls of airports in transit countries such as Malaysia and Indonesia to meet potential customers. If the smugglers were not there, participants and witnesses were able to contact them using phone numbers previously obtained. After making contact, the smugglers directed or took the refugees to hotels, arranged visas if required for the next part of their journey, and referred them to their smuggling partners in Indonesia. The Indonesia-based smugglers were able to arrange visas enabling entry into Indonesia for refugees just arrived in Malaysia. As Anness explained, "During the ten days I was in Malaysia, I dealt with agents to bring me to Indonesia. They gave me options. Did I want to buy a boat passage, a visa, or a passport? Did I want to go by land or air? It was multiple choice" (Anness, personal interview 2006–7).

On this point, Ameer described two phone conversations that took place with a smuggler who was in Indonesia. During the first call, Ameer was still in Amman, in Jordan. The smuggler told Ameer to go to a particular hotel in the capital city of Malaysia, Kuala Lumpur and wait there while the smuggler organized paperwork. When Ameer called the smuggler from Kuala Lumpur as instructed, he was told to wait three days, and then go to the Indonesian embassy in Malaysia to collect his visa for entry to Indonesia. This demonstrates the ease with which the smugglers were able to obtain false documents on behalf of their refugee customers. When smugglers delivered on their promises, the refugees were reassured as to the smugglers' ability, connections, and trustworthiness (Ameer, personal interview 2006–7).

Australia has sought to engage the cooperation of other countries in its attempt to stop people crossing borders using false papers and was successful in influencing Indonesia to tighten its immigration controls at Jakarta airport (Australian Government Department of Immigration and Citizenship 2008: 76). This made it more difficult for Middle Eastern refugees to enter Indonesia by plane. However, immigration controls at the seaports where ferries docked were known to be less stringent than at the airports, and smugglers' boats could land at one of thousands of Indonesia's small islands where there were no immigration controls. Australia's attempt to stop refugees arriving in Indonesia was therefore unsuccessful. Its main achievement was to force many of them to take a more dangerous route.

Getting from Malaysia to Indonesia by boat entails crossing the Strait of Malacca. The northwestern end of the Strait is about 370 kilometers wide and narrows to a funnel about 14 kilometers across. Although the waters of the Strait are usually calm, the two monsoon seasons, which together last for about nine months, bring brief but severe storms accompanied by strong winds and heavy rain (Roach 2005: 98ff).The Strait is one of the world's busiest shipping lanes, patrolled by multinational forces to counter the threats of piracy, armed robbery, illegal fishing, pollution, and the illicit movement of people and goods (Bateman 2009: 45ff). The high and growing density of traffic on the waterway has led to an increase in the number of collisions involving all types of vessels, big and small (Cleary and Goh 2000: 171). Refugees on smuggler boats are therefore at risk from the weather, criminal elements, and accidents, as well as from interception by security forces on watch for illegal people movement, which most likely lead to detention and deportation.

Of the fifty-eight study participants and trial witnesses I interviewed, eighteen took this route. While some opted to make the journey by boat because it was cheaper, others found that the alternative, flying, was no longer possible. "I tried to fly from Malaysia to Indonesia. I tried to get a visa but that was stopped for Iraqis. So I came by boat," said Aahad (personal interview 2006–7). Two men told me they traveled by commercial ferries, enjoying a safe journey. The rest were smuggled in wooden fishing boats, not intended to carry paying passengers. The journey was extremely dangerous. Kokeb described how his journey, which took a day and a night, was but a step away from death because of poor weather and an unstable boat. Taeseer gave a similar account:

> The boat journey took twenty-four hours and was like death. There were twenty-one people on the boat which was very small and not big enough for so many people. We changed boat two times. They put us on the bottom of the boat. We lay down. They covered us with a piece of wood maybe thirty centimetres from the ground, then put goods on top of that. We could not move. We had nothing to eat, our little girl took milk. It was October and the weather was rainy and stormy. The smuggler chose bad weather as the police don't patrol then and so won't find us (Taeseer, personal interview 2006–7).

The danger and discomfort of this journey was enough for Taeseer and his family to resolve not to attempt a second boat journey from Indonesia to Australia. "The experience from Malaysia to Indonesia was enough. We were afraid for the children," he told me (Taeseer, personal interview 2006–7).

Negotiating with People-Smugglers in Indonesia

Once in Indonesia, passengers waited in cheap hotels, wary of venturing outside for fear of capture and imprisonment by police and immigration officials. When a boat was ready to leave, the smugglers arranged transport for their passengers from the hotel to the embarkation point. Boats usually left at night to minimize the chance of detection by authorities. Many of the refugees realized their vulnerability exposed them to exploitation. Safaa recalled,

> People waited for us outside the airport and took us to a hotel. Someone came to see us in the hotel and asked for money. They just wanted money, they didn't care. So I refused to pay. The people-smuggler wanted a lot of money. I said I wouldn't pay until I was in the boat. Others paid and told me to pay. But I was worried that the people-smuggler would take the money and nothing would happen. So I went to the streets and asked people in Jakarta. I saw people who'd been there six months or one year and they all told me different stories (Safaa, personal interview 2006–7) (see Figure 11.2).

A few refugees mentioned to me how an Iraqi called Omeid had cheated them, taking their money but either not arranging a boat or not arranging one large enough for all the people who had paid for a passage. The next few paragraphs draw from de Crespigny's account of Ali Al Jenabi's experiences when he was in Indonesia (de Crespigny 2012). Al Jenabi (later convicted of people-smuggling) described how Omeid transported dozens more people to the embarkation point than the boat could carry. Places were guaranteed for those who had paid the most or who could, at the point of departure, pay

Figure 11.2. West Java, three hours south of the Indonesian capital of Jakarta, March 2007. Photographer: Sue Hoffman. Courtesy of Sue Hoffman.

extra. Al Jenabi described it as "bargaining with people at their most vulnerable.... [It was like] a human auction" (de Crespigny 2012: 156).

Al Jenabi was one of those who did not make it onto the boat. He wanted his money back, only to find that Omeid and his cronies had left the beach. Al Jenabi and other refugees, angry that Omeid had cheated them, demanded that Omeid meet with them. Omeid initially refused to return the refugees' money, instead promising that he would reserve places on the next boat he arranged. But that could be months away and Al Jenabi, like many of the other Iraqis, did not have enough money to support himself and his family in Indonesia for that long. Al Jenabi recorded that he stood his ground until Omeid capitulated and reluctantly returned people's money. "I can see how the people relax and glow. They have got back control of their lives and for a moment they are no longer powerless victims" (de Crespigny 2012: 158).

Following this incident, according to Al Jenabi's account, a group of about fifty refugees decided to stay together as they made their way across Indonesia to Bali where another smuggler was based. They wanted to check out whether he was reliable. Al Jenabi recalled that although Abu Qassey appeared pleasant enough, they instinctively did not trust him (de Crespigny 2012: 159). Abu Qassey later became notorious as the smuggler primarily responsible for organizing the ill-fated SIEV X boat that sank, killing 353 people.

By this time Ali Jenabi had met a number of smugglers and regarded each of them as untrustworthy individuals who took advantage of desperate Iraqis and other refugees. Al Jenabi decided that he could do what Omeid and Abu Qassey were doing: selling passages and arranging boats. These activities were not then an illegal activity in Indonesia. By his account, Al Jenabi resolved that he would provide a pathway to safety for refugees but he would be honest with them. In so doing he could help other refugees get to Australia at the same time as he earned the money he needed to help his family (de Crespigny 2012: 168).

Faris Kadhem Shohani was a passenger on SIEV X. Along with forty-four others, Faris survived the sinking. After the boat broke up, he spent at least twenty hours in the water before being rescued. However, his wife and seven-year old daughter drowned. Faris's son, mother, and two siblings had previously traveled to Australia without mishap on a boat organized by Al Jenabi. Despite his personal tragedy, Faris has been supportive of Al Jenabi's efforts to be granted a visa that would allow him permanent residence in Australia. In a newspaper interview, Faris spoke of how Al Jenabi reduced the price and described him as perhaps "the best smuggler. He had a good heart. He was not hard, not a greedy person" (de Crespigny 2012: 336).

Returning to my research, passengers on Asfoor's boats made similar comments. Ameer said he respected him. Mohammad, Hadeel, and Fajjer all said he was a good man, with Fajjer adding, "As long as a smuggler isn't stealing from people, then he's helping them. If people didn't have money, Keis Asfoor brought them for free" (Fajjer, personal interview 2006–7).

A participant in my study, Bahaa, benefited from a personal connection to the smuggler in that they had a mutual friend. Once the smuggler was satisfied that this was the case, Bahaa was able to travel for free. There was a further potential benefit to Bahaa for choosing to travel on a boat arranged by this particular smuggler. The smuggler's brother was planning the same journey and for this reason Bahaa was confident that the boat would be safe (Bahaa, personal interview 2006–7). Conversely, Aahad's account highlighted the inherent dangers of the trip and the difficulty of finding and traveling with a trustworthy smuggler: "After arriving in Indonesia in October 2000, I tried three times to go to Australia. One time I went to the coast. There was a bad storm, and we couldn't go. Another time, the police and immigration were there, so we could not leave. Maybe we would be caught and arrested. We paid for three attempts, and didn't get our money back. Each time we were advised by other people about which people-smuggler to use and we would go to a different smuggler and make a deal" (Aahad, personal interview 2006–7).

Smugglers, Boats, and Sea Crossings

The character of the smuggler made a big difference when negotiating price—and in getting a refund if something went awry—and could be the difference between life and death on the high seas. Smugglers purchased wooden boats from Indonesians. It was almost certain that the boat would be destroyed by Australian authorities after interception and the passengers were safely on dry land. This reduced the incentive to buy good quality boats. Some people-smugglers considered their role was over once they had their money and the boat had left Indonesian shores. However, other smugglers took a more responsible attitude. Najah recounted how the smuggler who arranged his passage, Keis Asfoor, came to the rescue when the boat broke down. He said, "After two days, we're still in Indonesian waters. The boat leaked and the engine broke down. The boat was blown to shore. We phoned the smuggler who brings another motor and pump to get rid of the water. On TV [and the] Internet, we see false reports that our boat has sunk. We stay in the sea twenty-three days. The smuggler came again, and brought food and other supplies, and a new motor" (Najah, personal interview 2006–7).

Despite the positive experiences of some passengers, the majority of participants and witnesses were critical of the smugglers, with two-thirds of those who commented on people-smugglers expressing negative views. Noor said, "I knew the word *smuggler* but I didn't realize what they are like. Now I think of them as being interested only in the money. They didn't want to help people, just wanted money, they are liars" (Noor, personal interview 2006–7).

Or more succinctly, is this comment from Nezal: "I view them as criminal" (Nezal, personal interview 2006–7).

The smugglers' failure to take steps that would have made the dangerous sea crossings safer put the refugees' lives directly at risk. Reports suggest that while the smugglers who run unsafe boats are well aware of the poor conditions of the wooden fishing boats used for the journey from Indonesia to Australia, they lie to the passengers about them. Safaa told me, "The people-smuggler brought a video camera and showed us the boat. It looked like a rich person's boat. Our boat was an old boat, overcrowded, and not like we were shown on the video.... The Indonesian crew and captain just had a small compass. There was no radio or technology on the boat" (Safaa, personal interview 2006–7). Najah had a similar experience with a smuggler: "Before we saw the boat, he told us the boat was very good, and in a safe condition. When we saw our boat, it was a miserable, small boat" (Najah, personal interview 2006–7).

It is common practice for the smugglers' boats to leave late at night, long after dark. Although this was done primarily to avoid authorities, it means that the refugees could not see the condition of their boat until it is too late. Usually the refugees are ferried in small boats to larger boats moored offshore.

In relation to his failed attempt to get on a boat, Ali Al Jenabi recounted just that scenario. He described how he saw people taken on small boats to a bigger boat. He was told that women and children and family groups went first. Once they were on board, it was too late for the men who followed; they were obliged to get on the boat to join their families. They were then were prevented from leaving the boat by the organizers and by the flow of people trying to get on (de Crespigny 2012: 153–55). According to Norres, who was one of a group of twenty-three Mandean passengers who left SIEV X before it sank, "The smugglers brought photos of the boat we were to get on. It was very large, two or three storeys, a five-star boat.... They told us 'you will not get on the boat at the beach. You get on small boats that will take you the next boat, then on that to the main boat'. When we got on the boat, we thought it would take us to the main boat. But it was the main boat" (Norres, personal interview 2006–7).

Similarly, a number of witnesses at Daoed's trial referred to armed men in uniforms being present as people boarded small boats that took them to a larger boat, moored at a distance from the shore (Hoffman 2005: 33, 45). One witness, who became distraught as he answered questions about the events that led to the deaths of 353 people when SIEV X sank, spoke rapidly in Arabic before breaking down. His words were not translated in open court but the Iraqis seated next to me in the public gallery told me he said that people were forced onto the boat against their will by men with guns.

As well as lying to refugees about the condition of the boats, three participants reported that smugglers misled them about the duration of the journey.

Bahaa was told that a thirty-six-hour journey would take just twenty hours. He fared better than Ethar who recounted, "I got on a boat to Australia. Four days they said. It took twenty-one days or more" (Ethar, personal interview 2006–7). Noor said, "They said thirty hours. It was eight days" (Noor, personal interview 2006–7).

Participants were aware that the boat journeys would be risky. As Nezal said, "It was a very dangerous trip but what can we do? My husband said to me, 'You know this is dangerous.' I said, 'I agree'" (Nezal, personal interview 2006–7).They had little or no option. According to Nazek, "We just needed to get on. We could not go back to Iran or Iraq. If we did that, we would be killed or imprisoned" (Nazek, personal interview 2006–7). For Charef, at least, the promise of the future outweighed concerns about the sea-crossing. "I was never afraid on the way. Whatever was on the way was not as dangerous as the danger I'd been through. I'm heading for safety, peace.... I didn't expect any danger except from the ocean. The only time I felt death would be very close was if the boat broke down" (Charef, personal interview 2006–7).

Thirteen participants reported engine breakdowns, leaking boats, getting lost, and running out of fuel. Anness was on a boat that was still close to Indonesia when it sank. A little girl, a twin, lost her life: "The journey to Australia was in a small boat with forty people. We travelled for twelve hours and then the boat sank. We were in the sea at night and scared to death. A 3-year-old girl drowned. One friend swam for twenty or thirty metres, and saw a fishing boat. Fishermen were repairing the boat. They threw a line to him ... and sent a small boat to collect us, one and two at a time. During that period, the little girl drowned. It was dark, we couldn't see" (Anness, personal interview 2006–7).

Norres described traveling on SIEV X.

> The waves were high. The boat began to break up, and water started to come in.... I was unconscious. I was sitting on the floor and behind me a piece of wood came loose. I was scared. I thought I would fall into the sea. We smelled smoke and a bad smell of burning. It seemed that we wouldn't arrive.... We saw a fishing boat and called to them. Then the twenty-three Mandeans left the boat we'd been on. The boat later sunk but we didn't know. We heard that the police captured the boat; then we heard that it sank; then we heard it had arrived. We didn't know. We decided to try again to go to Australia. After two or three days we heard the news, that the ship definitely sank, with very few survivors, forty to forty-five.... Once I heard the news, I didn't want to try again (Norres, personal interview 2006–7).

Traveling on the wooden fishing boats arranged by smugglers was inherently dangerous because of the conditions of the boats, and lack of safety and navigational equipment. Australia's policy of intercepting boats once they entered Australian waters placed passengers at further risk.

Messar was on a boat forcibly returned to Indonesia by the Australian navy in 2001. His account illustrates the determination of the navy to ensure the boat went back to Indonesia, and raises questions as to whether the safety of passengers was given due regard. He recounts how, after the naval escort left, it took his boat four hours to get to within three or four hundred meters of the Indonesian coastline, and six hours to cover the final few hundred meters.

> By this time, the boat was barely seaworthy and its passengers were exhausted. The engine of the boat broke down. The boat was tired and broken. The Australian Navy sent mechanics to repair the engine. For three days they tried to repair it. They could repair only two engines. After two hours, one engine broke down again, so only one was working. We had only one meal in three days; the navy gave us the meal on the third day. Otherwise there was no proper food. There were maybe fifteen to twenty kids on the boat. We only have water, water sufficient. We have biscuits, little cakes and snacks to survive. ...
>
> We had a ten-day journey on the water, then three days with the soldiers. We passengers were all very tired. We just sat and waited. ... During the three days, they hit us, especially those of us who were difficult. They brought a video camera and turned it on when there were problems. They videoed when people were shouting or fighting, not when people were calm. ...
>
> It is very difficult to erase from my mind. We were in between life and death. They left us in the sea, not on the shore, even though our boat was in bad condition. We thought we were going to our death. We were very scared in case that last engine broke down. If we sank, there was no-one who could help us. After the navy left, it took us four hours to get to the Kupang coast. The journey was very slow with a broken engine. ... The last three to four hundred metres took six hours. ... We could not get off the boat, as we were too far from the land. Everyone had lifejackets, but we were too exhausted, too tired to swim if the boat went down (Messar personal interview, 2006–7).

Deaths at Sea

The number of deaths at sea is difficult to establish. Sometimes authorities become aware that a boat may have sunk only after relatives make inquiries about loved ones who set off for Australia but never arrived. Hutton, who has analyzed many reports of drownings, concluded there were 375 confirmed deaths and 5 probable deaths between 1998 and 2001, and 314 confirmed deaths and between 854 and 864 probable deaths between 2009 and 2013 (Hutton 2014: 1–3). The increase in probable deaths from 2009 reflects the increase in the numbers of refugees attempting the hazardous journey from late 2008. Some drownings occurred close to Indonesia and others close to Australian territory.

No single incident has matched the loss of life that occurred when the SIEV X sank in October 2001 in waters between Australia and Indonesia. However, it was the event in December 2010 that, arguably, has had the most impact in recent years on the Australia psyche. After its engine broke down, the boat designated SIEV 221 crashed onto the rocks of Christmas Island, killing fifty people as locals watched on in horror. The severe weather conditions and the treacherous cliff-face hampered efforts by navy and customs personnel to rescue more than the forty-one people whose lives were saved. The coroner, in his report, stated that it appeared clear that the people-smugglers contributed to the deaths by failing to provide a vessel suitable for "the journey across open seas in the monsoon season to Christmas Island" (Coroner's Court of Western Australia 2012: 140). The boat, which was overcrowded, did not have enough lifejackets or other vital equipment. The crew members were not qualified for such a journey. The coroner also noted that the smugglers appeared to have lied to the passengers about the boat and safety equipment (Coroner's Court of Western Australia 2012: 140). The behaviors noted by the coroner accords with those attributed to other people-smugglers.

Reflecting on the Boat Journeys

For many of the refugees, the boat journey from Indonesia to Australia was simply terrifying. For those who made it to Australian shores, their hopes were high that their long and troubled journey was at an end. But for far too many, their lives, or the lives of their loved ones, were lost.

The tone of public discourse in Australia on the subject of refugees, people-smugglers, and boat journeys has long been toxic. While blame for deaths at sea has variously targeted the refugees for choosing to travel with smugglers, at smugglers for running unsafe boats, and at the Australian government for its deterrence policies, there is the underpinning reality that refugees, with little to lose, are driven by their need for a permanent, safe place to live. Smugglers, often from the host or refugee communities, respond to that need.

There is no question that some smugglers took advantage of the refugees' vulnerability and desperation. They took money for voyages that did not eventuate. They lied about the condition of boats. In the most extreme of cases, they sent people to their deaths. They demonstrated callousness and lack of regard for their refugee customers. But not all were like that. As described earlier in this chapter, there were a small number of refugees who viewed some people-smugglers in a positive light. They acknowledged those smugglers who helped refugees find a place of safety, and treated their customers with humanity. Ascribing a single stereotype, negative or positive, to people-smugglers is therefore mistaken. The data suggest the truth is more nuanced than this.

After more than one hundred refugees drowned on their way to Christmas Island in June 2012, politicians made tearful speeches in parliament, undertaking to "stop the boats" to ensure that there would be no more deaths at sea (Keane 2012). This became the catch-cry of Australia's Liberal Party led by Tony Abbott in the lead-up to an election in September 2013. The focus, unfortunately, was on stopping boats by forcing them back to Indonesia rather than developing a protection framework in the region such that refugees would not need to resort to buying a passage on a people-smuggler's boat.

Policy responses to refugees who have arrived by boat continue to be harsh and punitive. In early 2014, there were over a thousand children, including babies, locked up indefinitely in Australian-run immigration detention centers. Many commentators have pointed to human rights abuses of refugees by Australian authorities (Millar 2014). While the harsh deterrence policies, including the turning-back of refugee boats, appear to have stopped people buying passages to Australia on often-unsafe boats in their quest to find safety, they do nothing to address the wider issue of responding to the protection needs of people in the region who have fled war and persecution. Safaa voiced a sentiment expressed by other participants: "If there was a legal way, a better way than using smugglers, I would have done that" (Safaa, personal interview 2006–7).

At the time of writing this chapter, **Sue Hoffman** was an honorary research associate at Murdoch University, Perth, Western Australia. Her primary area of research concerned refugees, asylum seekers, and people-smuggling as they related to Australia. Her doctoral thesis examined refugee journeys from Iraq to Australia. To this end, she spent time in Indonesia, Syria, and Jordan with refugee communities and researchers. Sue sits on the board of a not-for-profit agency that provides services to torture and trauma survivors, has written for major newspapers and online media outlets, and appeared on national television and radio, commenting on refugee-related issues.

Notes

1. *The Queen and Keis Abd Rahim Asfoor* [2006] District Court of Western Australia.
2. Background to the SIEV X sinking is available at M. Hutton's Web site, www.sievx.com. Australian government policy in 2001 denied women and children any legitimate way to join husbands and fathers already in Australia, thereby creating a new market for people-smugglers: women and children. At least eight men in Australia lost their wives and children when SIEV X sank.

3. *The Queen and Khaleed Shnayf Daoed* [2005] Supreme Court of Queensland.
4. *The Queen and Keis Abd Rahim Asfoor* [2006] District Court of Western Australia: 3517.
5. *The Queen and Al Hassan Abdolamir Al Jenabi* [2004] NTSC 44, sentencing remarks.

Bibliography

Personal Interviews

Interviews were conducted in Indonesia and Australia in 2006 and 2007 with refugees who migrated, or had attempted to migrate, by boat between 1999 and 2001. Pseudonyms were used for all those involved in this research. A number of participants agreed to be interviewed only because of undertakings given to protect their identity. For this reason, the year and location of each interview is not provided.

Other Sources

Australian Government Department of Immigration and Citizenship. 2008. "Annual Report 2007–8." http://www.border.gov.au/ReportsandPublications/Documents/annual-reports/annual-report-2007-08-complete.pdf.

Bateman, Sam. 2009. "Regime building in the Malacca and Singapore Straits: Two Steps Forward, One Step Back." *Economics of Peace and Security Journal* 4, no. 2: 45–51.

Brown, Matt. 2011. "Indonesia passes laws criminalising people smuggling." *ABC News*, May 27, 2011. http://www.abc.net.au/news/2011-04-07/indonesia-passes-laws-criminalising-people/2624376.

Cleary, Mark, and Goh, Kim Chuan. 2000. *Environment and Development in the Straits of Malacca*. London/New York: Routledge.

Coroner's Court of Western Australia. 2012. *Inquest findings 2012–Christmas Island Tragedy*. Perth, http://www.coronerscourt.wa.gov.au/I/inquest_findings_2012.aspx?uid=4309-1981-1408-3425.

de Crespigny, Robin. 2012. *The People Smuggler*. Melbourne: Penguin.

Hoffman, Sue. 2005. "Notes from Trial of Khaleed Daoued." May/June: 1–66. http://sievx.com/articles/daoed/SueHoffmansNotes.pdf.

——. 2010. "Fear, Insecurity and Risk: Refugee Journeys from Iraq to Australia." Doctoral dissertation, Murdoch University, Western Australia.

Hutton, Marg. 2014. "Drownings on the Public Record of People Attempting to Enter Australia Irregularly by Boat since 1998." p. 1–12. http://sievx.com/articles/background/DrowningsTable.pdf.

Icduygu, Ahmet. 2005. "Transit Migration in Turkey: Trends, Patterns and Issues." Consortium for Applied Research on International Migration. http://cadmus.eui.eu/handle/1814/6277.

Icduygu, Ahmet, and Sule Toktas. 2002. "How Do Smuggling and Trafficking Operate via Irregular Border Crossings in the Middle East? Evidence from Fieldwork in Turkey." *International Migration* 40, no. 6: 25–52.

Keane, Bernard. 2012. "Substituting Treaties for Hard Thinking on Asylum Seekers." *Crikey*, June 28. http://www.crikey.com.au/2012/06/28/substituting-treaties-for-hard-thinking-on-asylum-seekers/.

Marfleet, Philip. 2006. *Refugees in a Global Era*. Hampshire, UK: Palgrave MacMillan.

Millar, Lisa. 2014. "Human Rights Watch Annual Report Says Australia's Record Damaged by Treatment of Asylum Seekers." *ABC News*, January 22. http://www.abc.net.au/news/2014-01-22/human-rights-watch-scathing-on-australia27s-treatment-of-asylu/5212038.

Phillips, Janet. 2004. "People Trafficking: Australia's Response." Canberra, Australia: Parliamentary Library.

———. 2014. "Boat Arrivals in Australia: A Quick Guide to the Statistics." Canberra, Australia: Parliamentary Library.

Roach, J. Ashley. 2005. "Enhancing Maritime Security in the Straits of Malacca and Singapore." *Journal of International Affairs* 59, no. 1: 97–116.

Rodgers, Emma. 2009. "Rudd Wants People Smugglers to 'Rot in Hell.'" ABC News, April 17. http://www.abc.net.au/news/2009-04-17/rudd-wants-people-smugglers-to-rot-in-hell/1653814.

Tailby, Rebecca. 2001. "Organized Crime and People Smuggling/Trafficking to Australia." *Trends and Issues in Crime and Criminal Justice* 208, Australian Institute of Criminology, Canberra.

United Nations High Commissioner for Refugees (UNHCR), 2002. "Jordan as a Transit Country: Semi-protectionist Immigration Policies and Their Effects on Iraqi Forced Migrants." *New Issues in Refugee Research 61*. http://www.refworld.org/docid/4ff3fcbe2.html.

12

En Route to Hell

Dreams of Adventure and Traumatic Experiences among West African 'Boat People' to Europe

Papa Sow, Elina Marmer, and Jürgen Scheffran

In recent years Western countries have introduced a variety of specific preventive measures to counter 'irregular migration' through their visa issuing and screening procedures (European Policy Evaluation Consortium [EPEC] 2004; Hamilton 2009; Hobolth 2012). Most of those drastic measures include the continuous training of staff at consulates and embassies, the assessment of willingness to return, cooperation and information exchange between countries, but also the use of biometric data. Other preventive measures include the identification of specific categories of migrants: the 'clandestine,' those who are mostly without formal education, and the 'swindlers'.

One of the main priorities of the European Commission (EC), for example, is to identify victims of trafficking early in the process. The EU Satellite Center and the European Maritime Safety Agency are usually enrolled in the general surveillance practices which demonstrates that security and fear of "invasion" (de Haas 2008, 2009; Wouters, Duquet, and Meuwissen 2013) are at the heart of the EU political agenda. Public threats (fences at Ceuta and Melilla, military forces, naval patrols, readmission agreements in return for aid, etc.) seem to be the most obvious alternatives used by the EU countries in their attempt to deal with irregular migration.

This chapter opens with an analysis of the EU visa policy for Africans and explains the lucrative visa market (foreign exchange earnings) set up by the European consulates in Africa. The fear of invasion and terrorism, and the drastic security measures implemented as well as the combined financial income behind the EU visa policy are explained thoroughly. This chapter also analyzes the root causes of despair in young 'clandestine adventurers', mostly fishers, who undertake dangerous long ocean journeys (in Wolof: *mbeuk-mi*) due to unemployment and lack of visas. An emphasis is placed on coastal countries, such as Senegal, where fishstocks have been depleted by European trawlers. This has put further stress on these young fishers. Primarily, it focuses on the organization of so-called 'clandestine journeys' and the division of tasks allotted to organizers. It explains the role of the *borom gaal* – the person who is the owner of the boat – and then explains in detail the activities of the *touts,* a kind of *coyote* (or tough negotiator and conveyor), who, through dense and diverse networks, is always looking for potential clients. Through qualitative interviews, it highlights the relationships forged while en route between the migrants themselves and between the migrants and the organizers. Promiscuity, privacy, and confidentiality become the unifying elements that bind adventurers during long ocean voyages and help to strengthen bonds of solidarity. In conclusion, this chapter emphasizes symbolic and emotional elements that create deep feelings both of bravery and of social failure.

Methodology

A compilation of several forms of data (in-depth interviews, reports, statistics, literature, etc.) was obtained from Senegalese fishers involved in migration (among them smugglers, intermediaries, captains, migrants, etc.) that try to make perilous ocean journeys to reach the Spanish Canary Islands. Furthermore, some of the literature search was conducted via Internet and especially targeted organizations of nature conservation and fisheries' resources, policymakers, artisanal fisher corporations, and owners of industrial fishing in order to get diverse information about the working conditions of fishers. The Senegalese portal Organization for the Promotion and Empowerment of Artisanal Fisheries' Actors in Mbour, Senegal (Association pour la Promotion et la Responsabilisation des Acteurs de la Pêche Artisanale à Mbour, or APRAPAM) provided many informative documents in its virtual library (www.aprapam.org). An excellent data set about fishing in this country and in the West African subregion is currently updated on that Web site every month. Publications from Frontex (European Agency for the Management of Operational Cooperation at the External Borders of the Member States of the European Union) as well as respective documents of the EC have also been used. These publications continuously update data on 'irregular' migration and entry attempts into the European continent. They focus on the trans-Mediterranean routes from West Africa that often end in European coastal countries. We also consulted recent literature on sea voyages in general and on migrant fishers from Africa, in particular, Senegal.

Some of the migrant fishers returned to Senegal after they reached the Spanish mainland and had been deported. Focus groups and individual interviews were done in July and September 2013 by one of the authors in Senegal, particularly in Rufisque, Thiaroye sur mer, and Kayar (Atlantic coast), with deported and returned migrant fishers, conveyors, and boat owners (*borom gaal*). Our interest focused on the population of fishers who after the ecological and environmental plunder of their fishery resources became sensitive to their situation and started emigrating toward Europe. Through our conversations, the traumatic experiences that these people have encountered as well as the spectrum of the causes (visa constraints, environmental stress, loss of food security, etc.) that have pressurized them to emigrate are shown. One of the authors interviewed individuals who were involved in the sea journeys including intermediaries, *borom gaal, coyotes,* captains, travel agencies, and so on.

Expensive Visa and Sophisticated Control System Contribute to 'Clandestine Emigration'

In the Western embassies in Africa, visas are highly priced, creating a lucrative visa market. Consistent with the logic of Western countries, financial revenues, austerity plans of embassy budgets, 'the myth of invasion', terrorism and security policies behind the consular system seem to be the main tightening measures that impede an easy access to visas (Sow and Alissoutin 2006; Nessel 2009). But among all these tightening measures, the debate on the cost of visas in Western embassies is the most discussed aspect in West African media (Seneweb, 2011). In addition to exorbitant visa fees, most embassies in West Africa require a life insurance policy prior to traveling. Expensive phone calls are also required prior getting an appointment that gives no guarantee of travel (Belaïsch and Petersel 2010).

The problem of exorbitant visa costs begins to emerge not only in the literature of major political institutions (such as the EC), but also among migration sociologists. Physical devices and sophisticated procedural blockages, technological and regulatory filtering as well as externalization processes of visa applications toward private travel agencies are increasingly being reported (Belaïsch and Petersel 2010; Di Bartolomeo, Fakhoury and Perrin 2010; Infantino 2010; Infantino and Rea 2012). In each consulate, consular agencies analyze, under the microscope, the risk factor of each visa applicant as to whether he or she might use the social services in the host country. A higher risk factor equates a lower chance of getting a visa.

Most applicants thus suspect that Western countries are taking the consular system for granted as a business that allows them to lessen their consular charges, and pay their staff and equipment as stated in Goudeyron's study (2007). This hypothesis is difficult to ignore if we analyze closely the recommendations contained in the report of the EC where an appeal is launched to Schengen states for a greater harmonization of conditions under which European consular missions outside Europe treat visa applications (EU 2014). The same report calls on Member States to adopt a differentiated treatment of applicants, between "primary applicants," "unknown applicants," and "frequent and regular applicants." Moreover, Goudeyron (2007) showed that "visa services" activities do not strain the budget of, for example, the French state. The filing fees for visa applications can cover all consulate costs and provide additional financial resources. The study estimates the profit earned by the French state for visa services from its abroad consulates to have reached 29 million euros in 2007 (Goudeyron 2007). Africans of all nationalities are not only considered a high risk for the EU due to their propensity to emigrate because of the harsh conditions of life in their countries, but also for their determination to sail to EU countries despite difficult weather conditions as often reported by Frontex (2014). Whether they have legal visa or not, Africans are often subject to thorough and humiliating checks at the borders.

EU types of visas are incorporated within a general European platform of visa policy called Visa Information System (VIS), which regulates the exchange of visa data between the Schengen states (figure 12.1).

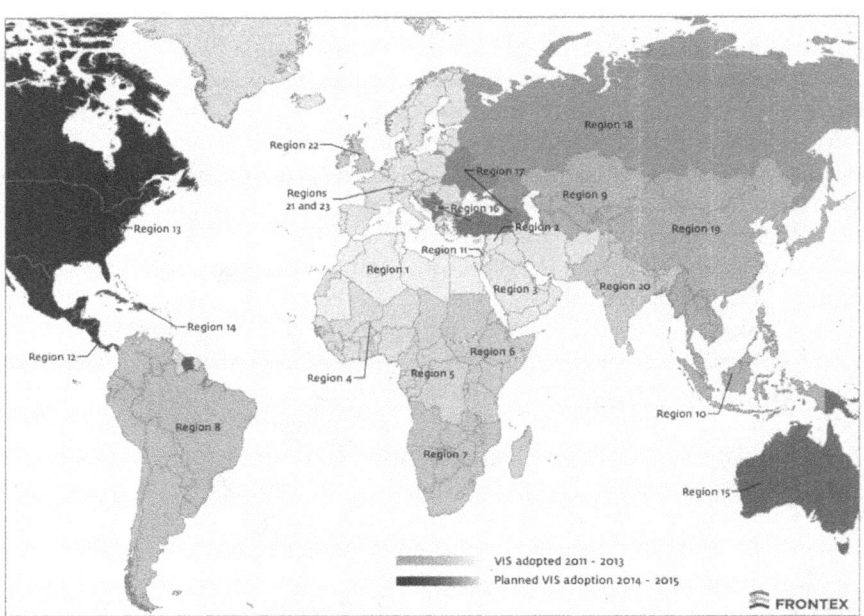

Figure 12.1. Visa Information System, May 2014. Courtesy of Frontex, Warsaw, Poland.

It helps to facilitate checks at external borders, to enhance security, to ease procedures, to prevent "visa shopping" and to prevent fraud. It is also used for the identification and the return of irregular emigrants from Europe to their home countries. As for the United States, Zonneveld et al. (2010: 553) reported that obtaining permanent residency can be a long and perilous path. The U.S. Immigration and Nationality Act (INA) provides four primary ways by which migrants can apply: (1) employment, (2) family, (3) asylum, and (4) the Diversity Visa Program. The latter, a kind of "lottery visa" or "green card," was enacted to further enhance and promote diversity in the United States, allowing more people from the "low admission foreign states" to apply. This type of visa is also a very selective one, because applicants have to be old enough to meet the education or work experience criteria. Within the EU, the highest rate of visa refusals in 2013 has been recorded for nationals from Maghreb and Egypt, according to the EU-DGHA (2013). For many years, it was mostly Senegalese, Nigerians, and Gambians (figures 12.2 and 12.3) who registered fraudulently at the EU border points, but they have been recently overtaken by Malians and Burkinabe (Frontex 2014).

Thus, for most African candidates to emigrate, the only legal way to reach Europe is through the visa system. But such an expensive, restrictive, and complicated system does not encourage candidates with various migration motives (fleeing misery, doing business, adventure, tourism, love, family, etc.), to engage in a process of legal emigration accepted by all stakeholders (consulates, African governments, etc.). The toughness of the visa system has created a class of 'excluded' peoples.

Annex Table 1. **Illegal border-crossing between BCPs**
Detections by border type and top ten nationalities at the external borders

Sea Border	2010	2011	2012	2013	Share of total	% change on prev. year
Syria	331	362	1 487	16 945	28	1 040
Eritrea	507	680	1 942	10 953	18	464
Afghanistan	3 074	2 598	3 331	5 102	8.5	53
Somalia	517	1 513	3 480	5 054	8.4	45
Nigeria	196	6 380	575	2 870	4.8	399
Egypt	713	1 948	1 283	2 749	4.6	114
Gambia	125	511	514	2 722	4.5	430
Mali	23	2 484	422	2 236	3.7	430
Pakistan	203	1 594	1 533	1 836	3.1	20
Senegal	10	453	145	1 391	2.3	859
Others	8 561	52 649	8 542	8 315	14	-27
Total Sea Borders	14 260	71 172	23 254	60 173	100	159

* This designation is without prejudice to positions on status, and is in line with UNSCR 1244 and the ICJ Opinion on the Kosovo declaration of independence

Figure 12.2. Illegal sea border-crossing between the Border Crossing Point (BCPS), May 2014. Courtesy of Frontex, Warsaw, Poland.

Annex Table 9. **Persons using fraudulent documents**
Detections on entry from third countries to EU or Schengen area by border type or nationality

	2011	2012	2013	Share of total	% change on prev. year
Border Type					
Air	3 652	4 401	7 068	72	61
Land	1 281	3 072	2 110	22	-31
Sea	356	405	615	6.3	52
Not specified	0	4	11	0.1	175
Top Ten Nationalities					
Syria	83	486	1 281	13	164
Unknown	370	191	1 219	12	538
Albania	155	2 110	1 044	11	-51
Morocco	496	397	619	6.3	56
Nigeria	244	277	482	4.9	74
Ukraine	437	284	347	3.5	22
Iran	199	243	334	3.4	37
Senegal	72	81	220	2.2	172
Afghanistan	90	202	211	2.2	4.5
Turkey	228	199	204	2.1	2.5
Others	2 915	3 412	3 843	39	13
Total	5 289	7 882	9 804	100	24

Figure 12.3. Top ten nationalities of persons entering the European Union or Schengen using fraudulent documents, May 2014. Courtesy of Frontex, Warsaw, Poland.

After the humiliation, frustration, and discouraging treatment received at Western embassies, there are basically two options left for applicants: first, working in the informal sector, or second, the sea journey, in Wolof called *yoonu guedj* or *mbeuk-mi*. If the informal sector employment is not an option because it often requires lots of financial resources, the sea journey to Europe is the only option left. Many applicants have tried to apply for a visa from four or five embassies before making the decision to migrate clandestinely by sea. There is a great temptation to make ocean journeys since in West Africa, and particularly in Senegal, the sea has always been the only way by which one could pirate, traffic, explore, challenge, and control the environment without attracting a close vigilance. Migration by sea takes place in "mixed migration flows" that can be described as "complex population movements including refugees, asylum seekers, economic and other migrants" (International Organization for Migration [IOM] 2010: 71). According to Arcand and

Mbaye (2013, 6), "Individuals will attempt illegal migration if they do not have any other legal possibility or if they assume that they have no chance of success in a legal migration due to their level of education and/or social condition."

Environmental and Job Insecurity among the Main Causes for Departures of Migrant Fishers

The high cost of visas and the complexity of the system make 'clandestine' migration by boat seem much more attractive, especially for people already familiar with the open sea. Several newspaper reports[1] and studies (Greenpeace 2012) have shown that many Senegalese migrants are former fishers who worked several years in artisanal fisheries in Senegal. The growing destruction of the marine ecosystem by ships and foreign fishing lodges (mostly from industrialized countries) has impoverished them. The overfishing these foreign vessels carry out off the Senegalese waters is difficult to monitor due to the lack of technical means and has made this one of the world's richest maritime spaces (Opic and Seret 2011) and a brigandage territory. More than five hundred boats from Russia, China, Eastern Europe, and some Western European countries have been charged for irregular fishing. These types of events are, for the most part, reported by the local press and the Senegalese government carries out arrests and detentions (mooring), often with the collaboration of the French navy.

The small pelagic fish provides work for more than 15,000 canoes, and totals 80 percent of the catches. It basically provides a living for more than six hundred thousand people directly or indirectly employed in the sector. Sea fishing accounted for 1.4 percent of real GDP in 2011 and fish products totalled nearly 90 billion FCFA, equivalent to 136 million euros (Cofrepêche at al. 2013). About forty thousand tons are exported annually, mainly to the EU, contributing about 12 percent to total exports of Senegal (Mpam 2013). Products exported to the EU market are exempt from customs duties. Moreover, the EU has funded the regional monitoring program and research on fisheries in Senegal, which can be seen as a way to keep an eye on the resources. Therefore, lack of fish causes severe food problems and falling incomes, which affects, in addition, the health and education of fishers who then try to make a living by emigrating to other countries.

Sanctions and fines do not seem to be very efficient, and overfishing is still a burning topic. One example is the recent scandal of a Russian ship, *Oleg Naydenov* that was illegally caught in the Senegalese waters, and that made a splash among politicians. Senegalese authorities are not indifferent to the current "fish wars" and they defend the argument that regulated fishing licences are needed to prevent other countries from illegally catching fish in the coastal countries of West Africa. Another proposal by the Senegalese government has been to sign an agreement with the EU for their fishing boats to ensure a steady supply of fish to Senegalese national companies that process tuna. This will enable Senegal to maintain the transformation of sea products within the country and create additional jobs with a local workforce (GSAC, 2013). This rush toward the "gold of the sea" has become a strategic and geopolitical issue as Senegal stands to lose about 230 million euro annually (Cofrepêche at al. 2013).

Additionally, the effect of climate change on ecosystems adds to the fear of fish stock migration, especially of small pelagic fish and tuna off the coast of Senegal to the north of Africa. A document funded by the EU (Cofrepêche et al. 2013: 53) states that the "development opportunities [of fishing in Senegal lie] ... in ... the restriction of access to fishery resources from artisanal fishers and the establishment of an effective system of control of that access [while at the same time] ... the optimization of the rights to access for foreign fleets [should be encouraged]." It also states that the Senegalese artisanal fishers are not under any effective control or monitoring when they fish outside the waters under Senegalese jurisdiction. This overexploitation has led the state of Senegal to pass fishing agreements with certain subregional states that allow Senegalese artisanal fishers to fish in their waters. However, environmental NGOs are convinced that the Senegalese authorities are complicit in this spoliation of seas; complicity also exists in the highest echelons of the state (Csag 2013; Environmental Justice Foundation [EJF] 2013; Greenpeace 2012).

In addition, some species caught in Senegalese waters have been overfished or are at risk of overexploitation because they are an important resource for traditional fishers who catch around four hundred thousand tons per year. That is one reason artisanal fishers are counted among the largest numbers of boat people who migrate to Europe by sea. Therefore, they can be called environmental migrants who are resilient in their use of migration as a way to adapt (Scheffran, Marmer, and Sow 2012; Sow, Adaawen, and Scheffran 2014).

The Wretched of the Sea en Route to Hell

In *La Pirogue* [The Boat], a film directed by Senegalese Moussa Touré (2012) and produced by Johanna Colboc in Studios Rezo Film, several men and a woman leave Senegal on board a large canoe together with other Guinean emigrants to reach the Spanish "Eldorado" and Europe via the Canary Islands. The film's characters face the loneliness of the sea, a violent storm, and at the end an engine failure that leaves them lost in the vastness of the ocean. Similar to the *La Méduse*,[2] to survive, the shipwrecked must throw dead victims' bodies overboard and uphold an incommensurate spirit of solidarity to stay alive. They consequently suffer long days without eating or drinking until finally the Spanish navy arrives to rescue them. After being collected by the Spanish Canary Islands Red Cross, the survivors were immediately and forcibly deported by plane back to their home countries. Upon arrival, a sandwich and a small amount of money is handed over to them.

The narrative of Moussa Touré's film is not very different from the life stories of most migrant fishers we have interviewed, with one difference being that the current shipwrecked people live in a time of sophisticated and modern telecommunications. The commitment and firmness of 'clandestine fishers' are surprising. To achieve their purposes, they set a whole organization in motion. They have powerful outboard engines and the latest fashion in compasses, and they use sophisticated satellite navigation systems to engage in careful preparation before leaving. During their dangerous journeys, for periods of approximately four to seven days, they have enough supplies: provision of all kinds, medicine to combat seasickness, fuel to run the engines, life jackets, GPS, gas cylinders, and so on. For direction, they often use benchmarks on the Spanish coast such as the Canarian mountain El Pico Viejo (3,000 meters) and the volcano El Teide that rises more than 3,700 meters (municipality of Santiago de Teide on Tenerife). These two formations are visible, in good weather, from six thousand nautical miles to sixty thousand nautical miles and migrant fishers pass on information about the safest routes once they reach land. Without this information many do not survive this dangerous journey, as explained here:

> I must say it is the powerful hand of Almighty that protected us. When we arrived in the Canary Islands, we called our friends that remained in our country and we explained them the harsh conditions of the sea journey. But to our surprise, there were still comrades who admired us and ask us all the time how to bring us back together here in the Canary Islands. Though we discourage them, some had already sailed without listening to us. Unfortunately they have to live over again the same nightmare as we did. Some even died along the way. (Rahim[3] 2013, personal interview)

Figures on the number of deaths far exceed several tens of thousands since the early 2000s (Frontex 2014). However, official figures are often far below lived realities. In Senegal, growing narratives estimate the numbers of recent deaths at approximately two thousand five hundred, more than the final assessment of victims on the *Joola* that sank in 2002.[4]

Exploiting the naivety of the 'clandestines,' some smugglers (journey organizers or *borom gaal*) ask candidates for huge lump sums ranging from 760 to 1,000 euros per person to organize the *beuk-mi*.[5]

> We ask all this money because at first, a boat must be built, which costs at least 3 million FCFA ([around 4,560 euro]. Boat construction takes at least three weeks and we must pay the wood and the labor. You have to order a tree trunk

that is the basis of the canoe from far in Casamance [southern Senegal] or even from the Gambia. And if the police catches you, you lose your canoe as it will be confiscated by law. Then you have to buy gasoline worth more than a million francs. This could ensure at least 7–8 days in the sea. Because we are fishers, we know what kind of boat to sail in the sea. The first emigrants left with medium sized canoes, called *fils à tourner,* that were usually used just to fish near the coast. However, these migrants never arrived all, there were many deaths. So when we organize trips, we mobilize a canoe conceived for the deep blue sea that has a long spur, which helps easily to manoeuvre in the deep water. We call them "boat for the tide" or *Gallu gueth* in Wolof. These are the only long canoes, 20m long, 4m wide and 2m deep with a capacity of 20–30 tons, with 40 hp outboard engines, which can withstand storms and carry a large number of people and take you far away. They can carry up to 350 people each. (Saliu 2013, personal interview)

Saliu explained also that it was on his third attempt that he managed to organize the trip by canoe for the first time, to the Canary Islands. Coming out from Thiaroye sur mer (one of the fishing port of Dakar's coastal suburb), Saliu's canoe was intercepted by the coast guard near Nouadibou in Mauritania; the boat was seized and returned to Senegal. For the second attempt, he organized a boarding in Kayar, north of Dakar. Again, the boat with its passengers did not go far before being intercepted near St. Louis by the Frontex, which is equipped with powerful means to stop canoes transporting 'clandestine migrants.' The third attempt was successful. Saliu explained that he initially invested his own resources in order to organize the third *beuk-mi* even though during the other two failed journey attempts police had taken away all his possessions. This time, he chose a location above St. Louis (northern Senegal) and organized a boarding overnight. Between 2008 and 2011, Saliu said he organized six trips successfully and has earned a lump sum of 30 million francs CFA net profit from the *beuk-mi* (around 45,600 euro).

Intermediaries are smugglers who organize papers and payments required by the leading journey organizer before boarding. They are also locally called *cocxeur, ki yepp gaal gui,* or *conveyors.* They usually collect photocopies of identity cards or passports as well as bank receipts to prove that fees were paid to the account of the *borom gaals.* They also act as negotiators and intermediaries travel from city to city to attract "clandestine" customers:

The first boat to which I helped to gather "clients," I brought a total of 47 people. Thereafter, the number varied between 45 and 53. I earned 25,000 CFA ([38 euro] for each person I brought. My role was also to bribe the police for not intervening during the boarding. There was thus a lump sum to give to the police and a special way to do it not to attract attention. Cops were corrupt. For each canoe departure, the police commissioner and his men received 500,000 FCFA ([ca. 760 euro] to close the eyes [look the other way]. Since 2008, I "smuggled" more than 500 people with an average of 50 per canoe. To be honest, I have received more than 5 million FCFA ([7,600 euro] commissions from different *borom gaal*.... There is a lot of scam in this job, but you must be tough to do the job. (Musa 2013, personal interview)

According to Musa, it is not only the former fishers who migrate, there are also people from the countryside who spend a lot of money on 'sea adventures' without having ever been to the sea. These departures are arranged after selling cattle or crops. Some intermediaries have also explained that they seek out 'clients' very close to the border villages with Mali, Guinea Bissau, and the Gambia – the deeper into the countryside the better. Many farmers and traders from these regions work hard to save enough money for the sole purpose of leaving the country. Not only do conveyors excel in their situational job search for new customers, but they are oral propaganda machines for the *borom gaal*.

Indeed, we have been told that intermediaries or conveyors are those who are best informed on how to travel and the latest news from Europe, but also they know about the safest hideouts and places of boarding. Their role, in fact, is to establish permanent trust among customers and to pretend to guarantee a safe trip without any risk. Some of them, having worked as intermediates in the fishing sector, are very familiar with various aspects of sea-faring activities; they also know how to acquire and present adequate information to potential migrants. According to several interviewees, some intermediaries have close relationships with the canoe owners; many of them have participated in sea journeys onboard large canoes, mostly serving as cooks. Finally, within the range of actors, there are captains, also called locally *jiitu gaal*. Captains are, in fact, people who want to migrate and leave the country because of the deterioration of their working conditions (the overfishing has left them without work also). They are paid by the *borom gaal* and conveyors who carrying the primary responsible in case there are any problems. Even though captains are the ones who commit to undertaking these journeys, it is the conveyors' role to shoulder the risks, and therefore, they are more vulnerable to lawsuits. Feared and/or respected by all the passengers, the captains are the ones who drive the canoes to the Canary Islands or other locations. During the long sea journey, captains and their assistants play the roles of sheriff and deputy sheriff on board the canoe, essentially they give orders and act like police officers on board. In his book on Senegalese 'clandestine migrants,' Mendy (2009: 147) explains the particular role of the captain when faced with an angry passenger who posed a potential danger during a trip to the coast of the Canary Islands: "In his state of stress, to prevent him from pushing people off the canoe, which could easily cause an accident, the captain decided that we should tie him. Four comrades were determined to hold him down to fasten him with ropes and lay him down at the bottom of the canoe. For three days, Balla remained fastened. His body was eventually swollen, but neither could we play on feelings towards him to unfasten him because it was a risk for the group" (translated by authors from French).

Captains are always experienced fishers who have often worked in this capacity since childhood. They would say that they know the sea like 'the back of their hand' and are masters par excellence of navigation. Equipped with their GPS equipment, they can perfectly master often, secret routes and they know the nooks and crannies of the coast to avoid problems. Their profession attitude and experience as fishers allow them to handle any technical engine failure, and to anticipate future weather conditions that may occur during the trip. Last but not least, they perform the role of medical professionals who are able to foresee health problems of the passengers that may lie ahead (like seasickness), but also to find solutions to conflicts, tensions, and bad attitudes. They make judgements, predictions, and decisions, and they can also be authoritarian:

> The job of a captain is not easy because you are the responsible for the "passengers" in front of the Nature's law and God. Whatever happens, they will blame you. Your opinion is requested for anything. Although that is only a journey of 8 to 10 days, you always have to manage egos and emotions of each person. For example: those who do not want to share their individual food once out of general stock, those who do not want to do their needs in front of the others, those who are greedy, those who see only what the others do not see [hallucinations].... In the deep sea, it is sometimes difficult to convince some passengers that it is impossible to cook and one has to eat dry food because the sea is often rough and the waves do not allow to cook. But it is more difficult to handle the "bewitched" or "hallucinated" people. For this, you have to be tough and authoritarian in order to be heard and also have accomplices among the passengers to restore order before they put disorder on board the canoe or even overturn it. (Modu 2013, personal interview)

Once on dry land, extraordinary phantasmagorical stories (hallucinations, sea ghosts, delusions, disputes, seasickness, etc.) are sometimes told by rescued migrant fishers. Some have described scenes of sorcery, latent tensions and conflicts between migrants and nonmigrant fishers that are also on board. At Rufisque, a conveyor told us how a captain was armed with a machete and a handmade gun in case he was threatened by those affected by seasickness and/or hallucinations:

> One of the captains told me he was faced once with serious problems at the deep sea: a migrant was saying he saw a strange shape with long arms that was pushing back the canoe. The arms, according to the migrant, were multiplying and going to overthrow the canoe. Because of his behavior, the migrant was a danger for others. The captain ordered him several times to stay calm, but

every time he followed doing his 'little games.' The captain ordered to catch him and to fasten him, but as he was strong he opposed a fierce battle in which several people were injured. The captain pulled out his machete and dealt him a heavy blow on the left leg. The other migrants arrived to handle him, deeply hurt, and finally to fasten him. Someone took care of him, feeding and curing him, for the rest of the trip until the arrival in the Canary Islands. (Samba 2013, personal interview)

Elders, wise men and women play religious and spiritual roles before and during the journey. These include wise men 'mining' with amulets and 'holy water' to protect sea travelers, but they also provide the captains with powerful talismans that preserve them from evil spell and curses. For example, according to several stories from conveyors and captains, there is always a night ritual observed by passengers before boarding. Wise men make travelers believe in their ability to fabricate amulets, which miraculously create what they call *mess menting*.[6] Some also report that when there is not enough food, some travelers throw their amulets into the sea, which allows them to go into a trance and forget their hunger. Elders and wise men also fix the days of embarking to avoid 'unnecessary deaths' as some interviewees reported, and they order the sacrifice of sheep, chickens, or cows. Huge amounts of money are paid for these sacrifices before departures. Needless to say, wise men often times abuse the 'amulets market system' and use witchery to convince everyone that their practices are essential for any sea journey, and therefore exploit passengers. Religious leaders and wise men have seen their trade increase during various *mbeuk-mi* campaigns and highly practiced witchery before boarding is still undertaken to ward off evil spirits and to ask for protection during the entire trip.

The 'ocean journey' of Senegalese migrant fishers has multiple causes. One of them is the decline of the fishing sector. However, their journeys actually begin even before the canoes they travel in are built. Several categories of people are involved in these 'clandestine trips.' The protagonists of the 'ocean journey' are people who want to live a new reality, but builders of fishing boats, carpenters, and fishers all see opportunities in this new market in terms of making an income. Captains play an important role because they sail the canoes from ports to outside destination. The dangers associated with the 'ocean journey' are obvious and the tensions endured during the trip, including possible death, are present at all times. Once migrants land in Spain, their dream is hardly ever fulfilled because of frequent repatriations. Severe frustration has been observed among repatriated individuals concerning failed migration attempts, which they may have been mentally and economically planning for years. Complex feelings of shame remain after having failed to meet the great expectations placed on the migrants in this position.

Discussion and Conclusions

Irregular migrations of fishers from Senegal to Europe are still on the news. They are broadcasted by the press and updated by different migration rules, regulations, and policies on both sides of the Atlantic. Powerful cultural fantasies, on both sides of the Atlantic, continue to feed them and to retro-feed them and ocean crossings continue to countries where emigration is an important resource (IOM 2009).

Dominant discourses define migration from Africa to Europe as a security problem, thereby obscuring the fact that it is mostly fueled by the structural job demand for cheap migrant labor in informal sectors in Europe (de Haas 2009). These discourses are counterproductive to humane treatment and justify extraordinary and costly reactive measures, such as military and police action, and a new arsenal of technologies and mechanisms actively deployed against migrants. Such measures aggravate the problem and lead to security dilemmas of a self-enforcing competition of measures and countermeasures that could turn security concerns into a self-fulfilling prophecy. They fail to address the underlying roots and pressures of forced migration, including those caused by the EU and other developed regions of the world such as globalization, climate change, and resource exploitation (including fishery).

One point to underline is the alarming situation of migrant fishers who are returned to Senegal by force, or even voluntarily. Often those whom return voluntarily decide to do so because they cannot withstand the pressures of life in Spain. One interviewee said that he "would rather be fishing in Senegal than collecting waste in Barcelona (Modu, July, 2013)." Some have solicited money from their families back home in order to return to Senegal. Most of them do not fish anymore and have turned to other small urban activities.

The hardest hit are those who are returned by force through repatriation agreements. They often explain that they are returned "without any explanation," and are obviously very discouraged after having spent all their savings on their journey. Many of them have fallen into alcohol and drugs, but also into aggressive activities in urban areas, and/or and banditry in rural areas. No monitoring program is set up to fight against this type of traumatic experience, which have detrimental consequences that should not to be overlooked by Senegalese society. Some returned migrant-fishers desire to become "spokesmen of the victims" in order to discourage new potential migrants through awareness campaigns funded by local and international NGOs. Even though these journeys continue to take place, the numbers are declining somewhat and they are becoming more secretive. Renowned Senegalese singers and youth icons are engaged in preventive TV programs warning about the dangers of adventurous migration by sea. In addition, the military Frontex patrols supported by the Senegalese state along the coast and at the open sea have become more intense. This has prompted narratives that argue that the 'security curtain' has moved from Europe to West Africa.

Papa Sow is a senior researcher at the Centre for Development Research, University of Bonn, Germany. He is currently working on the WASCAL project–West African Service Center on Climate Change and Adapted Land Use–funded by the German Ministry of Education. His research focuses on population dynamics issues with special links to African migrations and climate variability/uncertainties. His study countries are Senegal, The Gambia, Benin, Ghana, Burkina Faso, and Morocco.

Elina Marmer is lecturer at the Hamburg University of Applied Sciences and the University of Hamburg, Germany. She is a meteorologist and a social scientist. Marmer is particularly interested in the study of postcolonial racism, how it operates through policy, institutions, education, and media as well as how it affects interpersonal relations, focusing on African-European migration dynamics.

Jürgen Scheffran is professor at the Institute of Geography of Hamburg University, Germany and head of the Research Group Climate Change and Security in the CliSAP Cluster of Excellence. His research interests include climate change and energy security; environmental conflict and human migration; complex systems analysis and human-environment interaction; and sustainability science, technology assessment, and international security.

Notes

This research was partially supported by the Cluster of Excellence "Integrated Climate System Analysis and Prediction – CliSAP" (EXC177), University of Hamburg, funded by the German Science Foundation (DFG). The recent updated fieldwork interviews and the literature search of West African fishers were partially supported by BMBF – The German Ministry for Education – under the project WASCAL – West African Science Center for Climate Change and Adapted Land Use.
 1. Le Monde, July 13, 2011, "In Senegal, anger is brewing against the spoliation from the "foreigners' fishing boats". See also: APS–*Agence de Presse Sénégalaise,* May 15, 2014, "Fisheries Agreements: the fears of spoliation are "unfounded,", according to the Head of the EU Delegation in Dakar *(Translated by Authors).*
 2. On July 2, 1816, a French ship called *La Méduse,* departing from the Aix Island off the coast of Charente in France to Senegal (then a French colony) ran aground on a sandbank off Mauritania. Not having been rescued and having finished their food, 160 people died in the sinking within the first days and 137 others had been abandoned on a makeshift raft twenty by seven meters, which was later found by the French navy with only thirteen survivors. *La Méduse* was immortalized in 1819

by paintings that are now famous. One of the paintings is called *The Raft of the Medusa* and is by Théodore Géricault.
3. All the names have been changed.
4. The *Joola*, a Senegalese ship that ensured the maritime link between the capital Dakar and Ziguinchor (south Senegal) overturned on the high sea in the 26th of September 2002 due to a big storm and the negligence of the authorities who were responsible for its management, killing 1,863 people, mostly Senegalese. Almost 2000 people were on board.
5. This Wolof expression means sudden impulse, but also by extension illegal temptation to take to the sea in a situation of total disarray. It also refers to the sea journey itself and its entire corollary.
6. Amulets are thought to have the power to make people disappear while they are at sea, in case of an "emergency," without them being seen by other people.

Bibliography

Personal Interviews

Rahim, September 13, 2013, 29 years old, male, Conveyor (Kayar, Senegal)
Saliu, July 14, 2013, 47 years old, male, a canoe journey's organizer (Thiaroye sur Mer, Senegal)
Musa, July 17, 2013, 43 years old, male, Conveyor, (Rufisque, Senegal)
Samba, August 4, 2013, 32 years old, male, Conveyor (Kayar, Senegal)
Modu, July 17, 2013, 36 years old, male, Captain of a canoe expelled from Spain (Rufisque, Senegal)

Other Sources

Arcand, Jean-Louis, and Mously Linguère Mbaye. 2013. "Braving the Waves: The Role of Time and Risk Preferences in Illegal Migration from Senegal." IZA DP no. 7518, Bonn.
Belaïsch, Sarah, and Laura Petersel (eds.). 2010. "Visa refusé. Enquête sur les pratiques des consulats de France en matière de deliverance des visas." Paris : Cimade.
Cofrepêche, Neds, Poseidon, and Mrag. 2013. "Evaluation prospective de l'opportunité d'un accord de partenariat dans le secteur de la pêche entre l'Union Européenne et la République du Sénégal, sous le cadre MARE/2011/01-Lot 3, Contrat spécifique 5", Csag, 2013.
de Haas, Hain. 2008. "Irregular Migration from West Africa to the Maghreb and European Union: An Overview of Recent Trends. IOM, Geneva.
——. 2009. "The Myth of Invasion: The Inconvenient Realities of African Migration to Europe." *Third World Quarterly* 29, no. 7: 1305–22.
di Bartolomeo, Tamirae Fakhoury, and Delphine Perrin. 2010. *Senegal: Le cadre démographique, économique et sociale de la migration. Le cadre juridique de la migration. Le cadre socio-politique de la migration.* Florence : Carim.
Environmental Justice Foundation (EJF). 2013. "Transbordement en mer. Quand interdire la pratique relève de la nécessité." Environmental Justice Foundation, London.

European Policy Evaluation Consortium (EPEC). 2004. "Study for the Extended Impact Assessment of the Visa Information System." European Policy Evaluation Consortium (EPEC), Brussels.

European Union (EU). 2014. "Report from the Commission to the European Parliament and the Council. A Smarter Visa Policy for Economic Growth." European Commission, Brussels.

"Fisheries Agreements: The Fears of Spoliation Are 'Unfounded,' According to the Head of the EU Delegation in Dakar." 2014. (Translated by authors). *Agence de Presse Sénégalaise,* May 15.

Frontex (European Agency for the Management of Operational Cooperation at the External Borders of the Member States of the European Union). 2014. *FRONTEX Risk analysis.* Report, Warsaw: Risk analysis unit.

Goudeyron, Adrien. 2007. *Rapport d'information fait au nom de la Commission des finances, du contrôle budgétaire et des comptes économiques de la Nation (I) sur les services des visas.* Paris: French Senate, no. 353.

Greenpeace. 2012. "The Plunder of a Nation's Birth Right. The Fishing Licence Scandal: A Drama in Five Acts."

Gsac. 2013. "Guide Sectoriel d'auto-contrôle (Gsac) pour le secteur pêche du Sénégal." Gaipes, Giei, Clpa, Upames, Dakar.

Hamilton, Donna. 2009. "The Transformation of Consular Affairs: The United States Experience." Discussion Papers in Diplomacy, Netherlands Institute of International Relations "Clingendael," The Hague.

Hobolth, Mogens Hvam. 2012. "Border Control Cooperation in the European Union: The Schengen Visa Policy in Practice." Doctoral thesis, London School of Economics, London.

Infantino, Frederica. 2010. "Politiques et pratiques des visas Schengen à l'Ambassade et au Consulat d'Italie au Maroc, Champ pénal/Penalfiel" [online], vol. 7.

Infantino, Frederica, and Andrea Rea. 2012. "La mobilisation d'un savoir pratique local: Attribution des Visas Schengen au consulat général de Belgique à Casablanca." *Sociologies Pratiques, Presse de Sciences* Po, 1, no. 24: 67–78.

"In Senegal, Anger Is Brewing against the Spoliation from the "Foreigners' Fishing Boats." 2011. *Le Monde,* July 13.

International Organization for Migration (IOM). 2009. "Migration au Sénégal. Profil national." IOM, Geneva.

———. 2010. International Migration Law and Policies: Responding to Migration Challenges in Western and Northern Northern Africa, Round Table. IOM, Dakar.

Touré, Moussa [Director]. 2012. *La Pirogue* [The boat]. [Film]. Produced by Johanna Colboc, Studio Rezo Films, Metz.

"Les Ambassades occidentales au Sénégal, se font-elles des chiffres d'affaires?" 2011. *Seneweb* September 22.

Mendy, Toumany. 2009. *L'immigration clandestine. Mythes, Mystères et réalités.* Paris: L'Harmattan.

Mpam. 2013. "Conseil Interministériel sur la Pêche au Sénéga. Document introductive." Mpam, Dakar.

Nessel, A. Lori. 2009. "Externalized Borders and the Invisible Refugee." *Columbia Human Rights Law, 624 (40) Review.*

Scheffran, Jürgen, Elina Marmer, Papa Sow. 2012. "Migration as a Contribution to Resilience and Innovation in Climate Adaptation: Social Networks and Co-development in West Africa." *Applied Geography* 33: 119–27.

Sow, Papa, and Rosnert. L. Alissoutin. 2006. "Emigration africaine vers l'Espagne. Des Pateras aux Cayucos: toujours la chienlit diplomatique." Contribution, Barcelona.

Sow, Papa, Stephen A. Adaawen, and Jürgen Scheffran. 2014. "Migration, Social Demands and Environmental Change amongst the Frafra of Northern Ghana and the Biali in Northern Benin." *Sustainability* 6: 375–98.

Wouters, Jan, Sanderijn Duquet, and Katrien Meuwissen. 2013. "The European Union and the Consulate Law." Working Paper no. 107, Lewen Centre for Global Governance Studies, Lewen.

Zonneveld et al. 2010. "Selective preservation of organic matter in marine environments; processes and impact on the sedimentary record", *Biogeosciences,* 7, 483–511.

13

Re-living *Janga*
Survivor Narratives

Linda Briskman and Michelle Dimasi

On December 15, 2010, the asylum seeker boat, *Janga,* subsequently known as Suspected Illegal Entry Vessel (SIEV) 221, crashed in wild stormy weather on rocks at Australia's Indian Ocean Territory of Christmas Island, killing fifty people, including fifteen children. Forty-one people, including crew, survived; only thirty bodies were recovered. Televised imagery of the crash created shockwaves around the nation but within days it was apparent that there were competing narratives. Distressed Christmas Islanders who made courageous efforts to save lives talked about the trauma of witnessing. Rapacious media reported stories of wild seas, rocks, bodies, the morgue, and grief. The government seized on a platform that produced a mantra: "We" do not want to see people drowning on "our" shores. Despite their pleas to be heard through the media, narratives of survivors remained hidden by the government from public view. This chapter aims to reverse the silencing by revealing experiences of survivors, drawing on interviews, testimony at the coronial inquest into the tragedy, and other means of survivor communication. One of the authors (Dimasi) was on the island at the time of the tragedy and witnessed the suffering of survivors; her observations are incorporated. The silencing of survivor voices and privileging of more-powerful declarations can be understood by the trope of boats and ensuing fear and politics.

Boats, Fear, Death, Politics: A Convergence

Fear of asylum-seeker boats has taken hold in Australia, frequently linked to the 2001 terrorist attacks in the United States. A politics of fear promotes conflation of terrorism, Islam, and asylum-seeker boat arrivals. Fear permits a criminalization discourse, which conveniently enables government to treat noncriminals more harshly than convicted criminals. This has enabled the entrenchment of mandatory immigration detention laws, which without exception apply to "unauthorized" asylum seekers during the refugee determination process until they are found to be refugees or removed from Australia. Those most fortunate are released into the community while their claims are heard, although with minimal rights and inadequate means of support. The least fortunate are transported, under Australia's offshore detention policy, to substandard detention facilities in the countries of Nauru and Papua New Guinea and told they will never be permitted to settle in Australia, even if they are determined to be refugees. The government through fear campaigns has been able to convince the Australian public that asylum seekers are a threat to both border and nation. Capturing community opinion in this way has been instrumental in achieving the quest for border control, a pursuit that trumps compassion, even following loss of life.

Regrettably, deaths at sea due to migrations by boat are a global phenomenon. Although deaths of "illegal migrants" occur in a variety of ways, drowning is the most common (Weber and Pickering 2009: 7). Asylum seekers often find doors closing (particularly Western doors) as they flee their countries of origin, and place themselves in the hands of travel facilitators, most commonly referred to as people-smugglers. The December 2010 tragedy was not the first time that people died in attempts to reach safe haven in Australia. The most tragic in scale was a boat known as SIEV X in 2001, when 353 asylum seekers, mainly women and children, perished in the Sunda Strait in Indonesian waters on their way to Australia, many with high hopes of reconciling with husbands and fathers who had traveled before them and who had been denied family reunion. Even though that event received significant media attention in its immediate aftermath, the SIEV X faded in time from Australian collective memory apart from the work of some academics, activists and those who built SIEV X memorials on Christmas Island and in the nation's capital of Canberra.

What singled out the *Janga* as a unique event is twofold. First, the accident did not happen far out in the ocean but occurred at the shore of Christmas Island in full view of horrified islanders who endeavored to save lives by throwing life jackets from land to water. Second, the disaster made Australian political leaders more attentive to deaths at sea. Using the rhetoric of compassion and saving lives was the political strategy while incrementally imposing cruel policies that were clearly aimed at deterring future boat arrivals.

Emerging from this tragedy and others that followed was the merciless cry of "Stop the boats!" that still reverberates throughout Australian society. Since this 2010 boat crash, a recurring image that appears on television portrays the *Janga* crashing into rocks surrounded by flailing bodies in the water. Ironically, the dominant narrative has been the suffering of Australian citizen observers (Briskman 2013). As well, the bravery of the navy in this rescue was heralded, while the actions of the Christmas Islanders were minimized. This chapter sets out to remedy this absence by not only providing survivor perspectives on the rescue and its aftermath, but also presenting their accounts of heroic attempts by islanders to rescue them.

Christmas Island: A Site of Trauma and Hope

Christmas Island is an isolated territory in the Indian Ocean, located 2,600 kilometers from the nearest mainland city of Perth (see figure 13.1.) Its close proximity to Indonesia (360 kilometers south of Java) has made it a port of

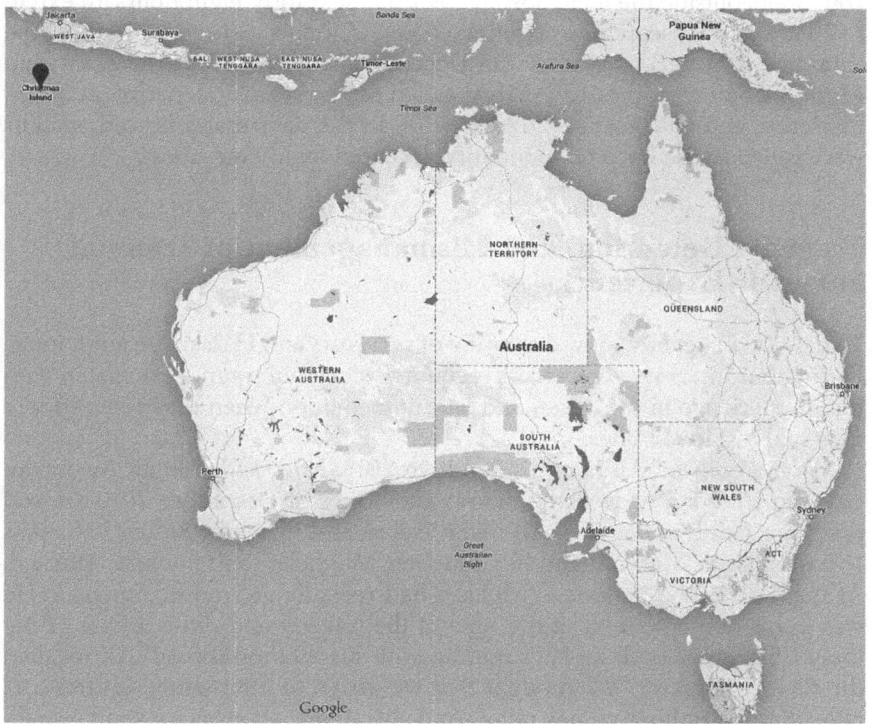

Figure 13.1. Christmas Island location. Courtesy of Google Maps (Map data @2015 Google).

entry for asylum seekers arriving to Australia by boat. The predominantly Chinese and Malay population have long witnessed arrivals of asylum seekers, but in recent years have experienced malevolent militarized attempts at deterrence by governments, including through the construction of detention facilities on the island. The compassion shown by Christmas Islanders to asylum seekers during and in the aftermath of the 2010 boat tragedy can be understood through the politics of proximity as well as solidarity that arises from their own experiences as indentured laborers, when up until the 1970s they experienced racial marginalization and were not afforded the same rights as mainland Australians (Dimasi and Briskman 2010: 206–7).

The tragedy unfolded in the early hours of December 15, 2010, when the island experienced a shocking swell during the monsoon season. Five-meter waves smashed the *Janga* apart on razor-sharp rocks as Christmas Islanders watched in horror. Islanders began a rescue effort by forming a human chain and throwing life jackets. By midmorning survivors and bodies were recovered from the water with many still missing. Survivors were transferred to the island's detention center, while bodies were stored in refrigerated shipping containers outside the local hospital. For the next forty-eight hours an extensive land and air search was conducted and islanders assisted by walking the shoreline in search of victims. On December 17 at 6:20 P.M., the Australian Maritime Safety Authority (AMSA) called off the search (Department of Immigration and Citizenship [DIAC] 2010). In the days that followed, victims were called to the hospital to identify deceased family members.

Tragedy, Detention, and Mismanagement of Trauma: Survivor Experiences[1]

To date we have interviewed a family of survivors and Hassan, an adult male. During our interviews, survivors recounted stories of trauma associated with their experience in the ocean and later in detention when they realized that they had lost loved ones.

We interviewed Ali[2] and his family in 2013. Now settled in an Australian city and studying or working, family memories of December 2010 are still raw. The family comprises Ali's wife Nahid and daughter Simin; his wife's widowed sister Maryam and her daughter Mahoobe; and her son, Mohsen. At the time of the interview, Mohsen had recently arrived in Australia. He was in his home country at the time of the tragedy and did not hear of the loss of his father until he later met up with his mother abroad. Ali recalled the day of tragedy: "We thought that we arrive to international water and after that everything comes okay. And the Army, Australian Army comes and catch me, helps me, save me and after that everything is okay. But it's not. When the boat went down, the family was in the water for 20 minutes"

(Ali personal interview August 18, 2013). Ali could not swim: "Just two boats from the Australian army came for help. If they come for help sooner this happened, this tragedy never happen. Why can't they help us right away." He had also told the coroner's inquest in Perth that "People from the houses–thanks to them–they threw life jackets–they saved my life."[3]

In August 2013 we interviewed Hassan in the rented house that he shared with other refugees. Hassan commenced the voyage with his wife and baby son. He began the interview by showing us photos from his wedding day. He also showed us the only piece of memorabilia from his baby boy–a pacifier attached to clothing that he had removed from the lifeless body. Hassan spoke of the rescue. When he could not find his wife he was ambivalent when the speedboat crew urged him aboard, saying "no my wife." He said around thirty people were saved by the lifejackets thrown by the islanders:

Some were just trying to throw themselves into the water to save some of the people but others were holding them back and they were saying, "No, the condition of the water and weather is not good and maybe something will happen to you" (Hassan, August 17, 2013, personal interview).

Hassan contemplated throwing his baby toward the rocks in the hope that the watching islanders might rescue his son. He expressed the view that it would have made a difference "if the Navy could have come a little bit closer to the rocks to save people.... I don't know what happened but one speed boat it came to save only one of the people, one person, then going back to the Navy boat, smoking and looking, but then staying there for a while before they came back. They could have picked up seven or eight people at one time [but] they didn't do so. It seems they didn't care about us. If they had been quicker, only by two or three minutes, they would have saved the people (Hassan August 17, 2013, personal interview).

Hassan also testified at the coroner's inquest in Perth, commending Christmas Islanders. "We owe our lives to the people of Christmas Island, not the Australian Navy. The life jackets they threw us made us to survive."[4]

In the days that followed the tragedy, some asylum seekers began protesting at the detention center, holding placards asking the United Nations to help them. They wanted more information about the boat crash and the rescue (King 2010a). Maryam spoke of the lack of information: "Some people were just lost.... Some people in the hospital maybe.... We don't know what happened, we don't know everybody is died or lost, we don't know.... It's a long time. It's five or six days after, some people came together and protest because they want information. Who died? What happened? Tell me?" (Maryam August 18, 2013, personal interview).

Hassan spoke about how traumatic it was when people moved to the Christmas Island detention center "because they were traumatised psychologically, impacted by the tragedy." After the event he was subjected to interviews and pages of paperwork. He was not ready to answer questions or to talk: "There was help given to us emotionally and mentally in the form of tablets only" (Hassan August 17, 2013, personal interview).

As a resident of Christmas Island at the time of the tragedy, Michelle Dimasi witnessed unfolding events. She offered solace to survivors and observed the silencing of their perspectives. While visiting asylum seekers at the detention center, she was approached by several detainees who had lost family members in the boat crash. They included a young orphan, Seena, who would run to the detention center fence every time a bus with new detainees arrived, asking, "Is my mum and dad on this bus?"

On February 12, 2011, one survivor (author unknown) gave Dimasi a letter titled, "The Painful Boat Incident" (2011); excerpts were later reprinted in *The Australian* newspaper (Neighbour and Taylor, 2011). Given that the DIAC would not release names, a group of survivors compiled their own list of those they believed were dead and alive, which was included in the letter. The writer queried the rescue effort, particularly as to why some people were in the water for at least two hours before being rescued, and raised questions about why twenty or more bodies were never recovered from the water although they were wearing life jackets. The letter also spoke of later events. At that time, survivors were not allowed to speak to the media despite requests. Children could not initially attend school. Health care provision was minimal. The women survivors were not permitted to join activities for women that were available to others. When survivors demanded that funerals be held for their loved ones they received no response. The letter stated, "In the last two months, we have been feeling psychologically down, many have lost interest in life.... At the moment the survivors' only request is to be released [transferred] from this camp, which has become too frightening and overwhelming.... We survivors would like to ask you to please help us so that our voices are heard."

Dimasi was approached by our interview respondent Maryam who asked her if she could find out which survivors were in the mainland hospitals, in the hope that her husband was there. She observed Maryam's distress in looking for her missing husband and her belief and hope that he was still alive. Dimasi was also contacted from abroad by Zahra, the sister of Nahid and Maryam, who was particularly concerned about her niece Mahoobe. She explained, "But now, her father died, her brother is in his country and her mother becomes almost mad. Whenever it is raining she terrified and remember that day. She was nearly sunk and she cannot forget this" (e-mail communication, February 20, 2011). Maryam asked Dimasi to write to the Joint Select Committee Inquiry on the Christmas Island Tragedy for her, saying, "Now after this tragedy, I am a helpless woman who don't know your language, don't know if my husband is dead or alive. Don't know what will happen for my son who is terribly in danger, don't know what should do with my little daughter when she is asking for her father and brother, don't know how to deal with the surrounding issues and most important of all don't know how I can satisfy myself that my dear husband died, while my feeling, my intuition and other evidences testify he is alive" (Maryam April 16, 2011, written communication).

The DIAC's management of survivors reveals a bureaucracy devoid of compassion. Survivors and relatives of the deceased were detained on Christmas Island for approximately three months, rather than being transferred to mainland Australia, where they would have been close to extended family, community and religious leaders. The DIAC released a number of community updates to the Christmas Island community stating that survivors were being well cared for and that the DIAC was working closely with medical and mental health service providers "to determine the most appropriate accommodation for the survivors of the SIEV 221" (DIAC 2011a).

The government's policy of mandatory detention dictated how victims were treated. This was clearly evident in the DIAC's handling of funeral services. On February 15, 2011, twenty-one survivors and family members were transported to Sydney to attend funeral and burial services and returned to Christmas Island three days later, much to their dismay. For those who had lost family, Christmas Island represented a place of pain and suffering to which they did not want to return. Fatima, who lost her sister and now cared for Seena, her sister's orphaned son, approached Dimasi on February 10. She queried why the immigration authorities would take them to Sydney for family members' funerals and then return them to a place of tragedy and trauma. Fatima had family in Sydney who would have supported her and her orphaned nephew.

The funerals received extensive media attention and relentless political debate. Internal rifts within the then opposition Coalition (conservative) Party occurred after Scott Morrison, Shadow Minister for Immigration, said that Australian taxpayers should not be paying for the funerals ("Opposition Demands to See Asylum Funeral Bill" 2011). Another conservative politician, Barnaby Joyce, proclaimed that compassion was not "limitless," and "you can't do it with a completely open cheque book" ("Opposition Demands to See Asylum Funeral Bill." 2011). Community responses that appeared in online public media outlets included such statements as, "We pay for their funerals, but their relatives are whingeing because they didn't get a traditional Muslim funeral. If they wanted Muslim traditions, they should have stayed in a Muslim country" (Haggis 2012: 22). Sara Wills's work on "pain and shame" and detention centers helps explain lack of empathy. "How can we respond to pain that we cannot claim as our own: how we respond in a way that does not take the testimony away from others as if it was only about our ability to feel the feelings of others.... The experience of pain has to be bound up in the loss of 'we'–the loss of the possibility of a certain kind of national body or community" (Wills 2008: 276).

The belief in "our" loss as Australians was apparent in indifference when video footage was released to television outlets of Fatima screaming over her relative's burial site and young Seena weeping at his father's grave. Survivors later reported to Dimasi that Seena wanted to throw himself into the gravesite to be with his father. Public debate ensued about the temporary release of Seena from Christmas Island to attend family funerals in Sydney with divided opinions in the Australian community about whether this traumatized child should be returned to Christmas Island or allowed to stay in Sydney to be close to family members (Tazreiter 2012: 31).

Fatima's question as to why the DIAC would return survivors to "a place of tragedy and trauma" was one that journalist Wendy Carlisle sought to answer. Under Australian Freedom of Information laws, psychiatric reports that assessed survivors, including the three orphans, were obtained, and submitted to the DIAC. Prior to the funeral services, pediatric psychiatrist Dr. Gosia Wojnarowska reported that it was "not in the best interests of the child to stay on the island," and that one of the orphans was self-harming and needed treatment. She also stated that, more importantly, his situation needed to be stabilized because the "current environment [was] not conducive to his recovery" (Carlisle 2012a). A psychiatrist who assessed the survivors in January 2011 told the DIAC that they "could now be managed in the mainstream facilities," but it was a crucial issue that they visit the site of the boat crash (Carlisle 2012b). Former Australian of the Year, psychiatrist Patrick McGorry, advocated for victims of torture and trauma to be moved into the community as soon as possible; he believed that the *Janga*'s victims would qualify for this move ("Opposition Demands to See Asylum Funeral Bill" 2011).

In his interview, Hassan reflected on the funerals in Sydney and how difficult it was for people to go back to Christmas Island. They had bad memories from what had happened on Christmas Island and did not wish to return. He also spoke at the coroner's inquest of the events preceding and following the funeral: "It is bad to put people in a cool room for two months. After two months I was taken to Sydney for ceremony for my son—why bring us back to the Island again? We have suffered enough. I can't sleep. The scenes and memories come back."[5]

The DIAC was aware of these concerns but failed to act. In a DIAC written communiqué for islanders, it stated, "The main concerns of the survivors have centred on the repatriation and burial arrangements of their loved ones and longer term placement options" (DIAC 2011b).

Christmas Islanders: A Compassionate Response

Not only were survivors affected by the boat tragedy, but so were the residents of Christmas Island. The tragedy was described by some islanders as an "unbelievable horror" (Perpitch, Guest, and Barress, 2010). Many ran to the rocks to assist after hearing the screams from their homes. Zainal Majid, president of the Christmas Island Islamic Council who assisted in the rescue, later said, "I cannot stop seeing the eyes, the faces, of the people on the boat as it was dashed against the rock, the father desperately clinging to the boat with one hand and with the other clutching his child to his side.... We are sorry for the families who have lost their loved ones in their attempt to find a better place to be. On behalf of the Islamic community we are sorry we could not put their loved ones to rest in peace earlier" (Majid 2011).

Shire of Christmas Island liaison officer Chris Su wrote, "What was so extraordinary that day was that strangers were prepared to go to such extraordinary lengths to help people whom they had never met. I heard of men being held back from diving off the cliff into the monstrous swell who felt the need to help the helpless. I saw human chains teetering on the edge of the cliff to get that extra foot of reach to throw out a lifejacket the furtherest they could.... For a short time, a stranger became a loved one" (Su 2011).

Dimasi spoke of her observations when she appeared before the official Joint Select Committee on the Christmas Island Tragedy in 2011:

> There was little opportunity for survivors and islanders to engage in the aftermath of what happened in December 2010. Many islanders had said that they wanted to meet with the survivors; they wanted to know what had happened to these people ... but there were no opportunities for that engagement to take place.... There was a memorial service and many island residents went to this service with the anticipation of meeting these survivors. On the day there were no survivors present. ... Christmas Islanders were very confused and puzzled as to why. (Dimasi 2011)

In conversations between Dimasi and islanders in the days that followed the tragedy, it was apparent that locals, particularly several who were involved in the emergency response, wished to meet with survivors and offer support. However, once again detention policies overrode compassion. Under detention center rules, in order for someone to visit a detainee, the visitor must know the name and immigration number of the person he or she wishes to meet; these were not made available.

Dimasi also told the committee that on March 5, 2011 when a memorial service was held for Christmas Islanders alone, survivors were taken to Tampa View, a street that overlooks the site where the boat tragedy occurred. At the service, shire president Gordon Thomson read speeches on behalf of survivors in which they expressed deep appreciation of help given by islanders. One stated, "Words are not enough to express our gratitude, we do not know how to thank them" ("SIEV 221 Thank You Statement" 2011: 4). At the service, hundreds of white lilies decorated the stage. Dimasi and Thomson later took the lilies into the detention center and handed them out to the survivors, and told them that the flowers were from the Christmas Islanders.

262 | Linda Briskman and Michelle Dimasi

One year after the tragedy in December 2011, a memorial service was held on the island. With money that some local residents raised from selling boat crash photographs to the media, a survivor trust fund was established. The funds were used to pay for the journeys of three survivors to return to the island for the first anniversary memorial service. A memorial was unveiled, which featured the propeller from the *Janga* (see figure 13.2). The inscription

Figure 13.2. *Janga* Memorial, Christmas Island, July 2011. Photographer: Michelle Dimasi. Courtesy of Michelle Dimasi.

on the memorial reads, "We reflect on this day with sadness. The loss of each person's life diminishes our own because we are part of humankind."

It was during this memorial event that islanders and survivors could at last shake one another's hands and hug one another. After the service, islanders and survivors went to the site where the crash took place. They threw flowers into the ocean and cried together. Hassan placed flowers into the sea that took the lives of his wife and child. He told the media, "I did not come to Australia to lose my family. I am always thinking about them when I am asleep, when I wake up, when I shower, when I am eating" (Hawke 2011).

Discussion

Former Australian diplomat Tony Kevin examined responses to sea rescues, expressing concern about adherence to international norms (Kevin 2012a). His revelations are supported by evidence from coronial inquests and media reporting (Briskman 2013: 7). In relation to *Janga,* Kevin confirms the musings of journalist David Marr whom he says provided a strong fact-based exposure of failures and delays in communication and command between government border protection agencies on that fatal day. He says the delays in response could have meant the difference between life and death (Kevin 2012b). The coroner criticized the federal government for failing to provide rescue vessels on Christmas Island, suggesting that the disaster was foreseeable (Needham 2012). He made fourteen recommendations about improving surveillance.

Following the 2010 crash, asylum seeker boats continued to arrive and there were more deaths en route, but none with the public visibility of the *Janga*. Policies were hardened by the Labor government in its last days in office, up to September 2013, and increased with the subsequent election of a conservative Coalition government. Tough measures have included the reopening of offshore detention sites on both Nauru and Papua New Guinea (Manus Island), increases in the numbers of children in closed detention, denial of permanent visas for those deemed to be refugees, and minimization of work rights for asylum seekers in the community. The centerpiece has been the design and implementation of Operation Sovereign Borders, with military personnel tasked to push back asylum-seeker boats to Indonesia. The arrival of boats have indeed slowed down, although the extent of attempts to enter Australia by boat is not known because of the secrecy shrouded in what are referred to as "on-water" matters. The whereabouts of those pushed back is largely unknown.

The *Janga* tragedy was particularly significant in influencing policy direction through opportunism rather than compassion. Nakhoul coined the term *wishful sinking fantasy* to suggest that the official mood appears to focus on "wishing to see a disaster unfold, in the hope of using it as a decisive deterrent to asylum seeker and smuggler alike" (Nakhoul 2011: 120). Afghanistan expert William Maley argues that those fleeing the Taliban will still die, but they will die by drowning in the Mediterranean or by suffocation in overcrowded trucks. He posits that the real message of the Australian approach is, "Die somewhere else" (Maley 2013).

The year of 2010 was not the first time that the Australian government had denied the release of names of those who died at sea. Perera points out that the Australian government refused to release the names of the 2001 SIEV X victims. For Perera these "nameless bodies of the dead" transform into "political bodies" and become "ongoing bearers of powerful political meaning" (Perera 2006: 638). Perera reminds us that some activists have ensured that these victims of government policy are not forgotten by reclaiming their bodies at the border (Perera 2006: 651). The emplacement of the *Janga's* propeller within the Christmas Island's landscape is a permanent reminder of those lost at sea. The Christmas Island community refused to allow the *Janga's* passengers to be nameless entities bound up in political opportunism. Instead, they reclaimed the humanity of the victims.

Haggis explains how, in the aftermath of the *Janga* tragedy, compassion circulated but was limited to "an emotion of disconnection rather than an empathic dimension of entanglement" (Haggis 2012: 21). Fenwick points to how lives of human beings are used for political purposes. Rather than risking lives at sea, most undertake the treacherous journey to save lives "because you would rather risk dying at sea ... than continue to face persecution and possible death in your home nation" (Fenwick 2014). And often there is little choice but to catch a boat from the staging post of Indonesia where people assessed as refugees by the United Nations High Commissioner for Refugees (UNHCR) face a ten- or twenty-year wait before they have the prospect of being resettled (Burnside 2014a: 29). Globally, protracted large-scale displacement situations are commonplace.

The convicted people-smuggler Khorram Heydarkhani was sentenced to fourteen years of imprisonment in Australia for organizing four boats to travel from Indonesia to Australia, one of which was the *Janga* (Menagh 2014). The coroner in his findings blamed people-smugglers as well as the boat crew (Needham 2012). The discourse moves according to the politics of the time from criminalizing asylum seekers to criminalizing those who transport them, and often to both in tandem. However, human smuggling has a long history and is in many ways a routine activity (Mountz 2010), and although the government speaks in such terms as "smashing the people-smuggler's business model" there is no evidence that such a model exists. In condemning smugglers, former prime minister Kevin Rudd proclaimed that Australians had enough of seeing people drown and that Australia has had enough of the exploitation of asylum seekers by people-smugglers (Rudd 2013).

At the time of this writing, there has been an announcement that legal action will be commenced by some of *Janga*'s survivors, arguing that Australia was responsible for the tragedy and that the Commonwealth breached its duty of care because government policies were putting lives at risk (Taylor 2014). Legal challenges are one way of ensuring that memories of the drowned and stories of the survivors are recognized. The memorial on Christmas Island not only immortalizes, but also recognizes that death is preventable, given political will.

Conclusion

Politics of control fail to recognize who is responsible for causing deaths. This is what May calls "vicarious dirty hands" in that "the problem of knowingly enabling or allowing others to do one's dirty work so that one can remain personally with clean hands" (May 2010: 165). We take liberty with the words of Australian academic Michael Hamel-Green who coined the phrase *circle of complicity* in relation to the offshore processing site of Manus Island where riots resulted in the death of an Iranian asylum seeker (Hamel-Green 2014: 19).The same questions can be posed for the *Janga* tragedy and lack of responsibility taken. How did Australia, obligated to protect asylum seekers in its care, allow this to happen? A contributing factor is government emphasis solely on border security, as opposed to human security, empathy, and compassion. If elected leaders and voters alike challenged what prominent Queen's Counsel Julian Burnside calls a moral question and not a political one (Burnside 2014b), we may be able to turn the discourse around from a focus on repelling those seeking our help to offering compassion and hospitality. Lessons from the moral acts of humanity seen in the actions of the Christmas Islanders provide some insights into how this might occur.

As Gilchrist rightly says, "Who could not be affected by images of the Christmas Island tragedy?" But as she further points out, "[W]hat hope is there for stopping these tragedies when so much energy seems consumed by political point scoring and an inability to compromise?" (Gilchrist 2013: 49). Despite such pessimism, the underlying story of unofficial rescue, from the heart, is narrated in the Indian Ocean, which became a site where human tragedy of great magnitude occurred. On the tiny outpost of Christmas Island, stories of islanders and survivors reveal prospects for humanity and compassion—of what happens when some strangers are in need and others come to their rescue, and when politics is pushed aside.

Linda Briskman is professor of Human Rights at Swinburne University of Technology. Her practice, policy, research, and advocacy focuses on the rights of asylum seekers and Indigenous rights. Her latest book is *Social Work* with *Indigenous Communities: A Human Rights Approach* (The Federation Press, 2014). Briskman coconvened the People's Inquiry into Detention on behalf of the Australian Council of Heads of Schools of Social Work. This civil society undertaking resulted in the coauthored (with Susie Latham and Chris Goddard) *Human Rights Overboard: Seeking Asylum in Australia* receiving the 2008 Australian Human Rights Commission Award for Literature.

Michelle Dimasi wrote a doctoral dissertation about Australia's asylum-seeker policy and Christmas Islander community responses at Swinburne University. She has worked with asylum-seekers and refugees in both Australia and internationally, including unaccompanied asylum-seeker children. She spent extensive periods on Christmas Island interviewing islanders about asylum-seeker policy. She was founding director of a nongovernmental organization (NGO), Asylum Seekers Christmas Island, which supported those in immigration detention. Dimasi has regularly visited Afghanistan with an interest in ethnic minorities and women's rights.

Notes

1. This ongoing research is funded by the Australia-Asia-Pacific Institute at Curtin University.
2. Pseudonyms (with the exception of Fatima and Seena whose names appeared in the public domain) are used to protect privacy of participants. Countries of origin are not identified.
3. This quote is taken from notes taken by Linda Briskman at the coronial inquest in Perth on July 26, 2011.
4. This quote is taken from notes taken by Linda Briskman at the coronial inquest in Perth on July 27, 2011.
5. This quote is taken from notes taken by Linda Briskman at the coronial inquest in Perth on July 27, 2011.

Bibliography

Briskman, Linda. 2013. "Voyages of the Damned." *Social Alternatives* 32, no. 3: 7–13.
Burnside, Julian. 2014a. "Asylum Seekers Can Be Managed with Cheaper and More Humane Options." *The Age,* June 18. http://www.theage.com.au/comment/asylum-seekers-can-be-managed-with-cheaper-and-more-humane-options-20140618-zscza.html.
———. 2014b. "How We Treat the Vulnerable Is a Moral Test Beyond Politics." *The Conversation,* March 17. http://theconversation.com/how-we-treat-the-vulnerable-is-a-moral-test-beyond-politics-24412.
Carlisle, Wendy. 2012a. "The Children of SIEV 221 Returned against Advice." *The Drum* February 21. http://www.abc.net.au/news/2012-02-21/carlisle-returned-against-advice-christmas-island/3840704.

———. 2012b. "Shipwrecked Survivors Returned to Christmas Island against Advice." *ABC, News.* http://www.abc.net.au/news/2012-02-20/doctors-advice-on-christmas-island-survivors-revealed/3840126.
Department of Immigration and Citizenship (DIAC). 2010. "Community Update," Christmas Island, December 18.
———. 2011a. "Community Update," Christmas Island, February 11.
———. 2011b. "Community Update," Christmas Island, February 25.
Dimasi, Michelle. 2011. "Official Committee Hansard: Joint Select Committee on the Christmas Island Tragedy," Canberra, May 27. http://www.aph.gov.au/~/media/wopapub/senate/joint/commttee/j73_pdf.ashx.
Dimasi, Michelle, and Briskman, Linda. 2010. "Let Them Land: Christmas Islander Responses to Tampa." *Journal of Refugee Studies* 23, no. 2: 199–218.
Fenwick, Shane. 2014. "Why 'Stopping the Boats' Doesn't Save Lives." *Agora Dialogue*, June 14. http://agora-dialogue.com/why-stopping-the-boats-doesnt-save-lives/.
Gilchrist, Michelle. 2013. "A personal reflection on the recent Australian discourse on Asylum seekers". Social Alternatives, 32, no. 3: 48–50.
Haggis, Jane. 2012. "White Australia and Otherness: The Limits to Hospitality." In *Cultures in Refuge: Seeking Sanctuary in Modern Australia,* edited by Anna Hayes and Robert Mason. Farnham, UK: Ashgate.
Hamel-Green, Michael. 2014. "Circle of Complicity." *The Age,* March 18.
Hawke, Sarah. 2011. "Service to Mark Year since Christmas Island tragedy." ABC News, December 15. http://www.abc.net.au/news/2011-12-15/xmas-memorial/3732006.
Kevin, Tony. 2012a. *Reluctant Rescuers: An Exploration of the Australian Border Protection System's Safety Record in Detecting and Intercepting Asylum Seeker Boats 1998–2011.* Canberra: Self-published.
———. 2012b. "Little SOLAS found in the wreck of SIEV 221." *Sydney Morning Herald,* March 2. http://www.smh.com.au/federal-politics/little-solas-found-in-the-wreck-of-siev-221-20120301-1u5nu.html.
King, David. 2010a. "Protest on Christmas Island." *Daily Telegraph,* December 17. http://www.dailytelegraph.com.au/riot-breaks-out-on-christmas-island/story-e6freuy9-1225972861759.
———. 2010b. "Protests on Hold as Mourning Begins." *Sydney Morning Herald,* December 18. http://www.smh.com.au/national/protests-on-hold-as-mourning-begins-20101218-1917r.html.
Majid, Zainal. 2011. "SIEV 221 Memorial Speech." *The Islander,* 478, March.
Maley, William. 2013. "'Die Somewhere Else.'" *Canberra Times,* July 27. http://www.canberratimes.com.au/comment/die-somewhere-else-20130726-2qq3s.html.
May, Larry. 2010. *Global Justice and Due Process.* New York: Cambridge University Press.
Menagh, Joanna. 2014. "Christmas Island Tragedy: Convicted People Smuggler Loses Appeal against 14-year Sentence." ABC News. http://www.abc.net.au/news/2014-03-12/appeal-for-people-smuggler-denied/5316538.
Mountz, Alison. 2010. *Seeking Asylum: Human Smuggling and Bureaucracy at the Border.* Minneapolis: University of Minnesota Press.
Needham, Kirsty. 2012. "Asylum Boat Deaths Avoidable, Coroner Rules." *Sydney Morning Herald,* February 24. http://www.smh.com.au/national/asylum-boat-deaths-avoidable-coroner-rules-20120223-1tqt7.html.

Nakhoul, Ghassan. 2011. *Overboard: You Would Not Believe What Really Triggered Australia's Controversial Policy on Boat People*. Merrylands: Dar Meera.

Neighbour, Sally, and Paige Taylor. 2011. "Lives Overboard: I Told Them Not to Come." The Australian, February 15, 2011. http://www.theaustralian.com.au/national-affairs/lives-overboard-i-told-them-not-to-come/story-fn59niix-1226005991927.

"Opposition Demands to See Asylum Funeral Bill." 2011. *Sydney Morning Herald*, February 16. http://www.smh.com.au/national/opposition-demands-to-see-asylum-funeral-bill-20110216-1avla.html.

"The Painful Boat Incident." 2011. Letter from SIEV 221 survivor.

Perera, Suvendrini. 2006. "They Give Evidence: Bodies, Borders and the Disappeared." *Social Identities: Journal for the Study of Race, Nation and Culture* 12, no. 6: 637–57.

Perpitch, Nicolas, Guest, Debbie, and Tony Barrass. 2010. "Locals Witness 'Unbelievable Horror' as Asylum Boat Tragedy Unfolds off Christmas Island." News.com.au, December 16. http://www.news.com.au/national/horror-christmas-island-crash-was-a-tragedy-waiting-to-happen-say-locals/story-e6frfkvr-1225971816485.

Rudd, Kevin. 2013. Kevin Rudd's Statement on Sending All Asylum Seeker Boat Asylum Seekers to PNG – Full Statement. *The Guardian*, http://www.theguardian.com/world/2013/jul/19/kevin-rudd-statement-asylum-seekers.

SIEV 221 "Thank You Statement." 2011. *The Islander*, 478, March.

Su, Chris. 2011. "People." *The Islander*, 478, March.

Taylor, Paige. 2014. "Families Sue over 221 Rescue Failures." *The Australian*, June 17. http://www.theaustralian.com.au/national-affairs/immigration/families-sue-over-siev-221-rescue-failures/story-fn9hm1gu-1226956496843.

Tazreiter, Claudia. 2012. "The Politics of Asylum and Identities in Exile: Negotiating Place and Meaning." In *Cultures in Refuge: Seeking Sanctuary in Modern Australia*, edited by Anna Hayes and Robert Mason. Farnham UK: Ashgate.

Weber, Leanne, and Sharon Pickering. 2009. *Globalization and Borders: Death at the Global Frontier*. London: Palgrave Macmillan.

Wills, Sara. 2009. "Between the Hostel and the Detention Centre: Possible Trajectories of Migrant Pain and Shame in Australia." In *Places of Pain and Shame: Dealing with 'Difficult Heritage'*, edited by William Logan and Keir Reeves. Oxon: Routledge.

Afterword

Lynda Mannik

In recent months (in particular April to October 2015) there has been a publicly articulated refrain, "Never have there been so many displaced people on the move globally since World War II," which has echoed across media venues in reference to what has also been described as the European refugee crisis. Just as the memory of World War II is fading along with a diminishing number of past refugees and survivors, it seems that a new "flood" or massive "flow" of refugees is on the move—individuals and families with children, from various countries, all trying to find a safe haven. In late September Europe finally "opened its doors" somewhat reluctantly, but out of necessity, to allow hundreds of thousands in. In particular, Germany stepped forward and said they would admit up to eight hundred thousand refugees by the end of 2015. Sadly, other nations were not as welcoming. The sheer numbers of desperate individuals and individual families who simply packed up a few belongings and traveled across land and water to escape traumatic situations strained international relations. Many suffered great hardships on their journeys due to the lack of international humanitarian aid. The majority of the people who are a part of this continuing crisis travel by boat at some point. At the time of this writing (mid-October 2015), the International Organization for Migration (IOM) in conjunction with the Missing Migrants Project (www .http://missingmigrants.iom.int) estimated that approximately 580,000 people attempted to cross the Mediterranean just between January and October 2015, which is double that of 2014. These statistics change on a daily basis. Again, it is unclear how many have drowned, but estimates state that over three thousand have lost their lives during the same ten-month period.

Of central importance is one photograph that will be remembered as the image that changed the world's perspective concerning the plight of refugees, and in particular Syrian refugees escaping civil war. A singular photograph of a small, three-year-old boy's dead body washed up on the beach on Bodrum, Turkey, sent thousands into action, changed and/or challenged government policies, and raised billions of dollars for resettlement. Alan Kurdi drowned while migrating by boat to the Greek island of Kos with his family on September 1, along with eleven others. The next day, Turkish journalist Nilufer Demir, took a photo of his wet lifeless body face down on the beach. This single image went viral within hours along with the hashtag, #KiyiyaVuranInsanlik (#humanity washed ashore). Reverberations continued into the following months and spawned an overwhelmingly compassionate, international response toward the rescue and resettlement of thousands of Syrian refugees, who for much of the past four years had been ignored. Alan Kurdi and his family will be remembered for many years to come, as will the single photograph that became instantly iconic. Even though this image of a dead child's body and the massive public circulation of it on the Internet can be considered obscene, it was also revolutionary in its global effect. For a period, it shifted the public focus away from long histories of negative stereotypical representations of refugees who migrate by boat that often depict refugees as a threat, to a focus on the desperate nature of their plights, and the individuals and families who are deserving of humanitarian aid.

Asylum seekers who risk their lives in small, overcrowded boats deserve to be recognized for their bravery and determination in the face of insurmountable odds. I hope this volume reflects the need for change in the narrow public mindset that has, up until recently, often ignored their suffering in favor of ignorance and dismissal. The indignities and heavy losses asylum seekers suffer in order to attempt these crossings are a high price to pay for the hope of safety. All refugees are in crisis and that includes the millions living in camps and detention centers around the world—an estimated 25 million worldwide. Without public support, the hope of finding new homes and new places of belonging will be overshadowed by policies aimed at curtailing their movements, and overshadowing legacies of despair and death.

Index

A

activists
  memory, 27, 31, 37, 42–43, 44n7, 254, 264; *see also* memory
  in Tunisian, 157, 162, 171
affect, 66, 74, 136, 139, 144, 148–49, 150n7, 155, 160, 165, 179, 241, 246, 265
  theory, 11–12, 122
affective communities, 71, 77
Afghanistan, 20, 85, 220, 264, 266
Africa, 12, 70, 126, 165, 198–99, 207, 236, 238
  border, 127
  government, 239
  media, 237
  migrants, 119, 165, 236, 238–39
  migrations, 240, 248
  North, 84, 118–19, 121, 126, 127, 128n1, 137, 150n4, 158, 197, 200, 206, 242
  South, 128
  Sub-Saharan, 119
  West, 236, 237, 240, 242, 249
Agamben, Giorgio, 117, 122, 137, 210
agency, 17, 54, 76
Ahmed, Sara, 34, 149, 182, 190
Albania, 18, 135, 144
  artists, 147
  diaspora, 144
  history, 137
  social construction of, 138
allegory, 72, 101, 110, 112
Alys, Francis, 117, 126–27

Amelie, 12, 178–79, 182–86, 192, 194n7
  passengers, 178, 182–84, 191
amnesia, 41
  historical, 106–9
anthropology, 111, 180–81
Arendt, Hannah, 103
art, 34, 58, 61, 84, 88–89, 125, 136
  artists, 159, 199, 212n7
  boats, 66, 90, 142
  commemorative, 88–89, 95, 97
  contemporary, 49, 58, 88–89, 96
  emotion, 145
  Holocuast, 58
  memory, 58, 61, 89
  naïve, 58
  painting, 58
  sculpture, 88, 93–95, 144
asylum-seekers, 4–5, 16, 19, 66, 70, 103, 104, 106, 141, 157–58, 193n2, 205–07, 210, 240, 254, 256–58, 264, 270
  Afghan, 56
  in Australia, 103–4, 105, 111
  boats, 254, 263
  in Canada, 178
  database, 169
  in Europe, 85–86
  Iranian, 265
  Iraqi, 55
  Vietnamese, 68, 74
Australia, 16, 48–49, 233, 265
  boat arrivals to, 58, 62, 104–6, 173n8, 226, 228–29, 263
  Chinese migrants, 56

government, 21
history, 55–57, 62, 112
indigenous, 55
immigration policy, 50–51, 54–55, 56, 101, 103–4, 227, 232
media, 54–56, 57, 63n5, 231
politics, 232, 264
navy, 230
novels, 107–8
Sydney, 56, 259–60
Australian National Maritime Museum (ANMM), 14, 16, 49–62

B
Bal, Mieke, 61
Balibar, Etienne, 84, 86–87, 90, 171
Barthes, Roland, 6
Bauman, Zygmund, 160, 171, 211
Berlin, 84, 88
 wall, 84, 90, 92, 118
Bible, 37, 38, 43
Binebine, Mahi, 17, 117, 120, 123–25
biometric border technologies, 170, 235
boat(s), 92, 199, 211
 arrivals in Australia, 101, 105, 219–20, 254, 256, 263
 arrivals in Canada, 181–82, 187, 188, 193n4
 art, 83, 98n3, 137, 141–45
 construction, 243
 in film, 208–9, 242
 fishing, 200–1, 224, 229, 242, 247, 249n1
 graveyard, 125, 158
 journeys, 29–30, 34, 67, 224–25, 229, 231–33
 law and, 203
 in literature, 34–36, 74–76, 77
 media, 86, 138, 141–42, 148, 159, 166, 253, 255
 memory, 66, 75, 92, 140, 145, 225
 migrant, 84–85, 90–92, 94–95, 120–21, 147, 198, 212n5
 migrations, 43, 66–68, 77, 77n5, 22, 128, 136, 146, 155–56, 200, 206, 211, 241, 244, 254; *see also* migration
 naval, 198
 as objects, 66, 77, 90–91, 124–25, 126–27, 139, 203

poems about, 154
refugee, 44n3, 70–71, 74, 101, 103, 219–20, 254
theory about, 66, 70–71, 73, 74, 197
tragedy, 260–261
unsafe, 228–30, 232, 254
boat people, 5, 66–67, 104, 112, 192, 193n2, 198–200, 202, 206, 242
 from Indonesia, 55
 from Vietnam, 51–52, 54, 66, 70, 72, 77n3
border(s), 84, 136, 264
 in Africa, 200
 anxiety, 182
 in Australia, 104–5, 254
 in Canada, 178, 182
 controls, 104, 155, 158, 168–70, 254
 death at, 120, 156, 160, 168
 definitions, 146
 in Europe, 83–84, 86, 95, 96, 98n3, 122, 129n10, 117, 154, 158, 198–99, 211, 238–39; *see also* Europe
 in Italy, 59, 136
 Mediterranean maritime, 120, 155–56, 165
 and no-border activists, 127, 155, 167
 protection, 55, 206, 208, 263
 securitization, 120, 148, 149n1, 198, 200, 223, 239, 265
 theory, 85–88, 94, 157
 violence, 91–92
borderless, 119
borderphilia, 140
borom gaals, 20, 236–237, 243–45
Brandenburg Gate, 17, 84, 90
British Home Children, 16, 27, 39, 45n10
Butler, Judith, 125, 136, 146–48, 161

C
Canada, 1, 16, 27–35, 42–43, 44n3, 54, 60, 62, 63n2, 77n5, 182, 185, 187–88, 190–92, 193n1, 194n8
Casey, Edward, 84, 85, 90
children(s)
 in detention, 232, 258, 263
 and displacement, 27, 35, 37, 43
 in film, 126–27, 129n17, 210
 home, 30, 42, 45n10
 and labour, 28–30, 44n1, 246

in literature, 27–28, 31–34, 37, 42-43,
    45n8
in media, 151n10, 270
in Morocco, 125
as objects, 188
and policy, 232
who are refugees, 44n1, 44n3, 151n10,
    157, 165, 200, 219, 221, 224, 228,
    253, 254, 270
Chimni, B.S., 2
China, 241
Chios, 17, 84, 90; *see also* islands
Christmas Island, 21, 57, 105, 113, 211,
    220, 231–32, 253–65; *see also* islands
citizens, 179, 182, 184, 185, 187
    of Canada, 191
    observers, 255
citizenship, 11, 70, 77, 84, 103, 123, 190
    activists, 165, 190
clandestine
    journey, 236
    migrants, 116, 119, 120–21, 122, 128,
        128n1, 128n4, 129n5, 129n14, 138,
        141, 148, 201
Coetzee, J.M., 17, 101, 107–12
Communism, 51, 59
    anticommunists, 2
Crialese, Emanuele, 198–99, 202, 207
culture, 191
    popular, 181, 201
cultural
    activism, 42, 95, 125
    amnesia, 87
    fantasies, 248
    heritage, 142
    identity, 65, 72, 88
    memory, 41, 137, 140
    multicultural, 182, 190–91
    performances, 186
    producers, 66–67, 106
    studies, 88, 192

D

dehumanizing, 4, 54, 62, 103, 180, 192
deportation, 205–206, 209, 224, 237, 239
Derrida, Jacques, 140
detention, 57, 96, 123, 129n11, 138,
    149n2, 151n10, 168, 206, 209–11,
    224, 241

in Australia, 104–6, 232, 254, 256–59,
    261, 263, 266
in Canada, 179, 183–86
in Italian centers, 162, 209–10
deterritorialization, 7, 168
diaspora
    and Albania, 144,
    studies, 71, 73
    and theory, 71
    and Vietnam, 66–68, 71–73, 76–77
digital
    data, 107, 170
    fingerprinting, 169–70
    museum, 42
    projection, 49, 54–57, 62
    scanning, 170
discrimination, 184–85, 187
disposability, 160
Douglas, Mary, 106
drowning, 21, 95–96, 120–21, 123, 125,
    127, 200–8, 229–32, 253–54,
    264–65; *see also* shipwrecks
dystopia, 197

E

England, 28
Eritera, 85
EU, 3, 85–86, 118, 137, 210
    consular missions, 238
    economy, 86, 241
    politics 85, 117, 121, 124, 145, 149n1,
        151n9, 203, 206, 235
    statistics, 4
    visa policy, 235
Europe, 83, 84, 203, 205, 211
    artists, 87–89, 94
    activists, 83
    border, 12, 15, 83–84, 86–87, 92,
        95–96, 116, 119, 122, 127, 148,
        198–200, 239
    Eastern, 87
    and identity, 86, 88
    and memory, 91, 92, 94, 96, 121, 144,
        198
    and media, 205
    migration from, 2
    migration into, 83, 85–87, 97, 120–21,
        135, 198, 237–38, 240, 242, 248
    Northern, 92

refugees in, 85
Southern, 17, 19, 84, 92, 94, 199
Western, 89
European Commission, 86, 235
European Convention on Human Rights, 203, 205–6

F
Facebook, 157, 172n4
forgetfulness, 41–42, 111, 146, 247, 258
Fortress Europe, 149n1, 157, 172n3, 173n9, 173n12, 199
Foucault, Michel, 70, 197
France, 238
Frontex, 84, 85–86, 98n2, 151n9, 158, 236, 238, 239, 243–44, 248

G
gate, 209
   art, 84, 95
   metaphor, 94, 96
Germany, 269
ghosts, 246
Greece, 137, 144–45, 200
grievability, 147–148

H
Halbwachs, Maurice, 14
Hall, Stuart, 72
Hammond, Breault Elaine, 32
Hannerz, Ulf, 6
Harrison, Troon, 33, 35, 36, 37–38, 40, 45n8
Haworth-Attard, Barbara, 32, 34–36, 38
heterotopia, 197–98, 202, 205, 208, 211
Hibernian, 27
historical amnesia, 106–109; *see also* amnesia
holing, 102–103
home, 248, 261, 264
   country, 243, 256
homelessness, 35, 200
hospitality, 18, 136–37, 140–41, 182, 187, 190, 265
host nations, 156, 231, 237, 262
human rights, 2, 8, 86, 96, 103, 109, 117, 155–156, 159, 203, 210; *see also* United Nations
   abuses, 9, 85, 87, 91, 173n13, 187, 192, 232
   activists, 83, 94, 187
   in media, 182
   law, 169–170, 203
   violations, 173n13
humanitarianism, 18, 84, 88, 96, 120, 122–23, 182, 188, 190–91, 222, 232, 248, 256, 261, 263–65
humanize, 49, 57, 208, 265
Huysmans, Jef, 138, 168
Huyssen, Andreas, 89

I
Icduygu, Ahmet, 221–22
identity, 127, 179
   cards, 244
   collective, 140
   and loss, 139, 166
   migrant, 128n1, 136, 155–56, 254
   national, 117, 188; *see also* nationalism
   politicized, 167
   Vietnamese, 65–67, 72–73
illegality, 5, 8, 120, 138, 192, 207, 209, 224, 226, 241, 250n5
immigration, 31
   agencies, 29, 34
   in Australia, 51, 55–56, 101, 104, 232, 254, 259, 261
   camps, 161
   in Canada, 27, 29, 43, 192, 181–83, 186–88, 191
   controls, 166, 203
   in the EU, 117, 154–55, 168, 171
   in Indonesia, 223–24
   in Italy, 137, 146
   museum, 45n10
   theory, 86
   in Tunisia, 162
   in U.S., 52, 239
Indonesia, 52, 219–32, 254, 255, 263–64
   fishing boat, 56
inhospitable, 129n7
international law, 203, 210
International Organization for Migration, 4, 83, 173n10, 240, 269
Iran, 20, 55, 220, 229, 265
Iraq, 9, 20, 61, 85, 199, 219–20, 222–29, 232

Ireland, 28–30
irregular migration, 83, 86, 91, 94, 95, 97, 98n3, 103, 112, 116, 119–20, 122, 128n1, 129n7, 129n9, 129n13, 65, 174n14, 205, 210, 235–36, 248; *see also* migration
island(s), 105, 210–12
  camps, 210–11
  Chios, 17, 84, 90
  Christmas Island, 21, 57, 105, 113, 211, 220, 231–32, 253–65
  in film, 208–10
  in Indonesia, 223
  Lampedusa, 17, 19, 84, 93–97, 148–49, 158–59, 161, 164, 166, 172n3, 173n12, 198–200, 202–7, 210–11, 212n7
  Linosa, 19–20, 198–99, 202, 207–9, 211
  Newfoundland, 44n5
  Prince Edward Island, 32–33, 37
  Spanish Canary, 236, 242–45, 247
islanders, 21, 209–10, 253–55, 256–57, 260–62, 265
Italy, 10, 60, 93–96, 137–40, 200, 204, 206–7
  and media, 137, 151n10
  navy, 155n9
  NGOs, 162

J
Janga, 9–10, 21, 253–57, 260, 262–65

K
Kafka, Franz, 109, 111
Kant, Immanuel, 140
Katër I Radës, 12, 18, 135–50
Kroeber, Alfred, 6

L
Lampedusa, 17, 19, 84, 93–97, 148–49, 158–59, 161, 164, 166, 172n3, 173n12, 198–200, 202–7, 210–11, 212n7; *see also* islands
Lemos, Kalliopi, 84, 87–94, 96
Libya, 83, 85–86, 158
  and refugees, 120
liminality, 7, 17, 136, 186
Linosa, 19–20, 198–99, 202, 207–9, 211; *see also* islands

Little, Jean, 33–34, 39–40, 45n9

M
Malkki, Liisa, 77, 122
Malta, 211
media
  in Africa, 237
  in Australia, 253–54, 259, 263
  Canadian, 178–81, 186–188, 190–92, 193n4
  consumers, 179, 184
  memory, 97, 180
  mediascape, 19
  print, 179, 181, 186, 188, 190–91
  and refugees, 54–55, 83, 86–87, 88, 91, 94–95, 137, 168, 173n9, 180, 182, 198–99, 206, 229
  representations, 63n5, 89, 121–22, 136, 138, 148, 178, 180, 186, 192, 197, 202, 205
  social, 88, 89, 172n5
  in Spain, 121
  in Tunisia, 157
  visual, 180
Mediterranean Sea, 85–86, 93–94, 119, 121, 128, 129n8, 136, 141, 197, 211
  border, 116, 128
  routes, 236
  shipwrecks in, 127, 147, 154, 156, 200, 203, 264; *see also* shipwrecks
memory, 49, 58, 62, 66, 73, 145, 147
  activism, 27, 31, 34, 37, 42–43, 44n7
  and art, 89, 95
  collective 14, 91, 97, 254
  diaspora, 17
  in literature, 34, 41, 42
  memory site, 14, 95
  objects, 37–39
  social, 14, 39, 106–8
  and trauma, 41–42, 61
migrant(s)
  African, 77, 210, 236, 238–39
  Albanian, 136–37, 141–42, 146
  in Australia, 50, 105
  boat, 55, 95, 98n3, 144, 150, 240
  British, 63n7
  child, 27, 29–32, 35, 39, 41–43, 44n3
  Chinese, 56
  clandestine, 244, 245

criminalization, 138, 168
crisis, 154
contracts, 29, 33, 44n2
definitions, 5, 44n4, 97n1, 128n1, 173n7, 235
deaths, 158, 160, 166–67, 168
deportation, 201
disappeared, 157–158, 161–62, 169
drowning, 95–97, 120, 125, 129n10, 136, 142, 146
environmental, 242
families of, 155–156, 174n14
in film, 205, 207–9
fishers, 236–37, 241, 243, 246–47, 248
hostility towards, 120, 154, 199–200, 211
identity, 154
illegal, 5, 8, 15, 154, 157, 254
irregular, 116, 120, 129n7, 129n13, 149n2
in Italy, 151n8, 204
labor, 248
Libyan, 198
longing, 56, 247
in media, 122, 123, 141, 151n10, 157, 168, 199, 206
and metaphor, 109, 112
North African, 137
and politics, 155–56
shelters, 174n14
suffering, 96–97
Turkish, 222
Tunisian, 155–57, 161–62, 164–65, 167
"war on," 203
Migrants Files, 158
migration, 44n4
  activism, 162
  from Africa, 236, 248
  art, 128n4, 129n6
  by boat, 32, 49–50, 55, 57, 62, 71, 76, 146, 148, 166, 241, 254
  to Canada, 27–35, 42–43, 44n3,
  and children, 27, 30, 32, 37
  depoliticization of, 154–55, 166
  and emotions, 121, 56
  Euro-Mediterranean, 155, 168, 200
  forced, 9, 29, 35, 42, 248
  history, 135,
  illegal, 241
  irregular, 116, 119, 121, 165, 167, 210, 235–36, 248
  lethal, 168
  in literature, 32–34, 41, 67
  memories, 31, 39, 43, 58, 136
  motivation, 239
  policing, 199, 203
  policy, 125
  stories, 50, 123,
  repoliticization of, 155–56, 166
  routes, 121, 240
  trauma, 58
  undocumented, 84–85, 90, 94, 98n1, 161–63
Missing Migrants Project, 4, 173n10, 269
mobilities, 35–36, 44n4, 117, 125–26, 128, 167
Montgomery, Lucy Maud, 31–32
Morocco, 83, 86, 116, 117, 121, 126–28, 129n6, 129n11, 210, 249
mourning, 95, 136, 148–49
museum, 14, 43, 55, 88, 145, 212n7
  Canadian Museum of Immigration, 45n10
  digital, 42
  Holocaust, 150n7
  maritime, 45n10, 50
  and migration by boat, 49, 188, 191
  objects in, 39, 50, 88
  photography, 58
myth of invasion, 12, 235, 237

N
nation, 49, 66, 92, 106
  building, 103, 137
  identity, 117, 188, 259
  security, 103, 105, 138, 146, 180, 182, 183, 186, 190, 254
  state, 75, 77, 86, 117,
nationalism, 49, 66, 70, 149, 181
  Australian, 50, 55–56
  Canadian, 181, 182, 190–91
  and mourning, 148–49
New Zealand, 58, 202, 207
Nyers, Peter, 11, 77

O
Otranto, 135–47

P

Paladino, Mimmo, 84, 87–88, 93–94, 96
Papua New Guinea, 105, 254, 263
Parr, Joy, 27–29, 44n1, 44n2, 44n3
Parr Traill, Catherine, 31
passports, 20, 103, 171, 209, 222–22, 244
pateras, 17, 116, 117, 120–21, 124, 128, 128n2
Perera, Suvendrini, 192, 202, 264
performance, 179, 183–86, 190, 246
  bond, 194n8
pmativity, 179–181
Peterson, Mark Allen, 179–81
photography, 148, 179–83, 186, 199, 204–5, 212n7, 228, 257, 262
Porta d'Europa, 10, 84, 93–96
Pugh, Michael, 3, 180
Pugliese, Joseph, 197, 202, 207, 211

R

racism, 106, 172n1, 185, 190–91, 203, 206, 256
Ravenhill, Louise, 33, 34–36, 37, 40–41
refugee(s), 86, 101, 178, 180, 230, 240, 263
  advocates, 187, 203, 212n3
  Afghanistan, 57
  agency, 76
  Albanian, 137–38, 146
  Baltic, 1
  boat, 44, 70–71, 74–75, 180, 197–98
  camps, 68, 105, 187
  crisis, 151, 182, 186
  Croatian, 49
  deaths, 203, 232
  definitions of, 5, 8, 67, 70, 179
  in film, 208–9
  Indonesian, 57
  Iraqis, 226
  Jewish, 56, 192
  Libyan, 120
  In narratives, 73, 108, 112, 225
  policies pertaining to, 105, 183, 187, 232
  and racism, 185–86, 188, 190
  representation, 199
  rights, 12, 103
  Sikh, 10, 179, 184, 188, 192
  status, 98n1
  Syrian, 199–200, 269
  stereotypes about, 11, 117, 122, 146, 180
  as terrorists, 179
  and trauma, 41, 193, 224, 231
  Vietnamese, 67–68, 73, 76, 193n2
  Yugoslavian, 137
Russia, 241

S

Sardiniana, 30
sea, 31, 70, 77, 217, 246, 253
  crossing, 229
  dangers, 221
  deaths at, 200–1, 205, 227, 229–31, 232, 254, 264
  in film, 127, 129n17
  journeys, 112, 198, 208–9, 219, 227, 237, 240, 243–46, 250n5
  in literature, 71–75, 109, 112
  and international law, 203
  in memory, 67, 229
  as metaphor, 65–67, 70–71
  ports, 223
  products, 242
  as a refugee space, 70, 104
  rescue, 199, 206, 210–12, 263
  sickness, 30, 35, 243, 246
  storms, 35, 74, 242, 250n4
  theory about, 70–71
seascapes, 36, 127
Schengen, 83–84, 98n2, 118–19, 129n5, 168, 238, 240
Scotland, 28
security, 129n12
  border, 155, 169, 224, 265
  discourses, 149, 235, 248
  food, 237
  insecurity, 119, 160, 182, 198, 241
  in media, 121, 123, 138, 149, 168
  policy, 237
  politics of, 148, 157, 171, 187, 203
securitization, 138, 146–49, 168, 190
semiotics, 136
Senegal, 236, 240, 241, 243–44
  "boat people" from, 20, 249n1, 245
  fishers, 236, 237, 239, 241–42, 247–48
  government, 241–42, 248
  organizations, 236

performers, 248
ships, 250n4
shipwreck(s), 30, 121, 136, 138–39 142, 146–47, 150n4, 154, 157–58, 161, 164, 166, 168, 173n9, 198, 205, 227, 229, 242–43, 257–58, 260–62
Sicily, 173n12, 206–7, 209
SIEV
   SIEV, 221, 253, 259, 261
   SIEV X, 4, 222, 226, 228–31, 232n2, 254, 264
SIVE, 120–21
silencing, 39–42, 67, 106, 151n10, 160–61, 164, 174n14, 253, 258
Sinozich, Gina, 58–62
smuggling, 104, 129n7, 155, 174n15, 223–29
   Indonesian, 57, 223
   intermediaries, 236, 237, 244–45
   people-smugglers, 20, 57, 68, 85, 105, 123–24, 182, 186, 223–29, 231–32, 236, 243, 254, 264
   rings, 182, 186
Sontag, Susan, 159
Sri Lanka, 20, 50
Stanner, W.E.H., 111
statelessness, 103
steamships, 27
Strait of Gibraltar, 17, 116–18, 120, 126, 129n8
Strait of Malacca, 223
Strait of Otranto, 18, 135, 137, 140–41
supernatural, 246–47, 250n6
Sweden, 1
Syria, 85, 158, 198–99, 200, 232, 269

T
MV *Tampa*, 51, 104, 261
Toure, Moussa, 242–43
tourism, 19, 89, 141, 150n7, 190–91, 209, 239
   dark, 190
   and images, 141
tourists, 89, 94, 95, 140–41, 188, 190–91, 198, 207–9
   site, 188, 190, 205
touts, 20, 236
trafficking rings, 119, 120–22, 220–21, 224, 235

transnational, 54, 70
trauma, 9, 13, 17, 42, 54, 58, 217, 237, 248, 253, 256–57, 260
   and forgetting, 41
   in media, 137
   and memory, 58, 61, 89
   in narratives, 42, 237
   and objects, 39, 58, 212n7
   and silencing, 41
   sites of, 150n5, 255–56, 259
Tunisia, 7, 19–20, 93, 96, 155–60, 200
   activists, 157, 162, 165, 171, 172n5
   flag, 163
   government, 162, 164, 174n17
   migrants, 155–57, 161–62, 164–65, 167
   revolution, 155, 161
Turkey, 86, 90, 91, 199, 221–22
Turner, Victor, 6, 179–81, 186, 190

U
unexpected arrivals, 5
United Nations, 68, 105, 203, 257, 264
United Nations Convention on the Law of the Seas (UNCLOS), 21n4, 203, 210
Universal Declaration of Human Rights, 1, 8, 206
United Nations High Commissioner of Refugees (UNHRC), 3, 104, 187, 203, 210, 222
United States, 54, 85, 173n8, 174n14, 239, 254
utopia, 15, 108, 117, 127, 201–2, 211

V
Van Alphen, 13
Varotsos, Costas, 14
Vietnam, 16, 52, 200
   diaspora, 10, 15, 17, 67–68, 71–73, 76–77
   and refugees, 9, 13, 17, 51–52, 54, 67–68, 70
   and refugee boats, 49, 62, 193n2
Visa Information System, 238–239
visas, 20, 104, 119, 162, 168, 171, 206, 223–24, 226, 237, 239, 263
   market, 237–38, 239, 241
   policy, 235–36, 240
Vlorë, 137

W

Wales, 28
Walnut, 1, 10
war, 65, 91, 140, 232
   Albanian Civil, 144
   Cold War, 91, 92
   and fishing, 241
   Greco-Turkish, 91
   Kosovo War, 137
   Libya, 158, 203–6, 212n7
   and memorialization, 74, 89
   "on migrants," 203
   Syria, 158
   "on terror," 105, 108, 149
   Trojan, 140
   Vietnam War, 56, 66–68, 76, 77n6
   World War I, 104
   World War II, 1, 8, 44n3, 45n11, 89, 137, 158, 269
Warsaw Pact, 137

water, 52–53, 59, 65, 71, 76, 109, 144, 178, 182, 220, 230, 255
   in boats, 227, 229
   dangerous, 119, 224, 257
   holy, 247
   as a metaphor, 180
   patrols, 186
   rescue, 254, 257–58
   in Vietnamese culture, 65–67, 72–73, 77
   as in watery graves, 120
Watts, Irene, 33, 35–36, 38–39, 41

Y

Yugoslavia, 59, 137

Z

zodiacs, 17, 116, 120–21
zombification, 102–3, 112

www.ingramcontent.com/pod-product-compliance
Lightning Source LLC
Chambersburg PA
CBHW070913030426
42336CB00014BA/2397